CONTENTS

D0552686

ON THE ROAD WITH FODOR'S

WHEN I PLAN A VACATION, the first thing I do is cast around among my friends and colleagues to find someone who's just been where I'm going. That's because there's no substitute for a recommendation from a good friend who knows your tastes, your budget, and your circumstances, someone who's just been there. Unfortunately, such friends are few and far between. So it's nice to know that there's *Fodor's Boston.*

In the first place, this book won't stay home when you hit the road. It will accompany you every step of the way, steering you away from wrong turns and wrong choices and never expecting a thing in return. It includes a wonderful, full-color map from Rand Mc-Nally, the world's largest commercial mapmaker. Most important of all, it's written and assiduously updated by the kind of people you *would* hit up for travel tips if you knew them. They're as choosy as your pickiest friend, except they've probably seen a lot more of Boston. In these pages, they don't send you chasing down every sight in the city but have instead selected the best ones, the ones that are worthy of your time and money. To make it easy for you to put it all together in the time you have, they've created itineraries and neighborhood walks that you can mix and match in a snap. Just tear out the map at the perforation, and join us on the road in Boston.

About Our Writers

Our success in achieving our goals—and in helping to make your trip the best of all possible vacations—is a credit to the hard work of our extraordinary writers.

Although **Fawn Fitter**'s conspicuous lack of a Boston accent gives her away as a transplant, she manages to pass for a native thanks to her fearsome eye for a Filene's Basement bargain and her offensive (in every sense) driving skills. After 14 years of hosting visiting friends and family, she's learned where to put them up and where to take them out—knowledge put to good use updating our Lodging and Nightlife chapters. A freelance writer whose work

has appeared in publications ranging from the *Boston Herald* to *Cosmopolitan,* she also teaches writing through the Cambridge Center for Adult Education and co-hosts an electronic discussion group for freelancers on the online service The WELL.

Carolyn Heller has lived in Cambridge since 1983. An avid foodie, she's proud to report that her five-year-old twins think that "restaurant" is synonymous with "Chinatown." As Boston Bureau Chief for On The Road, an online business travel newsletter, she covers the area restaurant scene, as well as arts, entertainment, and business events. Her recent travel articles have appeared in the *Boston Globe,* the *Los Angeles Times,* the *Philadelphia Inquirer,* the *Newark Star-Ledger,* the online Great Outdoor Recreation Pages, and in the book, *Travelers' Tales Paris.* She also contributed to Fodor's *New England's Best Bed & Breakfasts* guidebook.

Our dining critic, **Robert Nadeau,** has been reviewing Boston restaurants anonymously (and pseudonymously) for 25 years, with a longtime column in *The Boston Phoenix.* He is renowned as "the one critic in town who will publish a slam-dunk pan." A veteran journalist, editor, and writer under his real name, **Mark Zanger,** he edits a discount travel website, contributes regularly to food and business magazines, and moderates an on-line discussion group on current affairs for the Delphi computer on-line service.

Stephanie Schorow has yet to drop her r's despite seven happy years residing in the Boston area. A former newswoman for the Associated Press and editor for the TAB Newspapers, she now claims the title of assistant lifestyles editor for the *Boston Herald.* Thanks to her talents for coming up with the mots—both bon and juste—the Exploring chapters in this edition are now a charm to read. Her favorite haunts in Boston are the bookstores around Harvard Square, Chinatown bakeries, and the jogging path around Castle Island. A former Cantabrigian, she refuses to divulge her closely guarded secret for finding parking in Harvard Square. Normally a mild-mannered reporter, she has adopted some ferocious driving habits from cruising Boston streets—"but only out of self-preservation."

Anne Stuart, a New Englander by choice rather than by birth, has lived and worked in the Boston area since 1986, becoming familiar with the regions she updated for our Side Trips chapter. Her work, which has won numerous regional and national awards, has appeared in *The Los Angeles Times, The Washington Post, The Boston Globe, The Boston Herald* and *Boston* magazine, among others. When not writing or surfing the Internet, she can be found in-line skating along the Charles River or working in the large vegetable garden at her home on the South Shore.

When you use Fodor's maps to find your way to Filene's, you won't have to worry about getting lost: Map editor **Bob Blake** spent most of his life in Boston. Fortunately for Fodor's, Bob moved south to New York, where he labors to keep Fodor's maps as accurate as they are clear and easy to read.

Connections

We're pleased that the American Society of Travel Agents continues to endorse Fodor's as its guidebook of choice. ASTA is the world's largest and most influential travel trade association, operating in more than 170 countries, with 27,000 members pledged to adhere to a strict code of ethics reflecting the Society's motto, "Integrity in Travel." ASTA shares Fodor's devotion to providing smart, honest travel information and advice to travelers, and we've long recommended that our readers—even those who have guidebooks and traveling friends—consult ASTA member agents for the experience and professionalism they bring to your vacation planning.

On Fodor's Web site (www.fodors.com), check out the new Resource Center, an online companion to the Gold Guide chapter of this book, complete with useful hot links to related sites. In our forums, you can also get lively advice from other travelers and more great tips from Fodor's experts worldwide.

How to Use This Book

Organization

Up front is the **Gold Guide,** an easy-to-use section arranged alphabetically by topic. Under each listing you'll find tips and information that will help you accomplish what you need to in Boston. You'll also find addresses and telephone numbers of organizations and companies that offer destination-related services and detailed information and publications.

The first chapter in the guide, Destination: Boston, helps get you in the mood for your trip. New and Noteworthy cues you in on trends and happenings, What's Where gets you oriented, Pleasures and Pastimes describes the activities and sights that make Boston unique, Great Itineraries lays out a selection of complete trips, Fodor's Choice showcases our top picks, and Festivals and Seasonal Events alerts you to special events you'll want to seek out.

The Exploring chapters are divided into neighborhood sections; each recommends a walking or driving tour and lists neighborhood sights alphabetically, including sights that are off the beaten path. The remaining chapters are arranged in alphabetical order by subject (dining, lodging, nightlife and the arts, outdoor activities and sports, shopping, and side trips).

Icons and Symbols

★	Our special recommendations
✕	Restaurant
🏠	Lodging establishment
🐤	Good for kids (rubber duck)
☞	Sends you to another section of the guide for more information
✉	Address
☎	Telephone number
⊙	Opening and closing times
💰	Admission prices (those we give apply to adults; substantially reduced fees are almost always available for children, students, and senior citizens)

Numbers in white and black circles ③ ❸ that appear on the maps, in the margins, and within the tours correspond to one another.

Credit Cards

The following abbreviations are used: **AE**, American Express; **D**, Discover; **DC**, Diners Club; **MC**, MasterCard; and **V**, Visa.

Don't Forget to Write

You can use this book in the confidence that all prices and opening times are based on information supplied to us at press time; Fodor's cannot accept responsibility for any errors. Time inevitably brings changes, so always confirm information when it matters—especially if you're making a detour to visit a specific place.

Were the restaurants we recommended as described? Did our hotel picks exceed your expectations? Did you find a museum we recommended a waste of time? Keeping a travel guide fresh and up-to-date is a big job, and we welcome your feedback,

positive *and* negative. If you have complaints, we'll look into them and revise our entries when the facts warrant it. If you've discovered a special place that we haven't included, we'll pass the information along to our correspondents and have them check it out. So send us your thoughts via e-mail at editors@fodors.com (specifying the name of the book on the subject line) or on paper in care of the Boston editor at Fodor's, 201 East 50th Street, New York, New York 10022. In the meantime, have a wonderful trip!

Karen Cure
Editorial Director

Boston

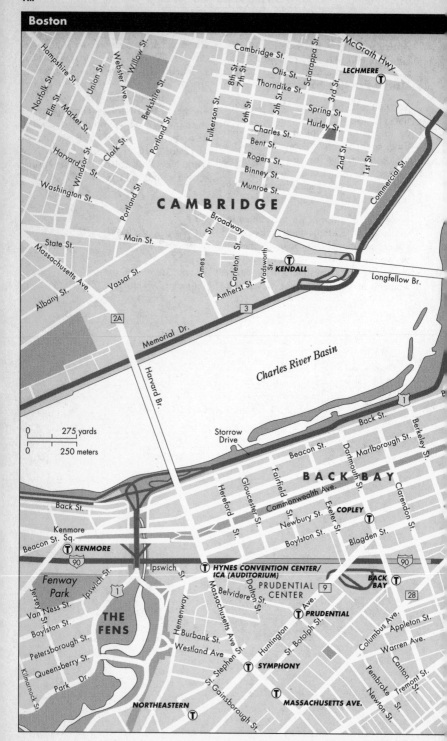

McGrath Hwy.

Hampshire St.
Norfolk St.
Union St.
Webster Ave.
Willow St.
Cambridge St.
Otis St.
Sciarappa St.
LECHMERE
Elm St.
Market St.
Berkshire St.
8th St.
7th St.
Thorndike St.
3rd St.
Harvard St.
Windsor St.
Clark St.
Portland St.
Fulkerson St.
6th St.
5th St.
Charles St.
Bent St.
Spring St.
Hurley St.
2nd St.
1st St.
Washington St.
Rogers St.
Binney St.
Commercial St.

CAMBRIDGE

Munroe St.

State St.
Massachusetts Ave.
Main St.
Broadway
Ames St.
Carleton St.
Wadsworth St.
KENDALL
Albany St.
Vassar St.
Amherst St.
Longfellow Br.

3

2A

Memorial Dr.

Harvard Br.

Charles River Basin

Back St.
Berkeley St.

0   275 yards
0   250 meters

Storrow Drive

Beacon St.
Marlborough St.

Fairfield St.
Dartmouth St.
Clarendon St.

BACK BAY

Commonwealth Ave.

Hereford St.
Gloucester St.
Newbury St.
Exeter St.
COPLEY
Blagden St.

Back St.
Boylston St.

Kenmore Sq.
Beacon St.
KENMORE

90

BACK BAY

28

Ipswich St.
HYNES CONVENTION CENTER/
ICA (AUDITORIUM)
PRUDENTIAL CENTER
9

Fenway Park

1

Belvidere St.
Dalton St.

Jersey St.
Van Ness St.
Boylston St.
Hemenway St.
Massachusetts Ave.
Ave.
PRUDENTIAL
Columbus Ave.
Appleton St.

THE FENS

Burbank St.
Westland Ave
Huntington
St. Botolph St.
Warren Ave.
Petersborough St.
Queensberry St.
St. Stephen St.
SYMPHONY
Canton St.
Pembroke St.
Tremont St.
Park Dr.
Klinarnock St.

St. Gainsborough St.

MASSACHUSETTS AVE.
Newton St.

NORTHEASTERN

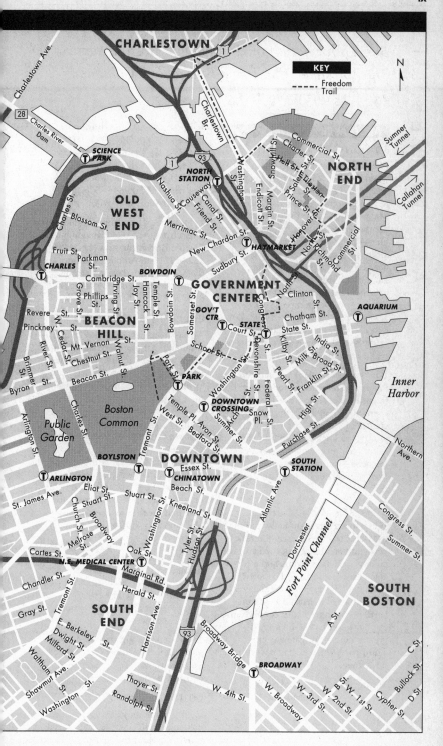

CHARLESTOWN

KEY

- - - Freedom
Trail

N

Charlestown Ave.

28

Charles River Dam

SCIENCE PARK

Charlestown Ave.

Charles St.

OLD WEST END

Blossom St.

NORTH STATION

Nashua St.

Causeway St.

Canal St.

Friend St.

Merrimac St.

Commercial St.

Charter St.

Snow Hill St.

Salem St.

Prince St.

NORTH END

Sumner Tunnel

Callahan Tunnel

Fruit St.

Parkman St.

CHARLES

Cambridge St.

BOWDOIN

New Chardon St.

Sudbury St.

Margin St.

Endicott St.

Hanover St.

North St.

Commercial St.

Richmond St.

HAYMARKET

Charles St.

Grove St.

Phillips St.

Irving St.

Hancock St.

Joy St.

Temple St.

Bowdoin St.

Somerset St.

GOVERNMENT CENTER

Clinton St.

Congress St.

Chatham St.

North St.

AQUARIUM

Revere St.

W. Cedar St.

Mt. Vernon St.

Walnut St.

BEACON HILL

GOV'T CTR

STATE

Court St.

Devonshire St.

State St.

Kilby St.

India St.

Pinckney St.

Chestnut St.

School St.

Milk St.

Broad St.

Byron St.

Brimmer St.

River St.

Charles St.

Beacon St.

Park St.

Washington St.

PARK

DOWNTOWN CROSSING

Temple Pl.

Avon St.

Summer St.

Snow Pl.

Federal St.

Pearl St.

Franklin St.

High St.

Purchase St.

Inner Harbor

Public Garden

Boston Common

BOYLSTON

West St.

Tremont St.

DOWNTOWN

Essex St.

CHINATOWN

Beach St.

Bedford St.

Arch St.

SOUTH STATION

Atlantic Ave.

Northern Ave.

Arlington St.

ARLINGTON

St. James Ave.

Eliot St.

Stuart St.

Church St.

Broadway

Stuart St.

Washington St.

Oak St.

Kneeland St.

Tyler St.

Hudson St.

Dorchester Ave.

Fort Point Channel

Congress St.

Summer St.

Melrose St.

Rose St.

Cortes St.

N.E. MEDICAL CENTER

Marginal Rd.

Chandler St.

Tremont St.

Herald St.

Gray St.

SOUTH END

E. Berkeley St.

Dwight St.

Milford St.

Harrison Ave.

93

Broadway Bridge

BROADWAY

A St.

SOUTH BOSTON

B St.

W. 1st St.

C St.

Bullock St.

Cypher St.

D St.

Waltham Ave.

Shawmut Ave.

Washington St.

Thayer St.

Randolph St.

W. 4th St.

W. Broadway

W. 3rd St.

W. 2nd St.

SMART TRAVEL TIPS A TO Z

Basic Information on Traveling in Boston, Savvy Tips to Make Your Trip a Breeze, and Companies and Organizations to Contact

AIR TRAVEL

BOOKING YOUR FLIGHT

Price is just one factor to consider when booking a flight: frequency of service and even a carrier's safety record are often just as important. Major airlines offer the greatest number of departures. Smaller airlines—including regional and no-frills airlines—usually have a limited number of flights daily. On the other hand, so-called low-cost airlines usually are cheaper, and their fares impose fewer restrictions, such as advance-purchase requirements. Low-cost carriers as a group have a good safety record—about equal to that of major carriers.

When you book, **look for nonstop flights** and **remember that "direct" flights stop at least once.** Try to **avoid connecting flights,** which require a change of plane. Two airlines may jointly operate a connecting flight, so ask if your airline operates every segment—you may find that your preferred carrier flies you only part of the way.

CARRIERS

When flying internationally, you must usually choose between a domestic carrier, the national flag carrier of the country you are visiting, and a foreign carrier from a third country. National flag carriers have the greatest number of nonstops. Domestic carriers may have better connections to your home town and serve a greater number of gateway cities. Third-party carriers may have a price advantage.

➤ MAJOR AIRLINES: **American** (☎ 800/433–7300). **Continental** (☎ 800/525–0280). **Delta** (☎ 800/221–1212). **Northwest** (☎ 800/225–2525). **TWA** (☎ 800/221–2000). **United** (☎ 800/241–6522). **US Airways** (☎ 800/428–4322).

➤ REGIONAL AIRLINES: **Business Express** (☎ 800/345–3400). **Cape Air** (☎ 508/771–6944 or 800/352–0714). **Colgan Air** (☎ 800/272–5488). **Comair** (☎ 800/354–9822). **Eastwind** (☎ 800/644–3592). **Jet Train** (☎ 800/359–4968).

➤ FROM THE U.K.: Three airlines fly direct from the United Kingdom to Boston: **British Airways** (☎ 0345/222–111) and **American Airlines** (☎ 0345/789–789), departing from Heathrow; and **Virgin Atlantic** (☎ 01293/747–747) from Gatwick.

CHECK IN & BOARDING

Airlines routinely overbook planes, assuming that not everyone with a ticket will show up, but sometimes everyone does. When that happens, airlines ask for volunteers to give up their seats. In return these volunteers usually get a certificate for a free flight and are rebooked on the next flight out. If there are not enough volunteers, the airline must choose who will be denied boarding. The first to get bumped are passengers who checked in late and those flying on discounted tickets, so **get to the gate and check in as early as possible,** especially during peak periods.

Although the trend on international flights is to drop reconfirmation requirements, many airlines still ask you to reconfirm each leg of your international itinerary. Failure to do so may result in your reservation being canceled.

Always **bring a government-issued photo ID to the airport.** You may be asked to show it before you are allowed to check in.

CONSOLIDATORS

Consolidators buy tickets for scheduled international flights at reduced rates from the airlines, then sell them at prices lower than those available directly from the airlines, usually without restrictions. Sometimes you can even get your money back if you need to return the ticket. Carefully read the fine print detailing penalties for changes and cancellations, and **confirm your consolidator reservation with the airline.**

➤ CONSOLIDATORS: **Cheap Tickets** (☎ 800/377–1000). **Discount Travel Network** (☎ 800/576–1600). **Unitravel** (☎ 800/325–2222). **Up& Away Travel** (☎ 212/889–2345). **World Travel Network** (☎ 800/409–6753).

CUTTING COSTS

The least-expensive airfares to Boston are priced for round-trip travel and usually must be purchased in advance. It's smart to **call a number of airlines, and when you are quoted a good price, book it on the spot**—the same fare may not be available the next day. Airlines generally allow you to change your return date for a fee. If you don't use your ticket, you can apply the cost toward the purchase of a new ticket, again for a small charge. However, most low-fare tickets are nonrefundable. To get the lowest airfare, **check different routings.** Compare prices of flights to and from different airports if your destination or home city has more than one gateway. Off-peak flights may be significantly less expensive.

When flying within the U.S., **plan to stay over a Saturday night** and **travel during the middle of the week** to get the lowest fare. These low fares are usually priced for round-trip travel and are nonrefundable. You can, however, change your return date for a fee ($75 on most major airlines).

Travel agents, especially those who specialize in finding the lowest fares (☞ Discounts & Deals, *below*), can be especially helpful when booking a plane ticket. When you're quoted a price, **ask your agent if the price is likely to get any lower.** Good agents know the seasonal fluctuations of airfares and can usually anticipate a sale or fare war. However, waiting can be risky: The fare could go *up* as seats become scarce, or your preferred flight could sell out. A wait-and-see strategy works best if your plans are

flexible. If you must arrive and depart on certain dates, don't delay.

FLYING TIMES

Flying time to Boston is one hour from New York, 2¼ hours from Chicago, 5½ hours from Los Angeles, 3¾ hours from Dallas, 1½ hours from Toronto, 7½ hours from London, and 21–22 hours from Sydney (including connection time).

HOW TO COMPLAIN

If your baggage goes astray or your flight goes awry, complain right away. Most carriers require that you **file a claim immediately.**

➤ AIRLINE COMPLAINTS: U.S. Department of Transportation **Aviation Consumer Protection Division** (✉ C-75, Room 4107, Washington, DC 20590, ☎ 202/366–2220). **Federal Aviation Administration Consumer Hotline** (☎ 800/322–7873).

AIRPORTS & TRANSFERS

AIRPORTS

The major airport is **Logan International**, across the harbor from downtown Boston.

➤ AIRPORT INFORMATION: **Logan International** (☎ 800/235–6426).

TRANSFERS

For recorded information about traveling to and from Logan Airport, contact the airport's **ground transportation hotline** (☎ 800/235–6426 around the clock). This is also your source for details on parking.

The **subway**'s Blue Line runs to downtown Boston in about 20 minutes; free shuttle buses connect the subway station with all airline terminals (5:30 AM–1 AM). Shuttle bus 22 runs between Terminals A and B and the subway; shuttle bus 33 goes to the subway from Terminals C, D, and E.

Taxis can be hired outside each terminal. Fares to and from downtown should average about $15, including tip, via the most-direct route, the Sumner Tunnel, assuming no major traffic jams. The new Ted Williams Tunnel, for taxis and commercial use only on weekdays, connects the airport to South Boston.

THE GOLD GUIDE / SMART TRAVEL TIPS

US Shuttle provides door-to-door van service 24 hours a day between the airport and many Boston area destinations. Call and request a pickup when your flight arrives. To go to the airport, call for reservations 24-48 hours in advance. Sample one-way fares are $8 to downtown or the Back Bay, $15.50 to Cambridge.

The **Airport Water Shuttle** makes seven-minute trips across Boston Harbor between Logan Airport and Rowes Wharf downtown (year-round, every 15 minutes weekdays 6 AM–8 PM; every 30 minutes Friday 8 PM–11 PM, Saturday 10 AM–11 PM, Sunday 10 AM–8 PM; ☞ Boat Travel *and* Subways & Trolleys, *below*). A free shuttle bus runs between the airport ferry dock and all airline terminals. One-way fare is $10 for adults. Connecting boats are available from Boston to Hingham on the South Shore (☞ Boat Travel, *below*).

The **Harbor Express boat service** takes passengers from Logan Airport to Long Wharf downtown (near the Aquarium) and to Quincy on the South Shore. The service makes 24 trips between 5 AM and 10 PM weekdays and 12 trips between 6 AM and 9:15 PM weekends. One-way fares are $8 between the airport and Long Wharf, $10 between the airport and Quincy.

From April 1 though mid-October, the **City Water Taxi** offers on-call boat service between Logan Airport and several downtown locations. One-way fares to or from the airport are $10, $8 each for parties of two or more. ☞ Boat Travel *below*.

If you're making bus or train connections at South Station, six **bus** companies offer non-stop service between Logan Airport and South Station for $6 each way. Buses run daily every 15–30 minutes. Logan Express buses travel to the suburbs of Braintree, Framingham, and Woburn. One-way fares are $8 weekdays and $6 weekends to Braintree or Framingham; Woburn fares are $6 each way.

➤ BOAT: The **Airport Water Shuttle** (☎ 800/235–6426). **Harbor Express** (☎ 617/376–8417).

➤ BUS: **Logan Express** or **Logan to South Station Service** (☎ 800/235–6426).

➤ SUBWAY: **MBTA** (☞ Subways & Trolleys, *below*).

➤ TAXI: **MASSPORT** (☎ 617/561–1751).

➤ VAN: **US Shuttle** (☎ 617/894–3100).

BOAT TRAVEL

Between April 1 and mid-October, water taxis ferry passengers between the World Trade Center, Congress St./Museum Wharf, Long Wharf, Rowes Wharf, North End/Burroughs Wharf, North Station/Fleet Center, Charlestown Navy Yard, Chelsea's Admiral's Hill, and other harbor destinations. One-way fares are $5 for non-airport stops, $10 to or from the airport. The service operates between 5 AM and 11 PM daily, but call ahead for reservations.

Commuter boat service operates weekdays between Rowes Wharf and Hewitt's Cove, off Route 3A in Hingham. Schedules change seasonally; call ahead.

➤ WATER TAXIS: **City Water Taxi** (☎ 617/422–0392 or 800/235–6426).

➤ COMMUTER BOATS: **Mass Bay Lines** (✉ 60 Rowes Wharf, ☎ 617/542–8000). **Boston Harbor Commuter Service** (✉ 60 Rowes Wharf, ☎ 617/439–4755).

BUS TRAVEL

Greyhound has direct trips or connections to all major cities in North America. Peter Pan Bus Lines connects Boston with cities elsewhere in Massachusetts, Connecticut, New Hampshire, and New York. Plymouth & Brockton Buses link Boston with the South Shore and Cape Cod. The South Station terminal's new multi-level bus deck simplifies making connections to other local public transportation.

➤ INTERSTATE BUSES: **Greyhound** (✉ At South Station, ☎ 800/231–2222). **Peter Pan Bus Lines** (✉ At South Station, ☎ 617/426–7838).

➤ INTRASTATE BUSES: **Plymouth & Brockton Buses** (✉ At South Station, ☎ 508/746–0378).

WITHIN BOSTON

Buses of the Massachusetts Bay Transportation Authority (MBTA) crisscross the metropolitan area and travel farther into suburbia than subway and trolley lines. Some suburban schedules are designed primarily for commuters. Current local fares are 60¢ for adults; you must pay an extra fare for longer suburban trips. Smart Traveler provides current service updates.

➤ SCHEDULE AND ROUTE INFORMATION: **Massachusetts Bay Transportation Authority** (MBTA, ☎ 617/222–3200). **Smart Traveler** (☎ 617/374–1234).

BUSINESS HOURS

Banks are generally open weekdays 9 to 4 (plus Saturday 9 to noon or 1 at some branches). Museums are generally open Monday through Saturday from 9 or 10 to 5 or 6 and Sunday noon to 5. Many are closed Monday. Post office branches do business weekdays 8 to 5 and Saturday 9 to noon, sometimes closing Thursday afternoon; the General Post Office (✉ 25 Dorchester Ave., behind South Station) is open around the clock. Public buildings are open weekdays 9 to 5. Shops and stores are generally open Monday through Saturday 9 or 9:30 to 6 or 7; those in malls or tourist areas may also be open Sunday noon to 5 or 6.

CAR RENTAL

Rates in Boston begin at $31 a day and $149 a week for an economy car with air conditioning, an automatic transmission, and unlimited mileage. This does not include tax on car rentals, which is 5%.

➤ MAJOR AGENCIES: **Alamo** (☎ 800/327–9633, 0800/272–2000 in the U.K.). **Avis** (☎ 800/331–1212, 800/879–2847 in Canada, 008/225–533 in Australia). **Budget** (☎ 800/527–0700, 0800/181181 in the U.K.). **Dollar** (☎ 800/800–4000; 0990/565656 in the U.K., where it is known as Eurodollar). **Hertz** (☎ 800/654–3131, 800/263–0600 in Canada, 0345/555888 in the U.K., 039/222–2523 in Australia, 03/358–6777 in New Zealand). **National InterRent** (☎ 800/227–7368; 0345/222525 in the U.K., where it is known as Europcar InterRent).

CUTTING COSTS

To get the best deal, **book through a travel agent who is willing to shop around.** When pricing cars, **ask about the location of the rental lot.** Some off-airport locations offer lower rates, and their lots are only minutes from the terminal via complimentary shuttle.

INSURANCE

When driving a rented car you are generally responsible for any damage to or loss of the vehicle. You also are liable for any property damage or personal injury that you may cause while driving. Before you rent, **see what coverage you already have** under the terms of your personal auto-insurance policy and credit cards.

For about $15 to $20 per day, rental companies sell protection, known as a collision- or loss-damage waiver (CDW or LDW), that eliminates your liability for damage to the car; it's always optional and should never be automatically added to your bill.

In Massachusetts the car-rental company must pay for damage to third parties up to a preset legal limit. Once that limit is reached, your personal auto or other liability insurance kicks in. However, **make sure you have enough coverage to pay for the car.** If you do not have auto insurance or an umbrella policy that covers damage to third parties, purchasing liability insurance and a CDW or LDW is highly recommended.

REQUIREMENTS

In Boston you must be 21 to rent a car, and rates may be higher if you're under 25. You'll pay extra for child seats (about $3 per day), which are compulsory for children under five, and for additional drivers (about $2 per day). Non-U.S. residents will need a reservation voucher, a passport, a driver's license, and a travel policy that covers each driver, in order to pick up a car.

SURCHARGES

Before you pick up a car in one city and leave it in another, **ask about**

drop-off charges or one-way service fees, which can be substantial. Note, too, that some rental agencies charge extra if you return the car before the time specified in your contract. To avoid a hefty refueling fee, **fill the tank just before you turn in the car,** but be aware that gas stations near the rental outlet may overcharge.

CAR TRAVEL

Driving is not easy in Boston. It's important **to look at a map *first* and have one with you at all times** due to the profusion of one-way streets and streets with the same names.

If you must bring a car, **keep to the main thoroughfares and park in lots**—no matter how expensive— rather than on the street.

FROM THE AIRPORT

If you are driving from Logan to downtown Boston, the most direct route is by way of the Sumner Tunnel ($2 toll inbound; no toll outbound).

When there is a very serious traffic delay in the tunnel, one alternative is to take Route 1A north to Route 16 west, then to the Tobin Bridge and into Boston: From the airport, follow 1A north about 2½ mi. At a traffic light, the road will fork, with 1A bearing right toward Revere Beach and Lynn. Stay right as if you were continuing on 1A, but just past the traffic signal, immediately bear left to reverse direction, following the airport signs. As soon as you are back through the intersection, heading south on 1A, exit right at the sign for "16 West, Tobin Bridge/Chelsea." Follow 16 west to the Tobin Bridge ($1 toll) into Boston.

GASOLINE

Gas stations are not plentiful in downtown Boston. Try Cambridge St. (behind Beacon Hill, near Massachusetts General Hospital), near the airport in East Boston, in Allston/Brighton along Commonwealth Ave. or Cambridge St., or off the Southeast Expressway in Dorchester. Cambridge service stations can be found along Memorial Drive, Mass Ave., and Broadway. In Brookline, try Beacon St. or Commonwealth Ave. Standard prices are $1.00–$1.30 per gallon.

PARKING

Parking on Boston streets is a tricky business. Some neighborhoods have residents-only rules, with just a handful of two-hour visitors' spaces; others have meters (25¢ for 15 minutes, one or two hours maximum). The meter maids are ruthless, and repeat offenders who don't pay fines may find the boot (an immovable steel clamp) secured to one of their wheels upon their return. In other words, **pay parking ticket fines** if you expect to come back to town.

Major public lots are at Government Center and Quincy Market, beneath Boston Common (entrance on Charles Street), beneath Post Office Square, at the Prudential Center, at Copley Place, and off Clarendon Street near the John Hancock Tower. Smaller lots are scattered throughout downtown. Most are expensive; the few city garages are a bargain at about $6–$10 per day.

ROAD MAPS

The American Automobile Association (AAA) provides good maps of Boston and vicinity, which conveniently indicate one-way streets in the downtown area. In Cambridge, look for the Arrow Map (carried in bookstores, newsstands, and some supermarkets), which combines a detailed street map with useful diagrams of the Harvard and MIT campuses.

➤ Map Source: **AAA** (✉ 125 High St., ☎ 617/443–9300 or 800/222–7448).

RULES OF THE ROAD

The speed limit on major highways in Massachusetts is 55 to 65 mph. Within the city of Boston and surrounding communities, speed limits on local streets are 20 to 30 mph. A right turn at a red traffic signal is permitted unless a "No Turn On Red" sign is posted. Rotary intersections are fairly common in Boston. When you are entering a rotary, state law dictates that you yield to any vehicle already in the rotary. Massachusetts state law requires all passengers in private cars to wear seat belts. Children under age 5 or weighing less than 40 pounds are required to ride in a child safety seat.

CHILDREN & TRAVEL

CHILDREN IN BOSTON

Boston is a great city for kids. It is home to world-class museums designed especially for children. Many of the historic sites in the city's compact and easily walkable center are outdoors along the Freedom Trail. The Boston Common and Public Garden, with boats and newly refurbished playgrounds, provides year-round fun for kids of all ages.

➤ LOCAL INFORMATION: Fodor's *Where Should We Take the Kids? Northeast* (available in bookstores, or ☎ 800/533–6478; $17). **Boston Parents Paper** (✉ Box 1777, Boston, MA 02130, ☎ 617/522–1515) lists events and resources; you'll find it at libraries, supermarkets, museums, children's shops, and nursery schools. *In and Out of Boston with (or without) Children,* by Bernice Chesler (**Globe Pequot Press,** ☞ *above*; 5th ed., $16 plus $2 postage) looks at the city from a child's point of view.

➤ BABY-SITTING: **Parents in a Pinch** (✉ 45 Bartlett Crescent, Brookline, MA 02146, ☎ 617/739–5437).

FLYING

If your children are two or older, **ask about children's airfares.** As a general rule, infants under two not occupying a seat fly at greatly reduced fares or even for free.

Experts agree that it's a good idea to use safety seats aloft for children weighing less than 40 pounds. Airlines, however, can set their own policies: U.S. carriers allow FAA-approved models but usually require that you buy a ticket, even if your child would otherwise ride free, since the seats must be strapped into regular seats. Airline rules vary, so it's important to **check your airline's policy about using safety seats during takeoff and landing.** Safety seats cannot obstruct the movement of other passengers in the row, so get an appropriate seat assignment as early as possible.

When making your reservation, **request children's meals or a free-standing bassinet** if you need them; the latter are available only to those seated at the bulkhead, where there's enough legroom. Remember, however, that bulkhead seats may not have their own overhead bins, and there's no storage space in front of you—a major inconvenience.

HOTELS

Most hotels in Boston allow children under a certain age to stay in their parents' room at no extra charge, but others charge them as extra adults; be sure to **ask about the cutoff age for children's discounts.** When planning your trip, **request a "Kids Love Boston" brochure** from the Greater Boston Convention and Visitors Bureau (☞ Visitor Information, *below*), which lists hotel packages for families and other discounts.

➤ BEST CHOICES: **Four Seasons Hotel** (✉ 200 Boylston St., Boston 02116, ☎ 617/338–4400). **Ritz-Carlton** (✉ 15 Arlington St., Boston 02117, ☎ 617/536–5700).

CONSUMER PROTECTION

Whenever possible, **pay with a major credit card** so you can cancel payment or be reimbursed if there's a problem, provided that you can supply documentation. This is the best way to pay, whether you're buying travel arrangements before your trip or shopping at your destination.

If you're doing business with a particular company for the first time, **contact your local Better Business Bureau and the attorney general's offices** in your state and the company's home state, as well. Have any complaints been filed?

Finally, if you're buying a package or tour, always **consider travel insurance** that includes default coverage (☞ Insurance, *below*).

➤ LOCAL BBBs: **Council of Better Business Bureaus** (✉ 4200 Wilson Blvd., Suite 800, Arlington, VA 22203, ☎ 703/276–0100, FAX 703/525–8277).

CUSTOMS & DUTIES

When shopping, **keep receipts** for all of your purchases. Upon reentering the country, **be ready to show customs officials what you've bought.** If you feel a duty is incorrect, appeal the assessment. If you object to the way your clearance was handled, get the inspector's badge number. In either case, first ask to see a supervisor, then write to the appropriate authorities, beginning with the port director at your point of entry.

IN AUSTRALIA

Australian residents who are 18 or older may bring back $A400 worth of souvenirs and gifts (including jewelry), 250 cigarettes or 250 grams of tobacco, and 1,125 ml of alcohol (including wine, beer, and spirits). Residents under 18 may bring back $A200 worth of goods.

➤ INFORMATION: **Australian Customs Service** (Regional Director, ✉ Box 8, Sydney, NSW 2001, ☎ 02/9213–2000, FAX 02/9213–4000).

IN CANADA

Canadian residents who have been out of Canada for at least seven days may bring in C$500 worth of goods duty-free. If you've been away less than seven days but more than 48 hours, the duty-free allowance drops to C$200; if your trip lasts 24–48 hours, the allowance is C$50. You may not pool allowances with family members. Goods claimed under the C$500 exemption may follow you by mail; those claimed under the lesser exemptions must accompany you. Alcohol and tobacco products may be included in the seven-day and 48-hour exemptions but not in the 24-hour exemption. If you meet the age requirements of the province or territory through which you reenter Canada, you may bring in, duty-free, 1.14 liters (40 imperial ounces) of wine or liquor *or* 24 12-ounce cans or bottles of beer or ale. If you are 16 or older you may bring in, duty-free, 200 cigarettes and 50 cigars.

You may send an unlimited number of gifts worth up to C$60 each duty-free to Canada. Label the package UNSOLICITED GIFT—VALUE UNDER $60. Alcohol and tobacco are excluded.

➤ INFORMATION: **Revenue Canada** (✉ 2265 St. Laurent Blvd. S, Ottawa, Ontario K1G 4K3, ☎ 613/993–0534, 800/461–9999 in Canada).

IN NEW ZEALAND

Although greeted with a "Haere Mai" ("Welcome to New Zealand"), homeward-bound residents with goods to declare must present themselves for inspection. If you're 17 or older, you may bring back $700 worth of souvenirs and gifts. Your duty-free allowance also includes 4.5 liters of wine or beer; one 1,125-ml bottle of spirits; and either 200 cigarettes, 250 grams of tobacco, 50 cigars, or a combo of all three up to 250 grams.

➤ INFORMATION: **New Zealand Customs** (✉ Custom House, ✉ 50 Anzac Ave., Box 29, Auckland, New Zealand, ☎ 09/359–6655, ☎ 09/309–2978).

IN THE U.K.

From countries outside the EU, including the United States, you may import, duty-free, 200 cigarettes or 50 cigars; one liter of spirits or two liters of fortified or sparkling wine or liqueurs; two liters of still table wine; 60 milliliters of perfume; 250 milliliters of toilet water; plus £136 worth of other goods, including gifts and souvenirs.

➤ INFORMATION: **HM Customs and Excise** (✉ Dorset House, ✉ Stamford St., London SE1 9NG, ☎ 0171/202–4227).

IN THE U.S.

Non-U.S. residents ages 21 and older may import into the United States 200 cigarettes or 50 cigars or two kilograms of tobacco, one liter of alcohol, and gifts worth $100. Prohibited items include meat products, seeds, plants, and fruits.

➤ INFORMATION: **U.S. Customs Service** (Inquiries, ✉ Box 7407, Washington, DC 20044, ☎ 202/927–6724; complaints, Office of Regulations and Rulings, ✉ 1301 Constitution Ave. NW, Washington, DC 20229; registration of equipment, Resource Management, ✉ 1301 Constitution Ave. NW, Washington DC 20229, ☎ 202/927–0540).

DISABILITIES & ACCESSIBILITY

ACCESS IN BOSTON

In general, Boston has a number of two- and three-century-old buildings that are difficult to modify within the strictures of the Historical Commission. The Back Bay is flat with well-paved streets. Beacon Hill is steep and difficult, with uneven, often narrow brick sidewalks. Quincy Market's cobblestone and brick malls are crisscrossed with smooth, tarred paths. The downtown financial district, Charles Street, and Chinatown are reasonably accessible, while South Boston and the North End may prove problematic for wheelchair users. The art and science museums, the Boston Common, and the historic Freedom Trail are all accessible.

➤ LOCAL RESOURCES: General information is available from the **Massachusetts Network of Information Providers for People with Disabilities** (☎ 617/642–0248 or 800/642–0249, TTY 800/764–0200). The **Massachusetts Office on Disability** (✉ 1 Ashburton Pl., 02108, ☎ 617/727–7440, TTY 800/322–2020) provides community outreach, advocacy, and education. The **Massachusetts Commission for the Deaf and Hard of Hearing** (✉ 210 South St., 5th Floor, 02111, ☎ 617/695–7500 or 800/882–1155, TTY 617/695–7600 or 800/530–7570, ℻ 617/695–7599) provides an interpreter referral service and listings of recreational activities and events in the deaf community. They also have a 24-hour emergency number (☎ 800/249–9949 voice or TTY) for medical interpreters. The **Boston Center for Independent Living** (✉ 95 Berkeley St., 02116, ☎ 617/338–6665) is a self-help organization run by and for people with disabilities.

MAKING RESERVATIONS

When discussing accessibility with an operator or reservations agent, **ask hard questions.** Are there any stairs, inside *or* out? Are there grab bars next to the toilet *and* in the shower/tub? How wide is the doorway to the room? To the bathroom? For the most extensive facilities meeting the latest legal specifications, **opt for newer accommodations,** which are more likely to have been designed with access in mind. Older buildings or ships may have more limited facilities. Be sure to **discuss your needs before booking.**

TRANSPORTATION

Boston is filled with narrow, sometimes hilly, often winding and congested streets not conductive to car travel. The substantial number of curb cuts throughout the city is increasing steadily. Taxi travel is easier for wheelchair users in Boston than in most other places in the nation as a result of a recent law requiring a certain percentage of every cab company's taxis to be accessible. As for sightseeing, many of Boston's most famous historic attractions are on or near the conveniently routed Freedom Trail, and most are wholly or partially accessible.

Currently half the bus routes in Boston can handle people with disabilities. The Call/Lift Bus Program facilitates the remaining routes; to **arrange for special pickups, contact the MBTA bus system** by 1PM on the day before you want to travel. Half the subway stations can accommodate people with disabilities; for **complete information, contact the subway system** (☞ Subways & Trolleys, *below*). The MBTA also offers a door-to-door pickup service called **The Ride.**

➤ AIRPORT TRANSPORTATION: **The Airport Handicapped Van** (☎ 617/561–1769) provides free service between terminals daily, on request.

➤ BUS/VAN TRANSPORTATION: Call **Lift Bus** (800/543–8287, or ☞ Bus Travel, *above*). **The Ride** (☎ 617/222–5123).

➤ COMPLAINTS: **Disability Rights Section** (✉ U.S. Department of Justice, Civil Rights Division, ✉ Box 66738, Washington, DC 20035–6738, ☎ 202/514–0301 or 800/514–0301, TTY 202/514–0383 or 800/514–0383, ℻ 202/307–1198) for general complaints. **Aviation Consumer Protection Division** (☞ Air Travel, *above*) for airline-related problems. **Civil Rights Office** (✉ U.S. Department of Transportation, De-

THE GOLD GUIDE / SMART TRAVEL TIPS

THE GOLD GUIDE / SMART TRAVEL TIPS

partmental Office of Civil Rights, S-30, ⊠ 400 7th St. SW, Room 10215, Washington, DC, 20590, ☎ 202/366–4648, FAX 202/366–9371) for problems with surface transportation.

TRAVEL AGENCIES & TOUR OPERATORS

As a whole, the travel industry has become more aware of the needs of travelers with disabilities. In the U.S., the Americans with Disabilities Act requires that travel firms serve the needs of all travelers. Note, though, that some agencies and operators specialize in making travel arrangements for individuals and groups with disabilities.

➤ TRAVELERS WITH MOBILITY PROBLEMS: **Access Adventures** (⊠ 206 Chestnut Ridge Rd., Rochester, NY 14624, ☎ 716/889–9096), run by a former physical-rehabilitation counselor. **Flying Wheels Travel** (⊠ 143 W. Bridge St., Box 382, Owatonna, MN 55060, ☎ 507/451–5005 or 800/535–6790, FAX 507/451–1685), a travel agency specializing in customized tours and itineraries worldwide. **Hinsdale Travel Service** (⊠ 201 E. Ogden Ave., Suite 100, Hinsdale, IL 60521, ☎ 630/325–1335), a travel agency that benefits from the advice of wheelchair traveler Janice Perkins.

➤ TRAVELERS WITH DEVELOPMENTAL DISABILITIES: **Sprout** (⊠ 893 Amsterdam Ave., New York, NY 10025, ☎ 212/222–9575 or 888/222–9575, FAX 212/222–9768).

DISCOUNTS & DEALS

Be a smart shopper and **compare all your options** before making any choice. A plane ticket bought with a promotional coupon may not be cheaper than the least expensive fare from a discount ticket agency. For high-price travel purchases, such as packages or tours, keep in mind that what you get is just as important as what you save. Just because something is cheap doesn't mean it's a bargain.

CREDIT-CARD BENEFITS

When you use your credit card to make travel purchases you may get free travel-accident insurance, collision-damage insurance, and medical or legal assistance, depending on the card and the bank that issued it. American Express, MasterCard, and Visa provide one or more of these services, so **get a copy of your credit card's travel-benefits policy.** If you are a member of an auto club, always **ask hotel and car-rental reservations agents about auto-club discounts.** Some clubs offer additional discounts on tours, cruises, and admission to attractions.

DISCOUNT RESERVATIONS

To save money, **look into discount-reservations services** with toll-free numbers, which use their buying power to get a better price on hotels, airline tickets, even car rentals. When booking a room, always **call the hotel's local toll-free number** (if one is available) rather than the central reservations number—you'll often get a better price. Always ask about special packages or corporate rates.

When shopping for the best deal on hotels and car rentals, **look for guaranteed exchange rates,** which protect you against a falling dollar. With your rate locked in, you won't pay more, even if the price goes up in the local currency.

➤ AIRLINE TICKETS: ☎ 800/359–4537. ☎ 800/359–2727.

➤ HOTEL ROOMS: **Accommodations Express** (☎ 800/444–7666).**Central Reservation Service (CRS)** (☎ 800/548–3311). **Quickbook** (☎ 800/789–9887). **RMC Travel** (☎ 800/245–5738). **Room Finders USA** (☎ 800/473–7829). **Steigenberger Reservation Service** (☎ 800/223–5652).

PACKAGE DEALS

Packages and guided tours can save you money, but don't confuse the two. When you buy a package, your travel remains independent, just as though you had planned and booked the trip yourself. Fly/drive packages, which combine airfare and car rental, are often a good deal. In cities, ask the local visitor's bureau about hotel packages. These often include tickets to major museum exhibits and other special events.

EMERGENCIES

Boston police officers patrol frequently in tourist areas, particularly during the peak travel seasons. Hotel staff or shopkeepers can also assist in getting help for an emergency situation.

➤ DOCTORS & DENTISTS: **Doctor Physician Referral Service** (☎ 617/726–5800); open weekdays 8:30–5. **Dental emergency** (☎ 508/651–3521).

➤ EMERGENCIES: **Dial 911** for police, fire, ambulance.

➤ HOSPITALS: **Massachusetts General Hospital** (☎ 617/726–2000).

➤ 24-HOUR PHARMACIES: **CVS** (✉ Porter Square Shopping Plaza, White St. at Massachusetts Ave., Cambridge, ☎ 617/876–5519), **Osco** (✉ 8 McGrath Hwy., Somerville, ☎ 617/628–2870), or **Walgreens** (✉ 757 Gallivan Blvd., Dorchester, ☎ 617/282–5246).

➤ OTHER EMERGENCIES: **Poison control** (☎ 617/232–2120). **Traveler's Aid Society** (✉ 17 East St., ☎ 617/542–7286, TTY 617/542–9482; FAX 617/542–9545); open weekdays 8:30–5; booths, open varying hours, at South Station (☎ 617/737–2880) and Logan Airport (✉ Terminal E, ☎ 617/567–5385); mayor's 24-hour traveler's aid hot line (☎ 617/635–4500).

GAY & LESBIAN TRAVEL

Boston has a vibrant lesbian and gay populace, a large portion of whom live in the South End (☞ Chapter 2), one of the city's most racially and ethnically diverse neighborhoods. To find out what's the latest in Boston's lesbian and gay scene, **stop by Glad Day, New Words,** or **We Think the World of You** bookstores (☞ Books *in* Chapter 8), where you can **pick up a copy of Bay Windows, IN Newsweekly,** and **Sojourner: The Women's Forum.**

➤ LOCAL RESOURCES: **AIDS Action Committee** (☎ 617/536–7733). **Gay and Lesbian Helpline** (☎ 617/267–9001). **Cambridge Women's Center** (✉ 46 Pleasant St., Cambridge, ☎ 617/354–8807).

➤ GAY- AND LESBIAN-FRIENDLY TRAVEL AGENCIES: **Corniche Travel** (✉ 8721 Sunset Blvd., Suite 200, West Hollywood, CA 90069, ☎ 310/854–6000 or 800/429–8747, FAX 310/659–

7441). **Islanders Kennedy Travel** (✉ 183 W. 10th St., New York, NY 10014, ☎ 212/242–3222 or 800/988–1181, FAX 212/929–8530). **Now Voyager** (✉ 4406 18th St., San Francisco, CA 94114, ☎ 415/626–1169 or 800/255–6951, FAX 415/626–8626). **Yellowbrick Road** (✉ 1500 W. Balmoral Ave., Chicago, IL 60640, ☎ 773/561–1800 or 800/642–2488, FAX 773/561–4497). **Skylink Travel and Tour** (✉ 3577 Moorland Ave., Santa Rosa, CA 95407, ☎ 707/585–8355 or 800/225–5759, FAX 707/584–5637), serving lesbian travelers.

HEALTH

MEDICAL PLANS

No one plans to get sick while traveling, but it happens, so **consider signing up with a medical-assistance company.** Members get doctor referrals, emergency evacuation or repatriation, 24-hour telephone hotlines for medical consultation, cash for emergencies, and other personal and legal assistance. Coverage varies by plan, so **review the benefits of each one.**

➤ MEDICAL-ASSISTANCE COMPANIES: **International SOS Assistance** (✉ 8 Neshaminy Interplex, Suite 207, Trevose, PA 19053, ☎ 215/245–4707 or 800/523–6586, FAX 215/244–9617; ✉ 12 Chemin Riantbosson, 1217 Meyrin 1, Geneva, Switzerland, ☎ 4122/785–6464, FAX 4122/785–6424; ✉ 10 Anson Rd., 14-07/08 International Plaza, Singapore, 079903, ☎ 65/226–3936, FAX 65/226–3937).

HOLIDAYS

Major national holidays include: New Year's Day (Jan. 1); Martin Luther King, Jr. Day (third Mon. in Jan.); President's Day (third Mon. in Feb.); Memorial Day (last Mon. in May); Independence Day (July 4); Labor Day (first Mon. in Sept.); Thanksgiving Day (fourth Thurs. in Nov.); Christmas Eve and Day (Dec. 24–25); and New Year's Eve (Dec. 31). Patriot's Day, the third Monday in April, is a Massachusetts state holiday. State, Suffolk County, and municipal offices (within the city of Boston only) also close on March 17 in honor of Evacuation Day and on June 17 for Bunker Hill Day.

INSURANCE

Travel insurance is the best way to **protect yourself against financial loss.** The most useful plan is a comprehensive policy that includes coverage for trip cancellation and interruption, default, trip delay, and medical expenses (with a waiver for preexisting conditions).

Without insurance, you will lose all or most of your money if you cancel your trip, regardless of the reason. Default insurance covers you if your tour operator, airline, or cruise line goes out of business. Trip-delay covers unforeseen expenses that you may incur due to bad weather or mechanical delays. Be sure to **compare the fine print regarding trip-delay coverage when comparing policies.**

For overseas travel, one of the most important components of travel insurance is its medical coverage. Supplemental health insurance will pick up the cost of your medical bills should you fall ill or be injured while traveling. Residents of the United Kingdom can buy an annual travel-insurance policy valid for most vacations taken during the year in which the coverage is purchased. If you are pregnant or have a pre-existing condition, make sure you're covered. British citizens should buy extra medical coverage when traveling overseas, according to the Association of British Insurers. Australian travelers should buy travel insurance, including extra medical coverage, whenever they go abroad, according to the Insurance Council of Australia.

Always **buy travel insurance directly from the insurance company**; if you buy it from a cruise line, airline, or tour operator that goes out of business you probably will not be covered for the agency or operator's default, a major risk. Before you make any purchase, **review your existing health and home-owner's policies** to find out whether they cover expenses incurred while traveling.

➤ TRAVEL INSURERS: In the U.S., **Access America** (⌂ 6600 W. Broad St., Richmond, VA 23230, ☎ 804/285–3300 or 800/284–8300). **Travel Guard International** (⌂ 1145 Clark St., Stevens Point, WI 54481, ☎ 715/345–0505 or 800/826–1300). In Canada, **Mutual of Omaha** (⌂ Travel Division, ⌂ 500 University Ave., Toronto, Ontario M5G 1V8, ☎ 416/598–4083, 800/268–8825 in Canada).

➤ INSURANCE INFORMATION: In the U.K., **Association of British Insurers** (⌂ 51 Gresham St., London EC2V 7HQ, ☎ 0171/600–3333). In Australia, the **Insurance Council of Australia** (☎ 613/9614–1077, FAX 613/9614–7924).

LODGING

See also Chapter 5, Lodging.

HOME EXCHANGES

If you would like to exchange your home for someone else's, **join a home-exchange organization,** which will send you its updated listings of available exchanges for a year and will include your own listing in at least one of them. It's up to you to make specific arrangements.

➤ EXCHANGE CLUB: **HomeLink International** (⌂ Box 650, Key West, FL 33041, ☎ 305/294–7766 or 800/638–3841, FAX 305/294–1148; $83 per year).

HOSTELS

No matter what your age, you can **save on lodging costs by staying at hostels.** In some 5,000 locations in more than 70 countries around the world, Hostelling International (HI), the umbrella group for a number of national youth hostel associations, offers single-sex, dorm-style beds and, at many hostels, "couples" rooms and family accommodations. Membership in any HI national hostel association, open to travelers of all ages, allows you to stay in HI-affiliated hostels at member rates (one-year membership is about $25 for adults; hostels run about $10–$25 per night). Members also have priority if the hostel is full; they're eligible for discounts around the world, even on rail and bus travel in some countries.

➤ HOSTEL ORGANIZATIONS: **Hostelling International—American Youth Hostels** (⌂ 733 15th St. NW, Suite 840, Washington, DC 20005, ☎ 202/783–6161, FAX 202/783–6171).

Hostelling International—Canada (⌗ 400-205 Catherine St., Ottawa, Ontario K2P 1C3, ☏ 613/237–7884, ℻ 613/237–7868). **Youth Hostel Association of England and Wales** (⌗ Trevelyan House, ⌗ 8 St. Stephen's Hill, St. Albans, Hertfordshire AL1 2DY, ☏ 01727/855215 or 01727/845047, ℻ 01727/844126); membership in the U.S. $25, in Canada C$26.75, in the U.K. £9.30).

MONEY

COSTS

Sample costs: sandwich $4–$7, slice of pizza $1–$1.50, cup of coffee $1–$2, and a bottle of beer $3–$3.50. Typical museum entrance fees range from $7 to $12.50. A taxi ride within the city of Boston starts at $1.50, plus $.25 for the first quarter mile and $.25 for each eighth of a mile thereafter.

EXCHANGING MONEY

For the most favorable rates, **change money through banks.** Although fees charged for ATM transactions may be higher abroad than at home, Cirrus and Plus exchange rates are excellent, because they are based on wholesale rates offered only by major banks. You won't do as well at exchange booths in airports or rail and bus stations, in hotels, in restaurants, or in stores, although you may find their hours more convenient. To avoid lines at airport exchange booths, **get a bit of local currency before you leave home.**

➤ EXCHANGE SERVICES: **Chase** *Currency To Go* (☏ 800/935–9935; 935–9935 in NY, NJ, and CT). **International Currency Express** (☏ 888/842–0880 on the East Coast, 888/278–6628 on the West Coast). **Thomas Cook Currency Services** (☏ 800/287–7362 for telephone orders and retail locations).

TRAVELER'S CHECKS

Do you need traveler's checks? It depends on where you're headed. If you're going to rural areas and small towns, go with cash; traveler's checks are best used in cities. Lost or stolen checks can usually be replaced within 24 hours. To ensure a speedy refund, buy your own traveler's checks— don't let someone else pay for them: irregularities like this can cause delays. The person who bought the checks should make the call to request a refund.

PASSPORTS & VISAS

When traveling internationally, **carry a passport even if you don't need one** (it's always the best form of I.D.), and make **two photocopies of the data page** (one for someone at home and another for you, carried separately from your passport). If you lose your passport, promptly call the nearest embassy or consulate and the local police.

➤ U.K. CITIZENS: **U.S. Embassy Visa Information Line** (☏ 01891/200–290; calls cost 49p per minute, 39p per minute cheap rate), for U.S. visa information. **U.S. Embassy Visa Branch** (⌗ 5 Upper Grosvenor St., London W1A 2JB), for U.S. visa information; send a self-addressed, stamped envelope. Write the **U.S. Consulate General** (⌗ Queen's House, ⌗ Queen St., Belfast BTI 6EO) if you live in Northern Ireland.

➤ AUSTRALIAN CITIZENS: **Australian Passport Office** (☏ 131–232).

➤ NEW ZEALAND CITIZENS: **New Zealand Passport Office** (☏ 04/494–0700 for information on how to apply, 0800/727–776 for information on applications already submitted).

➤ U.K. CITIZENS: **London Passport Office** (☏ 0990/21010), for fees and documentation requirements and to request an emergency passport.

SENIOR-CITIZEN TRAVEL

To qualify for age-related discounts, **mention your senior-citizen status up front** when booking hotel reservations (not when checking out) and before you're seated in restaurants (not when paying the bill). Note that discounts may be limited to certain menus, days, or hours. When renting a car, **ask about promotional car-rental discounts,** which can be cheaper than senior-citizen rates.

➤ EDUCATIONAL PROGRAMS: **Elderhostel** (⌗ 75 Federal St., 3rd floor, Boston, MA 02110, ☏ 617/426–8056).

SIGHTSEEING TOURS

ORIENTATION TOURS

Brush Hill/Gray Line picks up passengers from hotels for 3½-hour Boston–Cambridge tours with stops at the USS *Constitution* and the Tea Party Ship, March through November. Other tours are available to Plymouth, Plimoth Plantation, Cape Cod, Salem and Marblehead, New Hampshire, and Newport. Reserve in advance.

➤ BY BUS: **Brush Hill/Gray Line** (✉ Transportation Bldg., 14 Charles St. South, ☎ 617/236–2148).

Narrated **trolley** tours last about 1½ hours and make frequent stops near Freedom Trail sites, other attractions, and hotels; you can get on and off as you wish. Hours of service listed are for summer; departures may be more infrequent and end earlier off-season.

➤ BY TROLLEY: The red **Beantown Trolleys** (✉ Transportation Bldg., 14 Charles St. South, ☎ 617/236–2148) has 17 stops; cost is $18. Trolleys run every 20 minutes from 9 AM until 4 PM. **Minuteman Tours** (✉ 329 W. 2nd St., South Boston, ☎ 617/269–7010) run their blue trolleys every 20 minutes from 9 AM to 4 PM from May to October; tours cost $15, or $18 with a visit to the Tea Party ship. With the orange and green **Old Town Trolley** (✉ 329 W. 2nd St., South Boston, ☎ 617/269–7010), you can travel expediently, as trolleys run every 10 minutes from 9 AM to 4:30 PM, for $20; summer only, tours are also available through Cambridge. Call for details.

THEME TOURS

➤ BANKING: The **Federal Reserve Bank** (✉ 600 Atlantic Ave., ☎ 617/973–3451) schedules free tours of its money-processing operations every other Friday at 10:30 AM; reserve a week ahead. Children must be 12 or older and accompanied by an adult.

➤ CHILDREN: **Make Way for Ducklings Tours** (✉ Historic Neighborhoods Foundation, 99 Bedford St., ☎ 617/426–1885) follow the route taken by the ducks in Robert McCloskey's eponymous children's book; designed for youngsters five

and older, accompanied by adults, they're offered on Saturday in late spring and on Friday and Saturday from July 4 to Labor Day. Cost is $5 for kids, $7 for adults.

➤ GARDENS AND PARKS: **Beacon Hill Garden Club Tours** (✉ Box 302, Charles St. Station, 02114, ☎ 617/227–4392) are offered one day a year in mid-May. **Boston Park Rangers** (✉ Parks and Recreation Dept., ☎ 617/635–7383) lead free nature walks through many of the city's parks.

➤ HISTORY: **Bay Colony Historical Tours** (✉ Box 9186, JFK Post Office, Boston 02114, ☎ 617/523–7303) offers prearranged private tours of the greater Boston area and Cape Cod for corporate clients, groups, and individuals.

➤ MANUFACTURING: *The Boston Globe* (✉ 135 Wm. T. Morrissey Blvd., ☎ 617/929–2653), the city's largest newspaper, gives free hour-long tours, by appointment, Tuesday and Thursday; participants must be at least 12 years old. The tiny **Commonwealth Brewing Company** (✉ 138 Portland St., ☎ 617/523–8383), which began making English-style ales and stouts by traditional methods in 1986, has free tours by appointment. The 90-minute tours of the **Boston Beer Museum** and Samuel Adams brewery (✉ Boston Beer Company, 30 Germania St., Jamaica Plain, ☎ 617/368–5080), which end with a tasting, are given on Thursday and Friday at 2 and on Saturday at noon, 1, and 2. In July and August, there's an additional tour Wednesday at 2. A $1 donation is requested; it benefits a local charity.

WALKING TOURS

➤ AFRICAN-AMERICAN: **Black Heritage Trail** (☎ 617/742–5415 or 617/742–1854, ☞ Chapter 2, *below*), a self-guided walk, explores Boston's 19th-century black community, passing 14 sites of historical importance on Beacon Hill. Brochures are available at the Museum of Afro-American History (✉ 46 Joy St.) and the Visitor Information Center on the Boston Common (✉ Facing Tremont St.). Rangers lead 90-minute guided walks from April to October at 10, noon, and 2 daily, and in winter by appointment.

➤ BEACON HILL: The **Society for the Preservation of New England Antiquities** (SPNEA; ✉ 141 Cambridge St., ☎ 617/227–3956) conducts a walking tour of Beacon Hill that focuses on the neighborhood as it was in about 1810. Tours are given Saturdays May through October at 3 PM, with an added 10 AM tour in October, and cost $10.

➤ HISTORIC NEIGHBORHOODS: The nonprofit **Historic Neighborhoods Foundation** (✉ 99 Bedford St., ☎ 617/426–1885) covers the North End, Chinatown, Beacon Hill, the waterfront, and other urban areas on 90-minute guided walks Wednesday through Saturday from April through November. Tours cost $5 to $15.

➤ GENERAL-INTEREST: The 2½-mi **Freedom Trail** (☎ 617/242–5642) follows a red line past 16 of Boston's most important historic sites. National park rangers give free 90-minute guided tours daily from April to November. The nonprofit **Boston by Foot** (✉ 77 N. Washington St., ☎ 617/367–2345 or 617/367–3766 for recorded information) offers guided 90-minute walks daily from May to October with specially trained volunteers. Most tours are $8.

➤ MARITIME HISTORY: **Harborwalk,** a self-guided tour, traces Boston's maritime history. Maps are available at the information center on Boston Common.

➤ SPECIAL-INTEREST: The **Boston Center for Adult Education** (✉ 5 Commonwealth Ave., ☎ 617/267–4430) periodically offers walking tours with themes ranging from contemporary art to Jewish Boston, Back Bay mansions, and the Emerald Necklace. **Victorian Society in America/New England Chapter** (✉ Gibson House Museum, 137 Beacon St., ☎ 617/267–6338) tours specific sites, neighborhoods, and architecture representative of the Victorian era.

➤ WOMEN'S HISTORY: **Women's Heritage Trail** (☎ 617/522–2872) celebrates more than 80 accomplished women on four self-guided walks. The Old State House (✉ 206 Washington St.) and the National Park Service visitor center (✉ 15 State St.) sell maps for $5.

WATER TOURS

➤ AROUND THE HARBOR: **Boston Harbor Cruises** (✉ 1 Long Wharf, ☎ 617/227–4321) runs harbor tours from mid-April through October; other trips include sunset and evening entertainment cruises, a $2 lunchtime ride, and trips to the Boston Harbor Islands (Memorial Day–Labor Day). **Massachusetts Bay Lines** (✉ 60 Rowes Wharf, ☎ 617/542–8000) offers evening cruises with rock, blues, or reggae music and dancing, concessions, and cash bar, as well as daily harbor tours ($8) and sunset cruises.

➤ CHARLES RIVER BASIN: The **Charles Riverboat Co.** (✉ 100 CambridgeSide Pl., Suite 320, Cambridge, ☎ 617/621–3001) offers a 55-minute narrated tour of the Charles River Basin. Tours depart from the CambridgeSide Galleria Mall on the hour from noon to 5 daily from June through August and on weekends in April, May, and September; the fare is $8. **Boston Duck Tours** (✉ 790 Boylston St., Plaza Level, ☎ 617/723–3825) has 80-minute city tours that pair major landmarks with a half-hour ride on the Charles River. Tours begin and end at the Huntington Avenue entrance to the Prudential Center (✉ 101 Huntington Ave.). From April through November, tours leave every half hour, 9 AM till dark; fare is $19 ($10 for children 3–12). Tickets are sold inside the Prudential Center 9–8 weekdays and Saturdays, 9–6 Sundays; a limited number of tickets are available for purchase up to two days in advance.

➤ TO GLOUCESTER: **AC Cruise Company** (✉ 290 Northern Ave., ☎ 617/261–6633 or 800/422–8419) offers daily trips to Gloucester from Memorial Day through Labor Day, departing at 10 AM from its Northern Avenue pier; fare is $18.

➤ WHALE-WATCHING: Most whale-watching cruises run between April and the end of October. Cruises are available from the following operators: **AC Cruise Company** (✉ 290 Northern Ave., ☎ 617/261–6633 or

800/422–8419) for $19. **Boston Harbor Cruises** (⊠ 1 Long Wharf, ☎ 617/227–4321) for $22. **Massachusetts Bay Lines** (⊠ 60 Rowes Wharf, ☎ 617/542–8000) for $22. **New England Aquarium** (⊠ Central Wharf, off Atlantic Ave., ☎ 617/973–5277) for $24.

STUDENT TRAVEL

TRAVEL AGENCIES

To save money, **look into deals available through student-oriented travel agencies.** To qualify you'll need a bona fide student I.D. card. Members of international student groups are also eligible.

➤ STUDENT I.D.s & SERVICES: **Council on International Educational Exchange** (⊠ CIEE, ⊠ 205 E. 42nd St., 14th floor, New York, NY 10017, ☎ 212/822–2600 or 888/268–6245, FAX 212/822–2699), for mail orders only, in the United States. **Travel Cuts** (⊠ 187 College St., Toronto, Ontario M5T 1P7, ☎ 416/979–2406 or 800/667–2887) in Canada.

➤ STUDENT TOURS: **Contiki Holidays** (⊠ 300 Plaza Alicante, Suite 900, Garden Grove, CA 92840, ☎ 714/740–0808 or 800/266–8454, FAX 714/740–2034).

SUBWAYS & TROLLEYS

The **Massachusetts Bay Transportation Authority** (MBTA)—or "T" for short—operates subways, elevated trains, and trolleys along four connecting lines. *See also* individual sections for more information.

HOURS & FARES

Trains operate from about 5:30 AM to about 12:30 AM. Current T fares are 85¢ for adults, 40¢ for children ages 5–11. An extra fare is required heading inbound from distant Green and Red Line stops.

INFORMATION

MBTA dispenses information on bus, subway, and train routes; schedules; fares; and other matters including wheelchair access around the clock (☎ 617/222–3200 or 800/392–6100, TTY 617/722–5146).

MAPS

Get them free at the MBTA's Park Street Station information stand; open daily 7 AM–10 PM.

VISITOR PASSES

MBTA visitor passes are available for unlimited travel on city buses and subways for one-, three-, and seven-day periods (fares $5, $9, and $18 respectively). Buy passes at the following MBTA stations: Airport, South Station, North Station, Back Bay, Government Center, and Harvard Square. Passes are also sold at the Boston Common Information Kiosk (☞ Visitor Information, *below*) and at some hotels.

ROUTES

The **Red Line** originates at Braintree and Mattapan to the south; the routes join near South Boston and proceed to suburban Arlington. The **Green Line,** a combined underground and elevated surface line, uses trolleys that operate underground in the central city. It originates at Cambridge's Lechmere, heads south and divides into four routes; these end at Boston College (Commonwealth Avenue), Cleveland Circle (Beacon Street), Riverside, and Heath Street (Huntington Avenue). Buses connect Heath Street to the old Arborway terminus. The **Blue Line** runs weekdays from Bowdoin Square and weeknights and weekends from Government Center to the Wonderland Racetrack in Revere, north of Boston. The **Orange Line** runs from Oak Grove in north suburban Malden to Forest Hills near the Arnold Arboretum. Park Street Station (on the Common) and State Street are the major downtown transfer points.

TAXES

Sales tax of 5% is added to restaurant and take-out meals and to all other items except non-restaurant food and clothing valued less than $175. Hotel room charges in Boston and Cambridge are subject to state and local taxes of up to 12.45%.

TAXIS

Cabs may be hailed on the street; it's easiest to **go to a hotel taxi stand** or

call for a cab. All work around the clock and charge about $1.90 per mi, with a $1.50 base charge; one-way streets often make circuitous routes necessary and increase your cost.

➤ CAB COMPANIES: **Boston Cab Association** (☎ 617/262–2227). **Checker** (☎ 617/536–7000). **Green Cab Association** (☎ 617/628–0600). **Independent Taxi Operators Association or ITOA** (☎ 617/426–8700). **Town Taxi** (☎ 617/536–5000). In Cambridge, **Ambassador Brattle Cab** (☎ 617/492–1100). **Cambridge Taxi** (☎ 617/547–3000).

TELEPHONES

DIRECTORY & OPERATOR INFORMATION

To reach an operator, dial 0. For information, dial 411 for local numbers, or the area code plus 555–1212 for suburban Boston numbers and for long-distance numbers within the United States and Canada.

LOCAL CALLS

The area code for Boston, Cambridge, Brookline, and the innermost ring of suburban towns is 617. Communities in the next ring of suburbs, from Duxbury and Kingston to the south, Wellesley and Lincoln to the west, to Salem and Marblehead north of Boston, are in the 781 area. The area code for towns farther south, including those on Cape Cod, is 508, while communities to the north are in the 978 area.

LONG-DISTANCE CALLS

Competitive long-distance carriers make calling within the United States relatively convenient and let you avoid hotel surcharges.

➤ LONG-DISTANCE CARRIERS: **AT&T** (☎ 800/225–5288). **MCI** (☎ 800/888–8000). **Sprint** (☎ 800/366–2255).

PUBLIC PHONES

Local calls from public phones cost 25 cents.

TIPPING

In restaurants, the standard gratuity is 15%–20% of your bill. Many restaurants automatically add a 15%–18% gratuity for large groups, so if your party includes six or more, ask if a service charge is included. Tip taxi drivers 15% of the fare, airport and hotel porters at least $1 per bag.

TOUR OPERATORS

Buying a prepackaged tour or independent vacation can make your trip to Boston less expensive and more hassle-free. Because everything is prearranged, you'll spend less time planning.

Operators that handle several hundred thousand travelers per year can use their purchasing power to give you a good price. Their high volume may also indicate financial stability. But some small companies provide more personalized service; because they tend to specialize, they may also be more knowledgeable about a given area.

BOOKING WITH AN AGENT

Travel agents are excellent resources. In fact, large operators accept bookings made only through travel agents. But it's a good idea to **collect brochures from several agencies,** because some agents' suggestions may be influenced by relationships with tour and package firms that reward them for volume sales. If you have a special interest, **find an agent with expertise in that area**; ASTA (☞ Travel Agencies, *below*) has a database of specialists worldwide.

Make sure your travel agent knows the accommodations and other services. Ask about the hotel's location, room size, beds, and whether it has a pool, room service, or programs for children, if you care about these. Has your agent been there in person or sent others you can contact?

Do some homework on your own, too: Local tourism boards can provide information about lesser-known and small-niche operators, some of which may only sell direct.

BUYER BEWARE

Each year consumers are stranded or lose their money when tour operators—even very large ones with excellent reputations—go out of business. So **check out the operator.** Find out how long the company has been in business, and ask several travel agents about its reputation. If the package or tour you are considering is priced lower than in your wildest dreams, **be skeptical.** Try to **book with a company that has a consumer-protection program.** If the operator has such a program, you'll find information about it in the company's brochure. If the operator you are considering does not offer some kind of consumer protection, then ask for references from satisfied customers.

In the U.S., members of the National Tour Association and United States Tour Operators Association are required to set aside funds to cover your payments and travel arrangements in case the company defaults. It's also a good idea to choose a company that participates in the American Society of Travel Agent's Tour Operator Program (TOP). This gives you a forum if there are any disputes between you and your tour operator; ASTA will act as mediator.

➤ TOUR-OPERATOR RECOMMENDATIONS: **American Society of Travel Agents** (☞ Travel Agencies, *below*). **National Tour Association** (✉ NTA, ✉ 546 E. Main St., Lexington, KY 40508, ☎ 606/226–4444 or 800/755–8687). **United States Tour Operators Association** (✉ USTOA, ✉ 342 Madison Ave., Suite 1522, New York, NY 10173, ☎ 212/599–6599 or 800/468–7862, FAX 212/599–6744).

COSTS

The more your package or tour includes, the better you can predict the ultimate cost of your vacation. Make sure you know exactly what is covered, and **beware of hidden costs.** Are taxes, tips, and service charges included? Transfers and baggage handling? Entertainment and excursions? These can add up.

Prices for packages and tours are usually quoted per person, based on two sharing a room. If traveling solo, you may be required to pay the full double-occupancy rate. Some operators eliminate this surcharge if you agree to be matched with a roommate of the same sex, even if one is not found by departure time.

GROUP TOURS

Among companies that sell tours to Boston, the following have a proven reputation and offer plenty of options. The classifications used below represent different price categories, and you'll probably encounter these terms when talking to a travel agent or tour operator. The key difference is usually in accommodations, which run from budget to better, and better-yet to best.

➤ TOUR OPERATORS: DELUXE: **Globus** (✉ 5301 S. Federal Circle, Littleton, CO 80123–2980, ☎ 303/797–2800 or 800/221–0090, FAX 303/347–2080). **Maupintour** (✉ 1515 St. Andrews Dr., Lawrence, KS 66047, ☎ 913/843–1211 or 800/255–4266, FAX 913/843–8351). **Tauck Tours** (✉ Box 5027, 276 Post Rd. W, Westport, CT 06881–5027, ☎ 203/226–6911 or 800/468–2825, FAX 203/221–6866).

➤ FIRST CLASS: **Caravan Tours** (✉ 401 N. Michigan Ave., Chicago, IL 60611, ☎ 312/321–9800 or 800/227–2826, FAX 312/321–9845). **Gadabout Tours** (✉ 700 E. Tahquitz Canyon Way, Palm Springs, CA 92262–6767, ☎ 619/325–5556 or 800/952–5068). **Mayflower Tours** (✉ Box 490, 1225 Warren Ave., Downers Grove, IL 60515, ☎ 630/960–3793 or 800/323–7604, FAX 630/960–3575). **Trafalgar Tours** (✉ 11 E. 26th St., New York, NY 10010, ☎ 212/689–8977 or 800/854–0103, FAX 800/457–6644).

➤ BUDGET: **Cosmos** and **Trafalgar Tours** (☞ *above*).

PACKAGES

Like group tours, independent vacation packages are available from major tour operators and airlines. The companies listed below offer vacation packages in a broad price range.

➤ AIR/HOTEL: **Delta Vacations** (☎ 800/872–7786, FAX 954/357–4687).

➤ CUSTOM PACKAGES: **Amtrak Vacations** (☎ 800/321–8684).

➤ FROM THE U.K.: **Americana Vacations Ltd.** (✉ 11Little Portland St., London W1N 5DF, , ☎ 0171/637–7853). **British Airways Holidays** (✉

Astral Towers, Betts Way, London Rd., Crawley, West Sussex RH10 2XA, ☎ 01293/723–121). **Key to America** (⊠ 1–3 Station Rd., Ashford, Middlesex TW15 2UW, ☎ 01784/248–777). **Kuoni Travel** (⊠ Kuoni House, Dorking, Surrey RH5 4AZ, ☎ 01306/740–500). **Northwest Fly–Drive** (⊠ Box 45, Bexhill on Sea, East Sussex TN40 1PY, ☎ 01424/224–400). **Premier Holidays** (⊠ Westbrook, Milton Rd., Cambridge CB4 1YQ, ☎ 01223/516–516). **Trailfinders** (⊠ 50 Earls Court Rd., London W8 6EJ, ☎ 0171/937–5400; ⊠ 58 Deansgate, Manchester M3 2FF, ☎ 0161/839–6969).

THEME TRIPS

➤ FALL FOLIAGE: All of the group tour operators (*above*) offer these.

➤ SPAS: **Spa-Finders** (⊠ 91 Fifth Ave., #301, New York, NY 10003–3039, ☎ 212/924–6800 or 800/255–7727).

➤ WHALE-WATCHING: **Oceanic Society Expeditions** (⊠ Fort Mason Center, Bldg. E, San Francisco, CA 94123–1394, ☎ 415/441–1106 or 800/326–7491, FAX 415/474–3395).

TRAIN TRAVEL

Boston is served by Amtrak at South Station and Back Bay Station, which accomodates frequent departures for and arrivals from New York, Philadelphia, and Washington, D.C. South Station is also the eastern terminus of Amtrak's *Lake Shore Limited,* which travels daily between Boston and Chicago by way of Albany, Rochester, Buffalo, and Cleveland. Amtrak's *New England Express,* making the New York run twice a day, departs from South Station and Back Bay Station; reservations are required and travel time is approximately four hours.

The MBTA runs commuter trains to points south, west, and north. Those bound for Framingham, Needham, Franklin, Providence (RI), and Stoughton leave from South Station and Back Bay Station; those to Fitchburg, Lowell, Haverhill, Ipswich, and Rockport operate out of North Station (⊠ Causeway and Friend Sts.) (☞ Subways & Trolleys, *above*.)

➤ TRAIN INFORMATION: **Amtrak** (☎ 617/482–3660 or 800/872–7245). **South Station** (⊠ Atlantic Ave. and Summer St., ☎ 617/345–7451).

TRANSPORTATION

Most of Boston was laid out long before the automobile, so streets—particularly in older neighborhoods such as Beacon Hill and the West End—can lose their charm when you're a driver frustrated by the lack of parking. Boston's public transportation system, the T (☞ Subways & Trolleys, *above*) is superlative; it is easy and inexpensive and can get you quickly from one end of the city to another or from Boston to Cambridge or other outlying towns. If you're planning to try an out-of-the-way restaurant at an odd hour, a car will be helpful, and it will also make visiting Boston's farther-flung sights—such as those in the "streetcar suburbs" (☞ Chapter 2)—easier. For excursions outside the city, a car is practically required.

TRAVEL AGENCIES

A good travel agent puts your needs first. Look for an agency that has been in business at least five years, emphasizes customer service, and has someone on staff who specializes in your destination. In addition, **make sure the agency belongs to a professional trade organization,** such as ASTA in the United States. If your travel agency is also acting as your tour operator, *see* Buyer Beware in Tour Operators, *above*).

➤ LOCAL AGENT REFERRALS: **American Society of Travel Agents** (ASTA, ☎ 800/965–2782 24-hr hotline, FAX 703/684–8319). **Association of Canadian Travel Agents** (⊠ Suite 201, 1729 Bank St., Ottawa, Ontario K1V 7Z5, ☎ 613/521–0474, FAX 613/521–0805). **Association of British Travel Agents** (⊠ 55–57 Newman St., London W1P 4AH, ☎ 0171/637–2444, FAX 0171/637–0713). **Australian Federation of Travel Agents** (☎ 02/9264–3299). **Travel Agents' Association of New Zealand** (☎ 04/499–0104).

VISITOR INFORMATION

Before you go, contact the city and state tourism offices below for general information. The National Park Service has a Boston office where you can watch an eight-minute slide show on Boston's historic sites and get maps and directions. For general information when you get to Boston, look for the Welcome Center and Boston Common Information Kiosk. The Traveler's Aid Society helps distressed travelers.

➤ CITY: **Greater Boston Convention and Visitors Bureau** (✉ 2 Copley Pl., Suite 105, Boston 02116, ☎ 617/536–4100 or 800/888–5515). **Boston Common Information Kiosk** (✉ Tremont St., where the Freedom Trail begins, ☎ 617/426–3115); open Monday–Saturday 8:30–5 and Sunday 9–5). **Boston Welcome Center** (✉ 140 Tremont St., Boston 02111, ☎ 617/451–2227); open Sunday–Thursday 9–5 and Friday-Saturday 9–6 in winter, open till daily 9–7 (except Sundays 9–5) in summer **Traveler's Aid Society** (☞ Emergencies, *above*).

➤ NATIONAL PARKS: **The Boston National Historical Park Visitor Center** (✉ 15 State St., across from Old State House, ☎ 617/242–5642 ⊘ daily 9–5 in winter, daily 9–6 in summer).

➤ STATE: **Massachusetts Office of Travel and Tourism** (✉ 100 Cambridge St., 13th floor, Boston 02202, ☎ 617/727–3201 or 800/447–6277, FAX 617/727–6525).

➤ IN THE U.K.: **First Public Relations** (✉ Molasses House, Clove Hitch Quay, Plantation Wharf, London SW11 3TN, ☎ 0171/978–5233, FAX 0171/924–3134).

WHEN TO GO

Where the weather is concerned, it's best to **visit Boston in late spring and in September and October.** Like other American cities of the northeast, Boston can be uncomfortably hot and humid in high summer and freezing cold in the winter. Yet the city is not without its pleasures in these seasons. In summer, there are concerts on the Esplanade, harbor cruises, and sidewalk cafés. In winter there is Christmas shopping, First Night festivities on New Year's Eve, and music season. And a lot can be said for winter afternoon light on red brick.

Each September, Boston and Cambridge welcome thousands of returning students. University life is a big part of the local atmosphere, and it begins to liven considerably as the days grow shorter.

Autumn is a fine time to visit the suburbs. The combination of bright foliage and white church steeples will never become clichéd.

For a classic shore vacation, summer is the only time to go, but make your reservations early in the year.

➤ FORECASTS: **Weather Channel Connection** (☎ 900/932–8437), 95¢ per minute from a Touch-Tone phone.

Climate in Boston

Jan.	36F	2C	May	66F	19C	Sept.	71F	22C
	20	–7		49	9		55	13
Feb.	37F	3C	June	75F	24C	Oct.	62F	17C
	21	–6		58	14		46	8
Mar.	43F	6C	July	80F	27C	Nov.	49F	9C
	28	–2		63	17		35	2
Apr.	54F	12C	Aug.	78F	26C	Dec.	40F	4C
	38	3		62	17		25	–4

1 Destination: Boston

THE CITIES NAMED BOSTON

TWO DESTINATIONS NAMED BOSTON occupy the clutch of irregularly shaped peninsulas at the westernmost recess of Massachusetts Bay. The tourist's Boston is the old city, far older than the republic it helped to create, soul and anchor of that peculiar thing called New England civilization, and the cradle of American independence. Its most famous buildings are not merely civic landmarks but national icons; its great citizens are not the political and financial leaders of today but the Adamses, Reveres, and Hancocks who live at the crossroads of history and myth.

The other Boston, built no less by design than the original, is barely three decades old. This is the business traveler's destination, the new Boston created by high finance and higher technology, where granite and glass towers rise along what once had been rutted village lanes. In this new city, Samuel Adams is the name of a premium beer, and John Hancock is an insurance company with a dramatic headquarters tower designed by I. M. Pei.

It is entirely possible to come to Boston intent on visiting either the Freedom Trail or the 48th floor of Amalgamated Software and to get exactly what you want out of the experience. With a little extra time and effort, though, you can appreciate both the old and the new Boston and understand why they are really one and the same American city.

Boston is where the Mystic and the Charles flow together to form the Atlantic Ocean. That's the old attitude, and it has been reinforced by local anecdotes, such as the one about the Boston lady who said she had driven to the West Coast "by way of Dedham," and the one about the two Bostonians who blamed a spate of hot San Francisco weather on the fact that the sea was 3,000 mi distant.

The sayings and stories reinforce the popular notion that Boston is exceedingly self-important. Yet Bostonians are not the only people who take the place so seriously. Boston, in reality and in myth, surely looms larger than any other settlement of close to 600,000 souls in the United States, with the possible exception of San Francisco. The reason for this is hard to come by, but it has to be more than merely the result of masterful self-promotion on the part of a city where "the Lowells speak only to the Cabots, and the Cabots speak only to God" and the common folk used to vote "often and early for James Michael Curley."

Boston has an odd combination of reputations to live up to. For years, the standard line was that it was staid, respectable, and quick to raise its eyebrows at anything or anyone smacking of impropriety. It was a town in which the Watch and Ward Society recommended the books and plays that ought to be banned, where the major social outlets were evenings at the Symphony and afternoons at the Club, and where the loudest noise was the sound of dust and interest collecting on old Yankee money. More recently, word has gone around that Boston's enormous population of undergraduate and graduate students, artists, academics, wealthy Europeans, and smart young professionals who graduated and stayed on have made the town a haven for foreign movies, late-night bookstores, racquetball, sushi restaurants, unconventional politics, and progressive rock bands.

Neither view is closer to the truth than the other, and neither will do on its own. For all its age and small physical size, Boston is one of the least socially homogeneous cities on earth. Sure, men with three last names sit in leather wing chairs at the Somerset Club, but in most of the city the prevailing idea of a club is the Holy Name Society or the Sons of Italy. Yes, you will see lampposts plastered with ads for performances by radical dance collectives, but Boston's big political concerns revolve around which shade of Democrat is running for high city office (a Republican would as soon swim to Provincetown) and how he will dispense help to the homeless, asphalt to the potholes, and goodwill to the high-tech barons. Despite its small size, Boston compartmentalizes itself so neatly that you can come here and find as staid or as hip a city as you desire.

In considering the roots of the Boston image and the Boston reality, we have to recognize two overwhelming influences on the Boston we know today. The first is definitely Anglo-Saxon, which can be either Yankee or Brahmin. The second is unquestionably Irish. Though there may never have been much love lost between the two factions, Boston is their mutual creation.

Most of the Yankees' ancestors left England in the 17th or the 18th century with little more than the clothes on their backs. There was nothing aristocratic about them then, and there is nothing aristocratic about them today—assuming we encounter them as the unspectacular yeomen and urban-suburban bourgeoisie who constitute the base coat of New England's overlay of populations. In the 1700s and early 1800s, however, some of them began to acquire fortunes to go with their ancient lineage, and thus the Brahmin was born. The term was first used by Dr. Oliver Wendell Holmes in *The Autocrat of the Breakfast-Table*: "He comes of the Brahmin caste of New England. This is the harmless, inoffensive, untitled aristocracy." Holmes himself was a sterling example of a Brahmin, as was his son and namesake the Supreme Court justice. Although not spectacularly wealthy, the Holmeses were vastly learned and endowed with a sense of civic responsibility. When combined with pedigree, these qualities counted as much as money in establishing the Brahmin mystique.

Money counted less and less as the years separated the Brahmins from their merchant-prince and industrialist ancestors who provided them with their China-trade porcelain, Back Bay town houses, and summer homes in Nahant. It became something you had but didn't talk about, something you devoted no great amount of time to multiplying. One theory as to why Boston lost out to New York in the struggle for financial supremacy in post–Civil War America credits the practice of tying up family legacies in trusteeships so that potential venture capital was inaccessible to one's heirs. Making money with gusto began to seem gauche, a frenetic activity best left to ostentatious New Yorkers. It was thought far better to husband your resources and live a seemly life.

At worst, this attitude created a race of "cold-roast Bostonians," thin-lipped and tight with a dollar, as conservative in the realm of social and aesthetic ideas as they were with their portfolios. At best, it produced an atmosphere in which people spent their energies on public beneficence and the cultivation of the life of the mind. Such organizations as the Appalachian Mountain Club were talked into vigorous existence over sherry and biscuits in the homes of comfortable men. Colonel Henry Lee Higginson founded the Boston Symphony and financed it for years out of his own pocket. And men like Thomas Appleton cultivated salons in which good conversation for its own sake was the prized commodity.

MOST IMPORTANT, the old Yankee fortunes poured into education; putting money into college endowments was the logical extension of the acute concern with education that the Puritans brought to Boston in 1630 and that manifested itself during that first decade in John Harvard's donation of his library to form the cornerstone of Harvard College. Finally, it was the means by which the idea of Boston as stodgy, intolerant, and unchanging was laid to rest. The strains of liberality evident in the intellectual and economic climate today are owed to the tremendous influx of fertile minds that the great investment in education made possible.

As Boston is a city of colleges, it is also a city of neighborhoods. Neighborhoods are the bastions of continuity in a big city, places where a certain outlook and sense of parochial identity are preserved. Ironically, Boston's ethnic groups, the Irish in particular, have managed to maintain the conservative, tradition-minded neighborhood spirit cultivated by the Yankees when all Boston was the neighborhood. If any custom replaced beans and brown bread on Saturday night in the Back Bay, it was fish and chips during Lent in Charlestown and Southie. The Irish, in this century, have been the keel of Boston.

THE IRISH BEGAN to arrive in the late 1840s, when the potato famine devastated their home island. Boston had never seen such an invasion of immigrants and was anything but ready. The famous "No Irish Need

Apply" signs went up, although the rapid growth of the city made it necessary for the natives to give the Irish jobs. There were only so many farm girls willing to come to the city and enter domestic service, and few businesses during the boom time of the Civil War era could afford the Waltham Watch Company's "Yankees only" employment strictures.

The Irish found their way into jobs and into the social structure. Two avenues appealed to them especially: the civil service, particularly in the police and fire departments, and local politics. The venture into politics was in large part a defensive maneuver, a means of consolidating power in municipal institutions when it was denied them in the social and economic spheres. The first Irish mayor was elected in 1886, and by 1906 John F. Fitzgerald, the legendary "Honey Fitz," held the office. He was fiercely Irish, the most flamboyant and assertive Boston politician, until Mayor Curley himself appeared and defined big-city machine politics.

The wresting of political power from the Yankees allowed the Irish and their more recently arrived ethnic allies to take care of their own, and loyalty and votes were the mortar in the agreement. Similarly, civil service and other relatively secure blue-collar positions were a path to the kind of security that translated itself into stable, parish-oriented neighborhoods made up of row upon row of triple-decker apartment buildings, the wooden monoliths known in Boston as "Irish battleships." While you are in the area, read one of Mike Barnicle's *Boston Globe* columns, which often recall the spirit of these neighborhoods. (Barnicle has long since decamped for the suburbs.)

The Irish and other ethnics, then, are the heirs and guardians of the old Boston insularity and stability. It was neighborhood (not just Irish) discomfiture at the violation of this state of affairs that produced the terrible antagonisms associated with court-ordered school busing in the early 1970s. The new minorities—blacks, Hispanics, Asians—often find themselves in a situation similar to that faced by the new arrivals in the last century.

Nowadays working-class white enclaves and poor minority neighborhoods alike worry about the effects of gentrification, loosely defined as the migration of upper-middle-class, white-collar workers and professionals (including many gay men and lesbians and couples who haven't yet had children) into the core of the city, where there are town houses to be restored and apartments to be converted into condominiums. Places like Union Park in the South End and some of the streets around the Bunker Hill Monument in Charlestown look better than they have in years, and the city can certainly use the tax base. New businesses flourish, often selling gourmet scones and the *Wall Street Journal* across from Hispanic bodegas and tired old luncheonettes. There are people who insist that such blocks are pretty but sterile and that the old neighborhood identities have gone. One thing is certain: We have not seen the end of this movement.

The new gentry is evidence of the success of Boston's 30-year attempt to redefine its place in New England and the world. By the 1950s, Boston was living on its past. The industrial base had eroded, the population had begun to decrease (it is still about 100,000 below its peak), and the high-tech era had yet to begin. To successive mayors Hynes, Collins, and White, and to the fiscal nabobs who made up the private advisory group known as "the Vault," it seemed to make sense to play up the service aspects of the local economy and at the same time to launch vast tear-down-and-start-over projects like the Prudential Center and Government Center. By the '70s the emphasis had shifted from new construction to recycling old buildings, except downtown, where office towers rose at a frantic pace in the '80s.

To a significant degree the plan has worked, and the legions of condo buyers and townhouse restorers are part of a new order only temporarily slowed by the recession of the early '90s. What remains are the questions of how the old neighborhoods will fit in, whether the public school system can be salvaged, and whether there will be a middle class of any size in Boston as the century draws to a close.

Given a population with such divergent antecedents, it is difficult to point to a "typical" Bostonian, although you see a number of types—Cambridge academics, North Shore Brahmin ladies in town for the Friday afternoon symphony, business-suited young women with rucksacks and running shoes. Even the famous old Boston accent is hard to pin down, beyond a few broad *A*s and dropped *R*s; there are so many emigrants from other parts of the country that the native speech has become hopelessly diluted. (One thing is certain: *No one* talks like the Kennedys, who developed an Irish Brahmin accent all their own.)

Your essential Bostonian does love sports and politics, probably because both are vehicles for argument. The disputations could well be carried past recent Red Sox trades and the City Council to questions of whether Boston is on its way up or down, whether it is forward-thinking or preoccupied with the past, whether Boston is fashionable or dowdy, progressive or conservative, wise to the world or just kidding itself. Go into a bar, and pick your topic. You may well decide that it is sheer contentiousness, often mixed with respectable intelligence and more than a little rectitude, that put Boston on the map.

–William G. Scheller

The author of More Country Walks Near Boston *and* New Hampshire: Portrait of the Land and Its People, *William Scheller contributes frequently to national and regional publications.*

NEW AND NOTEWORTHY

Downtown Boston is in the midst of a massive multiyear construction project, known locally as **The Big Dig.** When completed, the elevated Central Artery that bisects the downtown area will be redirected underground, and the city center will be reunited with the North End and the waterfront. In the meantime, traffic delays and street closings abound. Allow extra time when traveling in this area.

The stained-glass **Mapparium** in the world headquarters of the Christian Science Church closed for renovations in March 1998 and will reopen in February 2000. The colorful globe depicts the world as it was in 1932. Tours of the Mother Church and other church exhibits will continue.

The Sports Museum, which recently opened a permanent venue in Lowell, Massachusetts, after a shaky history at the Cambridgeside Galleria, in March 1998 opened

a new exhibit at the FleetCenter on the 5th and 6th floor of the concourse level that celebrates the gone, but hardly forgotten Boston Garden (or *Gah*-den in Bostonspeak). The FleetCenter replaced the Boston Garden as the city's premiere site for sporting events.

This most Irish of cities got another reminder of its rich immigrant past in June of 1998 when a permanent **memorial to the Irish Famine** was scheduled to be completed in downtown Boston along the Freedom Trail, opposite historic Old South Meeting House. The $1-million park memorial consists of two sculptures by artist Rober Shure, one depicting an anguished family on the shores of Ireland, the other a determined and hopeful Irish family stepping ashore in Boston.

What goes around, comes around: A **furniture district**—in a location that was once a furniture district—is emerging near the intersection of Arlington and Boylston streets, in an area bounded by the South End, Back Bay, and the Theater District. In February 1998, the Cambridge-based Mohr & McPherson opened a branch (81 Arlington St.) of its ethnic and imported furniture business. Just blocks away are: veteran contemporary furniture store Adesso (200 Boylston St.); Repertoire (114 Boylston St.), a chic source for Italian and European design; and the Morson Collection (31 St. James Ave.). In the area also are standbys ranging from Laura Ashley Home (75 Arlington St.) to Jennifer Convertibles and Leathers and the Leather Center (all in the 300 block of Boylston St.).

Efforts to spiff and spruce up the venerable **Freedom Trail** continue. The city has replaced the red painted line with red brick (wherever brick was needed), sites are now identified by distinctive medallions, and colorful new banners help guide you en route. Most of the sites are individually owned and run; each fiercely guards its independence while seeking to make the trail work as a whole. (Sound like any colonies you know? Say, 13 back in the 1780s?)

The **Museum of Fine Arts,** in December 1997, opened three new galleries to highlight the arts of Africa, Oceania, and the ancient Americas. The African gallery focuses on masks, sculptures of figures, and many works that are less than 100 years old, representing items still used for celebrations and ceremonies in West and Central Africa. The Oceanic gallery displays works created by inhabitants of Melanesia and Polynesia. The works in the Ancient Americas gallery include Olmec stone sculptures, Mayan ceramics, Andean textiles and ceramics, and gold jewelry from a number of cultures across the Americas.

When was the last time you heard of an urban park expanding, much less by 24 acres? Usually parks must fight tooth-and-nail to keep developers at bay, but through a delicate series of negotiations, the **Arnold Arboretum** has acquired 24 acres to enhance the city's Emerald Necklace park lands. This parcel, the first land formally added to a Boston city park in more than a century and known as **Stony Brook Marsh,** will be retained as a wetlands without the kind of planting seen in the Arboretum proper. The arboretum plans to create a walking trail to lead from the Forest Hills MBTA station through the marsh area to the park's Forest Hills Gate, but a completion date has not been announced.

Finally, as you plan your trip to Boston in 1999, be sure to book a hotel or B&B room as far in advance as you can. **Few newly built hotels** means that Boston has one of the highest hotel occupancy rates of any city in the nation—and increased rates at many of the city's better hotels. Peak times of year when rooms can be particularly hard to come by are the graduation months of May and June and the fall-foliage season.

In the late fall of 1997, **Harborside Inn** was opened in a renovated warehouse building downtown near Faneuil Hall, the New England Aquarium, and the financial district by the family that owns the Newbury Guest House. The luxury **Seaport Hotel and Conference Center** opened in Boston off Northern Avenue opposite the World Trade Center on May 1, 1998. Clearly designed for the corporate executive, it has sophisticated electronic and communications amenites.

Boston's **restaurant** scene is booming: Weekend reservations for the city's newest spots are hard to come by unless you book at least a couple of weeks in advance.

WHAT'S WHERE

Boston, at least north and east of Massachusetts Avenue, is a compact city whose neighborhoods can be divided along precise lines. They share only their passion for the Red Sox, zip codes beginning with 02, and the "T," as they call the Massachusetts Bay Transit Authority, which unites them via trolleys, subways, elevated trains, and conventional buses. In many instances, their names recall their situation centuries ago, before land reclamations beginning after the American Revolution forever changed the shoreline.

The Back Bay

Extending along the Charles opposite Cambridge as far as Kenmore Square, south and west of Beacon Hill, it's the epitome of propriety, a veritable open-air museum of urban Victorian residential architecture, by turns French-influenced, Italianate, and reflecting revivals of gothic and other styles. Its streets recall Paris boulevards, which Baron Haussman had laid out not long before the Back Bay was developed on 19th-century landfill. The Public Garden, also built on landfill, is in character truly a part of the Back Bay, although just across Charles Street from the Common (which is more properly part of Beacon Hill). Copley Place, the Prudential Tower, and Symphony Hall are also here.

Beacon Hill

Earth scraped off the top of this height of land, named for the light that topped it in the 17th century, was put to use as landfill not far away. What remains is redolent of old Boston, with its gas lamps, shade trees, brick sidewalks, and stately brick town houses built between 1800 and 1850 in Federal style; many are now broken up into condominium apartments. Two of the loveliest thoroughfares are Chestnut and Mt. Vernon streets; the latter opens out onto Louisburg Square, where William Dean Howells and the Alcotts once lived.

Charlestown

This neighborhood on the north end of the Charlestown Bridge, across from the North End, is home to Bunker Hill and the USS *Constitution,* a tangle of masts and rigging moored at the Charlestown Navy Yard, now a National Historic Site for its long and continuous involvement in the American shipbuilding industry. Charlestown is becoming increasingly gentrified; you can glimpse home computers and house plants through newly gleaming windows, while the neighborhood eateries are developing devoted followers among the "Townies."

Downtown Boston and Chinatown

The city's retail and financial districts constitute downtown, anchored by Faneuil Hall and Quincy Market on the north; Chinatown, the Theater District, and South Station on the south; Tremont Street and the Common on the west; and the harbor and the New England Aquarium to the east. The main commercial thoroughfare is Washington Street. Elizabeth Pain, the model for Nathaniel Hawthorne's scarlet-letter-wearing Hester Prynne, is buried at King's Chapel here, not far from the Theater District, the Old State House, and those monuments to the mercantile mentality, Filene's and Macy's.

East Boston

With the airport, it's across the inner harbor to the north and east. Once a uniformly Italian neighborhood, East Boston is now also home to a thriving Latino population. Santarpio's Pizza is famous here, with a line stretching down Chelsea Street every night.

The Fens

This is the former swampland, south of Kenmore Square and southwest of the Back Bay, that Boston planners filled with green space rather than pavement, commissioning 19th-century American landscape architect Frederick Law Olmsted to do the work. In his hands, the landscape retains an aura of its marshy origins, by way of irregular, reed-bound pools. But between them are wide meadows, trees, and gardens of flowers. Nearby is a baseball stadium, Fenway Park—built in 1912 and still with a field that's real turf—plus two celebrated art museums, the immense, important Boston Museum of Fine Arts and the idiosyncratic, Venetian palazzo–inspired Isabella Stewart Gardner Museum.

The North End and Government Center

The northernmost tip of the peninsula, cut off from Boston's other neighborhoods by the Central Artery and Government Center, this is one of the city's oldest sections, and many of its earliest structures went up in the 17th century, when Shakespeare was a contemporary figure, albeit recently dead, and Louis XIV had just ascended to the French throne. The Old North Church, made famous in Longfellow's "Paul Revere's Ride," is here, along with—despite creeping gentrification—a voluble, zesty Italian population and the businesses that serve the neighborhood: restaurants, groceries, bakeries, churches, social clubs, and cafés.

The Old West End

Just a few brick tenements are all that remain of this area north of Beacon Hill across Cambridge Street and west of the Central Artery. Landmarks include the Charles River Park apartment and retail development, the Suffolk County Jail, and Mass General, as the local public hospital is known. However, you're more likely to find yourself in the area to visit the Museum of Science, to share a pint of Guinness with your mates at the Harp, or to watch the Celtics play basketball at the FleetCenter.

South Boston

This area juts due east toward the outer harbor and its cluster of islands; it is not to be confused with the South End. Another landfill project of the mid-1880s, it came into its own around 1900 with the influx of Irish immigration, and the Irish are still an important presence. It's the site of the Boston Children's Museum and the world's only Computer Museum, adjacent. Hundreds of artists have descended on A Street, once a stretch of abandoned warehouses next to the post office, now transformed into posh lofts and galleries.

The South End

Not to be confused with South Boston, this area hugging the Huntington Avenue flank of the Back Bay, southeast of the Back Bay and due south of Chinatown, is another 19th-century development. But with its park-centered squares and blocks of extravagantly embellished bowfront Victorian houses, it's less Parisian in style than

English. Today it's multiethnic and polyglot, both Spanish and Asian, with Middle Eastern groceries along Shawmut Avenue and some gentrification, including a new restaurant row along Tremont Street. Rainbow flags and window boxes decorate many of the brownstones, heralding its large gay population.

Cambridge

A kissing cousin just across the Charles River from Boston, Cambridge has long been a haven for writers, radicals, free thinkers and iconoclasts of all kinds. Home to two of the world's best universities—Harvard and MIT—and a huge population of students, Cambridge has an eclectic mix of cafés, bookstores, record shops, funky clothing outlets, and crafts galleries. Its Harvard University museums—the Fogg and the Peabody, most notably—are among the nation's best. Despite its rarefied reputation, Cambridge also has concentrated ethnic and working-class neighborhoods in East Cambridge and Cambridgeport, seemingly light years from the Colonial-era mansions on toney Brattle Street near Harvard Square.

Suburban Areas

South of the Back Bay Fens is Roxbury, a largely black neighborhood that merges along its eastern border with biracial but poorly integrated Dorchester, and Jamaica Plain, one of the first of the "streetcar suburbs" brought into existence by turn-of-the-century trolley lines. West of Kenmore Square is the separate municipality of Brookline, which almost completely cuts off Allston and Brighton, two residential and industrial Boston neighborhoods, from the rest of the city. Brookline, long home to many of the Boston area's Jewish families, now shares with Allston and Brighton an increasing number of Asian residents.

Farther south still are West Roxbury, Roslindale, Hyde Park, and Mattapan—virtual suburbs within the city. People here are more likely to identify themselves as coming from these neighborhoods than as hailing from Boston itself. After all, parts of them are farther from Beacon Hill than Cambridge, Medford, or Winthrop.

PLEASURES AND PASTIMES

Colleges

More than anything else, the Yankee investment in scores of colleges and universities in and around Boston has helped establish its present character. People come here for schooling and never go home. And every year in August and September, fleets of trucks, vans, and overloaded family sedans converge on the city as students of BC, BU, Harvard, MIT, Northeastern, and more than a dozen others welcome back the thousands of students who help rouse the city from its summer rest.

Day Trips

You've only to travel a short distance to visit sites connected with historic figures you started reading about back in grade school. *See* Chapter 9 for the many different destinations nearby.

Festivals

Though Boston has been a popular summer tourist destination for many years, the fact is that whatever time of year you visit, the town has some event going on. *See* Festivals and Seasonal Events, *below,* for a complete list of the best the city has to offer.

History

Perhaps no one today would speak of the Boston State House as "the hub of the solar system," as Oliver Wendell Holmes once did, yet it is very much at the heart of American history, both past and present. So much of the political ferment that spawned the nation took place here. The earthly remains of Cotton and Increase Mather, the 17th-century Boston theocrats, are in Copp's Hill Burying Ground; the chips in the headstones came about during British soldiers' target practices, and you can still see the pockmarks of musketballs. It was at Faneuil Hall that Samuel Adams first suggested, in 1772, that the Colonies organize a Committee of Correspondence to maintain lines of communication in the face of British oppression. In the North End is the Old North Church, famous for the two lanterns that glimmered from its steeple on the night of April 18, 1775, warning Americans of British troop movements by sea. Heroes of the American Revolution are buried in its Old Granary Burial Ground: Samuel Adams, John Hancock, James Otis, Paul Revere. American portraitist Gilbert Stuart is buried in the Central Burying Ground, along with scores of British casualties of the Battle of Bunker Hill. Moored in Fort Point Channel is a replica of one of the ships whose forcible unloading occasioned the famous Boston Tea Party. And all around these sights and sites are vintage buildings, both maintained and restored, so that the feeling of history surrounding you is almost palpable.

Parks and Gardens

The Boston Common, the oldest public park in the United States, is only one of Boston's green spaces. The Boston Public Garden, which abuts it across Charles Street, is the country's oldest botanical garden; the irregularly shaped pond in the center is famous for the swan boats that cruise it in warm months. The Fens, a landscape of meadows, trees, gardens, and reed-bound pools designed by noted landscape architect Frederick Law Olmsted, marks the beginning of Boston's famous Emerald Necklace, a chain of parks that extends along the Fenway, Riverway, and Jamaica Way to Jamaica Pond, the Arnold Arboretum, and Franklin Park. This loosely connected necklace of green has made Boston famous among 20th-century urban planners.

Walking

Boston is on a human scale, and it is best experienced by walking. The North End, Boston's Italian neighborhood, just a 20-minute walk from Beacon Hill, is quite another world. The highlight of any visit to Boston in '99 should be the memory of walks and sights around town: along the redbrick sidewalks of Beacon Hill (particularly Pinckney, Mt. Vernon, Chestnut, and Beacon streets), along the Freedom Trail through the crannied lanes of the North End, catching the Charles River breezes from the Esplanade, along the shores of the Public Garden's pond, along the Boston Harbor waterfront at the back side of the New England Aquarium, and through the Arnold Arboretum, especially in spring, when its lilacs, azaleas, rhododendrons, and fruit trees are in full bloom. Another memorable walk: from the Ritz-Carlton Hotel, down Newbury Street to Gloucester Street, right on Gloucester to Commonwealth Avenue, and right on Commonwealth to the Public Garden.

GREAT ITINERARIES

You could easily spend two weeks exploring Boston and its surrounding towns, but if you're here for just a short period you need to plan carefully so you don't miss the must-see sights. The following suggested itineraries will help you structure your visit efficiently. *See* the Boston neighborhood exploring tours in Chapter 2 and the Cambridge neighborhood exploring tours in Chapter 3. As small in size as it is large in history, Boston can be thoroughly explored by foot. Bring sturdy walking shoes and be prepared for the ever-unpredictable weather.

If You Have 2 Days

DAY 1➤ Start with a stroll through the **Public Garden.** Wander through the narrow streets of **Beacon Hill,** with a stop at the **Statehouse,** the **Old Granary Burying Ground,** and **King's Chapel.** Follow Beacon Street toward the Back Bay for a peek at the **"Cheers" Bar.** After lunch on Charles Street, cross the **Boston Common** into **Downtown Crossing.** From there, follow the **Freedom Trail** to **Fanueil Hall** and **Quincy Market** (stopping for a late afternoon drink) and into the North End for a visit to **Paul Revere's home** and the **Old North Church.** Dine at one of the neighborhood's trattorias, followed by cappuccino and cannoli at a pastry shop.

DAY 2➤ Spend the morning at the **Museum of Fine Arts,** accessible by the MBTA. Lunch in the **Gardner Museum.** Or spend the morning at the **New England Aquarium** and **Computer Museum.** In the afternoon, go by T into Cambridge to explore **Harvard Square,** or take the Green Line back to **Back Bay** for some elegant shopping on **Newbury Street.** As night falls, head for the Prudential Center's **Skywalk** for a romantic view of the city at sunset. Then it's time for dinner in the **Theater District,** followed by a late-night comedy show.

If You Have 5 Days

DAY 1➤ Walk **Beacon Hill** and explore the **Black Heritage Trail.** Antiques shop on **Charles Street.** Explore the **Boston Common** and the **Public Garden,** and then take a stroll along the **Esplanade.** Dine in the evening in the **Theater District,** and follow that with a show.

DAY 2➤ Visit the **Museum of Science,** and then take a stroll along the **Charles.** Hop the T into **Kenmore Square** for dinner and spend the evening club-hopping on Landsdowne Street. Or, on a more sedate Wednesday night, spend the evening at the **Museum of Fine Arts** with dinner in the Fine Arts Café.

DAY 3➤ Walk the **Freedom Trail,** pausing to shop at **Downtown Crossing** and **Fanueil Hall.** After visiting the **USS *Constitution*** in Charlestown, catch the water shuttle to downtown. Walk into the **North End** for dinner.

DAY 4➤ Visit the **Plimoth Plantation** and ***Mayflower II*** in Plymouth, south of Boston.

DAY 5➤ Walk through **Back Bay** to marvel at its mansions, with stops at the **Boston Public Library** and the **Gibson House.** Stroll east to **Newbury Street** for fine shopping and dinner.

If You Have 8 Days

You may wish to use an extended visit to linger at many sites. Although a car isn't necessary to explore Boston or Cambridge, you'll need it to get to sites some distance from the city. And if you don't venture out at rush hour, it takes just a short time to get outside the city limits.

DAY 1➤ Walk the **Freedom Trail** from the **Boston Common** to the **USS *Constitution.***

DAY 2➤ On Boston's waterfront, visit either the **New England Aquarium,** the **Children's Museum,** or the **Computer Museum.** Top any of these off with the **Boston Tea Party Museum.** In the early summer, consider a whale-watching tour that leaves from the **Aquarium.**

DAY 3➤ Drive north to **Salem** for a day at the **Salem Witch Museum** and **House of Seven Gables.**

DAY 4➤ Explore **Beacon Hill** and the **Public Garden.** Take the kids for a swan boat ride. On a fine day, walk to the **Charles River** and watch the sailboats. In inclement

weather, spend the day at the **Museum of Science.** Dine in the **South End** on Tremont Street and take in an avant-garde play nearby at the **Boston Center for the Arts.**

DAY 5➤ Visit the **Plimoth Plantation** and **Plymouth Rock.** Or, if the weather is good, pack a picnic lunch and spend the day swimming, sunning and exploring **Walden Pond** in Concord. In the fall, do some leaf peeping at Walden Pond, and stop off in **Lexington** on the way back.

DAY 6 ➤ After exploring the grand mansions in **Back Bay** and shopping on Newbury and Boylston streets, stop off at the **Institute of Contemporary Art.** Make your way back to **Copley Square** for a peek at **Trinity Church** and the **Boston Public Library.** Have dinner in **Chinatown.** See *Blue Man Group* in the **Theater District.**

DAY 7➤ Take the T into Harvard Square and explore **Harvard Yard** and its museums. Take kids to the university's complex of cultural and natural history museums; take yourself to the **Sackler** and **Fogg** art museums. Ride the T to **Kendall Square** for a stroll around the **MIT** campus; have dinner in one of the many ethnic restaurants in **Central Square** and check out the music scene at one of Central Square's funky night spots.

DAY 8➤ Take in a Red Sox game at **Fenway.** Or pack the kids off to the **Franklin Park Zoo** or **Arnold Arboretum.** Finish the day with a peek into the original "Cheers" bar, the **Bull & Finch** on Beacon Street.

FODOR'S CHOICE

No two people will agree on what makes a perfect vacation, but it's fun and helpful to know what others think. We hope you'll have a chance to experience some of Fodor's Choices yourself while visiting Boston. For detailed information about each, refer to the appropriate chapters within this guidebook.

Quintessential Boston

★ **Commonwealth Avenue when the magnolias are flowering.** The curved lines of these tree branches and the round shapes of their soft white-and-pink blossoms echo the elaborate detailing of the avenue's dark stone Victorian facades with their lacy wrought-iron balconies. Magnolia time happens during the middle of May.

⭐ **Concerts at the Isabella Stewart Gardner Museum.** Having built the Venetian palazzo of her dreams and stuffed it with innumerable curios and Old Masters, the celebrated Mrs. Gardner invited the rich and famous of her day—J. Pierpont Morgan, Henry James, Edith Wharton—to concerts in her resplendent Tapestry Room. Today, you, too, can be lulled by Bach and Scarlatti at the Gardner's Saturday and Sunday afternoon concerts, offered between October and April.

⭐ **Fourth of July along the Esplanade.** Everyone becomes a Liberty belle or beau at the Boston Pops's gala concert—the highlight: fireworks and *Stars and Stripes Forever.*

⭐ **The John Singleton Copleys at the Museum of Fine Arts.** Colonial Boston's most famous portraitist is represented by dozens of paintings on view here, including his famous image of Paul Revere—but don't miss the most spectacular painting in Boston, Copley's eye-knocking *Watson and the Shark.*

⭐ **Louisburg Square under a blanket of newly fallen snow.** It's easy to imagine former residents Jenny Lind and Louisa May Alcott emerging from one of the oh-so-prim-and-proper houses facing this tiny park. Mt. Vernon Street, which gives you access to this most decorous rectangle, is the home of the stateliest of the stately old Beacon Hill Houses, with their brilliantly polished brass door knockers.

⭐ **Paul Revere's Ride on Patriot's Day.** The ultimate Pony Express is reenacted every third Monday in April to celebrate Revere's speedy ride to salvation.

⭐ **The Public Garden in spring with the tulip beds in full bloom.** Best seen, perhaps, from the aptly named swan boats, the Public Garden is celebrated as the country's first botanic garden.

⭐ **The reflection of Trinity Church in the John Hancock Tower at Copley Square.** This capacious public gathering place, a harbor until it was filled in at the end of the 19th century, offers one of the most striking juxtapositions of 19th- and 20th-century building styles: the Renaissance Revival Boston Public Library (1885), designed by the American firm of McKim Mead & White; architect H. H. Richardson's powerful Romanesque Revival Trinity Church (1877), an American masterpiece that's solid as the rough-textured, multi-hued stone of which it's built; and, just adjacent, the rhomboid, I. M. Pei–designed John Hancock Tower (1976), whose 60 stories of shiny black glass brilliantly mirrors its neighbor. From its observatory, you can get a fine bird's-eye view of the square and beyond.

Buildings and Monuments

⭐ **Christian Science Church's Reflecting Pool.** The cool expanse of this mammoth pool and the surrounding plaza can be a refreshing pleasure on a hot summer's day.

⭐ **Holocaust Memorial.** The glass-and-steel structure of this tribute to Hitler's victims seems jarring against the 18th-century backdrop of Blackstone Block, but a walk through its disquieting configuration is a moving experience.

⭐ **Longfellow National Historic Site, Cambridge.** This splendid colonial mansion with period furnishings and elegant grounds is a reminder of the time when poets were the celebrities of the day.

⭐ **"Make Way for Ducklings" statue in the Public Garden.** If you have small children, run, do not walk, to the most child-friendly sculpture in the city.

⭐ **Paul Revere's statue in the Prado, North End.** Maybe this patriot overly benefited from Longfellow's poetic license. Still, few can match his record for revolutionary derring-do and sheer silver artistry.

⭐ **The State House seen from Boston Common at night.** Often described as a "beacon on the hill," the golden dome of the State House is a magnificent sight when illuminated at night.

⭐ **USS Constitution.** Old Ironsides upheld her nation's honor in battle and continues to do her proud as both a compelling exhibit and a fully commissioned warship.

Bars

⭐ **The Bay Tower Room.** By day, it's a private club, but after dark it opens to the public for panoramic views of the Boston harbor and the music of a jazz trio.

Bull & Finch. If the entrance to this pub looks strangely familiar, you might find yourself humming the words, ". . . where everybody knows your name." Yes, this is the watering hole that inspired the hit sitcom *Cheers,* though the interior has merely a passing resemblance to its TV counterpart.

The Cantab Lounge, Central Square, Cambridge. This is the city's real Cheers, a seedy but stately dive where Harvard professors and down-and-outs hold animated debates about Karl Marx. The bartenders, Joe and Judy, have poured heavy-handed drinks here for decades, and never forget a face.

The Plaza Bar at the Copley Plaza Hotel. It's plush and elegant yet very warm and intimate with its highly decorated coffered wood ceilings and its richly upholstered settees. Good for jazz.

The Ritz-Carlton. The sedate Street Bar, with its view of the Boston Public Garden, is a Boston institution.

Hotels

The Boston Harbor Hotel at Rowes Wharf. At one of Boston's newest and most elegant hotels, guest rooms have views of either the city or the harbor. The hundred or so paintings and other artwork in the lobby and other public spaces celebrate the city's historical and artistic traditions. *$$$$*

The Ritz-Carlton. In the old Yankee manner, this perennial favorite still stands for luxury combined with understatement. Coveted rooms and suites have fireplaces and views of the Public Garden across the street. *$$$$*

The Lenox Hotel. Built in 1900 and now renovated, it is better than ever—a first-rate choice for its traditional decor, original architectural details, and handsome, ornate lobby. *$$–$$$*

The John Jeffries House. A small hotel in a turn-of-the-century building across Charles Circle from Massachusetts General Hospital, complete with a graceful double parlor and Charles River views. *$–$$*

Restaurants

Biba. The restaurant all Boston just keeps talking about: Chef/owner Lydia Shire serves up giant portions of personality in the post-modern decor, surreal comfort food, desserts to study and devour, and a cross-cultural wine list. *$$$$*

Julien. Gilded cornices, weighty silver, and Queen Anne wing-back chairs help make this the handsomest dining room in the city. You half expect to see George Washington in such regal surroundings— and you just might: He figures in an N. C. Wyeth mural that adorns the adjacent bar. *$$$$*

L'Espalier. Set within a lovely Victorian Bay town house that has been updated with modern art and a "truffle"-hued color scheme, this restaurant serves what some say is the greatest dessert in Boston: the Chocolate Observatory Tower. *$$$$*

Rowe's Wharf Restaurant. Unruffled elegance, a view of the harbor, impeccable cuisine based on New England foodstuffs, and an extraordinary list of American wines make this a standout. *$$$$*

East Coast Grill. A classic Cambridge restaurant, it serves often atypical species of fresh fish, grilled in unusual herbal crusts by informal masters of condiments and barbecue. *$$$*

Elephant Walk. The cuisine of France meets southeast Asia's at these Brookline and Somerville favorites. *$$$*

Hamersley's Bistro. In a Red Sox cap instead of a toque, Gordon Hamersley runs one of the city's top dining rooms; it has the hearty spirit of a Parisian bistro. *$$$*

Lala Rokh. A memorable experience of Persian cuisine amid treasured medieval maps, calligraphy, and miniatures. *$$$*

Legal Sea Foods. Once a tiny adjunct to a fish market and now the chief resource for Bostonians who like their seafood straight from the sea, Legal has locations in the Prudential Center, Chestnut Hill, Park Square, Kendall Square in Cambridge, and Logan airport among others, and they're always busy. *$$$*

★ **Uva.** Wine lovers flock here for its radical pricing scheme: usually $10 over wholesale, which puts normally $40 and $50 bottles in the $25 price range. The savory cuisine is somewhere between new American and new Italian. *$$$*

★ **Pomodoro.** The playful decor and the winning country-Italian wine list make this bright, dynamic trattoria one of the nicest places in Boston's "Little Italy," the North End. *$$*

FESTIVALS AND SEASONAL EVENTS

"Great Dates in the Bay State" is the Massachusetts Office of Tourism's events hot line (☎ 800/227–6277). It lists six events and is updated every two weeks.

WINTER

➤ EARLY DEC.: **Thousands of tiny lights** are illuminated in the trees on Boston Common and on the big evergreen in front of the Prudential Center (☎ 617/635–4505 or 617/536–4100). The **Newbury Street Holiday Stroll** (☎ 617/267–7961) entertains shoppers with music, food, and holiday activities.

➤ MID-DEC.: At the Boston Tea Party ship and museum, a **Boston Tea Party Reenactment** (☎ 617/338–1773) takes place, and in Cambridge at Harvard's Sanders Theater, **Christmas Revels** (☎ 617/621–0505) celebrate the winter solstice with music, dance, and folk plays from around the world.

➤ NEW YEAR'S EVE: Bostonians turn out in force for the city's **First Night Celebration** (☎ 617/542–1399), a full day and night of outdoor and indoor concerts and festivities, culminating in fireworks over Boston Harbor.

➤ NEW YEAR'S DAY: To warm your spirit, stop by South Boston's Carson Beach to see the L Street Brownies, a group of elderly swimmers—many in their eighties and nineties—take their **annual icy plunge.**

➤ EARLY FEB.: Boston's Chinatown celebrates **Chinese New Year** (☎ 617/542–2574). The **Boston Wine Festival** (☎ 617/330–9355, held at the Boston Harbor Hotel at Rowes Wharf) includes a rare wine auction and the Anthony Spinazzola Gala, New England's premier culinary event.

➤ FEB.: The Museum of Afro-American History, in conjunction with the New England Conservatory of Music, sponsors the Roland Hayes/Marian Anderson Music Series to celebrate **Black History Month** (☎ 617/742–1854) on several Sundays through the month.

Hockey fans enjoy the annual **Beanpot Hockey Tournament** (☎ 617/624–1000) between area college teams.

SPRING

➤ MID-MAR.: The **Annual Spring New England Flower Show** blooms at the Bayside Expo Center (☎ 617/536–9280).

➤ MAR. 17: All of Boston turns out for the **St. Patrick's Day Parade** (☎ 617/536–4100). It's also officially **Evacuation Day,** which commemorates the expulsion of British troops from South Boston by General Washington in 1776 and which is observed as the de facto legal holiday.

➤ EARLY APR.–EARLY MAY: In conjunction with the Children's Museum (⌗ 66 Summer St., ☎ 617/439–7700), the **Big Apple Circus** comes to town.

➤ APR.: The **Red Sox** (☎ 617/267–1700 for tickets) open yet another hopeful season at friendly Fenway Park.

➤ MID-APR.: Bostonians know it's really spring when the **swan boats** return to the **Public Garden** (☎ 617/635–4505). On **Patriot's Day** (the Mon. nearest Apr. 19), celebrants reenact Paul Revere's ride from Hanover Street in Boston's North End to Lexington (☎ 617/536–4100). On the same day, the **Boston Marathon** (☎ 617/236–1652, Boston Athletic Association) fills the streets from Hopkinton to the Back Bay.

➤ MID-MAY: Franklin Park is the site for the **Greater Boston Kite Festival** (☎ 617/635–4505). The Arnold Arboretum (☎ 617/524–1718) celebrates the 400 varieties of lilac in bloom with **Lilac Sunday.** Everyone "makes way for ducklings" during their **Mother's Day** waddle over Beacon Hill to the Public Garden lagoon (☎ 617/635–7383 or 617/635–4505).

SUMMER

➤ EARLY JUNE: The week-long **Boston Early Music Festival** (☎ 617/661–1812) takes place biannually in odd-number years (head to Berkeley, CA, for the festival in even years), with dozens of lectures, classes, and performances and culminating in a rarely performed, fully staged Baroque opera. **Scooper Bowl** (☎ 617/439–7700) is an all-you-can-eat ice-cream festival; proceeds benefit the cancer-fighting Jimmy Fund.

➤ MID-JUNE: A weekend of activities culminates in a parade on **Bunker Hill Weekend** (☎ 617/242–5641), which recalls the battle in Charlestown. The **Boston Globe Jazz Festival** (☎ 617/929–2649) gets everyone swinging for over a week at venues throughout the city.➤ LATE JUNE–EARLY JULY: Boston's annual weeklong Fourth of July celebration, **Harborfest** (☎ 617/227–1528), takes place along the waterfront. It includes a concert synchronized to fireworks over the harbor.

➤ EARLY JULY: There's a pyrotechnical show above the Esplanade for the annual **Boston Pops Concert and Fireworks Display** (☎ 617/266–1492), a musical extravaganza at the Hatch Shell. **Chowderfest** (☎ 617/227–1528), on City Hall Plaza, lets you sample New England clam chowder from Boston's best restaurants.

➤ MID-JULY: On the weekend closest to July 18, at the Robert Gould Shaw and 54th Regiment Memorial on the Common, the National Park Service and the Museum of Afro-American History re-create the **Battle of Fort Wagner** (☎ 617/742–5415 or 617/742–1854), the Civil War battle fought by the first black regiment to be recruited in the North.

➤ LATE JULY: More than 100,000 music lovers make their way to Lowell for the **Lowell Folk Festival** (☎ 978/970–5000). Marblehead's **Race Week** (usually the last week of July; ☎ 781/631–2868) attracts boats from all along the Eastern seaboard .

➤ MID–LATE AUG.: A dragon parade enlivens Chinatown for the **August Moon Festival** (☎ 617/542–2574).

AUTUMN

➤ MID-SEPT.: Numerous events take place along the Charles River for the **Cambridge River Festival** (☎ 617/349–4380). September is also a huge month for **North End "feasts"** honoring a variety of saints with great food, great music (Italian), and great people-watching.

➤ EARLY OCT.: A big **Columbus Day Parade** (☎ 617/536–4100) moves from East Boston to the North End. On Columbus Day weekend south of Boston, the **Massachusetts Cranberry Harvest Festival** (☎ 508/295–5799 in service May–Oct.) is held in both Plymouth and neighboring South Carver's Edaville Cranberry Bog. Lowell honors its native son with **Lowell Celebrates Kerouac** (☎ 978/970–5000), presenting music, readings and "Beat Tours." The nation's oldest county fair, the **Topsfield Fair** (☎ 978/887–5000), harks back to our farm heritage.

➤ OCT.: The **Bruins** and **Celtics** (☎ 617/624–1000; 617/931–2000 Ticketmaster tickets for both) both open their seasons in October.

➤ MID-OCT.: College crew teams and spectators bearing blankets and beer come from all over for the **Head of the Charles Regatta** (☎ 617/864–8415). **Haunted Happenings** turns Salem into a witchy brew, climaxing on Halloween (☎ 978/744–0013).

➤ LATE NOV.–LATE DEC.: Modern-day Pilgrims stroll through **Plymouth's** historic homes the weekend before Thanksgiving (☎ 508/747–7533 or 800/872–1620). The **Boston International Antiquarian Book Fair** celebrates old tomes (☎ 800/447-9595). There's live Christmas music at **Faneuil Hall** (☎ 617/338–2323).

➤ LATE NOV.–EARLY JAN.: The Boston Ballet's **Nutcracker** (☎ 617/695–6950) heralds the return of another holiday season.

2 Exploring Boston

Genteel streets lined with elegant brick town houses, acres of public greens and gardens, more colleges than are found in many states, and a church on almost every corner: Boston serves up slices of history and culture at every turn. Savvy spin doctors of centuries past have made the town that cradled independence our nation's history and myth capital. More than ever, America's mother city serves up the bold and new with the old and true— reflecting skyscrapers mirror Colonial steeples and expressways zip around buildings whose hand-etched look recalls the scrimshaw era. Few places in America display their history so lovingly.

By Stephanie
Schorow and
William G.
Scheller

LIKE A MULTITIERED WEDDING CAKE, the city of Boston consists of discrete layers. The deepest layer is the historical base, the place where musket-bearing revolutionaries vowed to hang together or hang separately. The next layer, a dense spread of Brahmin fortune and fortitude, might be labeled the Hub. The Hub saw only journalistic accuracy in the hometown slogan "The Athens of America," and felt only pride in the label "Banned in Boston." Over that lies Beantown, home to the Red Sox faithful and the raucous Bruins fans who crowded Boston GAHden or order chowDAH; this is the city whose ethnic loyalties—Irish, Italian, Asian, and African-American—account for its many distinct neighborhoods. Crowded on top are the students who throng the city's universities and colleges every fall, infuriating not a few, but pleasing the rest with their infusion of high spirits and dollars from home.

The best part for a visitor is that all these Bostons can be experienced within a day or two. This is a remarkably compact city, whose labyrinthine streets will delight the walker, although they can—and often do—push drivers over the edge. An hour's stroll will take you from sites in the North End—where bewigged icons from dusty high school history books are transformed into flesh-and-blood heroes—to Beacon Hill's mansions where the Lowells spoke only to the Cabots, and the Cabots spoke only to God. You can explore the country's oldest public park, the Boston Common, in the morning, tour a Back Bay Victorian in the afternoon, and in the evening dine on Szechuan seafood in Chinatown or gnocchi in the North End. Even following the Freedom Trail—a self-guiding walking tour of famous American historic sites—traverses the layers: historical, Hub, and Beantown.

Ironically, Boston may be best known for the long-running television sitcom *Cheers,* the name of a convivial bar where everyone knew everyone else's name. In reality, a Bostonian would check to see if his wallet were missing if a stranger at a local bar knew his name. It's not that the natives are cold; it's rather that this city has all the reserve associated with New England. Instead of a hail-fellow-well-met bonhomie, there is a deep, abiding affection Bostonians have for old friends, family, and the city itself; they take perverse pride in mastering their M. C. Escher–like traffic patterns, in their frigid winters, and in their derring-do drivers. Boston has been first too many times—the first public library, the first public schools, the first subway system—to concede an inch of civic pride to bigger and bolder sister-cities. It still sees itself as a pioneer in culture—both popular and rarefied. This is the city that created First Night (a public participation showcase of arts and cultural events) as an alternative activity on New Year's Eve. It's still going strong after 20 years, and has inspired a string of imitators. This is the city that supports both the Boston Symphony and the Boston Pops, the grand Museum of Fine Arts and the offbeat Institute of Contemporary Art. And no citizenry—anywhere—loves fireworks more.

In 1858, Oliver Wendell Holmes—philosopher and author of *The Autocrat of the Breakfast Table*—called Boston "the hub of the solar system"; social inflation, however, soon raised the ante to "hub of the universe." For Bostonians that still feels about right.

BEACON HILL AND BOSTON COMMON

Enclave of Old Money grandees, contender for the "Most Beautiful" award among the city's neighborhoods, and hallowed address for many of its literary lights, Beacon Hill is Boston at its most Bostonian.

As if with a flick of a Wellsian time machine, the redbrick elegance of its narrow streets wafts visitors back to the 19th century. But make no mistake: Beacon Hill is no Williamsburg clone; here, people aren't living *in* the past, but *with* it. Increasingly, the district is less old guard than catch-you-off-guard: Residents are more likely to be college professors married to stockbrokers than D.A.R. matrons whose forebears were acquainted with Justice Oliver Wendell Holmes.

Even so, the Brahmin air of the Hill's cobbled streets still seems rarefied. From the splendidly gold-topped State House to mansions with neoclassical panache, Beacon Hill exudes power, prestige, and a calm yet palpable undercurrent of history. Once the seat of the Commonwealth's government, it was originally called "Tremont" or "Trimount" by the early Colonists. It had three summits: Cotton Hill, Beacon Hill, and Mount Vernon. Beacon, the highest, was named for the warning light (at first an iron skillet filled with lighted tallow and suspended from a mast) set on its peak in 1634. The location of the old beacon was directly behind the State House, on land now occupied by the building's 19th-century additions.

The classic face of Beacon Hill comes from its brick row houses, nearly all built between 1800 and 1850 in a style never diverging far from the early Federal norm. Even the sidewalks are brick, and will remain so by public fiat; in the 1940s, residents staged an uncharacteristic sit-in to prevent conventional paving. Since then, public law, the Beacon Hill Civic Association, and the Beacon Hill Architectural Commission have maintained tight control over everything from the gas lamps to the colors of front doors. Beacon Hill was finished quite nicely a century and a quarter ago, and as the Yankees say, "If it ain't broke, don't fix it."

When the fashionable families decamped for the "new" development of the Back Bay, not everyone left; enough residents remained to ensure that the south slope of the Hill never lost its Brahmin character. What is less well known, but no less interesting, is that Beacon Hill's north slope played a key part in African-American history. A community of free blacks lived here in the 1800s; many worshipped at the African Meeting House, established in 1805 and still standing, which came to be called the "Black Faneuil Hall" for antislavery activism. The area also housed a substantial Jewish population. Now both groups are among the inhabitants of both sides of the hill, but the south side retains its Brahmin character in the form of extremely high housing prices.

By the middle of the present century natives and newcomers alike realized that this was suitable ground for the new urban gentry. In what other city can one live on such an elegant plane within a 10-minute walk of the central business district? Thus, the unchanged facades of Beacon Hill were converted to condominium and apartment units rather than multistory single-family dwellings. These survive, too, but at prices in excess of a million dollars.

Today, Beacon Hill is the area bounded by Cambridge Street on the north, Beacon Street on the south, the Charles River Esplanade on the west, and Bowdoin Street on the east. Within these borders, residents distinguish three informal districts: the **"flat"** (the area west of Charles Street), the **south slope** (the area east of Charles Street and south of Pinckney Street), and the less architecturally distinguished **north slope** (the area east of Charles Street and north of Pinckney Street).

In contrast to Beacon Hill, the Boston Common, the country's oldest public park, exudes an attitude that is for, by, and of the people. From its first use as public land for cattle grazing, the Common has always accommodated the needs and desires of its citizens—whether for First Night, ice-cream festivals, the Corporate Challenge run, or rousing political rallies. Public hangings, however, have gone the way of the Puritans.

A good place to begin an exploration of the Common or Beacon Hill is at the Visitor Information Center on Tremont Street just east of the Park Street Station (☞ *below*). Here you can pick up a free map to Boston's Freedom Trail or buy a more extensive guide. The red line of the self-guiding trail begins just outside, in Parkman Plaza with its 1950s bronze monuments extolling religion, industry, and learning. Note that ranger-led tours leave frequently from the National Park Visitor Center on State Street in spring, summer, and fall (☎ 617/242–5642).

Numbers in the text correspond to numbers in the margin and on the Beacon Hill and Boston Common map.

A Good Walk

Few cities on earth are so ideally suited to walking and few sections of Boston are as tailored for a leisurely amble as the Boston Common/Beacon Hill nexus. Boston has a way of turning every stroll into a historical adventure, and this suggested tour is as much a journey back in time as it is a conveyor belt of interesting sights. Your starting point is the **Visitor Information Center** ① on Tremont Street. From here, head into **Boston Common** past the Parkman Bandstand and toward the Central Burying Ground—where Tories and Patriots are buried side by side (to skip a tour of the Common, head directly to the Park Street Church on Tremont Street). Walk back toward the bandstand, turn left, and head for the Common's highest ground to take a look at the Soldiers and Sailors Monument. Immediately below and to the north is the renovated Frog Pond—once Ye Olde Colonial Watering Hole for cows and now a delight for children. From the pond, walk uphill to reach Augustus Saint-Gaudens's moving Robert Gould Shaw Memorial—a commemoration of Boston's Civil War unit of free blacks (a regiment made famous by the 1989 Hollywood film, *Glory*). Here at the corner of Beacon and Park streets is where Beacon Hill—called "the Hill" by residents—the Common, and downtown Boston converge. If you head down Park Street along the Common—passing the Ticknor Mansion, the exclusive Union Club, and the Roman Catholic Paulist Center—you'll find the block ends at the **Park Street Church** ② and the **Old Granary Burial Ground** ③—final resting place of some of Boston's most illustrious figures, including John Hancock and Paul Revere (not to mention "Mother" Goose).

If you wish to view some of the grandest interiors in Boston, head up to **Beacon Street** and take a tour of the first two floors of the august **Boston Athenaeum** ④. From the **State House** ⑤—Charles Bulfinch's neoclassical masterpiece—continue along Beacon Street to soak up the local atmosphere; notable abodes include the Appleton Mansions and the third **Harrison Gray Otis House** ⑥. Continue along Beacon until you reach the **Bull & Finch Pub** ⑦ (a.k.a. *Cheers* Central) on your right, or turn right on Charles Street, then right on Chestnut Street and left on Willow to find **Acorn Street** ⑧—Boston's most photogenic byway—on your left. Continue on Willow across Mt. Vernon to reach quaint **Louisburg Square** ⑨, one of the few corners of Boston where Henry James would have little difficulty in recognizing his whereabouts. Turn right on **Pinckney Street** and follow to Joy Street: Two blocks to the left on **Smith Court** is the **African Meeting House** ⑩, a moving testament to Boston's historic African-American community. Next door, in the Abiel Smith School, is the **Museum of Afro-American History** ⑪. A visit to the north slope of the Hill should include a walk down Revere

Street and glances into Rollins Place, Phillips Street, and Bellingham Place. These trim residential courts all dead-end at a hidden cliff; the shuttered, white clapboard house at the blind end of Rollins Place is not a house at all but a false front masking a small precipice. You can follow Revere to Charles Street or backtrack on Joy Street to **Mt. Vernon Street,** passing the historic **Nichols House** ⑫, its bow window elegantly beveled by the hand of man and time. Take Mt. Vernon back to the main artery of **Charles Street.** On this itinerary, there are more than enough historic sites to go around, but pretty vistas—ready-made for the viewfinder of your video camera—also abound.

TIMING

Beacon Hill, one of the more compact areas of Boston, can be easily explored in an afternoon; add an extra few hours if you wish to linger on the Common and in the shops on Charles Street or plan to tour the Black Heritage Trail. It's a particularly lovely walk in spring and summer. In winter, the cobblestone streets can be difficult to navigate, but the convivial atmosphere makes it worth some effort, especially during the holidays—Christmas lights on the Common are an annual visual treat, while caroling and bell-ringing is a festive Christmas Eve tradition on elegant Louisburg Square. Other seasons bring other pleasures, particularly cherry blossoms on the Common in spring and Boston Pops concerts on the Esplanade in July—a lovely way to relax after a day of summer sight-seeing.

Sights to See

★ ⑧ **Acorn Street.** Surely the most photographed street in the city, Acorn is Ye Olde Colonial Boston at its best. Paved with cobblestones, the picturesque thoroughfare is considered by motorists to be Boston's roughest ride. Delicate, jewel-size row houses line one side, and on the other are the doors to Mt. Vernon's hidden gardens. Nineteenth-century artisans and small tradesmen once called these row houses home; today they are every bit as prestigious as their larger neighbors around the corners on Chestnut and Mt. Vernon streets.

⑩ **African Meeting House.** Built in 1806 and centerpiece of the historic **Smith Court African-American community** (☞ *below*), the African Meeting House is the oldest black church building still standing in the United States. It was constructed almost entirely with African-American labor, using funds raised in both the white and the black communities. The facade is an adaptation of a design for a town house published by the Boston architect Asher Benjamin. In 1832 the New England Anti-Slavery Society was formed here under the leadership of William Lloyd Garrison. When the black community began to migrate at the end of the 19th century to the South End and Roxbury, the building became a synagogue. In 1972, it was purchased by the Museum of Afro-American History, but that year a fire destroyed the slate roof and original pulpit. After its reconstruction, it was designated a historic site in 1974 and reopened in 1987. Additional renovations are planned for 2000, after renovation of the nearby Abiel Smith School. Tours are offered by employees of the National Park Service (☞ Black Heritage Trail, *below*). A ground-level gallery presents changing exhibits on African-American history. ⊠ *8 Smith Ct. (off Joy St., between Cambridge and Myrtle Sts.),* ☎ *617/742–1854.* ▨ *Suggested contribution $3.* ☉ *Memorial Day–Labor Day, daily 10–4; weekdays rest of yr. T stop, Park St.*

Appalachian Mountain Club. The bowfront mansion that serves as the headquarters of one of New England's oldest environmental institutions draws nature lovers from all over the world. The club is a great source of useful information on outdoor recreation throughout the

Beacon Hill and Boston Common

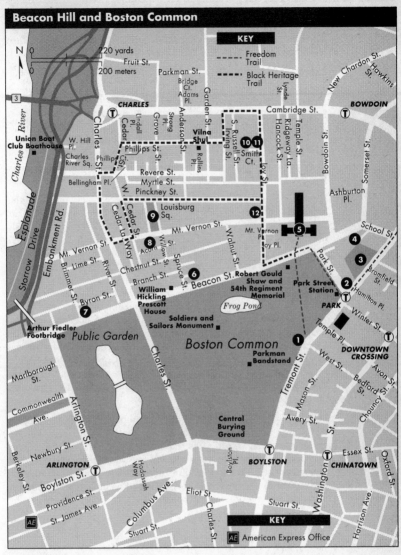

KEY

- - - Freedom Trail
━ ━ Black Heritage Trail

N

0   220 yards
0   200 meters

Fruit St.

Parkman St.

Bridge Ct.
Adams Pl.

CHARLES

Cambridge St.

New Chardon St.

Hawkins St.

BOWDOIN

Lyme St.

Ridgeway La.

Hancock St.

Temple St.

Lindall Pl.

Grove St.

Strong Pl.

Anderson St.

Garden St.

Vilna Shul

S. Russell St.

Irving St.

Joy St.

Smith Ct.

Bowdoin St.

Somerset St.

Union Boat Club Boathouse

W. Hill Pl.

Cedar St.

Phillips St.

Rollins Pl.

Charles River

Charles River Sq.

Phillips Ct.

Ashburton Pl.

Revere St.

Myrtle St.

Pinckney St.

Bellingham Pl.

Esplanade

Storrow Drive

Embankment Rd.

Mt. Vernon St.

Cedar St.

Cedar La. Way

Louisburg Sq. 9

Acorn St. 8

Willow St.

Spruce St.

Mt. Vernon St.

Walnut St.

Mt. Vernon Pl.

Joy Pl.

12

5

4

School St.

3

Bromfield St.

Lime St.

Brimmer St.

River St.

Chestnut St.

Branch St.

Beacon St.

Robert Gould Shaw and 54th Regiment Memorial

6

Park Street Station

2

Hamilton Pl.

Byron St.

7

William Hickling Prescott House

Frog Pond

PARK

Winter St.

Temple Pl.

Arthur Fiedler Footbridge

Public Garden

Soldiers and Sailors Monument

Boston Common

1

Tremont St.

Temple St.

West St.

Mason St.

DOWNTOWN CROSSING

Avon St.

Bedford St.

Chauncy St.

Marlborough St.

Commonwealth Ave.

Arlington St.

Charles St.

Parkman Bandstand

Avery St.

Newbury St.

Berkeley St.

ARLINGTON

Boylston St.

Hadassah Way

Central Burying Ground

Boylston Pl.

BOYLSTON

Essex St.

CHINATOWN

Oxford St.

Providence St.

St. James Ave.

Columbus Ave.

Eliot St.

Charles St.

Stuart St.

Washington St.

Harrison Ave.

AE

Stuart St.

KEY

AE American Express Office

Acorn Street, **8**

African Meeting House, **10**

Boston Athenaeum, **4**

Bull & Finch Pub, **7**

Harrison Gray Otis House, **6**

Louisburg Square, **9**

Museum of Afro-American History, **11**

Nichols House, **12**

Old Granary Burial Ground, **3**

Park Street Church, **2**

State House, **5**

Visitor Information Center, **1**

region. Architecturally, the building is notable for its carved cornices and spectacular oriel window decorated with vines and gargoyles. The club is around the corner from the **Nichols House** (☞ *below*). ⊠ *5 Joy St.,* ☎ *617/523–0636.* ☺ *Weekdays 8:30–5:15. T stop, Park St.*

Beacon Street. In New England, it used to be said wealth was a burden to be borne with a minimum of display. Happily, the residents of Beacon Street were all for showing off and lined the street with elegant architectural statements, from the magnificent State House to grand patrician mansions. Here you'll find some of the most important buildings of Charles Bulfinch—the ultimate designer of the Federal style in America—dozens of bowfront row town houses, the Somerset Club (the Parnassus of Boston's First Families), and the grand and glorious Harrison Gray Otis House.

After the **Boston Athenaeum** (☞ *below*), Beacon Street highlights begin with the headquarters of **Little, Brown.** Based at the corner of Beacon and Joy streets, this venerable mainstay of Boston's publishing trade was the firm responsible for bringing us Louisa May Alcott's *Little Women* and *Bartlett's Famous Quotations.* At 33 Beacon Street, the **George Parkman House** greets the eye, its gracious facade hiding more than a few secrets. One of the first sensational "Trials of the Century" involved the murder of Dr. George Parkman, a wealthy landlord and Harvard benefactor. He was bludgeoned to death in 1849 by Dr. John Webster, a Harvard medical professor and neighborhood acquaintance who allegedly became enraged by demands that he repay a personal loan. At the conclusion of the trial, the professor was hanged; he is buried in an unmarked grave on Copp's Hill in the North End. Parkman's son lived in seclusion in this house overlooking the Common until he died in 1908. The building is now used for civic functions.

Be sure to note the windows of the twin **Appleton Mansions,** built by the pioneer textile family at Numbers 39 and 40. These are the celebrated purple panes of Beacon Hill; only a few buildings have them, and they are as valuable as an ancestor in the China Trade. Their amethystine mauve color was the result of the action of sunlight on the imperfections in a shipment of glass sent to Boston around 1820. The mansions are not open to the public.

The quintessential snob has always been a Bostonian—and the **Somerset Club,** at 42 Beacon Street, has always been *the* inner sanctum of blue-nosed Cabots, Lowells, and Lodges. The mansion is a rare intrusion of the granite Greek Revival style into Beacon Hill. The older of its two buildings (the newer was built to match) was erected in 1819 by David Sears to a design by Alexander Parris, the architect of Quincy Market. Just a few doors down you'll find the grandest of the three houses Harrison Gray Otis built for himself during Boston's Golden Age (☞ Harrison Gray Otis House, *below*).

Farther along on Beacon, fans of the sitcom *Cheers* can visit the ☞ **Bull & Finch Pub.** If you wish to continue eastward along the street, an elegant coda to your stroll can be the **Fisher College,** housed in a stately bowfront (1903) whose Classical Revival style epitomizes turn-of-the-century elegance. Inside—and you can go inside—the marble stairway with its gold-plated balustrade, the Circassian walnut–paneled dining room, and the library's hand-carved rosewood doors with sterling silver knobs are among the many genteel touches. ⊠ *118 Beacon St.,* ☎ *617/236–8800.* ☎ *Free.* ☺ *Weekdays 8:30–4:30 . T stop, Arlington.*

FREE AT LAST:
THE BLACK HERITAGE TRAIL

THE MENTION OF BEACON HILL conjures up images of opulence, wealth, and proper Boston Brahmins. Yet until the end of the 19th century, its north side was home to a vibrant community of free blacks—more than 8,000 at its peak—who built houses, schools, and churches that stand to this day. In the African Meeting House, once called the Black Faneuil Hall, orators railed against slavery. The streets were lined with black-owned and operated businesses. The black community now has shifted to other parts of Boston, but the 19th-century legacy can be rediscovered on the **Black Heritage Trail.**

Established in the late 1960s, the self-guiding trail stitches together 14 sites in a 1.6-mile walk. Park Rangers give tours daily at 10 AM, noon, and 2 PM starting from the Shaw Memorial. Or you may follow directions in brochures available at the ☞ **Museum of Afro-American History** or the **National Park Service Visitor Center** (✉ 15 State St., ☎ 617/742–5415); park officials recommend you follow the brochure, as signs or plaques may be wrong or confusing. All but two houses on the trail remain private residences, but walking the twists and turns of the trail—often far less crowded than the better-known Freedom Trail—makes it easy to visualize an era when slavery was the nation's burning moral question.

Start at the stirring **Robert Gould Shaw and 54th Regiment Memorial** in the Boston Common. As depicted in the movie *Glory,* Shaw led the first black regiment to be recruited in the North during the Civil War. From here, walk up Joy Street to 5–7 Pinckney to see the 1797 **George Middleton House,** the oldest existing home built by blacks on Beacon Hill. Nearby, the **Phillips School** at Anderson and Pinckney streets was one of Boston's first integrated schools. The **John J. Smith House,** 86 Pinckney, was a rendezvous point for abolition-

ists and escaping slaves, and the elegant **Charles Street Meeting House,** Mt. Vernon and Charles streets, a former black church and community center. Unfortunately, the interior of the church has not been preserved; it now houses offices and a restaurant. The **Lewis and Harriet Hayden House,** 66 Phillips St., the home of freed slaves turned abolitionists, was a stop on the Underground Railroad. Harriet Beecher Stowe, author of *Uncle Tom's Cabin,* visited here in 1853 for her first glimpse of fugitive slaves. The Haydens reportedly kept a barrel of gunpowder under the front step, saying they'd blow up the house before they'd surrender a single slave. At 2 Phillips St., **John Coburn,** a clothing dealer and cofounder of a black military company, ran a gaming house, described as a "private place for gentlemen."

The five residences on **Smith Court** are typical of black Bostonian homes of the 1800s, including Number 3, the 1799 clapboard house where William C. Nell, America's first published black historian, lived. At the corner of Smith Court and Joy Street, the **Abiel Smith School,** the city's first public school for black children, is the permanent home for the ☞ **Museum of Afro-American History,** which jointly administers the trail with the Park Service. Next door is the venerable ☞ **African Meeting House,** which served as the community's center of social, educational, and political activity. The ground level now houses a gallery; in the airy upstairs, you can relax in the seats and imagine the fiery sermons that once rattled the upper pews.

The peeling wallpaper in the African Meeting House and the meager upstairs exhibits make clear that the Black Heritage Trail struggles for financial support and recognition. The Abiel Smith school was scheduled to be closed for two years starting in late 1997 for a major renovation; renovation of the African Meeting House was to follow.

★ ❹ **Boston Athenaeum.** One of the cofounders of the Boston Athenaeum is credited with coining an expression that has made politicians and newspaper editorialists rejoice ever since: William Tudor first compared Boston to Athens in an 1819 letter, and Bostonians now jealously guard the title "Athens of America." Tudor, the first editor of the *North American Review,* would surely have cited the Athenaeum, one of the oldest libraries in the country, as proof. Founded in 1807 from the seeds sown by the Anthology Club (headed by Ralph Waldo Emerson's father), it moved to its present imposing quarters—modeled after Palladio's Palazzo da Porta Festa in Vicenza, Italy—in 1849. Only 1,049 proprietary shares exist for membership in this cathedral of scholarship, and most have been passed down for generations (accredited researchers with references may, however, apply for annual memberships).

The public is permitted to walk through the first and second floors, to marvel at the marble busts, the exquisite porcelain vases, lush oil paintings, and leather-bound books of this Brahmin institution. A second-floor gallery has revolving art shows, most with a literary bent. A guided tour affords one of the most marvelous sights in the world of Boston academe, the fifth-floor Reading Room. In the words of critic David McCord, it "combines the best elements of the Bodleian, Monticello, the frigate *Constitution,* a greenhouse, and an old New England sitting room." Among the Athenaeum's holdings are most of George Washington's private library and the King's Chapel Library sent from England by William and Mary in 1698. (In reference to most of these volumes' uncut pages, a librarian once pointed out, "It appears that probably nobody ever read them, and now it is quite certain, I should say, that nobody ever will.") The venerable institution plans to launch an on-line catalog to prepare for its next century of operation. ⊠ *10½ Beacon St.,* ☎ *617/227–0270.* ✉ *Free.* ☉ *Weekdays 9–5:30; Sept.–May, also open Sat. 9–4. Free guided tours 3 PM Tues. and Thurs. by appointment 24 hrs ahead; closed holidays. T stop, Park St.*

Boston Common. Nothing is more central to Boston than the Boston Common, the oldest public park in the United States and undoubtedly the largest and most famous of the town commons around which New England settlements were traditionally arranged. Boston Common is not built on landfill like the adjacent Public Garden; nor is it the result of 19th-century park planning, as are Olmsted's Fens and Franklin Park. It is simply the Common: 50 acres where the freemen of Boston could graze their cattle. (Cows were banned in 1830.) Dating from 1634, it is as old as the city around it. Latin names are affixed to many of the Common's trees; it was once expected that proper Boston schoolchildren would have no problem translating them.

Although no building of substance ever stood here, the Common contains a variety of noteworthy sites. The **Central Burying Ground** may seem an odd feature for a public park, but remember that in 1756, when the land was set aside, this was a lonely corner of the Common. It is the final resting place of Tories and Patriots alike, as well as many British casualties of the Battle of Bunker Hill. The most famous person buried here is Gilbert Stuart, the portraitist best known for his likenesses of George and Martha Washington; he died a poor man in 1828.

The Common's highest ground, near the park's Parkman Bandstand, was once called **Flagstaff Hill**. It is now surmounted by the Soldiers and Sailors Monument honoring Civil War troops. The Common's most famous body of water is the **Frog Pond**, a tame and frogless concrete depression used as a children's wading pool during steamy summer days. It marks the original site of a natural pond that inspired Edgar Allan Poe to call Bostonians "Frogpondians." In 1848, the pond was the focal point for the inauguration of Boston's municipal water system, when a gushing fountain of piped-in water was created.

On the Beacon Street side of the Common sits the splendidly restored **Robert Gould Shaw Memorial,** executed in deep-relief bronze by Augustus Saint-Gaudens in 1897. It commemorates the 54th Massachusetts Regiment, the first Civil War unit made up of free blacks led by the young Brahmin Robert Gould Shaw, a stirring saga that inspired the 1989 movie *Glory.* Colonel Shaw died with nearly half of his troops in an assault on South Carolina's Fort Wagner. The monument—first intended to depict only Shaw until his abolitionist family demanded the monument honor his black regiment as well—figures in works by the modern poets John Berryman and Robert Lowell, both of whom lived on the north slope of Beacon Hill in the 1940s. This magnificent memorial makes a fitting first stop on the National Park Service's Black Heritage Trail (☞ *above*).

Also note the 1888 Boston Massacre Memorial on Tremont Street, near Boylston; the sculpted hand of one of the victims has a distinct shine from years of sightseers' caresses. *T stop, Park St.*

❼ Bull & Finch Pub. If the entrance to this pub looks strangely familiar, you might find yourself humming the words, ". . . where everybody knows your name." Yes, this is the watering hole that inspired the long-running NBC sitcom *Cheers,* as evidenced by the yellow *Cheers* flag and the (usually) long line of tourists outside. The interior has merely a passing resemblance to its TV counterpart, but that hasn't stopped the bar from generating a mini-industry of *Cheers* T-shirts and other goods. For the broadcast of the 275th—and final episode—in 1993, Gov. William Weld declared it "Cheers Day" in Boston. ⊠ *84 Beacon St.,* ☎ *617/227–9605. T stop, Arlington.*

Charles Street. With few exceptions, Beacon Hill lacks commercial development, and Charles Street more than makes up for it. The street is chockablock with antiques shops, bookstores, small restaurants, and flower shops. In keeping with the historic character of the area, even the 7-Eleven storefront has been made to conform to the prevailing aesthetic standards. Check out the chiropractor's sign (⊠ 83 Charles St.)—an unfleshed human spine. The contemporary activity would present a curious sight to the elder Oliver Wendell Holmes, the publisher James T. Fields (of the famed Bostonian firm of Ticknor & Fields), and many others who lived here when the neighborhood belonged to establishment literati. Charles Street sparkles at dusk from gas-fueled lamps, making it a romantic place for an evening stroll.

NEED A BREAK?

For a nice cappuccino, take your pick of coffee shops along Charles Street. **Rebecca's Bakery** (⊠ 119 Mt. Vernon St., ☎ 617/742–9542) has one of the more historic locations, as it sits on the ground floor of the ☞ Charles Street Meeting House, once an antislavery stronghold and, after the Civil War, a prominent black church.

Chestnut Street. With Mt. Vernon, Chestnut is one of the two loveliest streets in the city. Delicacy and grace characterize virtually every structure, from the fanlights above the entryways to the wrought-iron boot scrapers on the steps. Author and explorer Francis Parkman lived here, as did Richard Henry Dana (of *Two Years Before the Mast* fame) and actor Edwin Booth. Booth's sometime residence, 29A, dates from 1800 and is the oldest house on the south slope of the Hill. In particular, note the **Swan Houses,** at Numbers 13, 15, and 17, commissioned from Charles Bulfinch by Hepzibah Swan as dowry gifts for her three daughters. Complete with Adam-style entrances, marble columnnettes, and recessed arches, they are Chestnut Street at its most beautiful.

Club of Odd Volumes. The second-oldest book collectors' club in America is open to the public only for special exhibitions. An early 19th-century town house serves as its headquarters. ⊠ *77 Mt. Vernon St.,* ☎ *617/227–7003. T stop, Park St.*

⑥ Harrison Gray Otis House. Harrison Gray Otis, one of the Mount Vernon Proprietors, a U.S. senator, and Boston's third mayor, built in rapid succession three of Boston's most splendidly ostentatious Federal-era houses, all designed by Charles Bulfinch and all still standing. This, the third Harrison Gray Otis House, at 45 Beacon Street, was the last of these mansions—and the grandest. Here, Mr. Otis breakfasted on pâté de fois gras every morning (somehow he lived to a ripe old 80), fussed over his Simon Willard rocking-horse clock, and hosted musicales at the same pianoforte that Beethoven had used to compose his *Eroica* symphony. Now operated as the headquarters of the American Meteorological Society, the house was once freestanding and surrounded by English-style gardens. The **Second Otis House,** built in 1802 at 85 Mount Vernon Street, is today a private home. The **First Otis House**—the only one open to the public (☞ The Old West End, *below*)—is on Cambridge Street near the Old West Church. Otis moved into 45 Beacon Street in 1805 and stayed until his death in 1848. His tenure thus extended from the first days of Beacon Hill's residential development almost to the time when many of the Hill's prominent families decamped for the Back Bay, which was just beginning to be filled at the time of Otis's death.

★ ⑨ Louisburg Square. "Be unimpressed by reference to its being like London," essayist A. C. Lyons once wrote. "It is Boston to the hilt." One of the quaintest corners in a neighborhood that epitomizes quaint, Louisburg Square was an 1840s model for town-house development that was never repeated on the Hill because of space restrictions. Today, the grassy square—enclosed by a wrought-iron fence and considered the very heart of Beacon Hill—belongs collectively to the owners of the houses facing it. The statue at the north end of the green is of Columbus; the one at the south end is of Aristides the Just; both were donated in 1850 by a Greek merchant who lived on the square. The houses, most of which are now divided into apartments and condominiums, have seen their share of famous tenants: William Dean Howells at Numbers 4 and 16, the Alcotts at Number 10 (Louisa May not only lived but died here, on the day of her father's funeral). In 1852 the singer Jenny Lind was married in the parlor of Number 20.

There is no water in Louisburg (proper Bostonians always pronounce the "s") Square today, and the ground level is some 60 ft below the height of the original hill, yet the legend long persisted that this was the location of the Rev. William Blackstone's spring. Blackstone was the original Bostonian, having come here to live with his books and his apple trees four or five years before the arrival of the Puritans in 1630. It was he who invited them to leave Charlestown and come to where the water was purer, he who sold them all but 6 acres of the peninsula he had bought from the Indians. He left for Rhode Island not long after, seeking greater seclusion; a plaque at 50 Beacon commemorates him. (The name "Boston," given by the Puritans, comes from Boston, England, originally St. Botolph's Town.)

The square still boasts celebrity residents. One of the largest houses on the square was acquired several years ago by the woman dubbed the Ketchup Heiress—Teresa Heinz, who married Sen. John Kerry (D-Mass.). The house was purchased for a reported $2 million—unrenovated. The couple caused a flurry of sniffs when they pushed to have a fire hydrant moved from the front of their abode—apparently Ms. Heinz had been getting too many tickets. *T stop, Park St.*

Mt. Vernon Street. With Chestnut Street, Mt. Vernon has some of Beacon Hill's most distinguished addresses. Mt. Vernon is the grander of the two streets, with houses set back farther and rising taller; it even has a freestanding mansion, the Second Otis House, at Number 85 (☞ Harrison Gray Otis House, *above*). Henry James once wrote that Mt. Vernon Street was "the only respectable street in America," and he must have known, as he lived with his brother William at 131 in the 1860s. He was just one of many literary luminaries who resided on Mt. Vernon, including Julia Ward Howe, who composed "The Battle Hymn of the Republic" and lived at 32, and Robert Frost, who lived at 88.

⓫ **Museum of Afro-American History.** Ever since Crispus Attucks became one of the famous victims of the Boston Massacre of 1770, the African-American community of Boston has played an important part in the city's history. In the 19th century, Walt Whitman noted that "black persons" enjoyed a higher status in Boston than in New York. Throughout the century, abolition was the cause célèbre for Boston's intellectual elite and, during that time, blacks came to thrive in neighborhoods throughout the city, including Smith Court and Joy Street. The Museum of Afro-American History was established in 1964 to promote this history. Its headquarters occupies the **Abiel Smith School,** the first public school for black children in Boston. Funded by Abiel Smith, a white businessman, the school opened in 1835. The building was scheduled to be closed for two years starting in late 1997 for a major renovation focusing on the quest for equal education in Boston. A revamped gift shop and improved offices for the National Park Service are planned. In the meantime, the museum will have an office at Boston University and the National Park personnel are relocated at 14 Beacon St., room 506. Park service personnel continue to lead tours of the **Black Heritage Trail** (☞ *above*) starting from the Shaw Memorial. The museum also hosts a variety of activities during February, Black History Month, and in July stages a reenactment of the Civil War's black 54th regiment. ⊠ *46 Joy St.,* ☎ *617/742–1854.* ⊡ *Donations suggested.* ⊙ *Weekdays 10–4. T stop, Park St., Charles/MGH.*

⓬ **Nichols House.** Complete with a deep window seat straight out of a Henry James novel, the Nichols house is the only Mt. Vernon Street house open to the public. Beacon Hill eccentric, philanthropist, peace advocate, founder of the International Society of Pen Pals, and one of the first female landscape architects, Rose Standish Nichols (1872–1964) made this house—built in 1804 and attributed to Charles Bulfinch— her lifelong home. Nearly all the furnishings passed to Miss Nichols by descent, and the effect is of paying a call at a home already quaint a hundred years ago. The house gives a pervasive impression of how a Brahmin lady of modest means lived among the rich and comfortably aging possessions of her forebears. Nichols made arrangements in her will for the house to become a museum, and visitors have been calling since then. ⊠ *55 Mt. Vernon St.,* ☎ *617/227–6993.* ⊡ *$5 for tours only.* ⊙ *May–Oct., Tues.–Sat. noon–5; Nov.–Dec. and Feb.– Apr., Mon., Wed., and Sat. noon–4:15. Tours on the ¼ hr.; closed Jan., holidays. T stop, Park St.*

★ ➌ **Old Granary Burial Ground.** "It is a fine thing to die in Boston," A. C. Lyons, that old Boston wit, once remarked—alluding to Boston's cemeteries, among the most picturesque and historic in America. If you found a resting place here at the Old Granary, chances are your headstone would have been eloquently ornamented with skeletons and winged skulls—and your neighbors would have been mighty eloquent, too:

WHERE IT ALL BEGAN: THE FREEDOM TRAIL

THE FREEDOM TRAIL IS MUCH more than a 3-mi route of historic sites. As an eager army of bipeds discovers every year, it's a walk into history, to the events that exploded on the world during the Revolution, an odyssey whose 16 way stations allow you to reach out and touch the very wellsprings of American civilization. Try to allow a full day to complete the entire route comfortably, although some have been known to cram it into a few aerobic-paced hours. However long you take (just follow the route marked on the neighborhood maps), you will find the Freedom Trail exercises the spirit as well as the limbs. Perhaps some of its sights are more interesting than others, and perhaps it lacks the multimedia bells and whistles now becoming the norm at "historic" attractions. But that's what makes the Freedom Trail unique: It allows history to speak for itself.

With one foot in front of the other—just like the fledgling nation—begin at the very hub of the Hub, ☞ **Boston Common,** America's oldest public park. Get your bearings at the Visitors Information Center on Tremont Street and then head for the ☞ **State House,** Boston's finest piece of Federalist architecture; its 23-karat gilded dome looms magisterially above Beacon Hill. Several blocks away is the ☞ **Park Street Church,** whose steeple is considered by many to be the most beautiful in all of New England; here, the anthem "America" was first sung. Reposing in the church's shadows is the ☞ **Old Granary Burying Ground,** final resting place of Samuel Adams, John Hancock, Paul Revere, and "Mother" Goose. A short stroll beyond the **statue of Benjamin Franklin** will bring you to ☞ **King's Chapel,** built in 1754, and a hotbed of Anglicanism during the Colonial period. One of the poetry readings here in "the King's English"

will prep you up for the ☞ **Old Corner Bookstore,** onetime publisher of Hawthorne, Emerson, and Longfellow. Nearby is the ☞ **Old South Meeting House,** where pre-tempest arguments over a tax on tea were heard in 1773. Overlooking the ☞ **site of the Boston Massacre** is the earliest known public building in Boston, the ☞ **Old State House,** a stately Georgian beauty that houses a museum devoted to the city's yesteryears.

If it's midday, fuel up at **Faneuil Hall**(☞ *below*)—the first floor has numerous eateries—then explore its Assembly Room, the virtual "Cradle of Liberty," where Samuel Adams fired the indignation of Bostonians during those times that tried men's souls. Explore Quincy Market, then pass under the Expressway to enter the North End. Taking one step forward, into ☞ **Paul Revere's House,** takes you back 200 years—here are the hero's own saddlebags, toddy-warmer, and a pine cradle made from a molasses cask (Paul was papa to 16 children). Full-day trekkers might want to rest about now at the tranquil Paul Revere Mall, nearby. Next, tackle a place guaranteed to trigger a wave of oh-gosh patriotism: the ☞ **Old North Church** of "One if by Land, Two if by Sea" fame—sorry, the 154 creaking stairs leading to the belfry are out of bounds for visitors. From ☞ **Copp's Hill Burying Ground,** cross the bridge over the Charles and check out that revered icon, the ☞ **USS *Constitution*,** nicknamed "Old Ironsides" (cannonballs bounced off her copper-plated hull). The photo finish? A climb to the top of the ☞ **Bunker Hill Monument** for the incomparable vistas. Finally, head for the nearby Charlestown water shuttle, which goes directly to the downtown area, and congratulate yourself: You've just finished a unique cram course in American History.

Samuel Adams, John Hancock, Benjamin Franklin's parents, Paul Revere, and, last but not least, Elizabeth "Mother" Goose (whose nursery ditties were published by Thomas Fleet, who decided to illustrate the tome with a picture of a long-necked goose—an allusion to his mother-in-law's constant chattering—thereby creating her nom de plume). Note the winged hourglasses carved into the stone gateway of the burial ground; they are a 19th-century addition, made more than 150 years after this small plot began receiving the remains of Colonial Bostonians. ⊙ *Daily 8–4:30. T stop, Park St.*

② Park Street Church. If the Congregationalist Park Street Church, at the corner of Tremont and Park streets, could talk, what a joyful noise it would make. Inside the church, which was designed by Peter Banner and erected in 1809–10, Samuel Smith's hymn "America" was first sung on July 4, 1831. Here in 1829 William Lloyd Garrison began his long public campaign for the abolition of slavery. The church—called "the most impressive mass of brick and mortar in America" by Henry James—is earmarked by its steeple, considered by many critics to be the most beautiful in New England. Just outside Park Street Church at the intersection of Park and Tremont streets (and the main subway crossroads of the city) is **Brimstone Corner.** Does the name refer to the fervent thunderation of the church's preachers, the fact that gunpowder was once stored in the church's crypt, or the amazing story that preachers once scattered burning sulphur on the pavement to attract the attention of potential churchgoers? Historians can't agree. ⊠ *1 Park St.,* ☎ *617/523–3383.* ⊙ *Visitors: formal tours mid-June–mid-Aug., Tues.–Sat. 9:30–3:30. Sun. services at 9, 10:45, and 6:30; closed July 4. T stop, Park St.*

Park Street Station. Look out for Charlie, that poor soul immortalized in the 1950s Kingston Trio hit about a man "who never returned" for lack of a five-cent subway fare. The Park Street Station was one of the first four stops of the first subway in America. It was opened for service in 1897 against the warnings of those convinced it would make buildings along Tremont Street collapse. The copper-roof kiosks are national historic landmarks. The line originally ran only as far as the present-day Boylston stop. Outside the subway kiosks cluster flower vendors, street musicians, and partisans of causes and beliefs ranging from Irish nationalism to Krishna Consciousness—all making for a general dither and considerable litter.

Pinckney Street. Almost all the wooden houses on the north slope of Beacon Hill are gone now. Exceptions may be found at 5 and 7 Pinckney Street, near the corner of Joy Street, where a 1791 structure stands.

William Hickling Prescott House A modest but intriguing house museum has been installed in this five-story, 1808 Federal structure designed by Asher Benjamin, home to historian William Hickling Prescott from 1845 to 1859. Some rooms are furnished with period furniture, including the former study with Prescott's desk and "noctograph," which helped the nearly blind scholar write. Ask about his secret staircase, which allowed Prescott to escape into his study from boring guests in the parlor. Now the headquarters for the Massachusetts Society of Colonial Dames, the house also has a fine costume collection. ⊠ *55 Beacon St.,* ☎ *617/742–3190.* ⊡ *$4.* ⊙ *Tours only, Tues, Wed, Sat. noon–4 .*

St. Paul's Cathedral. Even a cursory comparison of this Episcopal church with its Tremont Street neighbor, Park Street Church, underscores the difference between 18th- and early 19th-century architectural aesthetics as they applied to large public buildings. Built just 10 years after the Park Street Church, St. Paul's is topped with an uncarved entablature; as with New York's Metropolitan Museum of Art, similarly adorned with uncut blocks of stone, the money ran out before stone carvers could be engaged. ⊠ *138 Tremont St.,* ☎ *617/482–5800.* ✆ *Weekdays noon–6. Sun. services at 8 and 10; daily services at 12:10 and 5:15; Holy Eucharist in Chinese at 12:30. Luncheon concerts Thurs. at 12:45. T stop, Haymarket.*

★ **Smith Court African-American Community.** In the neighborhood surrounding the African Meeting House (☞ *above*), one of Boston's most important 19th-century African-American communities came to thrive; today, you can soak up the historic atmosphere by viewing picturesque 3-ft-wide **Holmes Alley** (⊠ Between Joy and S. Russell Sts. at the end of Smith Court) and the five residential structures typical of the homes of African-American Bostonians in the 1800s. They include Number 3, a house purchased by clothes dealer James Scott; William Nell, the historian and famed crusader for school integration active in William Lloyd Garrison's circle, boarded here from 1851 to 1865. Built in 1799 and now a National Historic Landmark, this house is one of the most gracious clapboard structures remaining in Boston. Together, these sites bring Boston's African-American past very close.

❺ **State House.** It is hard to imagine a prouder or more hopeful moment: The nation was at peace, Massachusetts ships sailed every sea in pursuit of ever more lucrative trade, and the surviving fathers of the Revolution were on hand to enshrine the ideals of their new Commonwealth in a handsome and graceful State House designed by Charles Bulfinch. It was the Fourth of July, 1795. Governor Samuel Adams laid the cornerstone. Paul Revere made a speech; later, he would roll the copper sheathing for the dome.

Bulfinch's State House is one of the greatest works—perhaps the greatest—of classical architecture in America, so striking that it hardly suffers for having had appendages added in three directions by bureaucrats and lesser architects. It is arguably the most architecturally distinguished seat of state government in America; it was built well before the trend turned toward designs based on the Capitol in Washington. (Charles Bulfinch later held the position of architect of the U.S. Capitol.) The neoclassical design is poised between Georgian and Federal; its finest features are the delicate Corinthian columns of the portico, the graceful pediment and window arches, and the vast yet visually weightless golden dome (gilded in 1874). During World War II, the dome was painted gray so that it would not reflect moonlight during blackouts and thereby offer a target to anticipated Axis bombers.

Bulfinch's work would have stood splendidly on its own, but the growth of the state bureaucracy necessitated additions. The yellow-brick annex extending to the rear is clumsily ostentatious, but at least it is invisible from Beacon Street. The light-colored stone wings added to either side of the original structure early in this century serve no aesthetic purpose.

Inside the State House are Doric Hall, with its statuary and portraits, a part of the original structure; the chambers of the General Court (legislature) and Senate, including the carved wooden *Sacred Cod* that symbolizes the state's maritime wealth; and the Hall of Flags. In 1933, *Harvard Lampoon* wags stole the Cod; the uproar was so great it was speedily returned. Check out the giant, modernistic clock in the Great Hall designed by New York artist R. M. Fischer. Its installation in 1986 at a cost of $100,000 was roundly slammed as a symbol of legislative extravagance. The State House has a wealth of statuary: figures of Horace Mann, Daniel Webster, and, added in 1990, a youthful-looking President John F. Kennedy in full stride.

Two statues of American women stand on the front lawn. One is Anne Hutchinson, who challenged the religious hierarchy of the Massachusetts Bay Colony. She was excommunicated and banished from the colony in 1638. Her supporter Mary Dyer was also excommunicated; she later converted to the Quaker faith and was finally hanged for defending her beliefs. Her statue on the State House grounds overlooks the spot on the Boston Common where she mounted the gallows. ⊠ *Beacon St. between Hancock and Bowdoin Sts.,* ☎ *617/727–3676.* 🎫 *Free.* ☉ *Tours weekdays 10–4, last tour at 3:30.* ☎ *617/727–2590, Research library.* ☉ *Weekdays 11–5. T stop, Park St.*

Vilna Shul. This gem of a historical treasure is the focus of both renovation and research. The two-story brick synagogue was completed in 1920 by Jews from Vilna in what is now Lithuania. Of the more than 50 synagogues that once dotted Beacon Hill, it's the last intact example. The distinctive, L-shape second-floor sanctuary has separate seating for men and women in keeping with Orthodox tradition. The building, abandoned in 1985, was bought by the Vilna Center for Jewish Heritage, which is overseeing its restoration. ⊠ *14–18 Phillips St.,* ☎ *617/523–2324.* 🎫 *Donation.* ☉ *Sun. 1–3; hours may vary; call ahead. T stop, Charles/MGH.*

❶ **Visitor Information Center.** Information Central, this center is adjacent to the Common's Parkman Plaza. It's well supplied with stacks of free pamphlets about Boston, and the staff can field all questions. ☎ *617/536–4100 or 888/733–2678 general Boston information; center takes no incoming calls.* ☉ *Mon.–Sat. 8:30–5, Sun. 9–5.*

THE OLD WEST END

When Boston's 18th-century architects decided to go vertical with tall church steeples, they had no idea that their graceful edifices would one day be reposing in the shadow of 40-story skyscrapers. In this city, the startling contrast of old and new side by side is nowhere more evident than in the Old West End. Just a few decades ago, this district—separated from Beacon Hill by Cambridge Street—resembled the typical medieval city: thoroughfares that twisted and turned, maddening one-way lanes, and streets that were a veritable hive of laboring populations. Then, progress—or what passes for progress—all but eliminated the thriving communities of Irish, Italians, Jews, and Greeks to make room for a mammoth project of urban renewal, designed in the 1960s by that mandarin of modernism, I. M. Pei. Today, little remains of the *Old* West End except for a few brick tenements and a handful of historic monuments. But rambling around the Old West End can be a fascinating experience: Here, time seems to zoom by and then, a minute later, magically stand still. For sports fans, the Old West End is nirvana: The FleetCenter draws in crowds by the thousands.

The only surviving structures in the Old West End with any real history are two public institutions, the now disused **Suffolk County** (or Charles Street) **Jail** and the much-used **Massachusetts General Hospital.** Both are near the Charles Street Circle, where the Longfellow Bridge—called the Salt and Pepper Bridge because of the shakerlike stone shapes that ornament it—begins its reach across the Charles to Cambridge. The former jail is interesting chiefly for its central building, dating from 1849, designed by Gridley Bryant at the close of Boston's Granite Age. That made it too old for a secure jail, as well as terribly crowded and miserable for the inmates. The new Nashua Street Jail opened in 1991.

Behind Mass General and the sprawling Charles River Park apartment complex is a small grid of streets recalling an older Boston. Here are furniture and electric-supply stores, a good discount camping-supply house (Hilton's Tent City, on Friend Street; ☞ Sporting Goods *in* Chapter 8), and the Commonwealth Brewing Company on Portland Street (☞ Sightseeing *in* the Gold Guide). The main drag here is Causeway Street. North Station, on Causeway between Haverhill and Canal streets, provides service to commuters from the northern suburbs and can be jammed when there's a game at the FleetCenter.

Numbers in the text correspond to numbers in the margin and on The Old West End map.

A Good Walk

As this walk proves, Boston allows you to enjoy both the 21st and the 19th centuries in the space of a few hours. From Beacon Hill walk along the scenic paths of the **Esplanade** bordering the Charles River to reach the giga-mega-techno wonders of the **Museum of Science** ① and the **Charles Hayden Planetarium.** For views of old Boston, backtrack via Fruit Street and the **Massachusetts General Hospital** ② to Cambridge Street for a visit to the neoclassical salons of the first **Harrison Gray Otis House** ③ and the **Old West Church** ④. A visit to the **FleetCenter** ⑤ is best done via the T (North Station) or by car.

TIMING

Even with a kid or two in tow, it shouldn't take more than an hour to reach the Museum of Science via the Esplanade. The walk is not recommended in cold weather, but the locale is readily accessible by the MBTA's Green Line. After taking in the museum, catch dinner in the neighborhood, then return to the museum's Hayden Planetarium for an evening laser show or follow the throngs of arriving sports fans to nearby FleetCenter to see the Celtics or Bruins in action.

Sights to See

Esplanade. At the northern end of Charles Street is one of several footbridges crossing Storrow Drive to the Esplanade and **Hatch Memorial Shell.** The Boston Pops, made immensely popular by its former maestro, the late Arthur Fiedler, gives free concerts here during the week, up to and including the Fourth of July. For the almost nightly entertainment throughout the rest of the summer, Bostonians haul lawn chairs and blankets to the lawn in front of the shell; bring a picnic basket, find an empty spot, and you'll feel right at home, too. An impressive head, in stone, of the late Fiedler watches over the walkers, joggers, picnickers, and sunbathers who fill its paths on pleasant days. The Esplanade is home port for the fleet of small sailboats that dot the Charles River Basin. They belong to Community Boating, which offers membership on a monthly or seasonal basis. Here, too, is the **Union Boat Club Boathouse,** headquarters for the country's oldest private rowing club. The boathouse was built at the turn of the century.

⑤ **FleetCenter.** At first, when the name for the facility replacing aging Boston Garden was announced, hard-core fans swore that only the words "New Boston Garden" would ever pass their lips. But gradually, the name FleetCenter has won acceptance. For starters, this grand facility on Causeway Street, where the Celtics (basketball) and the Bruins (hockey) play their home games, is nothing like the old creaking, leaking Garden, the only court in the NBA where basketball games could be called on account of rain. Opening in 1928, the Garden hosted acts from the Beatles to the Grateful Dead, from Liberace to Frank Sinatra. Larry Bird made his NBA debut there in 1979; Bobby Orr's Number 4 was retired in 1979. The old Garden will continue to be mournfully hon-

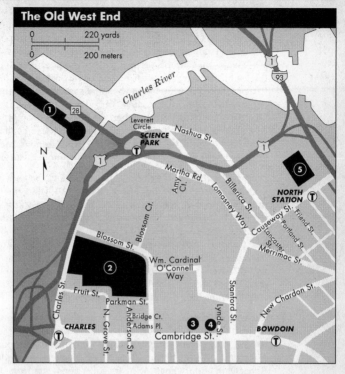

The Old West End

ored at after-game beer sessions in bars clustered around North Station. But since 1995 those same mourners have enjoyed the benefits and creature comforts of FleetCenter's amenities—air-conditioning, increased seating capacity, improved food selection, a 1,200-vehicle parking garage, and nearly double the number of bathrooms. The Bruins now play on a regulation-size rink, and there are no obstructed views. ☎ 617/624–1000 for recorded information on sports events and ticket availability. T stop, North Station.

❸ Harrison Gray Otis House. This is the first of three houses built for and bearing the name of Harrison Gray Otis, Boston's third mayor and prominent citizen and developer. Built in 1796, it now houses the headquarters of the Society for the Preservation of New England Antiquities (SPNEA), an organization that owns and maintains dozens of historic properties throughout the region. The society has restored the Otis House and opened two of its floors as a museum. The furnishings, textiles, wall coverings, and even the interior paint, specially mixed to match old samples, are faithful to the Federal period, circa 1790–1810. You may be surprised to see how bright and vivid were the colors favored in those days, and to learn that closets as we know them had not quite made their appearance. The dining room is set up as though Harry Otis were about to come in and pour a glass of Madeira; one gets the feeling he would have been good company. But Otis lived here only four years before moving to more sumptuous digs, designed by Charles Bulfinch, on Beacon Hill (☞ Harrison Gray Otis House in Beacon Hill and Boston Common, above). The SPNEA also conducts a Beacon Hill walking tour that originates here (☞ Sightseeing in the Gold Guide). ⊠ 141 Cambridge St., ☎ 617/227–3956. ☒ $4. ☺ Wed–Sun, 11–5; guided tours only, on the hour; last tour 4. T stop, Charles/MGH or Bowdoin.

❷ Massachusetts General Hospital. For doctors and medical students, paying a visit to Mass General is akin to art historians' visiting the Louvre. Incorporated in 1811 and the site of one of the most important breakthroughs in modern surgery—the use of ether—it traditionally has been regarded as the nation's premier general hospital. The domed, granite **Bulfinch Pavilion** was designed in 1818 by Boston's leading architect, Charles Bulfinch. It was in the hospital's amphitheater that, on October 16, 1846, Dr. John Collins Warren performed the first operation on a patient anesthetized by ether; the place was promptly nicknamed "The Ether Dome." You may visit the amphitheater today when it is not in use (use the hospital's North Grove Street entrance) and see a display describing the procedure that made modern surgery possible.

Mass General once housed the Harvard Medical School, and it was in a laboratory here around Thanksgiving 1849 that one of Boston's most notorious murders took place. Dr. George Parkman, a wealthy landlord and Harvard benefactor, was bludgeoned to death by Dr. John Webster (☞ George Parkman House *in* Beacon Hill and Boston Common, *above*). After several days of mystery over Parkman's disappearance, Webster's doom was sealed when part of the victim's jaw was discovered in the laboratory stove. Other grisly evidence turned up in the cesspool beneath Webster's privy. ⊠ *55 Fruit St.* ✆ *Free.* ⊘ *Amphitheater, daily 9–5. T stop, Charles/MGH.*

❶ Museum of Science. With 15-ft lightning bolts in the Theater of Electricity and a 20-ft-high *Tyrannosaurus rex* model, this is just the place to ignite any child's Jurassic spark. Occupying a compound of buildings that stand north of Mass General, the museum sits astride the Charles River Dam and its boat locks. Its collections date from 1830; its development as a rich educational resource evolved under the recent directorship of the explorer-mountaineer-cartographer Bradford Washburn, who is still active on the board. More than 600 exhibits cover astronomy, astrophysics, anthropology, progress in medicine, computers, the organic and inorganic earth sciences, and much more. Washburn and his curators made the Museum of Science a strong leader in hands-on education; "Investigate," a new permanent exhibit, lets kids explore such scientific principles as gravity by balancing objects—there are no wrong answers here, only discoveries. Other exhibits invite the participation of children and adults: The Transparent Woman's organs light up as their functions are described, and whole families can play "virtual volleyball." Eat at a first-floor café or browse the well-stocked gift and book shop. ⊠ *Science Park at the Charles River Dam,* ☎ *617/723–2500 or 617/523–6664.* ✆ *$9.* ⊘ *Daily 9–5, Fri. until 9 (extended hrs July 5–Sept. 5). T stop, Science Park.*

The Museum of Science's **Charles Hayden Planetarium,** with its sophisticated multi-image system based on a $2 million Zeiss planetarium projector, produces exciting programs on astronomical discoveries. Laser light shows, with laser graphics and computer animation, are scheduled Friday through Sunday evenings. The shows are probably best for children older than five.

The Museum of Science also contains the **Mugar Omni Theater,** which has state-of-the-art film projection and sound systems. The 76-ft-high, four-story domed screen wraps around and over you, and 27,000 watts of power drive the 84 loudspeakers. ☎ *617/523–6664, Museum.* ✆ *$7.50. Advance purchase of tickets recommended, 3–4 days ahead for weekends and holidays (V and MC accepted for phone orders with $1 handling fee).* ☎ *617/523–6664, Planetarium.* ✆ *Shows only: $7.50. Reduced price combination tickets available for museum, planetarium, and Omni Theater.* ⊘ *Shows from 11 AM.*

❹ Old West Church. Built in 1806 to a design of the great builder and architect Asher Benjamin, the imposingly elegant Old West Church stands, along with the Harrison Gray Otis house next door, as a reminder of the days when the West End near Bowdoin Square was a fashionable district. In the early 1960s, when the church served as a public library and polling place, Congressman John F. Kennedy voted here. ✉ *131 Cambridge St. (at Staniford St.),* ☎ *617/227–5088.* ☉ *Generally weekdays 9–5, but call to confirm. Sun. service at 11. T stop, Bowdoin.*

GOVERNMENT CENTER

This is the section of town Bostonians love to hate. Not only does **Government Center** house that which they can't fight—City Hall—it also contains some of the bleakest architecture since the advent of poured concrete. The sweeping brick plaza that marks **City Hall** and the twin towers of the **John F. Kennedy Federal Office Building** begins at the junction in which Cambridge becomes Tremont Street, an area once known as Scollay Square. An ambitious urban renewal project in the 1960s completely obliterated the raffish, down-at-heels square—a bawdy, raucous place where sailors would go when they came into port— that was also famous for its burlesque houses (such as the storied "Old Howard") and its secondhand bookstores. It is remembered more and more fondly as years go by.

The curving six-story **Center Plaza** building, across from the Government Center T stop and the broad brick expanse of City Hall Plaza, emulates the much older Sears Crescent, a curved commercial block next to the Government Center T stop. (A small plaque in the square behind the crescent-shape building marks the site of the old Howard Theater's stage.) The Center Plaza building separates Tremont Street from the higher ground to the west: Pemberton Square and the old and "new" courthouses.

The stark, treeless plain surrounding City Hall—like a man-made tundra of brick—has been roundly jeered for its user-unfriendly aura, but in recent years the expanse has been enlivened by feisty political rallies, free summer concerts, and the occasional festival.

Separating the North End from the Government Center area—and the rest of Boston—is the **Fitzgerald Expressway,** which appears to be not long for this realm. At some point it is due to be replaced with an underground highway as part of the multibillion dollar Central Artery project, (dubbed "The Big Dig" by natives) whose master plan includes the creation of the Ted Williams Tunnel, a third underwater tunnel to Logan Airport. All of this is intended to improve traffic flow; in the meantime, calling the area a mess is putting it mildly. Signs and maps explaining the project can be found posted on construction zones along Surface Artery. Driver alert: The rerouting of traffic and shifts in one-way signs are constantly changing what was once a conquerable maze into a nearly impenetrable puzzle. Trust no maps.

Numbers in the text correspond to numbers in the margin and on the Government Center and the North End map.

A Good Walk

The modern, stark expanse of Boston's **City Hall** ① and the twin towers of the **John F. Kennedy Federal Office Building** ② introduce visitors to Boston in the urban renewal age, but just across Congress Street is **Faneuil Hall** ③, a site of political speech-making since Revolutionary times, and just beyond that is **Quincy Market** ④, where shop-till-youdroppers can sample a profusion of international taste treats. For more Bostonian fare, walk back toward Congress Street to the city's oldest restaurant, the **Union Oyster House** ⑤, to partake of some oysters and ale. Near the restaurant is the recently dedicated **Holocaust Memorial** ⑥, a six-tower construction of glass and steel. Follow Marshall Street north and you pass the open-air stalls of **Haymarket** ⑦ on Blackstone Street, a flurry of activity on Fridays and Saturdays. To sample Italian goodies, make your way through a pedestrian tunnel underneath Fitzgerald Highway—destined to be a construction zone for the next decade due to Boston's massive Central Artery Project—and enter the **North End** at Salem Street.

TIMING

You can easily spend a whole day touring the myriad stores, boutiques, and historic sites of the Faneuil Hall and Quincy Market complex. On Fridays and Saturdays, you'll be able to join in the frenzied activity of the Haymarket. Nearly all the historic sites and plenty of the local stores and restaurants are open on Sundays.

Sights to See

❶ **City Hall.** Over the years, various plans—involving gardens, restaurants, music, and hotels—have been floated to make this area a more people-friendly site. Whether anything would ameliorate Bostonians' collective disregard for the chilly setting of Government Center is anyone's guess. But City Hall, an upside-down ziggurat design on a vast, sloping redbrick plaza, remains one of the most striking structures in the Government Center complex. The design by Kallman, McKinnell, and Knowles confines administrative functions to the upper floors and places offices that deal with the public on the street level: Despite those democratic intentions, the building is not much loved. ⊠ *Congress St. at North St. T stop, Government Center.*

★ ❸ **Faneuil Hall.** In some ways Faneuil Hall is a local Ark of the Covenant; a considerable part of Boston's spirit resides here. Learning to pronounce its name is the first task of any newcomer—say "Fan'l" or "*Fan*-yuhl." Like other Boston landmarks, Faneuil Hall has evolved over many years. It was originally erected in 1742, the gift of wealthy merchant Peter Faneuil, who wanted the hall to serve as both a place for town meetings and a public market. It burned in 1761 and was immediately reconstructed according to the original plan of its designer, the Scottish portrait painter John Smibert. In 1763 James Otis helped inaugurate the era that culminated in American independence when he dedicated the rebuilt hall to the "cause of liberty."

In 1772 Samuel Adams stood here and first suggested that Massachusetts and the other colonies organize a Committee of Correspondence to maintain semiclandestine lines of communication in the face of hardening British repression. In later years the hall again lived up to Otis's dedication, when Wendell Phillips and Charles Sumner pled for support of the abolitionist cause from its podium. The tradition continues to this day: In presidential election years, the hall hosts debates between contenders in the Massachusetts primary.

Faneuil Hall was substantially enlarged and remodeled in 1805 according to a Greek Revival design of the noted architect Charles Bulfinch, and this is the building we see today. Its purposes remain the same: The great balconied hall is available to citizens' groups on presentation of a request signed by a required number of responsible parties; it also plays host to regular concerts (when the grand hall itself is closed to the public—for an event like a concert—a closed-circuit TV gives visitors a glimpse of the famous podium).

Inside Faneuil Hall are the great mural *Webster's Reply to Hayne,* Gilbert Stuart's portrait of Washington at Dorchester Heights, and dozens of other paintings of famous Americans. On the top floors are the headquarters and museum of the **Ancient and Honorable Artillery Company of Massachusetts,** the oldest militia in the nation (1638). Its status is now strictly ceremonial, but it is justly proud of the arms, uniforms, and other artifacts on display.

Brochures about Faneuil Hall's history, distributed by the National Park Service, make light-hearted references to the ongoing commercialism nearby by reprinting a 1958 ditty by Francis Hatch: "Here orators in ages past/Have mounted their attack/Undaunted by the proximity/Of sausage on the rack." Faneuil Hall has always sat in the middle of Boston's main marketplace: Men like Andrew Jackson and Daniel Webster debated the future of the Republic here while the fragrances of bacon and snuff—sold by merchants in Quincy Market across the road—greeted their noses. Today, the aroma of cinnamon wafts throughout Faneuil Hall from a gourmet coffee and snack bar. There are still shops at ground level, but they cater mainly to the tourists seeking New England bric-a-brac. If you want an authentic Boston souvenir, visit the **City Store** (enter on the north side of the hall), which sells surplus municipal items ranging from real fire hydrants to hard hats to firemen's boots to vintage street signs (profits from City Store, which opened in 1995, support neighborhood youth programs).

Why is the gold-plated weather vane atop the cupola in the shape of a grasshopper? One story has it that Sir Thomas Gresham—founder of London's Royal Exchange—had been discovered in 1519 as a foundling babe by children chasing grasshoppers in a field, and placed an image of the insect over the Exchange to commemorate his salvation. Peter Faneuil liked the critter (it's the traditional symbol of good luck) and in his turn had one mounted over Faneuil Hall. The 8-pound, 52-inch-long insect remains as the only unmodified part of the original structure. Just across the way from Faneuil Hall is Quincy Market (☞ *below*), also known as the shopping extravaganza called Faneuil Hall Marketplace. ✉ *Faneuil Hall Sq.* 🕮 *Free.* ☉ *Daily 9–5; closed Thanksgiving, Dec. 25, Jan. 1. T stop, Government Center or Aquarium.*

NEED A BREAK? A homey landmark, the **Steaming Kettle**—a gilded kettle cast in 1873 that once steamed 'round the clock in Scollay Square—now adorns a branch of **Starbucks** (✉ 63-65 Court St. at Tremont, ☎ 617/227–2284). Stop in for a pastry and the day's brew.

❼ Haymarket. The Haymarket is an exuberant maze of a marketplace, packed with loudly self-promoting vendors who fill Marshall and Blackstone streets on Fridays and Saturdays from 7 AM until mid-afternoon. Pushcart vendors hawk fruits and vegetables against a backdrop of fish, meat, and cheese shops. The accumulation of debris left every evening has been immortalized in a whimsical 1976 public arts project—Mags Harries's "Asaroton," a Greek word meaning unswept floors—consisting of bronze fruit peels and other detritus smashed into pavement. It is now temporarily removed from the intersection of Blackstone and Hanover streets due to the Central Artery Project; officials promise to reinstall Ms. Harries's piece when the project is over. Another Harries piece, in bronze depicting a gathering of stray gloves, ornaments the Porter Square T station in Cambridge.

Not far from the Haymarket—between North and Hanover streets—lies Boston at its time-machine best: the **Blackstone Block,** now visited mostly for its culinary landmark, the **Union Oyster House** (☞ *below*).

Named for Boston's first settler, William Blaxton, it is the city's old-est commercial block, for decades dominated by the butcher trade. As a tiny remnant of Old Boston, the Blackstone Block remains the city's "family attic"—to use the winning metaphor of critic Donlyn Lyndon: more than three centuries of architecture on view, ranging from the 18th-century Capen House to the modern Bostonian Hotel. A Colonial-period warren of winding lanes—Scott Alley, Salt Lane, and Creek Square—surround the block, bursting with surprises and anachronis-tic storefronts at every turn.

Facing the Blackstone Block, in the vest-pocket-size **Union Park** framed by New Congress Street and Dock Square, are two bronze figures, one seated on a bench and the other standing eye to eye with passersby. Both represent James Michael Curley, mayor, governor, congressman, and questionable model for all urban bosses. It is well that he has no pedestal; the so-called Rascal King was much more a man than an idol. In 1946, he was sentenced to serve time in a federal penitentiary for fraud, but he refused to resign from his dual posts as mayor and con-gressman. His sentence was eventually commuted—his popularity only marginally diminished by the scandal—and he served out his term as mayor.

At Creek Square, near the Haymarket, can be found the **Boston Stone,** set into the brick wall of the gift shop of the same name. Older than the 1737 date the inscription suggests, it was long used as milepost zero in measuring distances from Boston.

⑥ Holocaust Memorial. At night, its six 50-ft-high glass-and-steel towers glow like ghosts who vow never to forget. During the day, Boston's newest monument seems at odds with the 18th-century streetscape of Blackstone Square behind it. Shoehorned into the north end of Union Park, the Holocaust Memorial is the work of Stanley Saitowitz, whose design was selected through an international competition; the finished memorial was dedicated in 1995. Recollections by Holocaust sur-vivors are set into the glass and granite walls; the upper levels of the towers are etched with 6 million numbers in random sequence sym-bolizing the Jewish victims of the Nazi horror. In the granite base, grates, aswirl in manufactured steam, cover pits of fiery electronic embers that make for a particularly haunting scene after dark.

② John F. Kennedy Federal Office Building. Looming up at the northwest edge of City Hall Plaza, these twin towers are noted structures for ar-chitecture aficionados: They were designed by the founder of the Bauhaus movement, Walter Gropius, who taught at Harvard toward the end of his illustrious career. **Gropius's house,** designed by him in textbook Bauhaus style, is in nearby suburban Lincoln (☞ Lincoln *in* Chapter 9 or inquire at SPNEA, ☞ The Old West End, *above*).

④ Quincy Market. Not everyone likes Quincy Market, also known as **Fa-neuil Hall Marketplace;** some people prefer grit to polish and disdain the new cafés and boutiques. But there is no denying that this pioneer effort at urban recycling set the tone for many similar projects through-out America and that it has brought tremendous vitality to a once-tired corner of Boston. Two decades after its inauguration, Quincy Market continues to attract huge crowds of both tourists and natives through-out the year. In the 1970s, demolition was a distinct possibility for these historic, yet decrepit, buildings. Fortunately, the primitive idea that urban renewal was accomplished with a bulldozer was beginning to yield to the more progressive idea of "recycling." With the participation of the Boston Redevelopment Authority, the architect Benjamin Thompson planned a renovation of all three Quincy Market buildings, and the

Government Center and the North End

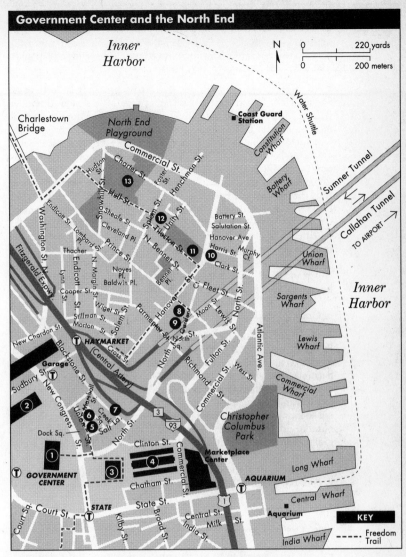

Inner Harbor

N

| 0 | | 220 yards |
| 0 | | 200 meters |

Charlestown Bridge

North End Playground

Coast Guard Station

Constitution Wharf

Water Shuttle

Commercial St.

Battery Wharf

Sumner Tunnel

Callahan Tunnel

TO AIRPORT

Hudson St.

Charter St.

Foster St.

Henchman St.

13

Hull St.

Snowhill St.

Sheafe St.

Cleveland Pl.

Snow St.

Unity St.

12

Union Wharf

Battery St.

Salutation St.

Hanover Ave.

Harris St.

Murphy Ct.

Endicott St.

Lombard Pl.

Prince St.

N. Bennet St.

11

Clark St.

10

Inner Harbor

Washington St. N.

Fitzgerald Expwy.

Thacher

N. Margin St.

Noyes Pl.

Baldwin Pl.

Bennet Ct.

Fleet St.

Sargents Wharf

Lynn St.

Endicott St.

Cooper St.

Wiget St.

Salem St.

Parmenter St.

Hanover St.

North St.

C

Moon St.

North St.

North St.

Lewis Wharf

Stillman

Morton

8

North Sq.

Sun Ct.

Lewis St.

New Chardon St.

T HAYMARKET

Cross St.

9

Fulton St.

Richmond St.

West St.

Atlantic Ave.

Commercial Wharf

Blackstone St.

Garage

T

Sudbury St.

New Congress St.

2

Hanover St.

Union St.

Marsh La.

Creek La.

Salt La.

7

6

5

North St.

3

93

Commercial St.

Christopher Columbus Park

Commercial Wharf

Dock Sq.

1

Clinton St.

Marketplace Center

Long Wharf

T GOVERNMENT CENTER

3

4

Chatham St.

Commercial St.

AQUARIUM

Central Wharf

Court Sq.

Court St.

Court St.

STATE

Chatham St.

State St.

Kilby St.

Broad St.

Central St.

India St.

Milk St.

T

AQUARIUM

Aquarium

India Wharf

KEY

- - - Freedom Trail

City Hall, **1**

Copp's Hill Burying Ground, **13**

Faneuil Hall, **3**

Haymarket, **7**

Holocaust Memorial, **6**

John F. Kennedy Federal Building, **2**

Old North Church, **12**

Paul Revere House, **8**

Paul Revere Mall (Prado), **11**

Pierce-Hichborn House, **9**

Quincy Market, **4**

St. Stephen's, **10**

Union Oyster House, **5**

Rouse Corporation of Baltimore undertook their restoration. Try to look beyond the shop windows to the grand design of the three monumental market buildings themselves; they represent a vision of the market as urban centerpiece, an idea whose time has certainly come again.

The market consists of three block-long annexes: **Quincy, North,** and **South Markets,** each 535 ft long and across a plaza from historic ☞ **Faneuil Hall.** The structures were built to the 1826 design Alexander Parris conceived to alleviate cramped retailers' conditions then common to Faneuil Hall. The central structure—of handsome granite, with a Doric colonnade at either end and topped by a classical dome and rotunda—has kept its traditional market-stall layout, but the stalls now purvey international and specialty foods: raw shellfish, cold pasta salads, frozen yogurt, bagels, calzone, sausage-on-a-stick, Chinese egg rolls, brownies, and baklava, plus all the boutique chocolate-chip cookies your heart desires. This is perhaps Boston's best locale for grazing, the hardest part being choosing what to sample. Along the arcades on either side of the Central Market are vendors selling sweatshirts, photographs of Boston, and other arts and crafts—some schlocky, some not—along with a couple of open-air bars and restaurants. The North and South Markets house a mixture of chain stores and specialty boutiques. Quintessential Boston remains here only in Durgin Park, the traditional New England dining experience. At the waterfront end of Quincy Market is **Marketplace Center,** another shopping complex.

A favorite tourist site for photos is the tacky but beloved bronze Bugs Bunny statue standing outside the **Warner Bros. Store.** An outdoor flower market on the north side of Faneuil provides a splash of color; at Christmastime, trees along the cobblestone walks are strung with thousands of sparkling lights. Year-round, these pedestrian walkways draw street jugglers and magicians—Peruvian instrumentalists often add their lilting sounds to the scene—and many summer visitors discover that the outdoor cafés are a great place to people-watch. Some people consider Quincy Market to be mall-style trendy, but 50,000 visitors a day enjoy the extravaganza. You'll want to decide for yourself. ⌂ *Quincy Market/Faneuil Hall Marketplace,* ☎ *617/338–2323.* ☉ *Mon.–Sat. 10–9, Sun. noon–6. Restaurants and bars generally open daily 11 AM–2 AM; food stalls open earlier. T stop, Haymarket, Government Center, State, or Aquarium.*

❺ Union Oyster House. Daniel Webster downed an occasional brandy and ate oysters by the dozen here in the 1830s. Charles Forster of Maine was the first American to use the curious invention of the toothpick on these premises. And John F. Kennedy was among more contemporary patrons; his favorite booth has been dedicated to his memory. The Union is the city's oldest restaurant, having opened its doors in 1826 in the former residence and dry goods shop of Hopestill Capen. The charming facade is constructed of Flemish bond brick and adorned with Victorian-style signage. For a time, the seignorial Duke of Chartres (who would later assume the French throne as Louis-Philippe) helped pay rent for his accommodations on the second floor by teaching French. ⌂ *41 Union St.,* ☎ *617/227–2750.* ☉ *Sun.–Thurs. 11 AM–9:30 PM, Fri.–Sat. 11 AM–10 PM. The distinctive semicircular oyster bar is open until midnight daily. T stop, Haymarket.*

THE NORTH END

This warren of small streets on the northeast side of the Central Artery that extends to the end of the peninsula was Boston before there was a Boston. Men and women walked these narrow byways when Shakespeare was not yet 20 years buried and Louis XIV was new to the throne of France. The town of Boston bustled and grew rich here for a century and a half before the birth of American independence. In the 17th century the North End *was* Boston, for much of the rest of the peninsula was still under water or had yet to be cleared.

Today's North End is almost entirely a creation of the late 19th century, when brick tenements began to fill up with European immigrants—first the Irish, then Central European Jews, then the Portuguese, and finally the Italians. For more than 60 years the North End attracted an Italian population base, so much so that one wonders whether wandering Puritan shades might scowl at the concentration of Mediterranean verve, volubility, and Roman Catholicism here. This is not only Boston's haven for Italian restaurants (there are dozens) but also for Italian groceries, bakeries, boccie courts, churches, social clubs, cafés, and street-corner debates over home-team soccer games. July and August are highlighted by a series of street festivals, or *feste,* honoring various saints, and by local community events that draw visitors from all over the city.

But although you'll see hordes of tourists following the redbrick ribbon of the Freedom Trail through the North End, there's still a neighborhood feeling to the jumbled streets, from the grandmothers gossiping on fire escapes to the laundry strung on back porches. Gentrification has made inroads—it is a rare block in which one or more tenements have not received the exposed-brick and track-lighting treatment—but it is unlikely that the North End will relinquish its ethnic strength any time soon; the people speaking with Abruzzese accents on Salem and Hanover streets are not paid actors, and they are not—fortunately—going to disappear tomorrow. If you wish to study up on this fascinating district, head for the North End branch of the Boston Public Library on Parmenter Street, where a bust of Dante acknowledges local cultural pride.

Numbers in the text correspond to numbers in the margin and on the Government Center and the North End map.

A Good Walk

History on two feet a day—that's the best way to view the sights of the North End: Parking is practically nonexistent here, so most people do this neighborhood by foot power, arriving via the T (Haymarket or Government Center). If you arrive by car, you can park at any of several garages near Quincy Market and cross under the Central Artery through a pedestrian tunnel that connects with **Salem Street.** (Be leery—the underpass is often a haven for the city's homeless.) The area between Faneuil Hall and the North End is ground zero of the massive Central Artery project; it's filled with construction equipment, pits, fences and ever-changing routes for cars and foot traffic. Plan to cross into the North only by the pedestrian tunnel; otherwise, you'll have to make heart-pounding dashes through traffic. Once through the tunnel, turn right on Cross Street and left on **Hanover Street,** one of the North End's main thoroughfares. Take Hanover to Richmond Street and turn left at North Square, following the Freedom Trail, to reach the fascinating (especially for kids) **Paul Revere House** ⑧—as the brochures state, "If Paul Revere were alive today, he'd still have a home in Boston." Right next door is the **Pierce-Hichborn House** ⑨, another venerable brick building. Take Prince Street back to Hanover Street and continue on Hanover to reach **St. Stephen's** ⑩, the only remaining church designed by the influential architect Charles Bulfinch. Directly across the street is the **Prado,** or **Paul Revere Mall** ⑪, dominated by a statue of the patriot and hero. At the end of the mall is the **Old North**

Church ⑫, of "One if by land, two if by sea" fame, from which twin lanterns warned of the invading British on the night of Revere's historic ride. Continue following the Freedom Trail to Hull Street and **Copp's Hill Burying Ground** ⑬, the resting place of many Revolutionary heroes. Then head back to Hanover Street to enjoy a well-deserved cappuccino and cannoli while savoring the character of this evocative neighborhood.

TIMING

Allow three to four hours for a walk through the North End. This part of town is made for strolling, day or night. Many people like to spend a day at nearby Quincy Market, then head under the Fitzgerald Expressway to the North End for dinner—the district has an impressive selection of traditional and contemporary Italian restaurants. Families should note that on Saturday afternoons from May to October the Paul Revere House schedules some of the most delightful events for children in the city (what seven-year-old would want to miss out on the mustering of the 10th Regiment Afoot?). And on Sundays, try to catch the ringing of the bells of Old North Church after the 11 AM service (they begin to ring at about 12:10 PM)—the bells today sound as sweet as when Paul Revere rang them on Sabbath mornings as a boy.

Sights to See

⑬ **Copp's Hill Burying Ground.** An ancient and melancholy air hovers like a fine mist over this Colonial-era burial ground. The extensive North End graveyard incorporates four cemeteries established between 1660 and 1819. Near the Charter Street gate is the tomb of the Mather family, the dynasty of church divines (Cotton and Increase were the most famous sons) who held sway in Boston during the heyday of the old theocracy. Also buried here is Robert Newman, who crept into the steeple of the Old North Church to warn of the British attack the night of Paul Revere's ride. Look for the tombstone of Captain Daniel Malcom; it is pockmarked with musket-ball fire from British soldiers, who used the stones for target practice. ⊗ *Daily 9–4. T stop, North Station.*

NEED A
BREAK?

From Copp's Hill head south and down on Snowhill Street, then, at the bottom, jog left briefly on Prince Street and right on Thatcher to arrive at **Pizzeria Regina** (⊠ 11½ Thatcher St.) for what some consider the best pizza in the North End—thin-crusted, oily, and wonderful. **Galleria Umberto** (⊠ 289 Hanover St.; closed Sun.) turns out pizza that rivals Regina's, but you have to sample its slices standing up—if you're lucky.

Ebenezer Clough House. At 21 Unity Street, hard by the Old North Church, this house warrants an exercise in imagination. Built in 1712, it is now the only local survivor of its era aside from Old North. Picture the streets lined with houses such as this, with an occasional grander Georgian mansion and some modest wooden frame survivors of old Boston's many fires—this is what the North End looked like when Paul Revere was young.

Hanover Street. This is one of North End's two main thoroughfares, named for the ruling dynasty of 18th-century England. Curiously, the label was retained after the Revolution, despite a flurry of patriotic renaming (King Street became State Street, for example). Hanover runs parallel to and one block east of Salem; its business center is thick with pastry shops and Italian cafés. It is also one of Boston's oldest public roads, once the site of the residences of the Rev. Cotton Mather and the Colonial-era patriot Dr. Joseph Warren, as well as a small dry-goods store run by Eben D. Jordan—who went on to launch Jordan Marsh.

Caffé Vittoria (✉ 296 Hanover St., ☎ 617/227–7606) specializes in cappuccino and other coffee concoctions; its café ambience makes it a great spot at any hour. President Clinton has stopped by **Mike's Pastry** (✉ 300 Hanover St., ☎ 617/742–3050) for the bakery's famous cannoli. Rumor has it that Secret Service agents made additional runs for him while he was in town.

★ ⓬ **Old North Church.** Standing at one end of the **Prado** (☞ Paul Revere Mall, *below*) is a church famous not only for being the oldest one in Boston, but for the two lanterns that glimmered from its steeple on the night of April 18, 1775. This is Christ Church, or the Old North, where a middle-aged silversmith named Paul Revere and a young sexton named Robert Newman managed that night to signal the departure by water to Lexington and Concord of the British regulars. Longfellow's poem aside, the lanterns were not a signal *to* Revere but *from* him to the citizens of Charlestown across the harbor. Newman, carrying the lanterns, ascended the steeple (the original tower blew down in 1804 and was replaced; the present one was put up in 1954 after the replacement was destroyed in a hurricane), while Revere began his clandestine trip by rowboat across the Mystic.

Although William Price designed the structure after he studied Christopher Wren's London churches, the Old North—still home to an active Episcopal congregation (including descendants of the Reveres)—is an impressive building in its own right. Inside, note the gallery and graceful arrangement of pews (reserved in Colonial times for the families that rented them); the bust of George Washington, pronounced by the Marquis de Lafayette to be the truest likeness of the general he ever saw; the brass chandeliers, made in Amsterdam in 1700 and installed here in 1724; and the clock, the oldest still running in an American public building. The pews—Number 54 was the Revere family pew—are the highest in America due to the little charcoal-burning foot warmers (used to accommodate parishioners back when). Try to visit when changes are rung on the bells, after the 11 AM Sunday service; recently restored and rehung, they bear the inscription, "We are the first ring of bells cast for the British Empire in North America." Every April 18, descendants of the patriots raise lanterns in the church belfry in a traditional reenactment.

One of the most peculiar mementos in the annals of American history is displayed in the small gift shop and museum next to the church. A glass container holds a vial of tea purportedly decanted from the boots of a participant in the notorious Boston tea party fracas. Other cases display such artifacts as a musket used in the battle of Lexington and a sword carried by Robert Gould Shaw, commander of the black regiment in the Civil War. Delightful souvenirs are for sale here, including bags of maple sugar candy and parchment copies of Longfellow's 1863 poem "Paul Revere's Ride".

Behind the church is the quaint **Washington Memorial Garden** where volunteers cultivate a plot devoted to plants and flowers favored in the 18th century. The garden is studded with several unusual commemorative plaques—including one for the Rev. George Burrough, who was hanged in the Salem Witch Trials in 1692; it was his great-grandson, Robert Newman, who had carried the famous pair of lanterns to the steeple. In another niche hangs the "Third Lantern," dedicated in 1976 during the country's bicentennial celebration. ✉ *193 Salem St.,* ☎ *617/523–6676.* ☉ *Daily 9–5. Sun. services at 9, 11, and 4; closed Thanksgiving, Dec. 25. T stop, Haymarket or North Station.*

"LISTEN, MY CHILDREN, AND YOU SHALL HEAR . . .": ALL ABOUT PAUL REVERE

THIS IS A TEST. PAUL REVERE WAS: (1) A great patriot whose midnight ride helped ignite the American Revolution; (2) a prominent dentist, expert in making false teeth; (3) a silversmith who crafted tea-caddies; (4) a printer who engraved the first American currency; (5) an authority on explosives and maker of gunpowder. The only correct response is "All of the above." But there's even more, much more, to this outsize revolutionary hero—leading bell ringer for Old North Church, major shareholder in the earliest fire-insurance company in the United States, founder of the copper mills that still bear his name, father of 16 children, coroner, and foreman of the jury of the most sensational murder trial of the day.

Although his life spanned eight decades (1735–1818), Revere is most famous for that one night when he became America's most celebrated Pony Express. *"Listen, my children, and you shall hear/Of the midnight ride of Paul Revere"* are the opening lines of Henry Wadsworth Longfellow's poem, which placed the event at the center of American folklore. Longfellow may have been an effective evangelist for Revere but he was an indifferent historian. Ever since, scholars have been analyzing the varying accounts of the events of the night of April 16, 1775, most recently in David Hackett Fischer's brilliant "remounting," *Paul Revere's Ride* (Oxford, 1994).

We now know that Revere was not the only midnight rider—William Dawes was also dispatched from Boston. We now know that Revere never looked for the "One if by Land" signal from Charlestown: He told Robert Newman to hang two lanterns from Old North's belfry— the Redcoats were on the move by water—but by that time, Revere was already on his way to Lexington astride Deacon Larkin's Brown Beauty. Nor did Revere ever raise the alarm in Concord. When he did make a little noise upon arriving, the duty sergeant told him to be quiet! Fischer further states that Revere never uttered the famous cry "The British are coming!" The reason? Bostonians considered themselves British.

Poetic license aside, this tale has become part of the collective American spirit. We dote on learning that Revere forgot his spurs, only to retrieve them by tying a note to his dog's collar, then awaiting its return with the spurs now attached. We're grateful for the temerity he showed in asking a lady to sacrifice her petticoat to muffle the sounds of his oars while crossing the Charles. Little wonder that this tale resonates in the hearts and imagination of America's citizenry, as well as in Boston's streets on the third Monday of every April, Patriot's Day, when Paul's ride is reenacted—in daylight—to the cheers of thousands of onlookers. The clickety-clack of hoofs announces Revere himself, costumed in tricorne, knickers, and Colonial ponytail.

☝ **❽ Paul Revere House.** It is an interesting coincidence that the oldest house standing in downtown Boston should also have been the home of Paul Revere, patriot activist and silversmith. And it *is* a coincidence, as many homes of famous Bostonians have burned or been demolished over the years, and the Revere house could easily have become one of them back when it was just another makeshift tenement in the heyday of European immigration. It was saved from oblivion in 1905 and restored, lovingly though not quite scientifically, to an approximation of its original 17th-century appearance.

The house was built in 1676 after the great fire of that year, nearly a hundred years before Revere's 1775 midnight ride through Middlesex County (for an in-depth look at the "Son of Liberty," ☞ Close-Up: "Listen, My Children, And You Shall Hear . . .", *below*). Revere owned it from 1770 until 1800, although he rented it out during the later part of that period. Pre-1900 photographs show it as a shabby warren of storefronts and apartments. The clapboard sheathing is a replacement, but 90% of the framework is original; note the Elizabethan-style overhang and leaded windowpanes. Few of Revere's furnishings are on display here, but just gazing at Paul's own toddy warmer brings the great man alive. The **Museum of Fine Arts** (☞ The Fens and Kenmore Square, *below*) has a splendid collection of Revere's silver work.

Special events are scheduled throughout the year, many designed to delight children. During the first week of December, the staff dresses in period costume and serves up apple pandowdy and other Colonial-era goodies, and silhouette makers show off their skills. From May to October, there's something going on every Saturday: A silversmith or broom maker may be on hand, a hammer-dulcimer player could entertain, or the 10th Regiment Afoot—in full antique British regalia—might muster on the premises. And if you go to the house on Patriot's Day, chances are you'll bump into the Middlesex Fife and Drum Corps.

The immediate neighborhood surrounding the Revere house also has Revere associations. The little park in North Square is named after Rachel Revere, his second wife, and the adjacent brick ☞ **Pierce-Hichborn House** once belonged to kin of his. ✉ *19 North Sq.,* ☎ *617/523–1676 or 617/523–2338.* 🎟 *$2.50.* ⊙ *Daily 9:30–4:15; Apr. 15–Oct. 31 until 5:15; closed holidays and Mon., Jan.–Mar. T stop, Haymarket.*

★ **⓫ Paul Revere Mall,** or the Prado. This makes a perfect time-out spot from the Freedom Trail. Bookended by two landmark churches—Old North and Bulfinch's St. Stephen's—the mall is flanked by brick walls lined with bronze plaques bearing the stories of famous North Enders of old. An appropriate centerpiece for this lovely cityscape is Cyrus Dallin's equestrian statue of Paul Revere. Despite Longfellow's "Paul Revere's Ride" and such statues as this, the gentle Revere was of stocky build and of medium height—whatever manly dash he possessed must have been in his eyes rather than his physique. That physique served him well enough, however, for he lived to be 83 and saw nearly all his revolutionary comrades buried.

❾ Pierce-Hichborn House. One of the city's oldest brick buildings, this structure—just to the left of the **Paul Revere House** (☞ *above*)—was once owned by relatives of Revere's mother. The lovely garden is planted with flowers and medicinal herbs favored in Revere's day. (Nearby, at 4 Garden Court Street, is the former residence of John F. "Honey Fitz" Fitzgerald. His daughter, Rose—mother of President John F. Kennedy—was born here.) ✉ *29 North Sq.,* ☎ *617/523–1676 or 617/523–2338.* 🎟 *Pierce-Hichborn House $2.50; combined admission for Paul Revere and Pierce-Hichborn houses $4.* ⊙ *Daily guided tours 12:30 and 2:30; call ahead to confirm. T stop, Haymarket.*

⑩ St. Stephen's. Rose Kennedy, matriarch of the Kennedy clan, was christened here; 104 years later, it held mourners at her funeral. This is the only Charles Bulfinch church still standing in Boston. A rebuilding in 1804 of an earlier structure, it was first used as a Unitarian Church. Since 1862 it has served a Roman Catholic parish. The building has been moved back 12 ft and raised 6 ft; it was restored in 1965. ⊘ *Daily 8:30–5. Sun. mass 8:30 and 11. T stop, Haymarket.*

Salem Street. This ancient and constricted thoroughfare, one of the two main North End streets, cuts through the heart of the neighborhood and serves as home to meat supply stores, hardware stores, an Italian ceramics shop, and more restaurants and cafés.

NEED A BREAK? The allure of **Bova's Bakery** (⊠ 134 Salem St., ☎ 617/523–5601), a neighborhood institution, is not only its Italian breads and pastries—it's open 24 hours a day (the deli closes at 1 a.m., however). Another modest but pleasant hang-out is **Biscotti's** (⊠ 95 Salem St., ☎ 617/227–8365), although espresso served in paper cups loses something.

CHARLESTOWN

Boston started here. Charlestown was a thriving settlement a year before Colonials headed across the Charles River to found the city proper. Today, the district lures visitors with two of the most visible—and vertical—monuments in Boston's history: the Bunker Hill Monument and the USS *Constitution*, whose indestructible masts continue to tower over the waterfront where she was built more than 200 years ago. As a neighborhood, Charlestown remains a predominantly Irish-American enclave, with yuppification setting in steadily since the 1980s. The area suffers some notoriety from its reputation as alleged home turf for Irish-led organized crime; a number of bloody murders that remain unsolved—due to the neighborhood's vaunted "code of silence"—hasn't helped. But Townies (as old-time Charlestown residents are called) are fiercely proud of their historic, elegantly maintained streets.

The blocks around the Bunker Hill Monument are a good illustration of a neighborhood in flux. Elegantly restored Federal and mid-19th-century town houses stand cheek by jowl with working-class quarters of similar vintage but more modest recent pasts. Gas lamps add a special charm. Nearby Winthrop Square also has its share of interesting houses. Farther north along Main Street is City Square, Charlestown's main commercial district. On Phipps Street you'll find the grave marker of John Harvard, a young minister who in 1638 bequeathed his small library to the fledgling Cambridge College, which was to be renamed in his honor. The precise location of the grave is uncertain, but a monument of 1828 marks its approximate site. John Harvard is also commemorated in the nearby Harvard Mall, a vest-pocket park.

To get to Charlestown, you may take Bus 93 from Haymarket Square, Boston, which stops three blocks from the Navy Yard entrance. A more interesting way to get here is to take the MBTA water shuttle from Long Wharf in downtown Boston, which runs every 15 or 30 minutes year-round.

Numbers in the text correspond to numbers in the margin and on the Charlestown map.

A Good Walk

Charlestown can be reached on foot across the Charlestown Bridge. From **Copp's Hill Burying Ground** (☞ *above*), follow Hull Street to

Commercial Street, and turn left to reach the bridge. You come upon the entrance of the **Charlestown Navy Yard** ① on your right after alighting from the bridge. Just ahead is the **USS *Constitution*** ② museum and visitor center; next door is Raytheon's **Bunker Hill Pavilion.** From here, you may follow the red line of the Freedom Trail to the **Bunker Hill Monument,** ③ which is visible from the yard.

TIMING

Give yourself two to three hours for a Charlestown walk; the lengthy stroll across the Charlestown Bridge calls for endurance in cold weather. You may want to save Charlestown's stretch of the Freedom Trail, which adds considerably to its length, for a second-day outing. You can always save backtracking the historic route by taking the MBTA water shuttle, which ferries back and forth between Charlestown's Navy Yard and downtown Boston's Long Wharf.

Sights to See

❸ Bunker Hill Monument. Three classic misnomers surround this famous monument. First, the Battle of Bunker Hill was actually fought on Breed's Hill, which is where the monument sits today. (The troops themselves originally called it the Battle of Charlestown.) Secondly, Americans actually lost the battle in a Pyrrhic victory for the British Redcoats, who lost nearly half of their 2,200 men; American casualties numbered 500 to 600. And third: The famous war cry, "Don't fire until you see the whites of their eyes," may not have been uttered by American Colonel William Prescott, but if he did shout it, he was quoting an old Prussian command. No matter. The Americans did employ a deadly delayed-action strategy on June 17, 1775, and conclusively proved themselves to be worthy fighters, capable of defeating the forces of the British Empire.

Among the dead were the brilliant young American doctor and political activist Joseph Warren, recently commissioned as a major general but fighting as a private, and the British Major Pitcairn, who two months before had led the Redcoats into Lexington. Pitcairn is buried in the crypt of the Old North Church. Warren lay in a shallow grave on Breed's Hill until the British evacuated Boston in 1776, when his remains were disinterred and buried ceremoniously in the Old Granary. How was the body identified? Warren's "dentist" recognized his own handiwork in a set of false teeth. The dentist was silversmith Paul Revere, a jack and master of many trades, who had made the teeth's silver springs.

In 1823, a committee was formed to construct a monument on the site of the battle, choosing the form of an Egyptian obelisk as a suitable tribute. Architect Solomon Willard designed a 221-ft-high obelisk constructed of blocks of granite cut from quarries in Quincy; transportation dilemmas led to the establishment of the country's first commercial railway; the rails were made first of pine, then granite, and finally iron. The Marquis de Lafayette laid the cornerstone of the monument in 1825, but, due to a nagging lack of funds, it wasn't dedicated until 1843. Poet and social reformer Sarah Josepha Hale and other women helped in 1840 with a yard and bake sale that netted $30,000. Daniel Webster's stirring words on its dedication have gone down in history: "Let it rise! Let it rise! Till it greets the sun in its coming. Let the earliest light of the morning gild it and painting day, linger and play upon its summit."

The monument's zenith is reached by a flight of 294 steps. There is no elevator, but the views from the observatory are worth the effort of the arduous climb. A statue of Colonel Prescott stands guard at the base. In the lodge at the base, dioramas tell the story of the battle, and ranger programs are conducted hourly. If you are in Boston on June

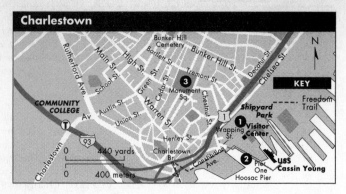

17, go to the hill to see a reenactment of the battle; it's quite a splendid production. ☎ 617/242–5641. 🎫 *Free.* ☉ *Lodge: daily 9–5;
Monument: daily 9–4:30. T stop, Community College.*

The Charlestown Historical Society runs a **museum** at 43 Monument
Square, open May to September. Another Bunker Hill presentation, the
multimedia show "Whites of Their Eyes," about the Battle of Bunker
Hill, is shown in the Bunker Hill Pavilion near the Navy Yard entrance.
✉ 55 Constitution Rd., ☎ 617/241–7576. 🎫 $3. ☉ Apr.–Nov., daily
9:30–4 (until 5 June–Aug.); shows every ½ hr.

❶ Charlestown Navy Yard. Now a National Park Service Historic Site,
the Charlestown Navy Yard was one of six established to build war-
ships. For 174 years, as wooden hulls and muzzle-loading cannons gave
way to steel ships and sophisticated electronics, the yard evolved to
meet the changing needs of a changing navy. It is a virtual museum of
American shipbuilding; here are early 19th-century barracks, workshops, and officers' quarters; a ropewalk (an elongated building for
making rope, not open to the public), designed in 1834 by the Greek
Revival architect Alexander Parris and used by the Navy to turn out
cordage for more than 125 years; and one of the two oldest dry docks
in the United States. The ☞ **USS *Constitution*** was first to use this dry
dock (in 1833). In addition to the ship itself, check out the *Constitution* Museum, the commandant's house, the collections of the Boston
Marine Society, and the USS *Cassin Young*, a World War II destroyer
typical of the ships built here during that era.

★ ☙ **❷ USS *Constitution*.** Better known as "Old Ironsides," the USS *Constitution* rides proudly at anchor in her berth at the Charlestown Navy Yard.
The oldest commissioned ship in the U.S. fleet is a battlewagon of the
old school, of the days of "wooden ships and iron men"—when she and
her crew of 200 succeeded at the perilous task of asserting the sovereignty
of an improbable new nation. Once a year—on July 4—she is towed
out for a turnabout in Boston harbor, the very place her keel was laid
in 1797.

The venerable craft, just over 200 years old, has narrowly escaped the
scrap heap several times in her long history. She was launched on October 21, 1797, as part of the nation's fledgling Navy. Her hull was
made of live oak, the toughest wood grown in North America; her bottom was sheathed in copper, provided by Paul Revere at a nominal cost.
Her principal service was during Thomas Jefferson's campaign against
the Barbary pirates, off the coast of North Africa, and in the War of
1812. Of her 42 engagements, her record was 42–0.

The nickname "Old Ironsides" was acquired during the War of 1812 when shots from the British warship *Guerriere* appeared to bounce off her tough oaken hull. Talk of scrapping the ship began as early as 1830, but she was saved by a public campaign sparked by Oliver Wendell Holmes's poem "Old Ironsides." A major restoration was done from 1992 to 1996; by now only about 8% to 10% of her original wood remains in place.

Today she continues, the oldest commissioned warship in the world, still a part of the U.S. Navy.

The men and women who look after her are regular Navy personnel and maintain a 24-hour watch. Sailors, dressed in 1812-era uniforms, show visitors around the ship, guiding them to two of the ship's three below decks: the places at the guns where the desperate, difficult work of naval warfare under sail was performed and, below that, the cramped living quarters. Another treat when visiting the ship: The view of Boston across Boston Harbor is spectacular. The nearby **Constitution Museum** has artifacts and hands-on exhibits pertaining to the ship—firearms, logs, and instruments. One section takes you step by step through the Constitution's most important battles. Old meets new in a video battle "fought" at the helm of a ship. ⊠ *Constitution Wharf,* ☎ *617/242–5670 ship; 617/426–1812 museum.* ⚑ *Ship, free; museum $4.* ☉ *Ship: daily 9:30–sunset, 20-min tours, last at 3:30 PM. Museum: daily 10–5; winter 10–4. T stop, Haymarket; then MBTA Bus 92 or 93 to Charlestown City Sq. or Boston Harbor Cruise water shuttle from Long Wharf.*

NEED A BREAK?   Stop for a drink or some food with an international twist at the **Warren Tavern** (⊠ 2 Pleasant St., ☎ 617/241–8142), built in 1780, a restored Colonial neighborhood pub once frequented by George Washington and Paul Revere. It was the first building reconstructed after the Battle of Bunker Hill, which leveled the town.

DOWNTOWN BOSTON

Boston's commercial and financial districts—the area commonly called downtown—are concentrated in a maze of streets that seem to have been laid out with little logic; they are, after all, only village lanes that happen to be lined with modern 40-story office towers. Just as the great fire of 1872 swept the old financial district clear, the downtown construction over the past two decades has obliterated many of the buildings where Boston businessmen of Silas Lapham's day sat in front of their expansive rolltop desks. Yet many historic sights remain in this thoroughly Manhattanized section of Boston: A good number of them have been linked together to make up a fascinating section of the Freedom Trail.

The area is bordered by **State Street** on the north and by **South Station** and **Chinatown** to the south. **Tremont Street** and the **Common** form the west boundary, and the **harbor** wharves the eastern edge. Natives may be able to navigate the tangle of thoroughfares in between, but very few of them manage to give intelligible directions when consulted, and you're better off trusting a map. The area is confusing, but it is mercifully small.

Washington Street is the main commercial thoroughfare of downtown Boston. South of the Old South, Washington is a pedestrian street that is home to two venerable anchors of Boston's mercantile district, Filene's and what was once Jordan Marsh (☞ Chapter 8). William Filene founded his Boston store in 1881 near the site of the present eight-story building (1912). Now a separate corporate entity, Filene's Basement grew to become more famous than its parent store—even though it operated without women's dressing rooms, a lack that necessitated shrewd undergarment planning and tortuous squirming in the aisles. Jordan Marsh was the creation of Eben Jordan, who arrived in Boston from Maine around 1840 with $1.25 in his pocket; he opened Jordan Marsh (Marsh was a partner) in 1851. The huge store expanded rapidly in the 1970s; the entire chain was eventually purchased by the Federated chain, which changed all of the Jordan Marsh stores into Macy's. For Boston shoppers, it was the end of an era.

Street vendors, food carts (including a particularly good burrito bar), flower carts, and gaggles of teenagers and shoppers throng the pedestrian mall outside the two stores.

Downtown, too, is home to some of Boston's most idiosyncratic neighborhoods. The old Leather District directly abuts **Chinatown,** which is also bordered by the **Theater District,** farther west (and the buildings of the Tufts New England Medical Center), while to the south, the red light of the once brazen and now decaying Combat Zone flickers weakly. The Massachusetts Turnpike and its junction with the Southeast Expressway cuts a wide swath through the area, isolating Chinatown from the South End in much the same way the Fitzgerald Expressway isolates the North End from downtown.

Numbers in the text correspond to numbers in the margin and on the Downtown Boston map.

A Good Walk

After viewing the dramatic interior of **King's Chapel** ① at the corner of Tremont (that's "*Tre*-mont," not "*Tree*-mont"), visit the burying ground next door, the oldest graveyard in the" city. From here, it's two blocks down School Street to the **Old Corner Bookstore Site** ②. From the corner of School Street and Washington turn right (south) to see the **Old South Meeting House** ③, which seethed with revolutionary fervor in the 1770s. A right turn (north) onto Washington Street from the doorstep of the Old South will take you past the Globe Corner Bookstore once again, past Pi Alley (named after the loose type, or "pi," spilled from the pockets of printers when upper Washington Street was Boston's newspaper row—or after Colonial pie shops, depending on which story you prefer to believe), and to the rear of the **Old State House** ④ near the intersection of Court Street. In a traffic island in front is a circle of stones that marks the **site of the Boston Massacre** ⑤. Following State Street east toward the harbor, you pass the **U.S. Custom House** ⑥, one of Boston skyline's most distinct entities. Then—if you have children in tow—head over to the **New England Aquarium** ⑦ on Central Wharf or skip directly to **Rowes Wharf** ⑧, Boston's most glamorous waterfront development. Or turn south on Atlantic Avenue—most likely a solid wall of traffic due to construction of a new underground Central Artery highway nearby—to the foot of Pearl Street where a plaque marks the **site of the original Boston Tea Party** ⑨. The **Boston Tea Party Ship and Museum** ⑩ lies a little farther beyond—cross the Fort Point Channel at Congress Street for a look at the *Beaver II,* a faithful re-creation of the hapless British ship that was carrying tea in 1773. Continue along Congress Street and you come to the 40-foot milk bottle that marks Museum Wharf, home to the **Children's Museum** ⑪ and **Computer Museum** ⑫, conveniently side by side. From here you can make your way toward **Chinatown** (and dinner) passing **South Station** ⑬ and the **Federal Reserve Tower** ⑭.

This section of Boston has a generous share of attractions, so it might be wise to save a full day to spend among the New England Aquarium, the Children's Museum, and the Computer Museum. There are optimum times to catch some sights: The golden dome of the State House shines best under sunny skies, while a stroll along the waterfront at Rowes Wharf is most romantic at dusk. No need to visit the Aquarium at a special hour to catch feeding time—this event happens continuously throughout the day.

Sights to See

Boston Harbor Islands State Park. In 1997, the Boston Harbor Islands— the 31 islands in the inner and outer harbors—were designated a national parks entity, administered by a public-private partnership. The focal point of the park is 30-acre Georges Island, on which the pre– Civil War Fort Warren stands, partially restored and partially in ruins. Confederate prisoners were once housed here. Other islands include Peddocks Island, which holds the remains of Fort Andrews, and Deer Island, where 200 Native Americans were interned and died during King Philip's War in 1675–76. From June to September, free water taxis run from Georges to Gallops, Lovells, Peddocks, Grape, and Bumpkin islands. Bumpkin and Gallops are small and easily explored within an hour or so; Lovells and Grape each cover about 60 acres. All the harbor islands are accessible by private boat, with the exception of Thompson's Island, a private research facility. You can fish and hike and picnic—there are plenty of ruins to explore, and beautiful views; Lovells and Gallops have a swimming beach. (☞ Participant Sports and Fitness *and* Beaches *in* Chapter 7). *Park offices,* ☎ *617/727–7676.* ⊠ *Boston Harbor Cruises,* ☎ *617/227–4321.* ☞ *Trip to George's Island, $7.50.* ☉ *Early June–Sept.*

⑤ Boston Massacre Site. Directly in front of the **Old State House** (☞ *below*), a circle of cobblestones (in a traffic island) marks the site of the Boston Massacre, which occurred on the snowy evening of March 5, 1770, when a small contingent of British regular soldiers fired in panic upon a taunting mob of more than 40 Bostonians. Five townsmen died. In the legal action that followed, the defense of the accused soldiers was undertaken by John Adams and Josiah Quincy, both of whom vehemently opposed British oppression but who were devoted to the principle of fair trial. All but two of the nine regulars charged were acquitted; the others were branded on the hand for the crime of manslaughter. Paul Revere lost little time in capturing the "massacre" in a dramatic engraving that soon became one of the Revolution's most potent images of propaganda.

⑩ Boston Tea Party Ship and Museum. The *Beaver II,* a handsome replica of one of the ships forcibly boarded and unloaded the night Boston Harbor became a teapot, bobs in the Fort Point Channel at the Congress Street Bridge. The ship was anchored here during the bicentennial festivities in 1976 and has remained ever since. The interpretive center on the adjacent pier contains exhibits explaining the significance of the events of that cold evening and what led up to it. Visitors receive a complimentary cup of tea, a nice touch. When there are enough visitors, kids may be pressed into donning feathers and war paint to reenact the tea drop. The site of the actual tea party is marked by a plaque on Pearl Street and Atlantic Avenue (☞ *below*). ⊠ *Congress St. Bridge,* ☎ *617/338–1773.* ☞ *$7.* ☉ *Memorial Day–Labor Day, daily 9–6; Labor Day–Dec. 1 and Mar.–Memorial Day, daily 9–5. T stop, South Station.*

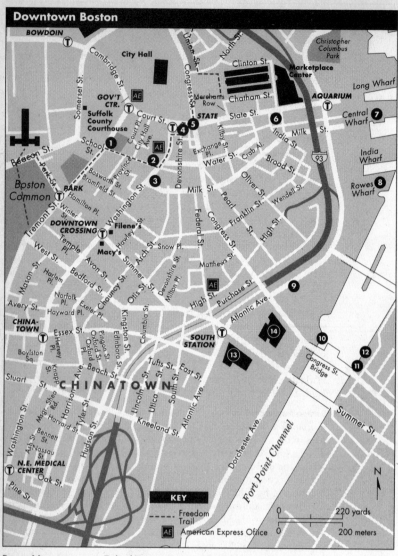

Downtown Boston

BOWDOIN

City Hall

Cambridge St.

Somerset St.

Union St.

North St.

Clinton St.

Christopher Columbus Park

Marketplace Center

Long Wharf

GOV'T CTR.

AE

Merchants Row

Chatham St.

AQUARIUM

Suffolk County Courthouse

Court St.

STATE

State St.

Central Wharf

School St.

Court Pl.

City Hall Ave.

Kilby St.

India St.

Milk St.

93

India Wharf

Beacon St.

Park St.

Bosworth St.

Province St.

Bromfield St.

Exchange Pl.

Water St.

Crab Al.

Broad St.

Oliver St.

Rowes Wharf

Boston Common

PARK

Hamilton Pl.

Washington St.

Milk St.

Pearl St.

Franklin St.

Wendell St.

High St.

Tremont St.

Winter St.

DOWNTOWN CROSSING

Filene's

Hawley St.

Arch St.

Snow Pl.

Federal St.

Congress St.

Temple Pl.

Macy's

Avon St.

Summer St.

Devonshire Pl.

Matthews St.

West St.

Bedford St.

Chauncy St.

Otis St.

Milton Pl.

AE

Purchase St.

Mason St.

Harlem Pl.

Norfolk Pl.

Exeter Pl.

Atlantic Ave.

Avery St.

Hayward Pl.

Kingston St.

Columbia St.

SOUTH STATION

CHINA-TOWN

Essex St.

Hersey Pl.

Edinboro St.

Pingon St.

Ping On St.

Oxford St.

Beach St.

Tufts St.

East St.

Congress St. Bridge

Boylston Sq.

Knapp St.

CHINATOWN

Lincoln St.

South St.

Utica St.

Summer St.

Stuart St.

Mgr Shea Rd.

Harrison Ave.

Tyler St.

Hudson St.

Kneeland St.

Atlantic Ave.

Dorchester Ave.

Fort Point Channel

Washington St.

Bennett St.

Ash St.

Nassau St.

N.E. MEDICAL CENTER

Oak St.

Pine St.

N

KEY

- - - - Freedom Trail

AE American Express Office

0   220 yards

0   200 meters

❾ Boston Tea Party Site. At the foot of Pearl Street, along Atlantic Avenue, a plaque is set into the wall of a commercial building to mark the site of the Boston Tea Party. That this was once Griffin's Wharf is only further evidence of Boston's relentless expansion into its harbor.

⑪ Children's Museum. Not for kids only. The whole family will enjoy the multitude of hands-on exhibits designed to help kids understand scientific laws, cultural diversity, their own bodies, and the nature of disabilities. Some of the most popular sights are also the simplest and most delightful: bubble-making machinery, a giant-size mug (big enough to hide a trio of 6-year-olds), and a two-story climbing sculpture. In "Teen Toyko," experience Japanese youth culture, including a Japanese subway car and karaoke booth. In the toddler room you can let kids under five go free in a fairly safe environment; the attached parent resource room has a great library of books and magazines on parenting issues. The downstairs museum shop overflows with children's books and gifts; upstairs, at Recycle, industrial raw material is sold in bulk. There's also a full schedule of special exhibits, festivals, and performances. ✉ *300 Congress St.,* ☎ *617/426–6500 or 617/426–8855 for recorded information.* 🎫 *$7, $1 Fri. 5–9.* ☉ *Mid-June–Labor Day, daily 10–5, Fri. until 9; Sept.–mid-June, Tues.–Sun. 10–5, Fri. until 9. T stop, South Station.*

Chinatown. Boston's Chinatown may be geographically small in the scheme of the city, yet it is home to one of the larger concentrations of Chinese-Americans in the United States. Beginning in the 1870s, Chinese immigrants began to trickle in, many setting up tents in Ping On Alley. The trickle increased to a flow when immigration restrictions were lifted after 1940. As in most American Chinatowns, the concentration of regional restaurants attracts numerous visitors; on Sundays, Bostonians traditionally head for Chinatown to feast on dim sum, the fragrant dumplings that are a popular choice for brunch. Today, the many Chinese establishments—most found along Beach and Tyler streets and Harrison Avenue—are interspersed with Vietnamese, Korean-Japanese, Thai, and Malaysian eateries. A three-story pagoda-style arch at the end of Beach Street welcomes visitors to the district. The community is centered around the Asian-American Civic Association, housed in the former Quincy School at 90 Tyler Street, built in 1848 to teach arriving Irish and Italian immigrants. An educational landmark, it was the first institution to assign pupils individual desks. Now a statue of Confucius ornaments the front yard, but its civic functions continue. *T stop, Chinatown.*

NEED A BREAK?	A treasure of a pastry shop in an out-of-the-way part of Chinatown is **May's Cake House** (✉ 223 Harrison Ave.). There's a delightful selection of pastries and treats—be sure to order the little cakes with fresh fruit toppings; they are deceptively light and entirely filling.

Christopher Columbus Park. It's a short stroll from the financial district to a view of Boston Harbor, once a national symbol of rampant pollution. These days, the harbor is making a slow comeback. Also known as **Waterfront Park**, the green space bordering the harbor and several of Boston's restored wharves is a pleasant oasis with benches and an arborlike shelter. Lewis Wharf and Commercial Wharf, which long lay nearly derelict, had by the mid-1970s been transformed into condominiums, apartments, restaurants, and upscale shops. Long Wharf's Marriott hotel was designed to look compatible with the old seaside warehouses. Sailboats and power yachts ride at anchor here. ✉ *Bordered by Atlantic Ave., Commercial Wharf, Long Wharf, and Atlantic Ocean.*

Combat Zone. The borders of Chinatown continue to expand—mostly at the expense of the Combat Zone, which has the dubious distinction of being one of the nation's first official red-light districts. It got its name more than 50 years ago when Boston-stationed troops would show up at the local tailor shops for uniform alterations and inevitably tussle with members of other branches of the military there for the same purpose. When the honky-tonk businesses were forced out of Scollay Square, they moved into this run-down area. Seeking to contain the spread of vice, city officials created the Lower Washington Street Adult Entertainment District, as Puritan ghosts shuddered. Today, due to the availability of X-rated tapes at most video outlets, the Combat Zone is a mere shadow of its sleazy self. The old Pilgrim Theater—where onetime Arkansas congressman Wilbur Mills ignited a media scandal by joining stripper Fanny Foxe on stage—is no more. Still, porn entrepreneurs continue to try to open new venues; even owners of the now-defunct Naked i keep attempting to reopen the notorious strip joint. But Chinatown merchants steadily object to the area's prostitution and illegal drug activity, and a major development firm has floated plans for a huge commercial, retail, and housing complex on lower Washington Street.

Computer Museum. Given the importance of high tech to the Boston economy, the establishment of this institution was an act akin to the hanging of the *Sacred Cod* in the State House. Standing conveniently next to the ☞ **Children's Museum,** the Computer Museum has more than 170 exhibits in which you and your kids can learn about the machines running our lives and about the men and women who created them. Exhibits include the two-story Walk-Through Computer™, a hands-on, interactive exhibit outlining all facets of the information highway, and a gallery to try out the best software for kids. Be sure to beam over to visit celebrity-robot-in residence R2-D2 from the *Star Wars* trilogy. And get a taste of creating your own reality in a new exhibit that allows young visitors to create fishes for a virtual fish tank. ⊠ *300 Congress St.,* ☏ *617/426–2800 or 617/423–6758; http://www.tcm.org.* 🎫 *$7; half-price Sun. afternoon.* ⊙ *July–Labor Day, daily 10–6; Sept.–June, Tues.–Sun. 10–5; closed holidays. T stop, South Station.*

Federal Reserve Tower. On Atlantic Avenue, across from South Station, is this striking aluminum-clad building, designed in 1976 by Hugh Stubbins and Associates. It houses a free art gallery and hosts occasional concerts. ⊠ *600 Atlantic Ave.,* ☏ *617/973–3453.* ⊙ *Weekdays 10–4. Tours Fri. 10:30; call 617/973–3451 to schedule.*

King's Chapel. Both somber and dramatic, King's Chapel looms over the corner of Tremont and School streets. Its distinctive shape was not achieved entirely by design; for lack of funds, it was never topped with the steeple that architect Peter Harrison had planned. The first chapel on this site was erected in 1688, when Sir Edmund Andros, the royal governor whose authority temporarily replaced the original Colonial charter, appropriated the land for the establishment of an Anglican place of worship. This rankled the Puritans, who had left England to escape Anglicanism and had until then succeeded in keeping it out of the colony. (In the 1780s King's Chapel became the first American church to embrace a new threat to congregationalist orthodoxy called Unitarianism.)

It took five years to build the solid Quincy granite structure. As construction proceeded, the old church continued to stand within the rising walls of the new, the plan being to remove and carry it away piece by piece when the outer stone chapel was completed. The builders then went to work on the interior, which remains today essentially as they finished it in 1754; it is a masterpiece of elegant proportion and Georgian calm (in fact, its excellent acoustics have made the use of a microphone unnecessary for Sunday sermons). To the right of the main entrance is a special pew, once reserved for condemned prisoners, who were trotted in to hear a sermon before being hanged on the Common. The chapel's bell is Paul Revere's largest and, in his judgment, his sweetest sounding. ⊠ *58 Tremont St. (at School St.),* ☎ *617/227–2155.* ⊙ *Mid-June–Labor Day, Mon., Fri.–Sat. 9:30–4, Tue.–Wed. 9:30–11, Sun. 1–3; Labor Day–mid-Nov., Mon., Fri.–Sat. 10–2; mid-Nov.–mid-Apr., Sat. 10–2; mid-April–mid-June, Mon., Fri., Sat. 10–2. Year-round music program Tues. 12:15–1, services on Sun., 11, Wed., 12:15. T stop, Park St. or Government Center.*

King's Chapel Burying Ground. Legends linger here in this oldest of the city's cemeteries. Take the path to the right from the entrance and then left by the chapel to the gravestone (1704) of Elizabeth Pain, the model for Hester Prynne in Hawthorne's *The Scarlet Letter.* Note the winged death's head on her stone—it was a common motif on Puritan gravestones, since those ever-dour folks favored reminders that life was harsh and fleeting. Elsewhere, you'll find the grave of William Dawes, Jr., who, with Dr. Samuel Prescott, rode out to warn of the British invasion the night of Paul Revere's famous ride; due to Longfellow's stirring poem, Revere's the one who gets all the glory today (which should show you what a good PR agent is worth). Other Boston worthies entombed here were famous for more conventional reasons, including the first Massachusetts governor, John Winthrop, and several generations of his descendants. The prominent slate monument near the entrance to the yard tells (in French) the story of the Chevalier de Saint-Sauveur, a young officer who was part of the first French contingent that arrived to help the rebel Americans in 1778. He was killed in a riot that began when hungry Bostonians were told they could not buy the bread the French were baking for their men, using the Bostonians' own wheat—an awkward situation only aggravated by the language barrier. The chevalier's interment here was probably the occasion for the first Roman Catholic mass in what has since become a city with a substantial Catholic population.

NEED A BREAK? **Rebecca's Café** (⊠ 18 Tremont St., ☎ 617/227–0020), with its fresh salads, sandwiches, and homemade pastries, is a comfortable place to stop for a casual lunch. It's open weekdays 7–7.

Leather District. Opposite South Station and nestled into the angle formed by Kneeland Street and Atlantic Avenue is a corner of downtown that has been relatively untouched by high-rise development, the old Leather District; it's probably the best place in downtown Boston to get an idea of what the city's business center looked like in the late 19th century. This was the wholesale supply area for raw materials in the days when the shoe industry was a regional economic mainstay, and a few leather firms are still located here. *T stop, South Station.*

⑦ **New England Aquarium.** More than just another pretty fish, the recently expanded New England Aquarium challenges visitors to really imagine life under (and around) the sea. Seal bark outside a new 17,400-square-foot West Wing, its glass and steel exterior constructed to mimic fish scales. This facility has a café, a gift shop, and changing exhibits, beginning with "Coastal Rhythms," a look at East Coast ecosystems. Inside the main facility, you'll find penguins, jellyfish, sea otters, a variety of sharks, and other exotic sea creatures—more than 2,000 species in all—some of which make their home in the aquarium's four-story, 187,000-gallon ocean reef tank, the largest of its kind in the world. Ramps winding around the tank lead to the top level and allow visitors to view the inhabitants from many vantage points. Don't miss the five-times-a-day feeding time; the procedure lasts nearly an hour and takes divers 23 ft into the tank. From outside the glassed-off Aquarium Medical Center, you can watch vets treat sick animals—if you've ever pictured an eel in a "hospital bed," here's where you'll see it. At the "Edge of the Sea" exhibit kids can gingerly pick up star fish and other creatures. They can learn something about environmental dangers in a multi-media exhibit on sewage systems, or "what happens when you flush." Sea lion shows are held aboard *Discovery,* a floating marine mammal pavilion; and whale-watch cruises (admission $24) leave from the aquarium's dock from April to October. There's also a "Science at Sea" educational cruise. Across the plaza is the aquarium's Education Center; it too, has changing exhibits. On the drawing boards is a new East Wing with a large-format movie theater and a million-gallon open ocean tank. Just watch your pennies in the gift shop—it seems to have every stuffed marine animal ever made. ⊠ *Central Wharf (between Central and Milk Sts.),* ☎ *617/973–5200; 617/ 973–5277 whale-watching information.* ☞ *$11.* ☺ *Memorial Day– Labor Day, Mon., Tues., Fri., 9–6; Wed., Thurs., 9–8; weekends and holidays, 9–7. Labor Day–Memorial Day, weekdays, 9–5; weekends and holidays, 9–6. T stop, Aquarium.*

New England Telephone Building. It was in a garret on one of the side streets off Scollay Square that Alexander Graham Bell first transmitted a human voice—his own—by telephone. When the building where Bell had his workshop was torn down in the 1920s, the phone company had the room dismantled and reassembled in the headquarters lobby of the New England Telephone Building. There the room looks just as it did on June 3, 1875, when Bell first coaxed his voice across a wire. (His famous call to Thomas Watson, "Come here, I want you," was made nearly a year later in another part of town.) Telephone memorabilia and a 160-ft mural tell the story of this exciting invention. ⊠ *185 Franklin St.,* ☎ *617/743–4886.* ☞ *Free.* ☺ *Weekdays 8:30– 5. T stop, Government Center.*

Old City Hall. Just outside this sight sits Richard S. Greenough's bronze statue (1855) of Benjamin Franklin, Boston's first portrait sculpture. Franklin was born in 1706 just a few blocks from here, on Milk Street, and attended the Boston Latin School, founded in 1635 near the City Hall site. (The school has long since moved to Louis Pasteur Avenue, near the Fenway.) As a young man, Franklin moved to Philadelphia, where he lived most of his long life. Boston's municipal government settled in to the new City Hall in 1969, and the old Second Empire building now houses business offices and a French restaurant. ⊠ *41– 45 School St.*

❷ Old Corner Bookstore Site. Through these doors, between 1845 and 1865, passed some of the century's greatest literary lights: Thoreau, Emerson, and Longfellow—even Charles Dickens paid a visit. Many of their greatest works were published here by James T. "Jamie" Fields, who in 1830 had founded the seminally important firm of Ticknor and Fields. In the 19th century, the graceful, gambrel-roofed early Georgian structure—built in 1718 on land once owned by religious rebel Anne Hutchinson—also housed the city's leading bookstore. ⊠ *1 School St., T stop, State St.*

③ Old South Meeting House. This is the second-oldest church building in Boston, and were it not for Longfellow's celebration of the Old North in "Paul Revere' Ride," it might well be the most famous. Some of the fieriest of the town meetings that led to the Revolution were held here, culminating in the tumultuous gathering of December 16, 1773, which was called by Samuel Adams to confront the crisis of three ships, laden with dutiable tea, anchored at Griffin's Wharf. The activists wanted the tea returned to England, the governor would not permit it—and the rest is history. To cries of "Boston harbor a tea-pot tonight" and John Hancock's "Let every man do what is right in his own eyes," the protesters poured out of the Old South, headed to the wharf with their waiting comrades, and dumped £18,000 worth of tea into the water.

One of the earliest members of the congregation was an African slave named Phillis Wheately, who had been educated by her owners. In 1773 a book of her poems was printed, making her the first published African-American poet. She later traveled to London, where she was received as a celebrity, but was again overtaken by poverty and obscurity and died at age 31.

The church suffered no small amount of indignity in the Revolution: Its pews were ripped out by occupying British troops, and the interior was used for riding exercises by Burgoyne's light dragoons. A century later it escaped destruction in the Great Fire of 1872, only to be threatened with demolition by developers. Aside from the windows and doors, the only original interior features surviving today are the tiered galleries above the main floor. The pulpit is a reproduction of the one used by Colonial divines and secular firebrands. Public contributions saved the church.

In late 1997, the Old South re-opened after its first renovation in more than 100 years with increased access for people with disabilities, air conditioning, and a new permanent exhibition, "Voices of Protest," which highlights Old South as a forum for free speech from Revolutionary days to the present. The renovation also created spaces for changing shows and for educational programs, such as lunchtime lecture series on Thursdays, October to April. ✉ *310 Washington St.,* ☎ *617/482–6439.* 🖅 *$3.* ☉ *Apr. 1–Oct. 31, daily 9:30–5; Nov. 1–Mar. 31, daily 10–4. T stop, State St. or Downtown Crossing.*

④ Old State House. This Colonial-era landmark has one of the most elegant facades in Boston, with its State Street gable adorned by a brightly gilded lion and unicorn, symbols of British imperial power. The original figures were pulled down in 1776. For proof that bygones are bygones, we may look not only to the restoration of the sculptures but to the fact that Queen Elizabeth II was greeted by cheering crowds on July 4th during the U.S. bicentennial celebration when she stood on the Old State House balcony (from which the Declaration of Independence was first read in public in Boston, and which overlooks the site of the Boston Massacre).

This was the seat of the Colonial government from 1713 until the Revolution, and after the evacuation of the British from Boston in 1776 it served the independent Commonwealth until its replacement on Beacon Hill was completed. John Hancock was inaugurated here as the first governor under the new state constitution. Like many Colonial-era landmarks, it fared poorly in the years that followed. Nineteenth-century photos show the old building with a mansard roof and signs in the windows advertising a variety of businesses. In the 1830s the Old State House served as Boston's City Hall. When demolition was threatened in the name of improving the traffic flow, the Bostonian Society organized a restoration, after which the Old State House reopened as home to a permanent collection that traces Boston's Revolutionary War history and, on the second floor, changing exhibits.

Immediately outside the Old State House at 15 State Street is a **visitors center** run by the National Park Service; you'll find free brochures and rest rooms. ⊠ *206 Washington St.,* ☎ *617/720–3290.* ☜ *$3.* ☉ *Daily 9:30–5. T stop, State St.*

8 **Rowes Wharf.** Take a Beacon Hill redbrick town house, cut loose with white clapboard trim, blow it up to the nth power, and you get this 15-story Skidmore, Owings, & Merrill extravaganza, one of the more welcome additions to the Boston Harbor skyline, and site of the Boston Harbor Hotel and the Rowes Wharf Restaurant. From under the complex's gateway six-story arch, you can get great views of Boston Harbor and the luxurious yachts parked in the marina. Water shuttles pull up here from Logan Airport—the most spectacular way to enter the city. Enjoy a windswept stroll along the Harborwalk; from this vantage point, it's easy to forget the intense construction for the Central Artery Project nearby on Atlantic Avenue. *T stop, Aquarium.*

13 **South Station.** The colonnaded granite structure at the intersection of Atlantic Avenue and Summer Street is the terminal for all Amtrak trains in and out of Boston. Catercorner from it is the terminal for Greyhound, Peter Pan, and other bus lines. Behind the station's grand 1900s facade, a major renovation project has created an airy, modern intermodal transit center. Thanks to its eateries, coffee bars, newsstand, flower stand, and other shops, waiting for a train can actually be a pleasant experience.

NEED A BREAK?   The **Blue Diner** (⊠ 178 Kneeland St., ☎ 617/338–4639) is everything the name implies—right down to the meat-loaf special on Monday—and great for a quick cup of coffee.

State Street. In the 19th century, State Street was headquarters for banks, brokerages, and insurance firms; although these businesses have now spread throughout the downtown district, "State Street" retains much the same connotation in Boston that "Wall Street" has elsewhere. The early commercial hegemony of State Street was symbolized by Long Wharf, built originally in 1710 and extending some 1,700 ft into the harbor. If today's Long Wharf does not appear to be that long, it is not because it has been shortened but because the land has expanded around it; State Street once met the water at the base of the Custom House. Landfill operations were pursued relentlessly through the years, and the old coastline is now as much a memory as such Colonial State Street landmarks as Governor Winthrop's 1630 house and the Revolutionary-era Bunch of Grapes Tavern, where Bostonians met to drink and wax indignant at their treatment by the British.

6 **U.S. Custom House.** This 1847 structure resembles a Greek Revival temple that appears to have sprouted a tower. It is just that. This is the work of architects Ammi Young and Isaiah Rogers. At least, the bottom part is. The tower (would skyscrapers have looked like this if they could have been built in the 1840s?) was added in 1915, at which time it became Boston's tallest building. In order to appreciate the grafting job done (not Custom House graft, but grafting in the horticultural sense), go inside and look at the great rotunda, surmounted by its handsome dome. The outer surface of that dome was once the roof of the building, but now the dome is embedded in the base of the tower.

The federal government moved out of the Custom Tower in 1987 and sold it to the city of Boston, which, in turn, sold it to the Marriott Corporation, which has converted the building into luxury time-share units. The move disturbed some historical purists, but the units have been selling briskly. Purchase prices range from $15,000 to $20,000 a week, depending on the season. But you don't have to buy a unit to step inside and enjoy the magnificent rotunda and view the maritime prints and antique artifacts now on display, courtesy of the Peabody Essex Museum in Salem. ✉ *3 McKinley Sq.,* ☎ *617/790–1400. T stop, Aquarium.*

THE BACK BAY

In the folklore of American neighborhoods, the Back Bay stands with New York's Park Avenue and San Francisco's Nob Hill as a symbol of propriety and high social standing. You still occasionally hear someone described as coming from "an old Back Bay family" as though the Back Bay were hundreds of years old and its stone mansions the feudal bastions of Puritan settlers from the time they got off the boat.

Nothing could be further from the truth. The Back Bay, at scarcely 125 years old, is one of Boston's newer neighborhoods. Before the 1850s it was a bay, a tidal flat that formed the south bank of a distended Charles River. Boston since time immemorial has been a pear-shaped peninsula joined to the mainland by an isthmus (the Neck) so narrow that in early Colonial times a single gate and guardhouse were sufficient for its defense; today's Washington Street, as it leaves downtown and heads toward the South End, follows the old Neck.

Filling in land along the Neck began in 1850 and resulted in the creation of the South End neighborhood. To the north, a narrow causeway called the Mill Dam (later Beacon Street) was built in 1814 to separate the Back Bay from the Charles. Bostonians began to fill in the shallows in 1858, using gravel brought from West Needham by railroad at a rate of up to 3,500 carloads per day. It took 30 years to complete the filling as far as the Fens. When the work was finished, the original 783-acre peninsula had been expanded by approximately 450 acres. Thus the actual waters of Back Bay became the neighborhood of Back Bay.

More important, city planners were able to do something that had never before been possible in Boston: to lay out an entire neighborhood of arrow-straight streets. Heavily influenced by the then-recent rebuilding of Paris according to the plans of Baron Haussmann, the Back Bay planners created thoroughfares that resemble Parisian boulevards more than they do the mews and squares of London. The main east–west streets—Beacon Street, Marlborough Street, Commonwealth Avenue, Newbury Street, and Boylston Street—were bisected by eight streets named in alphabetical order from Arlington to Hereford. Service alleys run behind the main streets. Though they are used now for waste pickup and parking, they were built so that provisioning wagons could be driven up to basement kitchens. That's how thorough the planning was.

Almost immediately, fashionable families began to decamp from Beacon Hill and the recently developed South End and establish themselves in the brick and brownstone row houses built upon the man-made land. Churches and cultural institutions followed, until by 1900 the streets between the Public Garden and Massachusetts Avenue had become, unquestionably, the smartest, most desirable neighborhood in all Boston. An air of permanence and respectability drifted in as inevitably as the tides once had, and the Back Bay mystique was born.

Some aspects of the Back Bay, such as the way households were distributed, became matters more of natural evolution than of intent. Old families with money congregated on Beacon Street; families with old Boston names but not much money gravitated to tree-lined Marlborough Street; and the nouveau riche tended to build on Commonwealth Avenue. Newbury and Boylston, originally residential rather than commercial streets, were the province of a mix of middle- and upper-middle-class families, as were the cross streets.

The Back Bay remains a living museum of urban Victorian residential architecture. The earliest specimens are nearest to the Public Garden (there are exceptions where showier turn-of-the-century mansions replaced 1860s town houses), and the newer examples are out around the Massachusetts Avenue and Fenway extremes of the district. The height of Back Bay residences and their distance from the street is essentially uniform, as are the interior layouts, chosen to accord with lot width. Yet there is a distinct progression of facades, beginning with French academic and Italianate designs and moving through the various "revivals" of the 19th century. By the time of World War I, when development of the Back Bay was virtually complete, architects and their patrons had come full circle to a revival of the Federal period, which had been out of fashion for only 30 years when the filling began. If the Back Bay architects had not run out of land, they might have gotten around to a revival of Greek Revival.

An outstanding guide to the architecture and history of the Back Bay is Bainbridge Bunting's *Houses of Boston's Back Bay*. A reading of this thorough study can be expanded upon only by visits to Back Bay houses. A few are open to the public.

The Great Depression brought an end to the Back Bay style of living, and today only a few of the houses are single-family residences. Most have been cut up into apartments and, more recently, expensive condominiums. Interior details have experienced a mixed fate—suffering during the years when Victorian fashions were held in low regard—and are at present undergoing careful restoration, now that the aesthetic pendulum has reversed itself and moneyed condo buyers are demanding period authenticity. The blocks and blocks of original facades have survived on all but Newbury and Boylston streets, so the public face of the Back Bay retains much of the original charm and grandeur.

Numbers in the text correspond to numbers in the margin and on the Back Bay, the South End, and the Fens map.

A Good Walk

A walk through the Back Bay properly begins with the **Boston Public Garden** ①, the oldest botanical garden in the United States. After wandering its meandering pathways, venture into the Back Bay through the gate near Arlington and Beacon streets. From here, if you're in the mood for greenery, take the Arthur Fiedler Footbridge to the Esplanade for a river view. For more urban fare, proceed on Beacon Street to the **Gibson House** ② museum. If you are interested in Back Bay mansions, you may wish to visit the **Baylies Mansion** at 5 Commonwealth Avenue at this point. If not, retrace your steps to Arlington, turn right, and proceed to the **Arlington Street Church** ③ at the corner of Boylston. Then, retrace your steps up Arlington to Newbury Street and turn left; ahead are **Emmanuel Church** ④ at Number 15 and the **Church of the Covenant** ⑤ at number 67. At the Church of the Covenant, follow Berkeley back to Commonwealth Avenue. One block to your left is the **First Baptist Church** ⑥. From here you can continue down the **Com-**

monwealth Avenue Mall to view its sumptuous mansions all the way to Massachusetts Avenue, and return via Newbury Street. Or, at any point before Mass. Ave. (as the natives refer to it), you can turn east to reach **Newbury Street** and backtrack along Boston's poshest shopping district, window-shopping all the way. At Dartmouth Street, turn right and head into **Copley Square,** where you will find the **"New" Old South Church** ⑦, **Boston Public Library** ⑧, **Trinity Church** ⑨, and the **John Hancock Tower** ⑩. For more shopping, followed by a movie, head for the upscale **Copley Place** ⑪ complex, which can be reached through the Westin Hotel at the corner of Dartmouth and Huntington streets. A walkway takes you over Stuart Street into the shopping galleries. Continue through to the Marriott Hotel, take another walkway over Huntington to the **Prudential Center** ⑫ for more shopping and a view of the city at the **Prudential Center Skywalk.** Exit onto Boylston Street and turn left to reach the **Institute of Contemporary Art** ⑬. Continue one block to Mass. Ave., turn left and walk several blocks to the reflecting pool and expansive plaza of the **Christian Science Church Center.** ⑭. Just across Mass Ave. at Huntington is **Symphony Hall** ⑮.

TIMING

The Back Bay may be the most well-ordered section of Boston, but it is spread out, so allow three to four hours for leisurely strolling and frequent stops. If you are an indefatigable shopper, give yourself another two hours to cover Newbury Street and/or the shops at Copley Place and the Prudential Center. The reflecting pool at the Christian Science Church is a great time-out spot—especially after an afternoon exploring the brownstones and boutiques of Newbury Street. Mid-April, the world descends on Copley Square—the finishing line for the Boston Marathon. A week later, magnolia time in Boston arrives (usually the third week of the month)—and nowhere do magnolias bloom more magnificently than along Commonwealth Avenue. In May, the Public Garden bursts with color, thanks to its flowering dogwood trees and thousands of tulips. Set aside a Sunday to enjoy the charms of the district's many historic churches. To help track your time, remember the north-south streets are arranged in alphabetical order, from Arlington to Hereford.

Sights to See

❸ **Arlington Street Church.** Opposite the Park Square corner of the Public Garden, this church was erected in 1861—the first to be built in the Back Bay. Following suit, many of the old downtown congregations relocated to the district's newly filled land and applied their considerable resources to building handsome churches. Often designed in Gothic and Romanesque Revival styles, these churches have aged well and blend harmoniously with the residential blocks, making the Back Bay a great neighborhood for ecclesiastical architecture (☞ **Emmanuel Church, Church of the Covenant, First Baptist Church,** and **Trinity Church,** *below*). Keynoted by its classical portico and modeled after London's St. Martin-in-the-Fields, Arlington Street Church is less picturesque and more Georgian in character—don't forget to note the beautiful Tiffany stained glass windows. During the year preceding the Civil War, the church was a hotbed of abolitionist fervor. Later, during the Vietnam War, it became famous as a center of peace activism. ⊠ *351 Boylston St.,* ☎ *617/536–7050.* ⊙ *Weekdays 10–5. Sun. service at 11. T stop, Arlington.*

Back Bay Mansions. If you like nothing better than to imagine how the other half lives, you'll suffer no shortage of elegant old homes to sigh over in Boston's Back Bay. Most, unfortunately, are off-limits to visitors, but there's no law against gawking from the outside.

The Back Bay, the South End, and the Fens

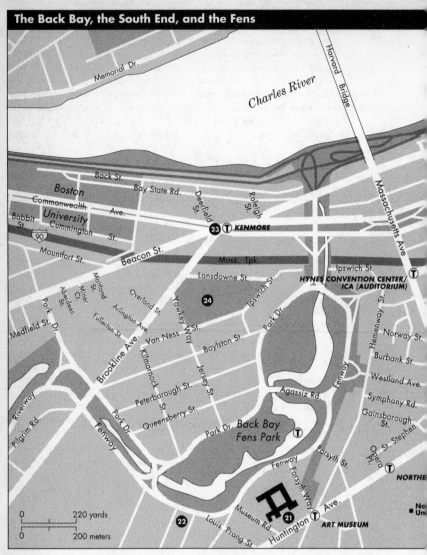

Among the grander Back Bay houses is the **Baylies Mansion** (⌂ 5 Commonwealth Ave.), of 1904, now the home of the Boston Center for Adult Education; you can enter to view its first-floor common. Another gem is the **Burrage Mansion** (⌂ 314 Commonwealth Ave.), built in 1899 in an extravagant French château style, complete with turrets and gargoyles, that reflects a cost-be-damned attitude uncommon even among the wealthiest Back Bay families. It now houses an assisted living residence for seniors, and walk-in visitors are not encouraged.

Other mansions of note include: The **Cushing-Endicott House** (⌂ 163 Marlborough St.), built in 1871 and later home to William C. Endicott, secretary of War under President Cleveland; this was once dubbed "the handsomest house in the whole Back Bay" by Bainbridge Bunting. The **Oliver Ames Mansion** (⌂ 55 Commonwealth Ave., corner of Massachusetts Ave.) was built in 1882 for a railroad baron and Massachusetts governor. This opulent château has been renovated and now houses offices. The **Ames-Webster House** (⌂ 306 Dartmouth St.), built in 1872 and remodeled in 1882 and 1969, is one of the city's finest houses.

Two Back Bay mansions are home to organizations that promote foreign language and culture: the **French Library in Boston** (⌂ 53 Marlborough St.) and the German-oriented **Goethe Institute** (⌂ 170 Beacon St.). See the *Boston Globe*'s "Calendar" section on Thursday or the *Boston Herald*'s "Scene" section on Friday for details on lectures, films, and other events held in the handsome quarters of these respected institutions.

★ ❶   **Boston Public Garden.** Although the Boston Public Garden is often lumped together with Boston Common, even in the minds of natives, the two are separate entities with different histories and purposes and a distinct boundary between them at Charles Street. The Common has been public land since Boston was founded in 1630. The Public Garden belongs to a newer Boston; it occupies what had been salt marshes on the edge of the Common's dry land. The marshes supported rope-manufacturing enterprises in the early 1800s, but by 1837 the tract was covered with an abundance of ornamental plantings donated by a private citizen. The area was fully defined in 1856 by the building of Arlington Street, and in 1860 (after the final wrangling over the development of this choice acreage) the architect George Meacham was commissioned to plan the park that survives to this day.

The central feature of the Public Garden is its irregularly shaped pond intended to appear, from any vantage point along its banks, much larger than its nearly 4 acres. The pond has been famous since 1877 for its foot pedal–powered **Swan Boats**, which make leisurely cruises during warm months. They were invented by Robert Paget, who was inspired by the popularity of swan boats made fashionable by Wagner's opera, *Lohengrin*. Paget descendants still run the boats, which have carried luminaries ranging from Shirley Temple to *Cheers*'s Ted Danson. The pond is favored by ducks and pairs of swans, and for the price of a few boat rides you can amuse children here for a good hour or more. Near the Swan Boat dock is what has been described as the world's smallest suspension bridge, designed in 1867 to cross the pond at its narrowest point.

The Public Garden has the finest formal plantings in central Boston. The beds along the main walkways are replanted for spring and summer. The tulips during the first two weeks of May are especially colorful, and there is a good sampling of native and European tree species.

The dominant work among the park's statuary is Thomas Ball's equestrian **George Washington** (1869), which faces the head of Commonwealth Avenue at the Arlington Street gate. This is Washington in a triumphant pose as liberator, surveying a scene that, from where he stood with his cannons at Dorchester Heights, would have comprised an immense stretch of blue water. Several dozen yards to the north of Washington (to the right if you're facing Commonwealth Avenue) is the granite and red marble **Ether Monument,** donated in 1866 by Thomas Lee to commemorate the advent of anesthesia 20 years earlier at nearby Massachusetts General Hospital. Other Public Garden monuments include statues of the pioneer Unitarian preacher and transcendentalist William Ellery Channing, at the corner opposite his Arlington Street church; the author (*The Man Without a Country*) and philanthropist Edward Everett Hale, at the Charles Street Gate; and the abolitionist senator Charles Sumner and the Civil War hero Colonel Thomas Cass, along Boylston Street.

The park may be one of the oldest botanical gardens in America, but it also contains a special delight for the young at heart; follow the kids quack-quacking along the pathway between the pond and the park entrance at Charles and Beacon streets to the *Make Way for Ducklings* **bronze statue group** sculpted by Nancy Schon, a tribute to the 1941 classic children's story, beloved for its drawings by Robert McCloskey. ☎ 617/635–4505. ⌫ *Swan boats $1.50.* ☉ *Swan boats mid-Apr.– late Sept., daily 10–4. Gardens: Dawn–10 PM. Not recommended after dark, even if you find a gate open. T stop, Arlington.*

★ ❽ **Boston Public Library.** This venerable institution is really two structures in one—a beautiful temple to literature and a functional research mecca. When the building was opened in 1895, it confirmed the status of architects McKim, Mead & White as apostles of the Renaissance Revival style, while reinforcing Boston's commitment to an enlightened citizenry that goes back 350 years, to the founding of the Public Latin School. Philip Johnson's 1972 skylighted addition emulates the mass and proportion of the original, though not its extraordinary detail; this skylighted annex houses the library's circulating collections.

You don't need a library card to enjoy the old library's magnificent art. Charles McKim saw to it that the interior of his building was ornamented by several of the finest painters of the day. The murals at the head of the staircase, depicting the nine muses, are the work of the French artist Puvis de Chavannes; those in the book-request processing room to the right are Edwin Abbey's interpretations of the Holy Grail legend. Upstairs, in the public areas leading to the fine arts, music, and rare books collections, is John Singer Sargent's marvelous mural series on the subject of Judaism and Christianity, still dazzling, although seriously darkened by time.

You enter the older part of the library from the Dartmouth Street side, passing through the enormous bronze doors by Daniel Chester French, the sculptor of the Lincoln Memorial (and under the library's motto— *Sicut Patribus Sit Deus Nobis*—sometimes translated by Bostonians as "O God, how sick we are of our ancestors"). Or you can walk around Boylston Street to enter through the newer addition. The corridor leading from the annex opens onto the Renaissance-style **courtyard**— an exact copy of the one in Rome's Palazzo della Cancelleria—around which the original library is built. A patio furnished with chairs rings a flower garden and fountain; from here the bustle of the city seems miles away. Beyond the courtyard is the main entrance hall of the 1895 building, with its immense stone lions by Louis Saint-Gaudens (brother of the more celebrated Augustus), vaulted ceiling, and marble staircase.

The corridor at the top of the stairs leads to **Bates Hall,** renovated in 1997 and one of Boston's most sumptuous interior spaces. This is the main reference reading room, 218 ft long with a barrel-arch ceiling 50 ft high. In an ongoing program slated to be completed by 2000, murals and paintings are being restored. ⊠ *Dartmouth St. at Copley Sq.,* ☎ *617/536–5400.* ⊙ *Mon.–Thurs. 9–9, Fri.–Sat. 9–5; Sept.–June, Sun. 1–5. Free guided art and architecture tours Mon. at 2:30, Tues. and Thurs. at 6, Fri. and Sat. at 11, Sun. at 2. T stop, Copley.*

Boylston Street. This broad thoroughfare is the southern commercial spine of the Back Bay. The ☞ **Hynes Convention Center** keeps company with a variety of interesting restaurants and shops, including an F.A.O. Schwarz store with an enormous teddy bear sculpture on the sidewalk in front. Here, too, is the severe, pale gray-stone mass of the **New England Building** (⊠ 501 Boylston St.)—housing the first chartered mutual life insurance company in the country. Interesting historical murals embellish the lobby. Across the street, at 500 Boylston Street, between Berkeley and Clarendon streets, is the company's newer building, a huge postmodern structure with an outdoor courtyard and fountain.

⑭ Christian Science Church Center. The world headquarters of the Christian Science faith mixes the traditional with the modern—marrying Bernini to LeCorbusier by combining an old-world basilica with a sleek office complex designed by I. M. Pei. The mother church of the Christian Science faith was established here by Mary Baker Eddy in 1879. Mrs. Eddy's original granite First Church of Christ, Scientist (1894) has since been enveloped by a domed Renaissance Revival basilica, added to the site in 1906, and both church buildings are now surrounded by the offices of the Christian Science Publishing Society, where the *Christian Science Monitor* is produced, and by Pei's complex of church administration structures completed in 1973. In the publishing society's lobby is the fascinating **Mapparium,** a huge stained-glass globe whose 30-ft diameter can be traversed on a glass bridge (don't look for political accuracy: Vietnam is still listed as French Indochina). Tying together the entire complex is a 670-ft reflecting pool, engineered so that water constantly spills over its inner banks—a lovely spot for a summer siesta. ⊠ *175 Huntington Ave.,* ☎ *617/450–3790.* ⊙ *Mother church, Mon.–Sat. 10–4, Sun. 11:15–2; free 30-min tours. On Mon. only, original edifice open for tours. Sun. services 10 AM and 7 PM. Mapparium open Mon.–Sat. 10–4, Closed Sun. T stop, Prudential.*

❺ Church of the Covenant. This 1867 Gothic Revival church at the corner of Newbury and Berkeley has more stained-glass windows by Louis Comfort Tiffany than any other structure in the world. It is crowned by a 236-ft-tall steeple—once the tallest in Boston—that Oliver Wendell Holmes called "absolutely perfect." ⊠ *67 Newbury St. (enter at church office),* ☎ *617/266–7480.* ⊙ *Tues.–Fri. 9–noon. Sun. service at 10. T stop, Arlington.*

Commonwealth Avenue Mall. The mall that extends down the middle of the Back Bay's Commonwealth Avenue also has its share of statuary. One of the most interesting memorials, at the Exeter Street intersection, is a portrayal of naval historian and author Samuel Eliot Morison seated on a rock as if he were peering out to sea. The other figures have only tenuous connections to Boston—Norwegian explorer Leif Ericsson and Domingo F. Sarmiento, president of Argentina, and Alexander Hamilton, who tried to block native son John Adams from the presidency. As one *Boston Globe* writer-wag pondered, "Have we forgotten how to hold a grudge?"

However, a dramatic and personal monument was added in 1997 near the Dartmouth Street: The **Vendome Monument,** dedicated to the nine firemen who died in 1972 putting out a fire at Back Bay's Vendome Hotel. Designed by Ted Clausen and Peter White, the curved black granite block, 29 feet long and waist-high, is etched with the names of the dead. A bronze cast of a fireman's coat and hat are draped over the granite, as if to say, "The fire is out, we can rest now." Its dedication brought an outpouring of emotion from Bostonians who saw the memorial as honoring the dedication of all firefighters. Just across the street from the monument, at 160 Commonwealth Ave., is the **Vendome Hotel** itself, which first opened in 1872 and is now used as office space.

⑪ Copley Place. Two bold intruders dominate Copley Square—☞ **the John Hancock Tower,** off the southeast corner, and the even more assertive Copley Place skyscraper, on the southwest. An upscale, glass and brass urban mall, Copley Place, built between 1980 and 1984, is comprised of two major hotels: the high-rise Westin, west, and the Marriott Copley Place, east. Dozens of shops, restaurants, and offices are attractively grouped on several levels surrounding bright, open indoor spaces. The large movie complex is a frequent venue for film festivals, including the popular Boston Film Festival. ☉ *Shopping galleries: Mon.–Sat. 10–7, Sun. noon–5. T stop, Copley.*

Copley Square. For thousands of folks in April, a glimpse of Copley Square is the most wonderful sight in the world; this is where the runners of the Boston Marathon end their 26-mi race. A square now favored by skateboarders (much to the chagrin of city officials), the civic space is defined by three monumental older buildings. One is the stately, bowfront 1912 **Copley Plaza Hotel,** which faces the square on St. James Avenue and serves as a dignified foil to its companions, two of the most important works of architecture in the United States: ☞ **Trinity Church**—Henry Hobson Richardson's masterwork of 1877, at the left—and the ☞ **Boston Public Library,** by McKim, Mead & White. The John Hancock Building looms in the background. To honor those runners who stagger over the marathon's finish line, bronze statues of the Tortoise and the Hare engaged in their mythical race were cast by Nancy Schon, who also did the much-loved *Make Way for Ducklings* group in the ☞ **Public Garden.**

❹ Emmanuel Church of Boston. Built in 1862, this Back Bay brownstone Gothic Episcopal church is popular among classical music–loving worshipers on Sunday mornings at 11. Every Sunday from September to May, a Bach cantata is included as part of the liturgy. Adjacent to the church is the Leslie Lindsey Chapel—a Gothic-style memorial created by parents in memory of their daughter, a young bride who perished with her husband on the *Lusitania*. It was said that the young girl's body washed ashore in Ireland, still bedecked with her family's wedding gift of rubies and diamonds, which were then sold to fund this chapel. ✉ *15 Newbury St.,* ☎ *617/536–3355.* ☉ *Mon.–Thurs. 10–4 by appointment. T stop, Arlington.*

Exeter Theater. The massive Romanesque structure was built in 1884 as a temple for the Working Union of Progressive Spiritualists. Beginning in 1914, it enjoyed a long run as a movie theater; as the *A.I.A. Guide to Boston* so charmingly points out, "it was the only movie theater a proper Boston woman would enter, probably because of its spiritual overtones." It now houses a restaurant and Waterstone's Booksellers (☞ Books *in* Chapter 8). ✉ *26 Exeter St. at Newbury St. T stop, Copley.*

68

BOSTON MARATHON: RUNNING FOR THE ROSES

MORE THAN A RACE, more than a social event, the Boston Marathon celebrates the art of endurance. For professionals like Bill Rogers, Joan Benoit Samuelson, Cosmas Ndeti and Uta Pippig, a marathon victory is the Holy Grail of the running world. For thousands of amateur runners, just finishing the tough 26.2 mi course is a spiritual quest. Though neither the nation's first marathon (from Stamford, CT, to New York City in 1896), nor the largest, the Boston Marathon is the nation's oldest continuously run marathon and, many would insist, the most prestigious.

came the sponsor, it was moved to its current location (☞ **Copley Square,**) in the shadow of the Hancock Tower.

The race's guardian spirit has been the indefatigable John A. Kelley, who ran his first marathon shortly after Warren G. Harding was sworn in as president. He won twice—in 1935 and 1945—and continued to run well into his eighties. Until his retirement in 1992, his arrival at the finish signaled the official end of the race. A double statue of an older Kelley greeting his younger self stands at the route's most strenuous incline—dubbed **"Heartbreak Hill"**—on Commonwealth Avenue in Newton.

Held every **Patriot's Day** (the third Monday in April), the course passes through Hopkinton, Ashland, Framingham, Natick, Wellesley, Wellesley Hills, Newton, Brookline, and Boston; only the last few miles are run in the city proper. The first marathon, organized by the Boston Athletic Association (BAA), was run on April 19, 1897, when Olympian Tom Burke drew a line in the dirt in Ashland (now the second town on the course) and began a 24 ½-mi dash to Boston with 15 men. For most of its history, the race concluded on Exeter Street outside the BAA's clubhouse. In 1965, after the Prudential Life Insurance Co. offered financial support, the finish was moved to the front of the Prudential Center. In 1986, when the John Hancock be-

Women weren't allowed to race until 1972; until then, the marathon was a battleground in the gender wars. In 1966 Roberta Gibb slipped into the throngs under a hooded sweatshirt; she was the first unofficial female winner. In 1967, cameras captured BAA organizer Jock Semple screaming, "Get out of my race," as he tried to rip off the number of Kathrine Switzer who had registered as K. Switzer. Semple later said he was just angry about the subterfuge. But the marathon's most infamous moment was when 26-year-old Rosie Ruiz came out of nowhere in 1980 to win the women's division. Ruiz apparently joined the race less than a 1 mi from the end, and her title was stripped eight days later. Bostonians still quip about her taking the T to the finish.

❻ First Baptist Church. This 1872 structure, at the corner of Clarendon Street and Commonwealth Avenue, is famed architect Henry Hobson Richardson's first essay in Romanesque Revival. It is landmarked by its soaring tower, adorned on high with figures sculpted by Bartholdi, of *Statue of Liberty* fame (his trumpeting angels have earned First Baptist its nickname, "Church of the Holy Bean Blowers"). ⊠ *110 Commonwealth Ave.* ⊘ *Weekdays 10–4; Sun. service at 11. T stop, Copley.*

❷ Gibson House. Through the foresight of an eccentric bon vivant, this house provides an authentic glimpse into daily life in Boston's Victorian era. One of the first Back Bay residences (1859), the Gibson House is relatively modest in comparison with some of the grand mansions built during the decades that followed; yet its furnishing, from its circa-1750 Willard clock to gold-trimmed wallpaper to a quaint Turkish pet pavilion, seems sumptuous to modern eyes. Unlike other Back Bay houses, the Gibson family home has been preserved with all its Victorian fixtures and furniture intact. That's the legacy of scion Charles Gibson, Jr., a poet, travel writer, and horticulturist, who continued to wear formal attire—morning coat, spats, and a cane—well into the 1940s when he dined daily at the Ritz nearby. As early as 1936, Gibson was roping off furniture and envisioning a museum for the house his grandmother built. His dream was realized in 1957, three years after he died. You can see a full-course setting with a China Trade dinner service in the ornate dining room and discover the elaborate system of servants' bells in the perfectly preserved 19th-century basement kitchen. The house also serves as the meeting place for the New England chapter of the Victorian Society in America and served as an interior for the Merchant-Ivory film *The Bostonians*. ⊠ *137 Beacon St.,* ☏ *617/267–6338.* ⊡ *$5.* ⊘ *Tours May–Oct., Wed.–Sun. at 1, 2, and 3; Nov.–Apr., weekends at 1, 2, and 3. T stop, Arlington.*

NEED A
BREAK?

You'll find a whiff of Parisian insouciance at the **Cafe de Paris** (⊠ 19 Arlington St., ☏ 617/247-7121), with its strong coffee, ample quiches, and delectable pastries. It's a great spot to people watch, but do expect less than speedy service and a European indifference to smoke.

Hynes Convention Center. From Star Trek confabs to the sports equipment shows, the Hynes plays host to thousands of visitors every week. Designed by Kallmann, McKinnell & Wood, architects of Boston's City Hall, it can hold 22,000 conventioneers. The building's official name is the John B. Hynes Veterans Memorial Convention Center, but everyone just calls it The Hynes. ⊠ *900 Boylston St.,* ☏ *617/954–2000; 617/424–8585. T stop, Hynes Convention Center.*

⓭ Institute of Contemporary Art. The fact that a 1989 exhibition of Robert Mapplethorpe photographs hardly raised an eyebrow here demonstrates the cutting-edge sensibility of this small showcase. Housed in a historic 19th-century police station and firehouse, the ICA has no permanent collection. One month it may present a show on cross-dressing, the next, a retrospective of Annie Leibowitz celebrity portraits, the next, an examination of pop icons Elvis and Marilyn. Videos, installations, and multimedia shows all push the envelope on the concept of "art." The multilevel galleries are compact, and a visit here could easily be combined with a visit to other Boston museums without risk of an art overdose or aesthetic redundancy. ⊠ *955 Boylston St.,* ☏ *617/266–5152.* ⊡ *$5.25, free Thurs. 5–9.* ⊘ *Wed.–Sun. noon–5, Thurs. noon–9. Tours weekends at 1 and 3. T stop, Hynes Convention Center.*

⑩ John Hancock Tower. In the early 1970s, the tallest building in New England became notorious as the monolith that rained glass. Windows were improperly seated in the sills of the stark and graceful reflective blue rhomboid tower, designed by I. M. Pei. After the building's 13 acres of glass were replaced and the central core stiffened, the problem was corrected. Bostonians originally feared the Hancock's stark modernism would overwhelm nearby Trinity Church, but its shimmering sides reflect the older structure's image, actually enlarging its presence. The 60th-floor observatory makes one of the two best vantage points in the city (the other is the ☞ **Prudential Center Skywalk**) and the "Boston 1775" exhibit shows what the city looked like before the great hill-leveling and landfill operations commenced. Also, several interactive machines let you test your knowledge of Boston trivia and another machine lets you target the horizon for the names and locations of specific buildings. ⊠ *Observatory ticket office, Trinity Pl. and St. James Ave.,* ☎ *617/247–1977 or 617/572–6429.* ☞ *$4.25.* ☉ *Mon.–Sat. 9 AM–11PM, May-Oct 10AM-11PM, Nov-April noon-11PM. T stop, Copley.*

NEED A BREAK?   **The Small Planet Bar and Grill** (⊠ 565 Boylston St., ☎ 617/536-4477) isn't just for extraterrestrials. This small but hip and always bustling bistro offers a galaxy of cuisines, from Asian stir-fries to pastas. Food is served until midnight daily.

Massachusetts Historical Society. The oldest historical society in the United States has paintings and a library of books and manuscripts from 17th-century New England. ⊠ *1154 Boylston St.,* ☎ *617/536–1608.* ☞ *Free.* ☉ *Weekdays 9–4:45. T stop, Hynes Convention Center.*

New England Historic Genealogical Society. Are you related to Miles Standish or Priscilla Alden? The answer may lie here. Pedigreed New Englanders trace their family trees with the help of the society's collections, which date from the 17th century. An introductory lecture on how to perform your own genealogical study is given every first Wednesday at 7 PM. The society itself dates from 1845. After renovations in 1996, the collections on the 5th and 6th floor are wheelchair-accessible. ⊠ *99–101 Newbury St.,* ☎ *617/536–5740.* ☞ *$10 fee to use facility.* ☉ *Tues.–Sat. 9–4:45, Wed.–Thurs. until 8:45; closed Sat. before Mon. holidays. T stop, Copley.*

❼ "New" Old South Church. Only in Boston could you call something the New Old South Church with a straight face. Members of the Old South Meeting House, of Tea Party fame, decamped to this new parish in 1875, a move not without controversy for the congregation. In a style inspired by the architecture of medieval Venice, with an ornate campanile and an interior decorated with Venetian mosaics and stained-glass windows, the "new" structure could not be more different from the plainer Meeting House. ⊠ *645 Boylston St.,* ☎ *617/536–1970.* ☉ *Weekdays 9–5. Sun. service at 11. T stop, Copley.*

Newbury Street. Eight-block-long Newbury Street has been compared to New York's Fifth Avenue, and certainly this is the city's poshest shopping area, with branches of Brooks Brothers, Armani, Burberry, and other top names in fashion. But here the pricey boutiques are more intimate than grand, and people actually live above the trendy restaurants and hair salons. Toward the Massachusetts Avenue end, cafés proliferate and the stores get funkier, ending with Newbury Comics, Tower Records, and the hipsters' housewares and clothing store, Urban Outfitters. (☞ Major Shopping Districts *in* Chapter 8.)

NEED A
BREAK? Care for a best-seller with your caffe latte? Folks gather at the **Trident Booksellers & Café** (⊠ 338 Newbury St., ☏ 617/267–8688) to review mostly New Age best-sellers, look for used-book bargains, and munch on homemade desserts, sandwiches, and soups. It's open until midnight daily.

⑫ Prudential Center. The only rival to the John Hancock's claim on Boston's upper skyline is the 52-story Prudential Tower, built in the early 1960s when the scale of monumental urban redevelopment projects had yet to be challenged. The Prudential Center, which dominates the acreage between Boylston Street and Huntington Avenue two blocks west of the library, adds considerably to the area's overabundance of mall-style shops and food courts. The "Pru" replaced the railroad yards that blocked off the South End. Its completely remodeled and enclosed shopping mall, connected by a glass bridge to Copley Place, was opened at the end of 1993. As for the Prudential Tower itself, Bainbridge Bunting made an acute observation when he called it "an apparition so vast in size that it appears to float above the surrounding district without being related to it." Later modifications to the Boylston Street frontage of the Prudential Center effected a better union of the complex with the urban space around it, but the tower itself will have to float on, vast as ever. Boston's Hynes Convention Center is connected to the Prudential Center, and it also contains a branch of Greater Boston Visitors Bureau. **Prudential Center Skywalk,** a 50th-floor observatory atop Prudential Center, offers spectacular vistas of Boston, Cambridge, and the suburbs to the west and south—on clear days, you can even see Cape Cod. You can see sailboats skimming the Charles River, the redbrick expanse of the Back Bay, and a great glimpse of the precise abstract geometry of the nearby Christian Science Church's reflecting pool. There are chairs for sitting and noisy interactive exhibits on Boston's history that ease the bite of the admission ticket. ⊠ *800 Boylston St.,* ☏ *617/536–4100 weekdays 9–5 or 800/374–7400; Skywalk, 617/859–0648.* ▣ *Skywalk, $4.* ⊙ *Weekdays 8:30–6, Sat. 10–6, Sun. 11:30–6; Skywalk, daily 10–10. T stop, Prudential.*

⑮ Symphony Hall. With commerce and religion accounted for in the Back Bay by the Prudential Center and the Christian Science headquarters, the neighborhood still has room for a temple to music: Symphony Hall, home of the Boston Symphony Orchestra, the Boston Pops, and frequent guest performers. Symphony Hall was another contribution of McKim, Mead & White to the Boston landscape. But acoustics rather than aesthetics make this hall so special for performers and concertgoers. Although acoustical science was a brand-new field of research when Professor Wallace Sabine planned the interior, not one of the 2,500 seats is a bad one—the secret is the box-within-a-box design. ⊠ *301 Massachusetts Ave.,* ☏ *617/266–1492; 800/274–8499 box office.* ⊙ *Tours by appointment with volunteer office (1 wk notice suggested). T stop, Symphony.*

★ ⑨ Trinity Church. In his 1877 masterpiece, architect Henry Hobson Richardson brought his Romanesque Revival style to maturity; all the aesthetic elements for which he was famous come together magnificently—bold polychromatic masonry, careful arrangement of masses, sumptuously carved interior woodwork. Today, the church remains the crowning centerpiece of Copley Square. A full appreciation of its architecture requires an understanding of the logistical problems of building it here. Remember, the Back Bay is a reclaimed wetland with a high water table; bedrock, or at least stable glacial till, lies far beneath the wet clay near the surface. Like all older Back Bay buildings,

Trinity Church sits on submerged wooden pilings. But its central tower weighs 9,500 tons, and most of the 4,500 pilings beneath the building are under that tremendous central mass. The pilings are checked regularly, by means of a hatch in the subbasement. Much to the dismay of churchgoers and Back Bay residents, skateboarders have designated the church steps as the most radical ride in town.

Don't miss the interior. Richardson engaged some of the great artists of his day—John LaFarge, William Morris, and Edward Burne-Jones among them—to execute the paintings and stained glass that make this a monument to everything that was right about the pre-Raphaelite spirit and the nascent aesthetic of Morris's Arts and Crafts movement. LaFarge's brilliant paintings, including the intricate ornamentation of the vaulted ceilings, have been cleaned only once, in the late 1950s, and have never been substantially retouched. Today they look as though the paint were barely dry. Along the north side of the church, note the Augustus Saint-Gaudens statue of Phillips Brooks—the most charismatic rector in New England—who almost single-handedly got Trinity built and decorated. Shining light of Harvard's religious community and lyricist of "O Little Town of Bethlehem," he is shown here— amazingly—with Christ touching his shoulder in approval. ⊠ *206 Clarendon St., ☎ 617/536–0944. ☉ Daily 8–6. Sun. services at 8, 11, and 6. T stop, Copley.*

THE SOUTH END

History has come full circle in the South End. Once a fashionable neighborhood created with landfill in the mid-19th century, it was deserted by the well-to-do for the Back Bay toward the end of the century. Solidly back in fashion today, its redbrick row houses in states of refurbished splendor or elegant decay are home to a polyglot mix of ethnic groups and a substantial gay community.

The South End is an anomaly of planning and architecture. It neither rose haphazardly among cow paths and village lanes, like the old sections, nor followed the strict, uniform grid typical of the Back Bay. Bainbridge Bunting called its effect "cellular," and it is certainly more a sum of random blocks and park-centered squares than of bold boulevards and long vistas. An observation often made is that the Back Bay is French-inspired while the South End is English. The houses, too, are noticeably different; although they continue the bowfront style, they aspire to a more florid standard of decoration.

Even if the South End was a kind of Victorian Levittown, it is an intimate and nicely proportioned neighborhood that deserved a better reputation than it earned at the outset. Consider the literary evidence: William Dean Howells's Silas Lapham abandoned the South End to build a house on the waterside of Beacon as material proof of his arrival in Boston society. In *The Late George Apley,* John P. Marquand's Brahmin hero tells how his father decided, in the early 1870s, to move the family from his South End bowfront to the Back Bay—a consequence of his walking out on the front steps one morning and seeing a man in his shirtsleeves on the porch opposite. Regardless of whether Marquand exaggerated Victorian notions of propriety (if that was possible), the fact is that people like the Apleys did decamp for the Back Bay, leaving the South End to become what a 1913 guidebook called a "faded quarter."

A more practical reason the South End was relegated to the status of a social backwater was that it was literally out of the way. Railroad tracks separated it from the Back Bay, and disunity between state planners in the Back Bay and their city counterparts in the South End left the two districts with conflicting grid patterns that have never comfortably meshed. The rail tracks are now gone, but the South End is still cut off from the rest of the city by the I–90 underpass, Copley Plaza, and the Prudential Center.

The South End by 1900 was a neighborhood of lower-middle-class families and rooming houses. It had not lost its association with upward mobility, however, and African-Americans, many of them holders of the prestigious Pullman porter jobs on the railroads, began to buy the old bowfronts and establish themselves in the area.

About 25 years ago, middle-class professionals, mostly white, began looking at the South End as though it had just been filled in and built over, and this group didn't care who might be walking around in shirtsleeves. A gentrification process began and continues today.

There is still a substantial black presence in the South End, particularly along Columbus Avenue and Massachusetts Avenue, which marks the beginning of the predominantly black neighborhood of Roxbury. Boston's gay community also has a large presence in the South End, with most of the gay-popular restaurants and businesses located on Columbus Avenue and Tremont Street between East Berkeley Street and Massachusetts Avenue. Along East Berkeley, neighbors have created a lush community garden. At the north end of the South End, where Harrison Avenue and Washington Street lead to Chinatown, you'll find several Chinese supermarkets.

Numbers in the text correspond to numbers in the margin and on the Back Bay, the South End, and the Fens map.

A Good Walk
Although it would take years to understand the South End completely, you can capture some of its flavor within a few hours. Begin a stroll from Symphony Hall in the Back Bay. Walk down Massachusetts Avenue to Columbus Avenue, turn left and follow it to the tiny park of **Rutland Square** ⑯ on your right. Continue on Tremont until you turn right on **Union Park** ⑰. Both parks are quiet, shady examples of a more elegant time. Follow Union Park street across Shawmut to Washington Street for a view of the huge **Cathedral of the Holy Cross** ⑱. If you like, detour to Shawmut Street, a mixture of ethnic outlets and upscale retail spaces. Walk along Shawmut to East Berkeley Street, turn left and head back to Tremont. On Tremont Street near Clarendon Street is the **Boston Center for the Arts** ⑲. After a break at one of the many trendy restaurants and shops along Tremont Street, retrace your steps on Tremont to Arlington and cross the Massachusetts Turnpike on an overpass to find **Bay Village** ⑳ on your right; it's another 19th-century oasis in the center of Boston.

TIMING

You can walk through the South End in two to three hours. It's a good option on a pleasant day; go elsewhere in inclement weather, as most of what you'll want to see here is outdoors.

Sights to See
⑳ **Bay Village.** It seems improbable that such a fine, serene neighborhood (Edgar Allen Poe was born here) could exist so close to the busy Theater District and the Massachusetts Turnpike. Yet here it is, another Boston surprise. This pocket of early-19th-century brick row houses is near Arlington and Fayette Streets. Its quaint window boxes and short, narrow streets make the area seem a toylike replica of Beacon Hill. Note that, owing to the street pattern, it's nearly impossible to drive here, and it's easy to miss on foot.

⑲ Boston Center for the Arts (also known as the **Cyclorama Building**). Of Boston's multiple arts organizations, the city-sponsored arts and culture complex is the one that is closest "to the people." Here you can see the work of budding playwrights, view exhibits on Haitian folk art, or walk through an installation commemorating World AIDS Day. The BCA houses three small theaters, the Mills Gallery, and studio space for some 60 artists. It's a bit of a leap from the original purpose of the Cyclorama Building, which was built by William Blackall in 1884 to house a 400-by-50-ft circular painting of the Battle of Gettysburg. After the painting was sent to Pennsylvania, the building was used as a boxing ring, a bicycle ring, and a garage (Alfred Champion invented the spark plug here). The building now hosts frequent antiques shows and fund-raisers. Its distinctive copper dome got a face-lift in 1997 and plans were pending for development of the space next door, created when the old National Theater was razed.⊠ *539 Tremont St.,* ☎ *617/426–5000 or 617/426–7700; 617/426–8835, Mills Galleries.* ▭ *Free.* ☉ *Weekdays 9–5; Mills Galleries Wed.–Sun., 1–4, Thurs.–Sat. 7 PM– 9 PM. T stop, Back Bay.*

⑱ Cathedral of the Holy Cross. Irish Roman Catholics are no longer well represented in the South End, which is ironic, as this enormous 1873 Gothic cathedral dominates the corner of Washington Street and Monsignor Reynolds Way. Although it is now used principally for special occasions (such as the Pope's 1979 visit), it remains the premier church of the Archdiocese of Boston, New England's largest Catholic church, and the episcopal seat of Bernard Cardinal Law. ⊠ *Washington St.,* ☎ *617/542–5682.* ☉ *Mass Sun. at 8, 9:30, weekdays at 9; in Spanish, Sun. at 11, Tues., Thurs. at 7 PM. T stop, Chinatown; then Bus 49 to Cathedral.*

⑯ Rutland Square. Reflecting a time in which the South End was the most prestigious Boston address, this slice of a park, between Columbus Avenue and Tremont Street, is framed by lovely Italianate bowfront houses.

⑰ Union Park. Cast-iron fences, Victorian-era town houses, and a lovely grassy knoll all add up to one of Boston's most charming cityscapes, dating from the 1850s, located between Tremont Street and Shawmut Avenue.

NEED A BREAK?	**To Go Bakery** (⊠ 312 Shawmut Ave., ☎ 617/482–1015) is a charming neighborhood hangout, perfect for a pastry or a sinfully rich dessert. There are only a few tables; on nice days, people congregate outside.

THE FENS AND KENMORE SQUARE

The marshland known as the **Back Bay Fens** gave this section of Boston its name, but two quirky institutions give it its character: **Fenway Park,** where hope for another World Series pennant springs eternal, and the **Isabella Stewart Gardner Museum,** the legacy of a bon vivant Brahmin who once attended a concert at Symphony Hall wearing a headband that read, "Oh, You Red Sox." **Kenmore Square,** a favorite haunt for Boston University and Northeastern University students, adds a bit of funky flavor to the mix.

After the outsize job of filling in the bay had been completed, it would have been small trouble to obliterate the Fens with gravel and march row houses straight through to Brookline. But the planners, deciding that enough pavement had been laid between here and the Public Garden, hired none other than Frederick Law Olmsted—cocreator of New

York's Central Park—to turn the Fens into a park. Olmsted applied his genius for heightening natural effects while subtly manicuring their surroundings; today's Fens park consists of irregularly shaped reed-bound pools surrounded by broad meadows, trees, and flower gardens.

The Fens mark the beginning of Boston's **Emerald Necklace,** a loosely connected chain of parks designed by Olmsted that extends along the Fenway, Riverway, and Jamaicaway to Jamaica Pond, the Arnold Arboretum, and Franklin Park (for more on the arboretum and Franklin Park, ☞ The "Streetcar Suburbs" *below*). Farther off, at the Boston–Milton line, the vast Blue Hills Reservation offers some of the Boston area's best hiking, scenic views, and even a ski lift.

Numbers in the text correspond to numbers in the margin and on the Back Bay, the South End, and the Fens map.

A Good Walk

With Boston's two most spectacular art museums on this itinerary, a case of museum feet could set in. Happily, both the Museum of Fine Arts and the Isabella Stewart Gardner Museum are surrounded by the sylvan glades of the Fens—a perfect oasis and time-out location when you're suffering from gallery gout. From the intersection of Huntington and Massachusetts avenues, with the front entrance of Symphony Hall on your right, walk down Huntington Avenue. (A note of caution: This neighborhood becomes deserted at the end of the day, so this outing is not recommended at night.) On your left is the New England Conservatory of Music and, on Gainsborough Street, its recital center, Jordan Hall. Between Huntington and the Fenway is the **Museum of Fine Arts** ㉑ and, just around the corner, the **Isabella Stewart Gardner Museum** ㉒. If you prefer to pay homage to the Red Sox: From Symphony Hall, go north on Massachusetts Avenue, turn left on Commonwealth Avenue, and continue until you reach **Kenmore Square** ㉓; from here it's a 15- to 20-minute walk down Brookline Avenue to Yawkey Way and **Fenway Park** ㉔.

TIMING

Although this area can be walked through in a longish afternoon, art lovers could spend a week here—thanks to the glories of the Museum of Fine Arts and the Isabella Stewart Gardner Museum. To cap off a day of culture, plan for an area dinner, then a concert at nearby Symphony Hall. This district is most easily traveled via branches of the MBTA's Green Line; trains operate above ground on Commonwealth and Huntington Avenues.

Sights to See

㉔ **Fenway Park.** Belief in the "Curse of the Bambino" runs so strong that in 1995 Babe Ruth's daughter felt compelled to publicly dismiss it. To little avail. Red Sox fans will continue to blame the shadow of Babe Ruth—traded away as a rookie by the Sox to the New York Yankees—for their beloved team's inability to repeat its 1918 World Series win. But although Fenway may be one of the smallest parks in the major leagues (capacity 34,000), it is one of the most loved (although, granted, the looming left-field wall continues to carry the moniker The Green Monster). It was built in 1912, when the grass on all baseball fields was real, as it still is here today. Fenway has been bittersweet for the Red Sox, with pennants in 1946, 1967, 1975, and 1986, and a divisional championship in 1988—but long droughts in between. There has been no shortage of heroics: Babe Ruth pitched here when the stadium was new; Ted Williams and Carl Yastrzemski slugged out their entire careers here. Yawkey Way is named for the late Tom Yawkey, who bought the team in 1933 as a 30th-birthday present for himself and spent the next 43 years pursuing his elusive grail. ⊠ *4 Yawkey Way, between Van Ness and Lansdowne Sts., ☎ 617/267–1700 box office; 617/267–8661 recorded information.*

㉒ **Isabella Stewart Gardner Museum.** A spirited young society woman, Isabella Stewart had come from New York—where ladies were more commonly seen *and* heard than in Boston—in 1860 to marry John Lowell Gardner, one of Boston's leading citizens. "Mrs. Jack" promptly set about becoming the most un-Bostonian of the Proper Bostonians, devoting her life not only to shocking the Brahmins with her flamboyance but also to her energetic acquisition of art. When it came time finally to house the Old Master paintings and Medici treasures she and her husband had acquired in Europe (with *her* money—she was heir to the Stewart mining fortune), she decided to build the Venetian palazzo of her dreams along Commonwealth Avenue. Always resenting the lack of privacy symbolized by the bay-windowed houses of Beacon Hill—and wanting to escape the prying eyes and raised lorgnettes of Boston grande dames—she built her palace to center around a spacious inner courtyard. On New Year's Day 1903, she threw open the entrance to Fenway Court (to use the museum's original name)—then as now, a monument to one woman's individuality and taste. Today, it probably is America's most idiosyncratic treasure house.

In a city where expensive simplicity was the norm, her palazzo was an amazing sight: A trove of spectacular paintings—including such masterpieces as Titian's *Rape of Europa,* Giorgione's *Christ Bearing the Cross,* Piero della Francesca's *Hercules,* and John Singer Sargent's *El Jaleo*—overflow rooms bought outright from great European houses. Spanish leather panels, Renaissance hooded fireplaces, and Gothic tapestries accent salons; eight "Romeo, Romeo, wherefore art thou, Romeo?" balconies adorn the majestic Venetian courtyard. There is a Raphael Room, a Spanish Cloister, a Gothic Room, a Chinese Loggia, and—to entertain such guests as Henry James and Edith Wharton—a magnificent Tapestry Room for concerts. Throughout the two decades of her residence, Mrs. Jack continued to build her collection under the tutelage of the young Bernard Berenson, who became one of the most respected art connoisseurs and critics of the 20th century.

Mrs. Gardner lived on the top floor at Fenway Court until her death in 1924. When she died, the terms of her will stipulated that Fenway Court remain exactly as she left it—paintings, furniture, everything, down to the smallest object of *virtu* in a hall cabinet. The courtyard, fully protected from the rigors of New England winters by a glass roof, is often decorated with fresh poinsettias at Christmastime, lilies at Easter, chrysanthemums in the fall—just as when Mrs. Jack lived here. Almost everything is just as it was back then.

Well, not quite everything. On March 19, 1990, the Gardner was the target of one of the world's most sensational art heists. Thieves disguised as police officers stole 13 works of art with an estimated value of $200 million from Mrs. Jack's collection. Vermeer's *The Concert* was the most famous painting taken, along with works by Rembrandt, Manet, and Degas. To date, none of the art has been recovered, despite a $1 million reward. Because Mrs. Gardner's will prohibited substituting other works for any stolen art, and because of high premiums, the Gardner Museum had chosen not to insure its collections. Empty expanses of wall and small white cards identify the spots where the art once hung; these are studied with great curiosity by museum goers. Today, with more than 2,000 works in the collection and rates dramatically lower because of increasing recoveries of stolen art, the Gardner carries insurance. Mrs. Jack never believed in making a contribution to the Metropolitan Life Insurance Company, putting her faith in her mansion's entry portal, which carries Renaissance-period figures of both St. George and St. Florian, the patron saints protecting believers from theft and fire.

An intimate restaurant overlooks the garden, and in spring and summer tables and chairs spill outside. To fully conjure up the spirit of days past, try to attend one of the concerts still held from September to May in the elegant Tapestry Room. A first floor gallery has revolving exhibits of historic and contemporary art. ⊠ *280 The Fenway,* ☎ *617/ 566–1401 (also for recorded concert information Sept.–May); 617/ 566–1088 for café.* 🎫 *$10; concert and galleries $15; admission free to café and gift shop; children under 18 free.* ☉ *Museum: Tues.–Sun. 11–5, some Mon. holidays; café: Tues.–Fri. 11:30–4, weekends 11–4. Weekend concerts at 1:30. T stop, Museum.*

㉓ Kenmore Square. Two blocks north of Fenway Park is Kenmore Square, home to fast-food parlors, rock-and-roll clubs, an abundance of university students, and an enormous sign advertising Citgo gasoline. The red, white, and blue neon sign put up in 1965 is so thoroughly identified with the area that historic preservationists have fought, successfully, to save it—proof that Bostonians are an open-minded lot who do not insist that their landmarks be identified with the American Revolution. Beneath the sign, at 660 Beacon Street, is the **Barnes & Noble at Boston University,** a literary hangout that often sponsors readings and book signings by authors. A few blocks away, at 528 Commonwealth, is the **Rathskeller,** known to one and all as The Rat, a grubby hangout that was among the first Boston clubs to headline New Wave bands and still knows how to rock.

In the shadow of Fenway Park is **Lansdowne Street,** a mecca of nightlife for young Bostonians and those who some (less than affectionately) dub Eurotrash. Dance clubs like Avalon and Axis go for the can't-hear-yourself-think sound; Jake Ivory's has dueling pianos; and, around the corner on Commonwealth Avenue, **Boston Beer Works** attracts the suds-seekers. Keep an eye out for Steve Tyler of Aerosmith, who often makes the local scene. The Bad Boy of Rock and other partners opened **Mama Kin,** a large music club (with the names of Aerosmith songs carved into its bar).

The urban campus of **Boston University** begins farther west on Commonwealth Avenue, in blocks thick with dorms, businesses—including the popular **Nickelodeon movie theater**—and restaurants.

★ ㉑ Museum of Fine Arts. When you walk past Cyrus Dallin's *Appeal to the Great Spirit* at this museum's main entrance, between Huntington Avenue and the Fenway, with its grand stairway and rotunda whose cupola is decorated with frescoes by John Singer Sargent, or through the doors of the newer West Wing, count on staying at this celebrated museum a while if you have any hope of even beginning to see what is here. Eclecticism and thoroughness, often an incompatible pair, have coexisted agreeably at the MFA, as it's known locally, since its earliest days. From Renaissance and Baroque masters to impressionist marvels to sublime samples of American Indian pottery and contemporary crafts, an afternoon here is better than a packed semester of art history, shorn of both cultural snobbery and short-sighted trendiness.

Founded in 1870, the museum first had quarters on the upper floors of the Boston Athenaeum, then a Gothic structure on the site where the Copley Plaza Hotel now stands. As the MFA was beginning to outgrow this space, the Fenway area was becoming fashionable, and in 1909 the move was made to Guy Lowell's somewhat severe Beaux Arts building, to which the West Wing, designed by I. M. Pei, was added in 1981. The move helped to cap the half century of expansion of the Back Bay area.

The MFA's vast collections—only a third to two-thirds is on display at any one time—was built from a core of paintings and sculpture from the Boston Athenaeum, historical portraits from the city of Boston, and donations by area universities. The early MFA connoisseurs were as enamored as any cultured Victorians with the great art of European civilizations; nevertheless, they sought out American works as well; today, the MFA's holdings of American art surpass those of all but two or three U.S. museums, supplemented by intensive acquisitions in the early 1990s. It has more than 60 works by John Singleton Copley—Colonial Boston's most celebrated painter—including his amazing *Watson and the Shark,* which depicts a shark attack on a young man in Havana Harbor (Mr. Watson lost his leg but went on to become an 18th-century celebrity and government official). It has major paintings by Winslow Homer, John Singer Sargent, Fitz Hugh Lane, and Edward Hopper, as well as a galaxy of American works ranging from native New England folk art and Colonial portraiture to New York abstract expressionism of the 1950s and 1960s.

American decorative arts are also amply represented, particularly those of New England in the years before the Civil War. Rooms of period furniture, much of it from the matchless Karolik collection, show the progression of taste from the earliest Pilgrim pieces through the 18th-century triumphs of the Queen Anne, Hepplewhite, Sheraton, and Empire styles.

If you think of Paul Revere simply as a sounder of alarms, linger over a gleaming display of his superb silver teapots (more than 13 of them), ornate sauceboats, and other tableware; the patriot was one of the greatest artists ever to turn his hand to silver. An extra pleasure is seeing his silver Liberty Bowl, then viewing the museum's Copley portrait of Revere with the same bowl.

The museum also boasts one of the world's most extensive collections of Asian art under one roof. The **Japanese Buddhist art** is the finest outside Japan, and **Chinese porcelains** of the Tang Dynasty are especially well represented. The **Egyptian rooms** display statuary, mummies, furniture, and exquisite gold jewelry, and the **Nubian gallery** showcases the art and culture of this ancient kingdom. The gathering of classical treasures proceeds chronologically through the Hellenistic and Roman eras, recalled by marble busts, jewelry, and glassware.

French Impressionists abound and are perhaps more comprehensively represented here than at any other New World museum outside the Art Institute of Chicago; many of the 38 Monets, the largest collection of his work outside France, vibrate with their original colors. There are canvases by Renoir, Pisarro, Manet, and the American painters Mary Cassatt and Childe Hassam.

The museum has strong collections of textiles and costumes and prints dating from the 15th century, including many works by Dürer and Goya. The museum's collection of antique **musical instruments,** expanded in 1979 by the acquisition of an important group of early keyboard instruments, is among the finest in the world. It includes Benjamin Franklin's keyboard "armonica." (The hours for viewing this collection differ from the regular museum hours; call for the schedule.) The MFA also has a regular concert season (☞ Music *in* Chapter 6).

Fifteen galleries contain the MFA's recently rehung and reorganized European painting and sculpture collection, dating from the 11th to the 20th centuries. Among the highlights in the Renaissance sculpture gallery on the second floor is Donatello's marble relief *The Madonna of the Clouds.* Most striking, however, is the newly reinstalled **William I. Koch** (pronounced "coke") **Gallery,** a former tapestry room whose vast 40-ft-high marble walls are now hung—nearly floor to ceiling—with fifty-three Renaissance and Baroque paintings by El Greco, Claude Lorraine, Poussin, Rubens, Tintoretto, Titian, Van Dyck, Velázquez, Veronese, and other masters. Given the vastness of many of these canvases, the scenes of high drama that predominate, and just how *many* paintings there are, the Koch gallery now offers a surprising revelation to museum goers: that the city widely recognized as America's most genteel has, in fact, long had an appetite for flamboyance and sensuousness.

The **West Wing,** a handsome, airy, well-lighted space, is used primarily to house traveling exhibitions, temporary shows drawn from the museum's holdings, and lively contemporary art and photography exhibits. It also has a refurbished restaurant, a cafeteria, and a gallery café serving light snacks. In the newly re-opened **Fraser Court,** a charming oasis of green trees and statuary, beverages are served on the terrace from April to October. From October to April, a "Ladies Tea" is served from 2:30 to 4:30 inside near the main entrance. The Morse Study Room for prints, drawings, and photographs, which opened in December 1997, lets visitors study (by appointment only) more than 200,000 works from the museum's collection. Upcoming major exhibits include a retrospective of Mary Cassatt from February to May 1999.

Outside, on the Fenway Park side of the MFA, the **Tenshin-En** or **Japanese Garden,** the "garden in the heart of heaven," allows visitors to experience landscape as a work of art. A stone wall separates the formal garden from the nearby park, and a curved, graceful gate of Japanese cypress opens onto a path of Mexican river stones that leads to a solitary bench surrounded by white gravel. An assortment of Japanese and American trees and shrubs are used to combine the elements of the Japanese garden with elements of the New England landscape. Stone lanterns are placed at intervals, and a bridge at the center symbolically links longevity on the one side with prosperity on the other. Access to the garden is free with admission to the museum. ⊠ *465 Huntington Ave.,* ☎ *617/267–9300.* ⌷ *$10; pay what you wish Wed. 4– 9:45; children under 17 free.* ⊙ *Entire museum: weekdays 10–5, weekends 10–6, Wed. until 10. West Wing only: Thurs. and Fri. until 10 with admission reduced by $2. 1-hr tours available weekdays. Garden: Apr.–Oct., Tues.–Sun. 10–4. T stop, Museum.*

Northeastern University. Northeastern students are largely commuters, and their noses are seldom far from the grindstone. For their great numbers, they keep a low local profile. The campus was established in 1898 and now has an enrollment of about 34,000, including part-time students. It is one of the world's largest cooperative education plan universities, where students in a wide variety of disciplines alternate periods of classroom study with employment in related professions. Northeastern's engineering school is strong, and the university offers important programs in nursing, computers, business administration, pharmacology, criminal justice, marine sciences, the human development professions, and law—yet another law school in a city of lawyers. ⊠ *360 Huntington Ave.,* ☎ *617/373–2000.*

THE "STREETCAR SUBURBS"

The expansion of Boston in the 1800s was not confined to the Back Bay and the South End. Toward the close of the century, as the working population of the downtown district swelled and public transportation (first horsecars, then electric trolleys) linked outlying suburbs with the core city, development of the "Streetcar Suburbs" began. These areas answered the housing needs of the rising native middle class as well as the second-generation immigrant families already outgrowing the narrow streets of the North and West Ends.

The landfill project that became South Boston—not to be confused with the South End—is not a true streetcar suburb; its expansion predates the era of commuting. Some of the brick bowfront residences along East Broadway in City Point date from the 1840s and 1850s, but the neighborhood really came into its own with the influx of Irish around 1900, and the Irish-Americans still hold sway here. "Southie" is a Celtic enclave, as the annual St. Patrick's Day parade attests.

Inland from Columbia Point are **Dorchester, Roxbury,** and **Jamaica Plain**—rural retreats barely more than a century ago that are now thick with tenements and the distinctive three- or six-family triple-decker apartment houses of Boston's streetcar suburbs. Both Dorchester and Roxbury are almost exclusively residential, tricky to navigate by car, and accessible by the T (the Red or Orange lines) only if you know exactly where you are going. Dorchester and Roxbury are contiguous and border **Franklin Park,** an Olmsted creation of more than 500 acres, noted for its zoo.

Due to its geography, **Brookline** seems like a neighborhood of Boston, but it is a separate civic entity, composed of a mixture of the affluent, the middle-class, and students, proud of their government and school system.

Numbers in the text and margin correspond to numbers on The "Streetcar Suburbs" map.

A Good Walk

Except for the Arnold Arboretum, the sights covered here aren't particularly walkable from the center of town; your best bet is to make separate trips, either via public transportation or car. If you do have a car, **Castle Island Park** ①, **Dorchester Heights Monument** ②, and the **John F. Kennedy Library and Museum** ③ make a sensible joint excursion, as do the **Franklin Park Zoo** ④ and the **Arnold Arboretum** ⑤, especially if you are not inclined to take the suggested walk to or from it. You'll probably want to make separate trips to the **John F. Kennedy National Historic Site** ⑥, the **Frederick Law Olmsted National Historic Site** ⑦, and **Garden in the Woods** ⑧.

If you *do* have the time and stamina for a jaunt of approximately 3½ mi, it is possible to walk almost the entire distance from Arnold Arboretum to **Kenmore Square** (☞ The Fens and Kenmore Square, *above*) within the Emerald Necklace, Boston's loosely connected chain of Olmsted-designed parks. Just follow the Jamaicaway north from its beginning at the circle that marks the northern tip of the arboretum. Within the equivalent of one long block you'll reach Jamaica Pond. Continue along the Jamaicaway through Olmsted Park, past Leverett Pond. From a point just north of here, either Brookline Avenue or the Riverway will take you to the Fens and Kenmore Square. Along the way you will pass many of the spacious freestanding mansions built around the turn of the century along the park borders of Jamaica Plain, when this was the choicest of the streetcar suburbs. Not the least of your pleasures as you move along this stretch will be that you are walking, not driving. The Jamaicaway was one of Boston's first attempts at increasing the pace of traffic, and it worked extremely well for horse-drawn carriages and the slower and narrower early-model automobiles. If you think that Boston still isn't very good at hurrying cars around, remember that, unlike most American cities, it has been inhabited almost exclusively by pedestrians for two-thirds of its history.

TIMING

To enjoy the "Streetcar Suburbs"—the city at its country best—wait for pleasant weather. Who would want to view the Arnold Arboretum's Lilac Sunday and flowering crab-apple trees (mid-May), its spectacular rhododendron display (June), or any of its other special floral displays under cloudy skies?

South Boston

❶ Castle Island Park. South Boston projects farther into the harbor than any other part of Boston except Logan Airport, and the views of the Harbor Islands from along Day Boulevard or Castle Island are very fine. At L Street and Day Boulevard is the L Street Beach, where an intrepid group called the L Street Brownies swims all year long, including a celebratory dip in the icy Atlantic every New Year's Day. Castle Island Park is no longer on an island, but Fort Independence, when it was built here in 1801, was separated from the mainland by water. The circular walk from the fort around Pleasure Bay, delightful on a warm summer day, has a stunning view of the city's skyline late at night (South Boston is considered one of the city's safest neighborhoods). The statue near the fort is of Donald McKay, whose clipper ships once sped past this point on their way to distant California and the Orient. To get here by the T, take the Red Line to Broadway Station. Just outside the station, catch Bus 9 going east on Broadway, which will take you to within a block of the waterfront. From the waterfront park you can walk the loop, via piers, around the island.

Dorchester and Roxbury

❺ Arnold Arboretum. This 265-acre living laboratory, administered by Harvard University is incongruously set in a dense urban area. Established in 1872 in accordance with the terms of a bequest from New Bedford merchant James Arnold, it contains more than 14,000 varieties of trees and shrubs, many of them native to the North Temperate Zone. The rhododendrons, azaleas, lilacs, magnolias, and fruit trees are spectacular when in bloom, and something is always in season from early April through September. In October, the park puts on a spectacular scarlet and neon orange display that will more than satisfy leaf peepers. The bonsai collection has individual specimens more than 300 years old imported from Japan. The visitor's center has a 40-to-1 scale model of the arboretum (with 4,000 tiny trees), installed for its 125th anniversary in 1996, plus an exhibit on "Science in the Pleasure Ground," a kind of "green" history of the landscape. The arboretum, 6 mi from downtown Boston, is accessible by MBTA Orange Line (Forest Hills stop) or Bus 39 from Copley Square to Centre Street. Walk four blocks south. ⊠ *Rtes. 1 and 203, Arborway,* ☎ *617/524–1718.* ☉ *Grounds, daily dawn–dusk; visitor center, weekdays 9–4, weekends noon–4. Extensive tours and programs. T stop, Forest Hills or Arborway.*

❷ Dorchester Heights Monument. Off Telegraph Street, near the juncture of the South Boston peninsula with the Dorchester mainland, stands the high ground of Thomas Park, where you will find the Dorchester

The "Streetcar Suburbs"

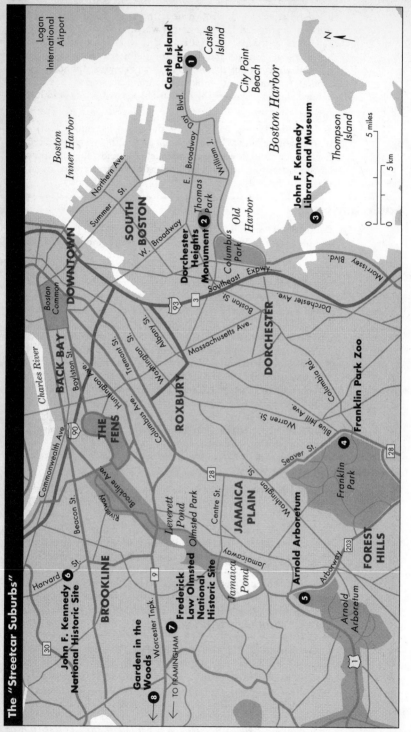

Logan International Airport

Boston Inner Harbor

Castle Island Park ➊

Castle Island

City Point Beach

Boston Harbor

Day Blvd.

E. Broadway

Northern Ave.

Summer St.

SOUTH BOSTON

W. BOSTON

Broadway

E. Broadway

William J.

Thomas Park

Dorchester Heights Monument ➋

Columbus Park

Old Harbor

Thompson Island

John F. Kennedy Library and Museum ➌

DOWNTOWN

Boston Common

BACK BAY

Charles River

Southeast Expwy.

Morrissey Blvd.

93

3

Boston St.

Dorchester Ave.

DORCHESTER

Massachusetts Ave.

Columbia Rd.

Albany St.

Washington St.

Tremont St.

Boylston St.

Huntington Ave.

THE FENS

ROXBURY

Columbus Ave.

Commonwealth Ave.

90

Brookline Ave.

Warren St.

Blue Hill Ave.

Beacon St.

Franklin Park Zoo ➍

28

Seaver St.

Franklin Park

Riverway

Leverett Pond

Olmsted Park

Washington St.

JAMAICA PLAIN

Centre St.

28

Jamaica Pond

Jamaicaway

Arnold Arboretum

FOREST HILLS

203

BROOKLINE

Harvard St.

John F. Kennedy National Historic Site ➏

9

Frederick Law Olmsted National Historic Site ➐

Arborway

Arnold Arboretum

➎

Worcester Tnpk.

30

Garden in the Woods ➑

TO FRAMINGHAM

1

N

5 miles

5 km

Heights Monument and National Historic Site. In 1776 Dorchester Heights commanded a clear view of central Boston, where the British had been under siege since the preceding year. Here George Washington set up the cannons that Henry Knox, a Boston bookseller-turned-soldier, and later secretary of war, had hauled through the wilderness following their capture at Fort Ticonderoga. The artillery did its job of intimidation, and the British troops left Boston, never to return. The site has a spectacular view of Boston; otherwise you may find more history at the Bunker Hill Monument. ⊠ *Thomas Park (near G St.).* 🎫 *Free.* ☉ *Grounds with interpretive plaques open daily; monument not open to public. T stop, Broadway; then City Point Bus to G St.*

❹ **Franklin Park Zoo.** After a decade of decline, the Franklin Park Zoo (now under the direction of the nonprofit Zoo New England, which also oversees the Stone Zoo in Stoneham), has begun to rock and roar. New exhibits of lions and cheetahs (separate) opened in 1997. A four-acre mixed-species area, called "Bongo Congo," showcases antelope, zebras, ostriches, ibex, and warthogs. The African Tropical Forest, with its popular gorilla cage, continues to be a draw, although the facilities are somewhat outdated. Scheduled for opening in spring of 1998 are an Australian Outback trail, with wallabies and kangaroos, and a butterfly enclosure. If you see a man in a 10-gallon hat inspecting the zoo on horseback, that may just be director Brian Rutledge, who lives on the grounds. Unfortunately, the zoo continues to struggle with concerns about its location on the outskirts of a high-crime area. The Children's Zoo, which is limited in scope, is scheduled for a new site, with groundbreaking in late 1998. The park, 4 mi from downtown, is reached by Bus 16 from Forest Hills (Orange Line) or Andrew (Red Line). If you drive, you would hardly guess that the area has a bad reputation, and there's plenty of parking. ⊠ *1 Franklin Park Rd.,* ☎ *617/442–2002 or 617/442–4896.* 🎫 *$6 adults, $3 children 2–15.* ☉ *Nov.–Mar., daily 10–4; Apr.–Oct., daily 10–5; closed Thanksgiving, Dec. 25.*

❸ **John F. Kennedy Library and Museum.** Chronicling a time now passing from memory to history, the library/museum is both a center for serious scholarship and a focus for Boston's nostalgia for her native son. The stark, white, prowlike building (another modernist monument designed by I. M. Pei) at this stunning harbor-enclosed site pays homage to the life and presidency of John F. Kennedy, an Irish-American blessed with distinctive style, intellect, and passion, and to members of his family, including his wife, Jackie, and brother Robert.

The Kennedy Library—which is opened only to serious, accredited researchers—is the official repository of his presidential papers; the museum displays a trove of Kennedy memorabilia, including re-creations of his desk in the Oval Office and of the television studio in which he debated Richard M. Nixon in the 1960 election. At the entrance, high and dry during the summer months, is the president's 26–foot sailboat; inside, two theaters show a film about his life. The exhibits, ranging from the Cuban missile crisis to his assassination, include 20 video presentations. A more recent addition is a permanent display on Jackie Kennedy, including some samples of her distinctive wardrobe and personal mementoes. As a somber note in an otherwise gung-ho museum, continuous videos of the first news bulletin of the assassination and the funeral are shown in a darkened hall. The Steven M. Smith Wing provides space for meetings and events; the facility also includes a store and a small café. The harbor-front site, at the tip of Columbia Point, alone is worth a visit. ⊠ *Columbia Point,* ☎ *617/929–4523.* 🎫 *$6.* ☉ *Daily 9–5. Free shuttle bus every 20 min from JFK/UMASS T stop 9–5.*

Brookline

❻ John F. Kennedy National Historic Site. This was the home of the 35th president from his birth on May 29, 1917, until 1920, when the family moved to nearby Naples and Abbottsford streets. Mrs. Rose Kennedy provided the furnishings for the restored 2½-story, wood-frame structure. Devoted Kennedyphiles may pick up a brochure for a walking tour of young Kennedy's school, church, and neighborhood. To get here, take the MBTA Green Line to Coolidge Corner and walk north on Harvard Street four blocks. ⊠ 83 Beals St., ☎ 617/566–7937. ☒ $2. ☉ Mid-Mar.–Nov. 30, Wed.–Sun. 10–4:30; tours every hr from 10:45. Last tour at 4. T stop, Coolidge Corner.

★ **❼ Frederick Law Olmsted National Historic Site.** Frederick Law Olmsted (1822–1903), the first person to call himself a "landscape architect," is considered the founder of the profession and the nation's preeminent creator of parks. In 1883 at age 61 while immersed in planning Boston's Emerald Necklace of parks, Olmsted set up his first permanent office at Fairsted, an 18-room farmhouse dating from 1810, to which he added another 18 rooms for his design offices. The site is primarily a mecca for researchers and planners; there are displays of plans and drawings for such high-profile and diverse projects as the U.S. Capitol grounds, Stanford University, and Mount Royal Park in Montreal. You can also tour the design rooms (some still in use for preservation projects) where Olmstead and staff drew up their plans; highlights include a 1904 "electric blueprint machine," a kind of primitive photocopying process. The 1.76-acre site incorporates many trademark Olmstedian designs, including areas of meadow, wild garden, and woodland; Olmsted believed body and spirit could be healed through close association with nature. The site became part of the National Park Service in 1979; Olmsted's office played an influential role in the creation of this federal agency. In 1916, Olmsted's son, who carried on his father's work here, wrote the words that were to serve as a statement of purpose for legislation establishing the park service in 1916: "To conserve the scenery and the natural and historic objects and the wildlife therein and to provide for the enjoyment of the same in such manner and by such means as will leave them unimpaired for the enjoyment of future generations." ⊠ 99 Warren St., ☎ 617/566–1689. ☒ Free. ☉ Fri.–Sun. 10–4:30, and by appointment; 40-min tours every hr from 10:30. Last tour at 3:30. T stop, Brookline Hills.

Framingham

❽ Garden in the Woods. In springtime, garden-loving Bostonians make the pilgrimage to Garden in the Woods in Framingham to glimpse the first blossoming trees, wildflowers, and shrubs. Run by the New England Wild Flower Society, the 45-acre garden has nearly 3 mi of trails and is planted with more than 1,600 kinds of plants, 200 of them rare or endangered. Even in summer and fall, the majestic trees and naturalistic woodland landscapes can be a welcome escape from urban strife. Self-guiding booklets are available, and there's a well-stocked gift shop that remains open through the winter. The garden also offers numerous garden and wildflowers classes and workshops. ⊠ 180 Hemenway Rd., Framingham, ☎ 508/877–6574 or 508/877–7630. ☒ $6. ☉ Apr. 15–Oct. 31, Tues.–Sun. 9–5, plus Memorial Day. Last admission 1 hr before closing. Call for taped directions.

3 Exploring Cambridge

Home to Harvard and MIT, Cambridge has more geniuses per capita than any other town in America. It's also home to the Fogg Art Museum, a bevy of bookstores, and hipster hangouts by the dozen. Harvard remains America's finest university; it is also a Yard and a Square that are a few feet and a few light-years apart. Begin by walking into the rarefied air of the college quadrangle. Love it or leave it, this is the Ivy League—ground zero.

By Stephanie
Schorow

PRONOUNCED WITH EITHER PRIDEFUL SATISFACTION
or the occasional smirk, the nickname "The People's
Republic of Cambridge" sums up this independent
city of 95,000 west of Boston. Cambridge not only houses three of the
country's greatest educational institutions—Harvard University, Radcliffe College, and the Massachusetts Institute of Technology—it has
a long history as a haven for freethinkers, writers, activists, and iconoclasts of every stamp. Cambridge also functions as Boston's con-
science; when a new social experiment or piece of progressive legislation
appears on the local scene, chances are it grew out of local political
activism. Once a center for publishing, Cambridge has become a high-
tech mecca; more than a few MIT students have launched software companies even before they graduated.

Yet Cambridge, like Boston, is a city of neighborhoods; the rarefied
air of Harvard Yard and the mansions of Brattle Street are within a
mile of the ethnic enclaves in Central Square and East Cambridge.
Cantabrigians, as residents are known, are a mixed breed, ranging from
French-cuisine doyenne Julia Child to detective novelist Robert Parker
(author of the gritty Spencer books) and William F. Weld, the former
governor. The more than 300,000 students ensure a cornucopia of cafés,
record stores, music clubs, street-chic boutiques, and bookstores, many
of which stay open until the wee hours.

The city dates from 1630, when the Puritan leader John Winthrop chose
this meadowland as the site of a carefully planned, stockaded village
he named Newtowne. Eight years later the town was renamed in honor
of the university in England at which most Puritan leaders had been
educated. In 1636, the Massachusetts Bay Colony established the
country's first college here, which was later named after one of its first
benefactors, John Harvard.

The old Cambridge that took shape around the 17th-century college
was a considerable journey from the several villages that grew up
within its borders. In time they broke away to form Lexington, Watertown, Arlington, and other towns, and in 1846 Cambridge itself was
incorporated as a city. It then included the industrial communities of
Cambridgeport and East Cambridge, which lie below it on the west
bank of the Charles River. Settled in the 19th century, these villages
produced furniture, brushes, caskets, bricks, glass, and reversible shirt
collars. By 1900, the population of these communities, made up of Irish,
Polish, Italians, and French Canadians, was eight times that of the Harvard end of town. MIT moved to Cambridge in 1916, and after World
War II heavy industry was rapidly replaced by firms engaged in camera manufacturing, electronics, and space research; these activities
were in turn succeeded by software developers in the 1980s and biotech-
nology in the '90s.

Cambridge, just minutes from Boston by MBTA, is easily reached on
the Red Line train to **Harvard Square.** The area is notorious for limited parking, so do consider taking the T. If you insist on driving, avoid
the local circling ritual by pulling into a garage. Your sanity may well
be worth the parking fees. Cambridge now has an office of tourism;
you may reach the very helpful staff at 617/441–2884 or 800/862–
5678.

HARVARD SQUARE

If elsewhere all roads lead to Rome, in Cambridge the street patterns
all point to Harvard Square. In addition to being the gateway to Har-

vard University and its various museums, the square boasts the venerable Passim folk-music club, the House of Blues, three movie theaters, one of the country's first cybercafés, and a bounty of clothing and home furnishings stores. Although Harvard Square draws the most tourists, other neighborhood squares exude their own charms. Inman Square, at the intersection of Cambridge and Hampshire streets, has a fine concentration of restaurants; Central Square has funky eateries and music clubs; Porter Square, farther west on Massachusetts Avenue, has several shopping centers, and, within the nearby Porter Exchange, a minimall of Japanese noodle and food shops. Kendall Square, near MIT, is home to a new independent movie complex and a branch of Legal Seafoods, a favorite restaurant for students to take visiting " 'rents" (parents). Still, Harvard Square is the best place to begin to feel like a native on a first visit to Cambridge.

Numbers in the text and margin correspond to numbers on the Cambridge map.

A Good Walk

A good place to begin your tour is the **Cambridge Information Booth** in **Harvard Square** ① near the MBTA station entrance, where you will find maps and information about the entire city (plus brochures that cover walking tours of Old Cambridge, seasonal events and—the most requested item—a guide to the local bookstores. Walk past the **Wadsworth House** ②, a clapboard house on Massachusetts Avenue that dates from 1726, and enter the dignified hush of **Harvard University**'s ③ Yard. After a stroll through the university's rarefied climes, exit the yard and cross Massachusetts Avenue to view the **Old Burying Ground and First Parish Church** ⑤ on the corner of Church Street and Massachusetts Avenue. Through the iron railing of the cemetery, you can make out a number of 17th- and 18th-century tombstones of ministers, early Harvard presidents, and Revolutionary War soldiers. Turn right and cross over to **Dawes Island** ⑥ in the middle of Garden Street to see the historical plaques mounted on signposts and the bronze horseshoes embedded in the sidewalk. Continue up Garden Street to **Christ Church** ⑦, designed in 1759 and still an active parish. The Cambridge Common, across Garden Street, makes a nice place for a picnic or break.

The next portion of this walk is particularly good if you have children. Retrace your steps along Massachusetts Avenue, crossing Mass. Ave. at the crosswalk near the First Parish Church. Cut through Harvard Yard bearing to your left and look for the striking Victorian architecture of **Memorial Hall.** (Ask any student for directions if you're disoriented.) Just past Memorial Hall is Kirkland Street; turn right and follow it to Divinity Avenue, onto which you turn left. At 6 Divinity, you'll find **Harvard Semitic Museum** ⑧, a fine place to view Egyptian art, and at 11 Divinity, an entrance to the extensive complex of **Harvard Museums of Cultural and Natural History** ⑨. You and your offspring can happily spend the rest of the afternoon here. If you are inclined toward art, it's about a 15-minute walk through Harvard Yard to Harvard's impressive **Fogg** ⑩ and **Arthur M. Sackler** ⑪ museums on Quincy and Broadway streets, respectively.

In good weather, beginning back at Harvard Square, you can walk along Massachusetts Avenue to reach the bustle and ethnic diversity of urban Central Square (where there are some wonderful Middle Eastern and Indian spots for lunch), and into the warehouselike openness of the Kendall Square area, where the 135-acre campus of the **Massachusetts Institute of Technology** ⑫ dominates the neighborhood. If the weather is poor, take the T Red Line heading inbound from Harvard Square two stops to Kendall Square. The **MIT Museum** ⑬ merits a visit.

TIMING

Budget at least two hours to explore Harvard Square, plus at least three more if you plan to go to either Harvard's cultural and history museums or the art museums. The walk down Massachusetts Avenue to MIT will take an additional 30 to 45 minutes (much less if you catch the T, as suggested just above), and you could easily spend an hour or two on the MIT campus admiring its architecture and visiting its museum or the List gallery. Even in cold weather the distances between sites should not be off-putting.

Sights to See

⑪ **Arthur M. Sackler Museum.** The richness of the Orient and artistic treasures of the ancient Greeks, Egyptians, and Romans fill three of the four floors of this modern structure. The permanent collections, which include Chinese, Japanese, Buddhist, Indian, and Islamic works, are installed on a rotating basis. The admission fee also grants you entrance to the Fogg Museum. ⊠ *485 Broadway,* ☎ *617/495–9400.* 🎟 *$5, free Sat. 10–noon and after 4:30.* ☉ *Mon.–Sat. 10–5, Sun. 1–5.*

☾ **Cambridge Multicultural Arts Center.** Ranging from colorfully creepy Mexican Day of the Dead festivals to gospel concerts, from African drumming to Argentine tangos, from Korean dance to Jewish storytelling, the multiethnic events the center hosts are aimed at promoting cross-cultural understanding. While many events are geared for youngsters, adults can also enjoy lectures, workshops, ongoing art exhibits, and concerts. ⊠ *41 2nd St.,* ☎ *617/577–1400.* 🎟 *Gallery free, admission charge for events.* ☉ *Gallery, weekdays 10–5; open during events.*

Cambridge Visitor Information Booth. At this volunteer-staffed kiosk, just outside the MBTA station entrance, you will find maps, brochures and guides—in several languages—about the entire city. Material available includes a historic walking tour, an excellent guide to the bookstores in the Square and beyond, and a guide to seasonal events. The booth is supervised by the Cambridge Tourism office (⊠ 18 Brattle St., ☎ 617/441–2884 or 800/862–5678). ⊠ *Zero Harvard Sq.,* ☎ *617/ 497–1630.* ☉ *Mon.–Sat. 9–5, Sun. 1–5.*

❼ **Christ Church.** This picturesque structure was designed in 1761 by Peter Harrison, the country's first trained architect. During the Revolution, its mostly Tory congregation fled for their lives and the church was used as a soldiers' barracks during the Siege of Boston. Washington ordered it reopened for services on New Year's Eve, 1775. Step into the vestibule to look for the bullet hole left by either British or Revolutionary forces. The church was reopened in 1790 and has an active parish to this day. The interior is airy and elegant in its simplicity. ⊠ *Zero Garden St.,* ☎ *617/876–0200.* ☉ *Sun.–Fri. 7:30–6, Sat. 7:30–3. Sun. services at 8, 10, 12:30, 5 during academic yr. Services at 8, 10 in June, July, Aug.*

❻ **Dawes Island.** Paul Revere, move over. The traffic island in the middle of Garden Street, called Dawes Island, is studded with bronze horseshoes, a bicentennial gift from descendants of William Dawes, a tanner who galloped through Cambridge spreading the alarm "The British are coming," on the eve of the 1775 Battle of Lexington (although, of course, in those days, he wouldn't have used those exact words, as the colonists considered themselves British). Dawes, unlike fellow rider Revere, managed to elude capture by the British. Signs on the island provide additional information. Across Garden Street, through an ornamental arch, is **Cambridge Common,** a public park since 1631. Here, on July 3, 1775, George Washington is said to have taken command of the Continental Army under a large elm. A bronze plaque now marks the site of the "Washington Elm." A striking recent addition is the Irish Famine Memorial by Derry artist Maurice Herron, unveiled in 1997 to coincide with the 150th anniversary of "Black '47," the deadliest year of the potato famine. It shows a desperate Irish mother sending her child off to America.

★ ⑩ **Fogg Art Museum.** Seldom has so much been packed into so small a space. Harvard's most famous art museum is a virtual history of art in the world, stunningly arranged in a way intended to stimulate, not overtax. Opened in 1895, and occupying its current space since 1927, the collection of more than 80,000 works focuses primarily on European, American, and East Asian works; it has notable collections of Italian Renaissance paintings and 19th-century French Impressionists, including Renoir and Monet. There are also works by Gauguin, Van Gogh, Whistler, Klee, and Kandinsky. A landscape by John Singer Sargent was labeled controversial because it was obtained while Singer was still alive, the first time the museum had collected a contemporary work. The museum's exterior design was deliberately kept simple and dignified to reflect the institution's academic as well as artistic mission. The interior courtyard, however, is grand; it reproduces an Italian Renaissance court of the 16th century. The museum has an impressive collection of decorative arts, including American and English silver, and the most curious and distinctly uncomfortable Harvard University "President's Chair," used only at commencement.

A ticket to the Fogg also gains admission to Harvard's **Busch-Reisinger Museum,** in the Werner Otto Hall entered through the Fogg. From the serenity of the Fogg's old masters, you step into the jarring and mesmerizing world of German Expressionists and other 20th-century artists. The museum was founded in 1902 as the university's "Germanic Museum," but its collections now include the modern art considered "degenerate" by the Nazis and art from Central and Northern Europe. ⊠ *32 Quincy St.,* ☏ *617/495–9400.* ✉ *$5.* ☉ *Mon.–Sat. 10–5, Sun. 1–5.*

☝ ⑨ **Harvard Museums of Cultural and Natural History.** Many museums promise something for every member of the family; the Harvard museum complex actually delivers. This vast brick building fulfills the plan of the Swiss naturalist Louis Agassiz; his idea was to bring under one roof the study of all kinds of life: plants, animals, and humankind. It contains four distinct museums within its walls, all accessible through one admission fee.

The **Peabody Museum of Archaeology and Ethnology** (⊠ 11 Divinity Ave., ☏ 617/495–2248) holds one of the world's outstanding anthropological collections; exhibits focus on Native American and Central and South American cultures, along with displays on Africa. Learn to pronounce the clicks in the bush country language of Ju wasi or marvel at plaster reproductions of pre-Columbian obelisks. The Hall of the North American Indian is particularly outstanding.

The **Museum of Comparative Zoology** (⊠ 26 Oxford St., ☏ 617/495–3045) traces the evolution of animals and humans. You can't miss—literally—the 42-foot-long skeleton of the underwater *Kronosaurus.* A live fire-ant farm and a zoo of stuffed exotic animals can occupy young minds for hours.

Oversized garnets and crystals sparkle at the **Mineralogical and Geological Museum** (⊠ 24 Oxford St., ☏ 617/495–4758), founded in 1784. The museum also contains an extensive collection of meteorites, as well as scale models of volcanoes and well-known mountains.

Cambridge

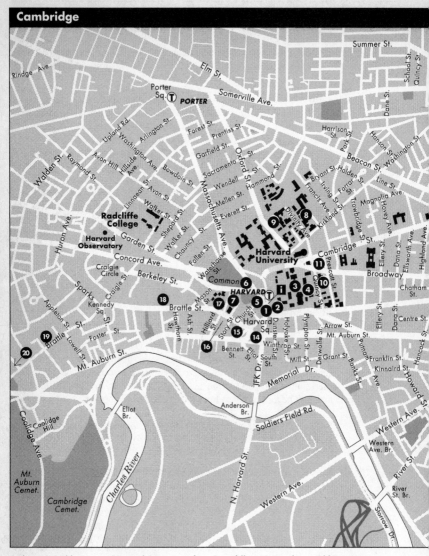

Arthur M. Sackler
Museum, **11**

Brattle House, **15**

Christ Church, **7**

Dawes Island, **6**

Dexter Pratt
House, **16**

Fogg
Art Museum, **10**

Harvard Museums of
Cultural and Natural
History, **9**

Harvard Semitic
Museum, **8**

Harvard Square, **1**

Harvard University, **3**

Hooper-Lee-Nichols
House, **19**

Longfellow National
Historic Site, **18**

Massachusetts
Institute of
Technology, **12**

MIT Museum, **13**

Mt. Auburn
Cemetery, **20**

Old Burying
Ground and First
Parish Church, **5**

Radcliffe College, **17**

Wadsworth House, **2**

Widener Library, **4**

Winthrop Park, **14**

But perhaps the most famous exhibits of the museum complex are the glass flowers in the **Botanical Museum** (⊠ 26 Oxford St., ☎ 617/495–3045), which were created as teaching tools that would never wither and die. Renting the taped tour will help you to appreciate fully these 3,000 models of 847 plant species, meticulously re-created in glass by a father and son in Dresden, Germany, who worked continuously from 1887 to 1936. Even more amazing than the colorful flower petals are the delicate roots of some plants; frequent signs assure the viewer everything is, indeed, of glass. ⊡ $4; free Sat. 9–noon. ⊙ Mon.–Sat. 9–5, Sun. 1–5.

8 **Harvard Semitic Museum.** This Harvard institution serves as an exhibit space for Egyptian and ancient Middle East artifacts and as a center for archaeological exploration. Here you may discover *how* the pyramids were excavated, not just *what* was discovered inside. The small gift shop is stocked with such intriguing items as a papyrus-making kit. Rotating exhibits treat varied subjects, such as the history of writing. The building also houses the Department of Near Eastern Languages and Civilization—the permanent exhibit space upstairs serves as a classroom. ⊠ *6 Divinity Ave.*, ☎ *617/495–4631.* ⊡ *Free.* ⊙ *Weekdays 10–4, Sun. 1–4.*

1 **Harvard Square.** Gaggles of students, street musicians—known as buskers—homeless people hawking the paper *Spare Change* (as well as asking for some), end-of-the-world preachers, and political-cause proponents make for a nonstop pedestrian flow at this most celebrated of Cambridge crossroads. Not a square at all, Harvard Square is where Massachusetts Avenue (locally, Mass Ave.), coming from Boston, turns and widens into a triangle broad enough to accommodate a brick peninsula (beneath which the MBTA station is located). Sharing the peninsula is the Out-of-Town newsstand, a local institution that occupies the restored 1928 kiosk that used to be the entrance to the MBTA station. Harvard Square is walled on two sides by banks, restaurants, and shops, and on the third by Harvard University.

3 **Harvard University.** Although its name is often cited to exemplify Boston-speak, as in "paak the caa in Havaad Yaad," the shade-dappled expanse of Harvard Yard—the very center of Harvard University—itself exudes peace and gentility. It has been that way for more than 300 years. In 1636 the Great and General Court of the Massachusetts Bay Colony established the country's first college here. Named in 1638 for John Harvard, a young Charlestown clergyman who died·that year, leaving the college his entire library and half his estate, Harvard remained the only college in the New World until 1693, by which time it was firmly established as a respected center of learning. Today, the country's finest university encompasses various schools or "faculties," including the medical school, law school, Radcliffe College, the John F. Kennedy School of Government, and the Faculty of Arts and Sciences.

Although the college dates from the 17th century, the oldest buildings in Harvard Yard are of the 18th century; together the buildings chronicle American architecture from the Colonial era to the present. **Holden Chapel,** built in 1742, is a Georgian gem. The graceful **University Hall** was designed in 1815 by Charles Bulfinch. An 1884 statue of John Harvard by Daniel Chester French stands outside; ironically for a school with the motto of "Veritas," the model for the statue was a member of the class of 1882, as no contemporary likeness of Harvard himself survived. **Sever Hall,** designed in 1878 by Henry Hobson Richardson, represents the Romanesque revival that was followed by the classical (note the pillared facade of Widener Library) and the neo-Georgian (represented by the sumptuous brick houses along the Charles River).

Harvard's four oldest buildings—Massachusetts Hall, Holden Chapel, Hollis Hall, and Harvard Hall—were occupied by patriot regiments during the Revolution. Just north of the Yard is **Memorial Hall,** completed in 1878 as a memorial to Harvard men who died in the Union cause; it is high Victorian both inside and out. It also contains the 1,200-seat Sanders Theater, site of concerts by national and local talent and the festive Christmas Revels. **Memorial Church,** a graceful steepled edifice of modified colonial design, was dedicated in 1932. One of the more striking examples of public art on the campus, in front of the Science Center, is the 1984 Tanner Fountain, a 60-foot round environmental work combining stone, steam, and water, by Peter Walker.

Many of Harvard's cultural and scholarly facilities are important sights in themselves; for complete information on the Arthur M. Sackler Museum, the Fogg Art Museum, the Harvard University Museums of Cultural and Natural History (including the Peabody Museum), and Widener Library, *see* their separate listings.

The **Harvard University Information Office,**run by students, offers maps of the university area and a free hour-long walking tour of Harvard Yard. The tour does not include visits to museums, but it provides a fine orientation and will give you ideas for further sightseeing. ⊠ *Holyoke Center, 1350 Massachusetts Ave.,* ☎ *617/495–1573.* ⊘ *During academic year, weekdays at 10 and 2, Sat. at 2; mid-June–Aug., Mon.–Sat. at 10, 11:15, 2, and 3:15, Sun. at 1:30 and 3.*

List Visual Arts Center. Founded by Albert and Vera List, pioneer collectors of modern art, this MIT center has three galleries showcasing exhibitions of cutting-edge art and mixed media that often seek to challenge conventional ideas about culture. ⊠ *Weisner Bldg., 20 Ames St.,* ☎ *617/253–4680.* ▧ *Free.* ⊘ *Oct.–June, Tues.–Thurs. noon–6, Fri. noon–8, weekends 12–6; closed July–Sept.*

⑫ **Massachusetts Institute of Technology.** Celebrated for both its brains and its cerebral sense of humor, the Massachusetts Institute of Technology occupies 135 acres bordering on the Charles River. The campus may once have been dismissed as "the factory," particularly by its Ivy League neighbor, and its graduates considered confirmed eggheads, but with true "Revenge of the Nerds" flair, MIT and its graduates are sharpening the cutting edge of the information revolution. MIT students are also renowned for their brazen "hacks," or tricks, which often spoof the university's image.

Founded in 1861, MIT moved to Cambridge from Copley Square in the Back Bay in 1916 with great panoply, and it has long since fulfilled the predictions of its founder, the geologist William Barton Rogers, that it would surpass "the universities of the land in the accuracy and the extent of its teachings in all branches of positive science." Its emphasis shifted in the 1930s from practical engineering and mechanics to the outer limits of scientific fields. World War II stimulated war research, and MIT has played a major role in producing instrumentation and guidance devices for NASA.

Obviously designed by and for scientists, the MIT campus is divided by Massachusetts Avenue into the West Campus, devoted to student leisure life, and the East Campus, where the heavy work is done. The West Campus has some extraordinary buildings. The **Kresge Auditorium,** designed by Eero Saarinen, with a curving roof and unusual thrust, rests on three, instead of four, points. The nondenominational **MIT Chapel,** a circular Saarinen design, is lighted primarily by a roof oculus that focuses natural light on the altar, and by reflections from the water in a small surrounding moat; it is topped by an aluminum sculpture by Theodore Roszak. The serpentine **Baker House** was designed in 1947 by the Finnish architect Alvar Aalto in such a way as to provide every room with a view of the Charles River. Sculptures by Henry Moore and other notable artists dot the campus.

The East Campus, which has grown around the university's original neoclassical buildings of 1916, also has outstanding modern architecture and sculpture, notably the high-rise **Green Building** by I. M. Pei, which houses the Earth Science Center. Just outside is Alexander Calder's giant stabile, entitled *The Big Sail*, designed as a wind baffle so that the revolving doors in Pei's building would function despite unplanned-for wind resistance. Another Pei work on the East Campus is the **Wiesner Building**, designed in 1985, which houses the **List Visual Arts Center** (☞ *above*). The **Great Dome**, which looms over Killian Court, has at various times supported a telephone booth with a ringing phone, a life-size statue of a cow, and a campus police cruiser—all traditional student hacks, or pranks. Another domed structure is the **Rogers Building** (✉ 77 Massachusetts Ave.). From its front doors, students can walk throughout the East campus without ever coming up for air, via a series of hallways and tunnels. MIT wags have dubbed this "the infinite corridor."

The Institute maintains an information center and offers free tours of the campus weekdays at 10 and 2. ✉ *77 Massachusetts Ave., Bldg. 7,* ☎ *617/253–4795.* ☼ *Weekdays 9–5.*

⓭ MIT Museum. A place where art and science meet, the MIT Museum showcases photos, paintings, and scientific instruments and memorabilia. A popular ongoing exhibit is the "Hall of Hacks," a look at the pranks MIT students have played over the years; the exhibit includes the campus police cruiser, lights flashing, which was "parked" atop the Great Dome in 1994. The museum also has an extensive collection of alluring holograms, including the "Light Forest Gallery"—a holographic room filled with the sights and sounds of the rain forest. ✉ *265 Massachusetts Ave.,* ☎ *617/253–4444.* 💰 *$3.* ☼ *Tues.–Fri. 10–5, weekends noon–5; closed Mon. and holidays.*

Administered by the MIT Museum, the **Hart Nautical Gallery** harbors a small but outstanding collection of ship models plus changing exhibits on the history of shipbuilding. ✉ *77 Massachusetts Ave., Bldg. 5, 1st floor,* ☎ *617/253–5942.* 💰 *Free.* ☼ *Daily 9–8.*

❺ Old Burying Ground and First Parish Church. Next to the imposing church on the corner of Church Street and Massachusetts Avenue is a spooky-looking colonial graveyard. You can make out through the iron railing of the cemetery a number of 17th- and 18th-century tombstones of ministers, early Harvard presidents, and Revolutionary War soldiers. The wooden Gothic Revival church was built in 1833 by Isaiah Rogers. Today, it provides space to the Nameless Coffeehouse, one of New England's oldest donation-run coffeehouses. The church also sponsors a popular crafts fair during the Christmas season. ✉ *3 Church St.,* ☎ *617/876–7772; 617/864–1630 for recorded Nameless Coffeehouse information.* ☼ *Church: Winter, weekdays 8–4; summer, weekdays 8–2. Sun. service at 10:30, church open until 1.*

❷ Wadsworth House. On the Harvard University side of Harvard Square stands the Wadsworth House, a yellow clapboard structure built in 1726 as a home for Harvard presidents. It served as the first headquarters for George Washington, who arrived on July 2, 1775 to take command of the Continental Army, which he did the following day.

❹ **Widener Library.** One of the country's largest collections of books, Harvard University's Harry Elkins Widener Library was named for a young book lover who went down with the *Titanic*—it is said that he went back to his stateroom for a first edition of Bacon's *Essays* which he had left behind. The Widener boasts a Gutenberg Bible, a Shakespeare folio, and dioramas of Cambridge as the city appeared in 1667, 1775, and 1936. The building is open to the public, but access to its stacks is reserved for those with a Harvard affiliation or special permission, and visits are not especially encouraged. ⊠ *Harvard Yard*, ☎ *617/495–2411.* ☺ *During academic yr, weekdays 9 AM–10 PM, Sat. 9–5, Sun. noon–5. Hrs may vary during class breaks, particularly on weekends and evenings.*

BRATTLE STREET/TORY ROW

Brattle Street remains one of New England's most elegant thoroughfares. Elaborate mansions line both sides from where it meets John F. Kennedy Street to the Fresh Pond Parkway. Brattle Street was once dubbed "Tory Row" because during the 1770s its mansions (numbering seven), situated on lands that stretched to the river, were owned by staunch supporters of King George. These properties were appropriated by the patriots when they took over Cambridge in the summer of 1775. Many of the historic houses are marked with blue signs, and although only two are open to the public, it's easy to imagine yourself back in the days of Emerson and Thoreau as you stroll the brick sidewalks. Less than 2 mi down Brattle Street from Harvard Square, Mt. Auburn Cemetery, an exquisitely landscaped garden cemetery, is a fitting finale.

Numbers in the text correspond to numbers in the margin and on the Cambridge map.

A Good Walk

Begin your walk at **Winthrop Park** ⑭, a small open space surrounded by bookstores, music shops, clothing stores, and restaurants near the juncture of Mt. Auburn and John F. Kennedy Street. From here, walk one block along Mt. Auburn as it curves to your right to reach Brattle Street. Proceeding on Brattle Street past a shopping complex that includes a huge HMV Records, you pass on your left the **Brattle Theater,** followed by the **Brattle House** ⑮, an 18th-century colonial that now serves as headquarters of the Cambridge Center for Adult Education. Another block and you pass on the left the yellow **Dexter Pratt House** ⑯, also known as the **Blacksmith House,** which was immortalized in Longfellow's "The Village Blacksmith" (it, too, houses activities of the Cambridge Center for Adult Education, as well as a small eatery). Continue up Brattle just past Hilliard Street. On your left is the Loeb Drama Center, home to the American Repertory Theatre, which takes up nearly the entire block at 64 Brattle Street. Across Brattle Street on your right is **Radcliffe College** ⑰.

Continue on Brattle to the next corner with Ash Street to find the **Stoughton House,** at the corner of Ash and Brattle streets. Just one block farther is the **Henry Vassall House,** at the intersection of Hawthorn Street. Across Brattle Street to your right, and just yards farther at 105 Brattle, is **Longfellow National Historic Site** ⑱, a mansion built in 1759 by John Vassall, Jr. Inside this well-appointed mansion, which is open to the public, you can pick up more detailed information about the houses on this tour. Continuing along Brattle, you'll reach 149, the **Lechmere-Riedesel House.** At 159 Brattle, you can see the interior of one of these houses: The **Hooper-Lee-Nichols House** ⑲ is open for tours on Tuesday and Thursday afternoons. At 175 Brattle, the **Ruggles-Fayerweather**

House, a white Georgian structure built in 1764, was taken over by revolutionaries in August of 1775 and served as a hospital after the Battle of Bunker Hill. At the corner of Elmwood Avenue and Fresh Pond Parkway is **Elmwood** (⊠ 33 Elmwood).

Continue west, cross the Fresh Pond Parkway and follow Brattle to where it meets Mt. Auburn Street. **Mt. Auburn Cemetery** ⑳ is a few blocks up on your left. After exploring the cemetery (maps are provided) you can retrace your steps or catch bus Number 71 or 73 just outside the cemetery to get back to the Square. Or you can follow Mt. Auburn east, cross over to Memorial Drive on your right and walk back along the Charles River to JFK Street. This is especially nice on summer Sundays when this section of Memorial Drive is closed to car traffic. The annual Head of the Charles Regatta, held in October, can be seen from along the paths that line the Charles.

TIMING

If you opt to walk all the way to Mt. Auburn Cemetery (it is about 1½ mi from Longfellow National Historic Site), allot three to four hours for a leisurely stroll. This trip is not recommended in inclement weather.

Sights to See

⑮ **Brattle House.** This 18th-century gambrel-roof Colonial once belonged to the Loyalist William Brattle, who moved to Boston in 1774 to escape the patriots' anger, then left in 1776 with the British troops. From 1831 to 1833 it was the residence of Margaret Fuller, feminist editor of *The Dial;* today it is the headquarters of the Cambridge Center for Adult Education and is listed on the National Register of Historic Places. It is one of the seven Tory Houses. ⊠ *42 Brattle St.,* ☎ *617/547–6789.* ▨ *Free.* ☉ *Mon.–Thurs. 9–9, Fri. 9–7, Sat. 9–2.*

Brattle Theatre. The square's longtime independent movie house, the Brattle, survived the home video revolution and now shows foreign, obscure, or classic films, from nouveau to noir. In conjunction with the nearby bookstore WordsWorth, it also hosts free readings by well-known authors. ⊠ *40 Brattle St.,* ☎ *617/876–6837.*

NEED A
BREAK?

Algiers Café (⊠ 40 Brattle St., ☎ 617/492–1557), upstairs from the Brattle Theatre, is a favorite student hangout. Linger over your mint tea and hummus, and don't expect rapid service. It's open until midnight weekdays, until 1 AM Fridays and Saturdays.

⑯ **Dexter Pratt House.** Also known as the **"Blacksmith House,"** the yellow Colonial Dexter Pratt House is now owned by the Cambridge Center for Adult Education. The tree itself is long gone, but this spot inspired Longfellow's lines: "Under a spreading chestnut tree, the village smithy stands." The blacksmith's shop, now commemorated by a granite marker, was next door, at the corner of Story Street. ⊠ *56 Brattle St.,* ☎ *617/547–6789.* ▨ *Free.* ☉ *Mon.–Sat. 9–6.*

NEED A
BREAK?

The Hi-Rise Bread Company at the Blacksmith House Bakery (☎ 617/876–8766), on the first floor of the Dexter Pratt House, is the perfect stop for a pick-me-up coffee and fresh-baked treat or sandwich. The bakery here was first known as the Window Shop, which evolved during World War II to provide employment for German and Eastern European refugees from Nazism.

Elmwood. A three-story Georgian house built in 1767 by the colonial Governor Thomas Oliver and later home to the Lowell family, Elmwood House is now the residence of Harvard University's president. ⊠ *33 Elmwood Ave.*

Henry Vassall House. One of the seven Tory Houses occupied by wealthy families linked by friendship, if not blood, the house may have been built as early as 1636. In 1737 it was purchased by John Vassall, Sr.; four years later he sold it to his younger brother, Henry. It was used as a hospital during the Revolution, and the traitor Dr. Benjamin Church was held here as a prisoner. The 8-foot square chimney dates from the mid-17th century. The house was remodeled during the 19th century. ✉ *94 Brattle St.*

⑲ Hooper-Lee-Nichols House. Home to the Cambridge Historical Society, this is one of three Tory-era homes on Brattle Street open to the public. (The Emerson family gave it to the society in 1957). Built between 1685 and 1690, the house has been remodeled at least six times; your tour guide will obligingly pull off false fronts to show layers of the various eras. The downstairs is elegantly, although sparsely, appointed with period books, portraits, and wallpaper. An upstairs bedroom has been preserved to represent the 1850s; in the children's room there's a Victorian dollhouse and other toys. The house's models of Brattle Street in pre-Revolutionary times evoke the days when there were only seven homes along the street, all surrounded by formal gardens and farmland. Visits by tour only. ✉ *159 Brattle St.,* ☎ *617/547–4252.* ▨ *$5.* ☉ *Tues., Thurs. 2–5.*

Lechmere-Riedesel House. During the revolution, this Georgian gem and architectural conundrum became the prison/home of the loyalists Baron and Baroness Riedesel. Still, the Baroness managed to entertain lavishly during her house arrest, writing, "Never have I chanced on such an agreeable situation." In 1869, the structure was lifted and a new first story inserted. In 1886, the entire house was moved from 145 Brattle to its current location and its top story was removed. ✉ *149 Brattle St..*

★ ⑱ Longfellow National Historic Site. This elegant mansion was once home to Henry Wadsworth Longfellow—the poet whose stirring renditions about the Village Blacksmith, Evangeline, Hiawatha, and Paul Revere's midnight ride thrilled 19th-century America (and who was, surname to the contrary, a short man). Formally called the Vassall-Craigie-Longfellow House after its various occupants, the house was used by George Washington as his residence during the siege of Boston from July 1775 to April 1776. He and wife Martha celebrated their 17th anniversary here with a Twelfth Night party in January of 1776. The house, built in 1759 by John Vassall, Jr., is one of the seven original Tory Row homes on Brattle Street. Longfellow first boarded here in 1837 and later received the house as a gift from his new father-in-law on his marriage to Frances Appleton, who burned to death here in an accident in 1861. For 45 years Longfellow wrote his famous verses here and filled the house with the exuberant spirit of his own work and that of his literary circle, which included Ralph Waldo Emerson, Nathaniel Hawthorne, and Charles Sumner, an antislavery senator. Even in Longfellow's day, the house was a draw for visitors who wanted to tread the floors where Washington once stood.

Among the lovely antiques and furnishings of the house, most of which Longfellow himself would remember fondly, note the Gilbert Stuart family portraits, the bust of Washington set upon sections of the Washington Elm, and the simple but haunting portrait of Fanny Longfellow hung in their bedroom. But the place of pride goes to the intricately carved "Spreading Chestnut" chair, handcrafted from the tree under which the village smithy stood—a present from the schoolchildren of Cambridge after the city cut down the tree to widen Brattle Street. Across Brattle Street is **Longfellow Park,** created to preserve the beautiful view—which extends almost to the river—immortalized in the poet's "To the River Charles." Ironically, a monument here to Longfellow, sculpted by Daniel Chester French, partially blocks the view the park was intended to safeguard. Among the many pamphlets offered for sale is "Footprints on the Sands of Time," a self-guiding tour of Longfellow's Cambridge. ⌂ *105 Brattle St.,* ☎ *617/876–4491.* ⌦ *$2.* ☉ *Mid-Mar.–May and Nov.–mid-Dec., Wed.–Fri. noon–4:30, weekends 10–4:30; June–Oct., Wed.–Sun. 10–4:30 for guided tours only; last tour departs at 4. Gardens open year-round for a self-guided tour.*

⑳ Mt. Auburn Cemetery. This was one of the country's first garden cemeteries, and it remains one of the loveliest. Since it opened in 1831, more than 80,000 people have been buried here, among them Henry Wadsworth Longfellow, Mary Baker Eddy, Winslow Homer, Amy Lowell, Dorothea Dix, and Charles Bulfinch. Buckminster Fuller's stone bears an engraved geodesic dome. The warbler migrations in the fall and the glorious spring blossoms make this a popular spot with bird-watchers and nature lovers. Two tour maps are available at the gate: one for horticultural points of interest, the other for tombstones of note. Picnicking, jogging, and bicycling are not permitted. ⌂ *Mt. Auburn St., Cambridge,* ☎ *617/547–7105.* ☉ *Summer, daily 8–7; winter, daily 8–5. T stop, Harvard; then Watertown or Waverly Bus to cemetery.*

⑰ Radcliffe College. More than just the "female" half of Harvard, Radcliffe continues to strive to redefine its mission in a time of coeducation. Its lovely and serene yard is the heart of the college, founded in 1879 "to furnish instruction and the opportunities of collegiate life to women and to promote their higher education." Still an independent corporation within Harvard University—to which it was wedded in 1977—Radcliffe maintains its own physical plant, including the Agassiz Theater. The college also sponsors events, programs, and workshops devoted to women's issues. ⌂ *10 Garden St.*

Stoughton House. Built circa 1883, this shingled house was designed by the noted architect H. H. Richardson, who also planned Austin and Sever Halls at Harvard and **Trinity Church** in Boston (☞ Chapter 2). ⌂ *Corner of Ash and Brattle Sts..*

| NEED A BREAK? | Once beyond the vicinity of Harvard Square, Brattle Street lacks eateries, so consider stocking up before your walk at **Dawin's Ltd.** (⌂ 148 Mt. Auburn St., ☎ 617/354–5233) which offers Cambridge-inspired sandwiches and other "comestibles and spirituous provisions." |

⑭ Winthrop Park. Once an 18th-century marketplace and now part and parcel of **Harvard Square** (☞ *above*), this grassy knoll is a great time-out spot (its benches are hotly contested) and is surrounded by a panoply of shops and restaurants, including the largest Swatch store in the world and Grendel's Den, a favorite student hangout.

4 Dining

Victorian Boston's ideal of yeoman food in aristocratic surroundings influenced all America, and all America still imagines Bostonian gentry dining on fish cakes and yesterday's baked beans. Today, in fact, the great dining rooms are gracefully yielding to a flush of creative little bistros. Boston dining can be world class, a world tour, worlds to come, or a world in 10 tables. It's often seafood; sometimes challenging flavors; sometimes comfort food. And still a great place for a lobster dinner whether you like yours simply boiled or nouvelle-fangled wood-grilled with wild seasonings.

Updated by
Robert
Nadeau

IT IS ONLY A MYTH THAT THE BOSTONIANS OF HISTORY hated food. Really, it was only unfamiliar food they disdained. Their chowders and codfish cakes, baked beans and apple pies rolled across America and sailed around the world—why would they need anything else to eat? The boiled dinner and breakfast hash that fed the farm hands could be served in fine dining rooms just as well—it was only thrifty common sense.

Their successors and descendants have reversed priorities. Bostonians now want innovative food without formality. They get it in some of the best casual restaurants in the world. Today's Boston certainly has palaces of grand cuisine to rival those of the cultural capitals, but Boston—and especially Cambridge—also has a kind of great restaurant that is similar only to those of San Francisco and New Orleans: restaurants overseen by creative masterminds concocting apparently divinely inspired food, served in very human surroundings by waiters and waitresses who are less suave than enthusiastic and knowledgeable.

Boston now has caught the passion for craft-baked breads, brew-pubs with homemade ales, espresso shops with fine cakes or with computers, and all other exquisite and unique specialties. Ice creams have been central to Boston living for 150 years, and every gourmet restaurant here has a few unusual flavors.

What Boston diners most enjoy is what every Boston visitor should seek out as well—the fish and shellfish that have always inspired the best Boston cooking. Although the city has many notable restaurants specializing in seafood, you can find at least two or three offerings from the sea *anywhere* you choose to eat. Where the treatments used to be limited to lobsters boiled or baked, fish broiled or fried, nowadays sauces are permitted. If the chef has pretensions, you may be offered a lobster sausage or wood-roasted lobster with a vanilla sauce. In a Chinese restaurant, the lobster will be stir-fried with ginger and scallion, and the gray sole served with the fried whole fins. Your chowder may be traditional with milk and potatoes, or experimentally Caribbean. To get the real flavor of Boston today, eat seafood at a place that's small.

Currently, the New England commercial fishery for cod, haddock, and flatfish has been almost shut down to conserve stocks. But the shortage has provoked a wonderful burst of creative cooking with lesser-known delicacies such as monkfish, wolf fish, tilefish, ocean perch, ocean catfish, skate wings, and squid. Striped bass, once fished to near-extinction, are back on the summer table, followed by New England's seasonal delicacies: harpooned swordfish and tuna steaks, Maine shrimp, bay scallops, steamer clams, and Wellfleet oysters. When lobster prices rise too high, tasty deep-sea crabs appear.

You don't operate a seaport for 350 years without developing a few outside interests, but Boston has developed an appetite for exotic, foreign cuisines that would have shocked a clipper captain. Anything spicy and different has long been popular in the university culture of Cambridge, but the high immigration of recent decades has given Bostonians and visitors a special chance to taste all the world's delicacies. A few are in settings that evoke the bygone aristocracies—and the cuisines—of Russia, Persia, Thailand, Afghanistan, or Cambodia. Many more serve large immigrant communities from Latin America, Asia, and some countries of Europe and Africa—but welcome the merely curious to their tables. These restaurants are not especially Bostonian except in their use of seafood, and in the way Boston diners now foster authentic foreign restaurants.

BONUS MILES MAKE
GREAT SOUVENIRS.

Earn Miles With Your MCI Card.

Take the MCI Card along on this trip and start earning miles for the next one. You'll earn frequent flyer miles on all your calls and save with the low rates you've come to expect from MCI. Before you know it, you'll be on your way to some other international destination.

Sign up for MCI by calling 1-800-FLY-FREE

Is this a great time, or what? :-)

Earn Frequent Flyer Miles.

AmericanAirlines
A'Advantage

Continental Airlines
OnePass

▲ Delta Air Lines
SkyMiles

HAWAIIAN AIRLINES.

MIDWEST EXPRESS AIRLINES

NORTHWEST AIRLINES
WORLDPERKS

Rapid Rewards
SOUTHWEST AIRLINES

MILEAGE PLUS.
United Airlines

US AIRWAYS
DIVIDEND MILES

You've read the book. Now book the trip.

For all the best deals on flights, hotels, rental cars, and vacation packages, book them online at www.previewtravel.com. Then click on our Destination Guides featuring content from Fodor's and more. You'll find hotels, restaurants, attractions, and things to do around the globe. There are even interactive maps, videos, and weather forecasts. You'll have everything you need to make your vacation exactly what you want it to be. All it takes is a trip online.

Travel on Your Terms™
www.previewtravel.com
aol keyword: previewtravel

preview travel℠

New England's own food is still widely served in the tourist version, but a young generation of highly trained and well-traveled chefs are reclaiming the regional cuisine by treating the six-state region as though it were a province of France or Italy. It turns out that our wild mushrooms work in a ragout, cheddar makes a fine quiche, and butternut squash or lobster fit into savory ravioli.

Boston is resistant to chain restaurants and puts its own twists upon food fads. Yes, it went through a Mediterranean period, followed by a spate of bistros with a little plate of Pan-Asian everything. But the Mediterranean era quickly turned to Tunisian and Moroccan flavors. And the recent rush of fusion bistros is doing great things with Atlantic seafood.

The dominant trend however, is homegrown. Boston is the special home for small bistro-style restaurants with highly flavored food. Gifted chefs have scattered out among the neighborhoods, infiltrated the established places on the restaurant rows, and now dominate the scene in Cambridge.

To find the best of Boston—gustatorily speaking—follow the roads that radiate out from downtown like the spokes of a giant wheel. Smack inside the hub are the huge, and hugely famous, waterfront seafood restaurants—but go north, or west and south, and you're suddenly into the neighborhoods, home to numerous smaller restaurants on the way up.

Restaurant Reservations and Dress Codes

Reservations are always a good idea; we note only when they're essential or when they are not accepted. Book as far ahead as you can, and reconfirm when you get to town. Unless otherwise noted, the restaurants listed are open daily for lunch and dinner. We mention dress only when men are required to wear a jacket or a jacket and tie.

CATEGORY	COST*
$$$$	over $40
$$$	$25–$40
$$	$15–$25
$	under $15

*per person for a three-course meal, excluding drinks, tip, and 5% sales tax

BOSTON

Back Bay/Beacon Hill

This upscale neighborhood is home to Newbury Street, Commonwealth Avenue, and lots of enticing restaurants. Toward Beacon Hill, restaurants and the dining rooms of the large hotels get to be more dressy. Around Massachusetts Avenue, the Back Bay's western border, things are looser at the bistros and espresso bars that predominate.

Contemporary

$$$$ ✕ **Ambrosia.** Chef Tony Ambrose likes his flavors vivid and his platters tall, from an ostrich meat appetizer to "grilled lamb rack and saddle on a crisp potato layered with morbier cheese and served with a caper eggplant vinaigrette." Take down the French decorations, and the food is haute Yankee, based on native ingredients. The decor is designer-chic: burnished woods, floor-to-ceiling glass windows, and an ever-changing arrangement of modern art on the walls. ⊠ *116 Huntington Ave.,* ☎ *617/247–2400. Reservations essential. AE, MC, V. No lunch weekends.*

$$$$ ✕ **Aujourd'hui.** The formula for Aujourd'hui's success has been to speak softly and attract a discreet crowd. This formal dining room of the Four Seasons Hotel has become one of the city's power rooms. The food reflects an inventive approach to regional ingredients and new American cuisine. Some entrées, such as rack of lamb with fontina polenta, can be extremely rich, but the seasonal menu also offers "alternative cuisine" and vegetarian choices. Window tables overlook the Public Garden. ⊠ *200 Boylston St.,* ☎ *617/351–2071. Reservations essential. Jacket required. AE, DC, MC, V.*

$$$$ ✕ **Biba.** Arguably Boston's best restaurant, and surely one of the most
★   original and high-casual restaurants in America, Biba is a place to see and be seen, from the vividness of the dining room's rambling mural to the huge street-level people-watching windows of the downstairs bar. The menu encourages inventive combinations, unusual cuts and produce, haute comfort food, and big post-modern desserts. Take your time, and don't settle for the "classic lobster pizza" if something like "crusted ocean perch" is available. The wine list is an adventure. ⊠ *272 Boylston St.,* ☎ *617/426–7878. Reservations essential. D, DC, MC, V.*

$$ ✕ **Brew Moon.** Instead of the usual industrial decor of a brewpub, the flagship of this minichain looks like a California Zen health food palace and has rather flashy food, although with an emphasis on the salty and peppery morsels that call out for beer. Save room for serious desserts. Also in Harvard Square, Cambridge. ⊠ *115 Stuart St.,* ☎ *617/742–5225.* ⊠ *Cambridge: 50 Church St., Harvard Square,* ☎ *617/499–2739. AE, DC, MC, V.*

$$ ✕ **Cena.** Brand new and red hot, Cena (pronounced like Latin, "*kaynah*") is capturing the Symphony crowd with a bistro menu of worldbeat flavors that quietly drops red meat and barely mentions chicken and cheese. They do it with a full palette of vegetables and starches, herbal oils, and exotic spices.⊠ *14 Westland Ave.,* ☎ *617/262–148. AE, D, MC, V.*

$$ ✕ **Sonsie.** Café society blossoms along Newbury Street, particularly at the elegant Sonsie, where much of the clientele either sips coffee up front or angles for places at the bar. The restaurant is famous for breakfasts (open daily at 7) that extend well into the afternoon for late risers. During warm weather months, the entire front of Sonsie becomes an open-air café looking out on upper Newbury Street. The dishes on the menu are basic bistro with an American twist, such as pan-seared fish sandwich with spicy tartar sauce. ⊠ *327 Newbury St.,* ☎ *617/351–2500. AE, MC, V.*

Continental

$$$$ ✕ **Ritz-Carlton Dining Room.** A traditional restaurant in the best sense of the word, The Ritz has subly modernized the menu while keeping the classic rack of lamb, roast beef hash, broiled scrod, and such seasonal Yankeeisms as shad roe in May and June. The true glory of the Ritz is the service, aristocratic in its detail, democratically offered to all. Second-floor windows provide a commanding view of the Public Garden. All in all, it's the perfect place to allow your grandmother to take you after college graduation. ⊠ *15 Arlington St.,* ☎ *617/536–5700, ext. 6286. Reservations essential. Jacket and tie. AE, D, DC, MC, V.*

Cuban

$$ ✕ **Mucho Gusto Cafe.** On a bohemian block full of jazz students from Berklee College sits this hospitable Cuban restaurant with *I Love Lucy* decor (most of it for sale) and terrific food. The kitchen excels at black bean soup, eggplant salad, french-fried onions, and Cuban sandwiches. The coffee makes you want to get up and dance to the old mambos that are always playing. ⊠ *1124 Boylston St.,* ☎ *617/236–1020. Reservations for fewer than five not accepted. No credit cards. No lunch Mon.–Wed.*

French

$$$$ ✕ **L'Espalier.** An elegantly modernized Victorian Back Bay town house
★ is the setting for what some critics consider Boston's best restaurant. Chef-owner Frank McClelland creates an intoxicating blend of new French and newer American cuisine. You can simplify the opulent menu by choosing a prix fixe tasting menu, such as the innovative vegetarian *dégustation*. With two fireplaces and subtle decor in truffle colors, the downstairs is among Boston's most romantic places—the front salon is known as the Courtship Room, the back parlor as the Seduction Room. Upstairs is the Library, more masculine and clubby. ⊠ *30 Gloucester St.,* ☎ *617/262–3023. Reservations essential. Jacket and tie. AE, D, DC, MC, V. Closed Sun. No lunch.*

Japanese

$$ ✕ **Miyako.** A very competitive sushi bar amid many at this end of Back Bay, this little spot also offers estimable hot dishes, including *age shumai* (shrimp fritters), *hamachi teriyaki* (yellowtail teriyaki), and *age dashi* (fried bean curd). Ask for one of the tatami rooms if you have a big party. ⊠ *279A Newbury St.,* ☎ *617/236–0222. AE, DC, MC, V.*

Persian

$$$ ✕ **Lala Rokh.** This is one of the best western Asian restaurants in the
★ United States, a beautifully detailed and delicious fantasia upon Persian food and art, specifically the Azerbaijanian corner that is now Northwest Iran. The wall art is treasured Persian miniatures and medieval maps. The food includes exotically flavored specialties, and dishes as familiar (but superb here) as eggplant purée, pilaf, kebabs, *fesanjoon* (the classic pomegranate-walnut sauce), and lamb stews. The staff obviously enjoys explaining the menu, and the wine list is well selected for foods that often defy wine matches. ⊠ *97 Mount Vernon St.,* ☎ *617/720–5511. AE, DC, MC, V. No lunch.*

Seafood

$$$ ✕ **Legal Sea Foods.** What began as a tiny restaurant upstairs over a
★ Cambridge fish market has grown to important regional status, with locations in Chestnut Hill, Kendall Square in Cambridge, and now Washington, DC. The hallmark, as always, is extra-fresh seafood. As the organization has matured, it has applied the same standards to the trimmings and the wine list. Once puritanically simple preparations have loosened up to include Chinese and French sauces, and woodgrilling is now the preparation of choice. Rhode Island clam chowder *with tomatoes* has been allowed onto the menu alongside the traditional Boston milk chowders. The smoked bluefish pâté is one of the finest appetizers anywhere. Dishes come to the table in whatever order they come out of the kitchen, as freshness is held to be more important than the order of courses. If you miss a flight at Logan Airport, a Legal restaurant there can make it the most delicious missed flight of your life. Or you can stop in at the Legal shop at Logan (⊠ Terminal C, ☎ 617/568–2809) and pick up some chowder, pâté, shellfish, and lobster to take home with you. ⊠ *35 Columbus Ave., Park Sq.,* ☎ *617/ 426–4444.* ⊠ *Cambridge: 5 Cambridge Center, Kendall Sq.,* ☎ *617/*

Boston Dining

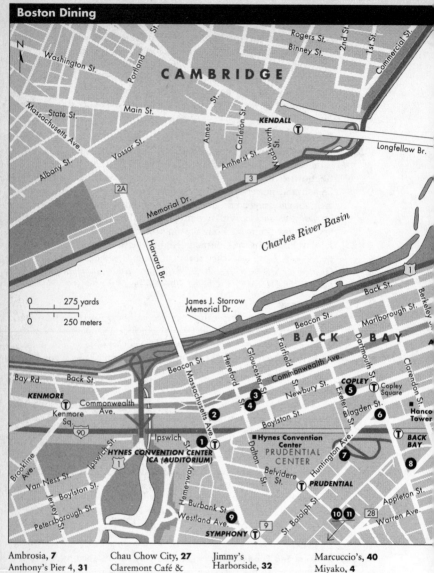

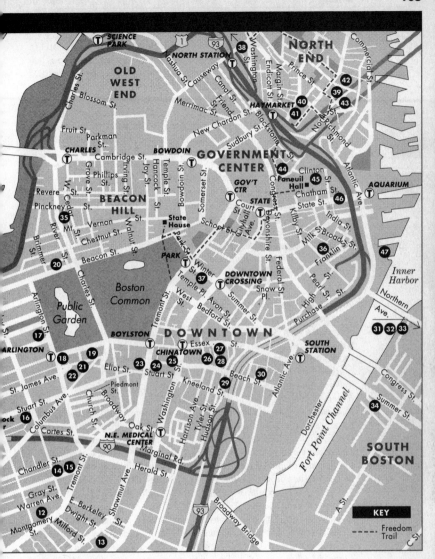

Rabia's Ristorante, **41**

Red Herring, **20**

Ritz-Carlton Dining
Room, **17**

Rowes Wharf
Restaurant, **48**

Sonsie, **2**

Tatsukichi-Boston, **46**

Turner Fisheries of
Boston, **6**

Union Oyster
House, **44**

864–3400. ⊠ *Logan Airport: Terminal C,* ☎ *617/569–4622. Reservations not accepted. AE, D, DC, MC, V.*

$$$ ✕ **Turner Fisheries of Boston.** On the first floor of the Westin Hotel in Copley Square, Turner Fisheries is second only to Legal Sea Foods (☞ *above*) in its traditional appeal and has outstripped it in trimmings and service. Turner broils, grills, bakes, fries, and steams everything in the ocean, but also applies classic and modern sauces, vegetables, and pasta with panache. Any meal should begin with the creamy chowder (the restaurant having won Boston's yearly Chowderfest competition too many times to contend any more). ⊠ *10 Huntington Ave.,* ☎ *617/ 424–7425. Reservations essential. AE, D, DC, MC, V.*

$$ ✕ **Legal C Bar.** What a headline: "Staid Legal Sea Foods Backs Haitian Chef Novilus Petit-Frère in Caribbean Restaurant!" You get the standard, superb Legal fried calamari or wood-grilled scallops with tropical side dishes, or impeccable conch fritters, Bermuda fish chowder, and acra (St. Lucia-style codfish cakes). There are great rum drinks, too. Efforts at Island atmosphere (Caribbean gear hung on white tile walls) don't quite make Boston into a beach, but the food is outstanding. ⊠ *27 Columbus Ave.,* ☎ *617/426–5566. Reservations not accepted. AE, D, DC, MC, V.*

Steak

$$$ ✕ **Grill 23.** Gray business suits predominate at this steak house while dark paneling, comically oversized flatware, and waiters in white jackets give it a men's-club ambience: Yet seafood, such as the roasted monkfish with caramelized golden beets, outsells beef by a narrow margin. Outstanding is the word for the rotisserie tenderloin with Roquefort mashed potatoes and for the only meatloaf in the world served with mashed potatoes and truffle oil. ⊠ *161 Berkeley St.,* ☎ *617/542–2255. Reservations essential. Jacket and tie. AE, D, DC, MC, V. No lunch.*

$$$ ✕ **Library Grill at the Hampshire House.** Downstairs, usually marked by a massive line of tourists, is the Bull & Finch Pub, the model for the TV sitcom *Cheers.* Upstairs, the Library Grill serves classic steak and lobster in an elegant setting overlooking the Public Garden, making this an apt choice for dinner after the Brahmin tour of Beacon Hill or before the theater. There is valet parking after 5 PM. ⊠ *84 Beacon St.,* ☎ *617/227–9600. Reservations essential. AE, D, DC, MC, V.*

$$$ ✕ **Morton's of Chicago.** A Chicago-based chain with an un-Bostonian display of raw meat and live lobsters, but the best, dry-aged, prime Angus steak in town, Morton's is packed and often noisy. If you brave the 1½ hour-Saturday wait, you deserve the 24-ounce T-bone.⊠ *1 Exeter Plaza,* ☎ *617/266–5858. Reservations essential. AE, DC, MC, V. No lunch weekends.*

Charlestown

This little neighborhood across Boston Harbor contains the Bunker Hill Monument, the USS *Constitution,* and one culinary landmark, the famous Olives, a standout among otherwise homey taverns that serve the locals.

Mediterranean

$$$ ✕ **Olives.** The pacesetting bistro is named for an important Mediter-
★ ranean flavor and for Olivia English, who runs the front of the house while her husband, Todd English, minds the wood-fired brick oven and the spit-roasting in the kitchen. It set the local standards for grilled pizza, piled-on platters of delicious things, "vertical food," and such smart signature offerings as the open-face roast lamb sandwich. The crowded seating, noise, long lines, and abrupt service only add to the legend. Come early or late—or be prepared for an extended wait: Reservations

are taken only for groups of six or more at 5:30 or 8:30 PM, and there are few nearby alternatives. ⊠ *10 City Sq.,* ☎ *617/242–1999. AE, DC, MC, V. Closed Sun., Mon. No lunch.*

Chinatown

Boston's large Chinatown is the focal point for Asian cuisines of all types, from authentic Cantonese and Vietnamese to Malaysian, Korean/Japanese, and Mandarin food. Many places are open after midnight while the rest of the city sleeps or lurks. It's definitely worth the adventure, especially if you're tracking down the current rage: live-tank seafood prepared in Hong Kong or Chiu Chow styles.

Chinese

$$ ✕ **Chau Chow.** *Chiu Chow* (or Chaozhou in China) is the word for
★ people from Shantou (formerly Swatow) in China's Guangdong province. They and their wonderful seafood cuisine migrated all over Southeast Asia and around the world, introducing other cultures to clams in black bean sauce, steamed sea bass, gray sole with its fried fins, or any dish with their famous ginger sauce. Chau Chow has expanded to a larger storefront called **Grand Chau Chow**, right across the street, which has live-fish tanks, accepts credit cards, and looks a little nicer on the outside. Your best bet is not to order from the menu per se, but to look around at what others are eating and order that way. It's not as rude as it sounds. ⊠ *50-52 Beach St.,* ☎ *617/426–6266. No credit cards.* ⊠ *41–45 Beach St.,* ☎ *617/426–6266. AE, D, MC, V.*

$$ ✕ **Chau Chow City.** This is the newest, biggest, glitziest, and most versatile production yet from the Chau Chow dynasty, on three floors, with dim sum by day and live-tank seafood by night. Chiu Chow cooking is so attuned to seafood that the "Swatowese-style braised duck" has more seafood than duck meat. Overwhelmed? Order the clams in black bean sauce. ⊠ *83 Essex Street,* ☎ *617/338–8158. AE, D, MC, V.*

$$ ✕ **Imperial Seafood.** On the first floor is a wonderful (and seldom crowded) Cantonese restaurant specializing in seafood. The livelier second floor is a large, airy dining room with the most extensive dim sum selection in Chinatown. Dim sum denotes both the meal (a veritable Chinese brunch, served daily 8:30–3:30) and the variety of dumplings and buns, tiny spareribs, morsels of pork, chicken, clams, shrimp, and other foods that you select from roving carts and pay for by the item. Pointing is fine. The selection is wider when the restaurant is more crowded with weekend shoppers, mostly suburban Chinese-Americans. ⊠ *70 Beach St.,* ☎ *617/426–8543. AE, DC, MC, V.*

$$ ✕ **New Shanghai.** Boston's Chinese restaurants aren't generally of the linen-tablecloth variety found on New York's East Side, but New Shanghai is moving that way. The "old" Shanghai was an island of Mandarin-Szechuan food in the Chinatown sea of southern cuisines; the new one does Szechuan dishes well but has concentrated on Shanghai-style braises and such cold appetizers as red-cooked beef and crisp eels. ⊠ *21 Hudson St.,* ☎ *617/338–6688. AE, MC, V.*

Malaysian

✕ **Penang.** Penang is a resort island with a history like that of nearby Singapore and an extraordinary cuisine of many influences—Malaysian, Chinese, Indian, Thai, and a bit of British Trader Vic. It all comes together in this very popular restaurant that has people coming back repeatedly for favorites like the mashed-taro "yam pot" stir-fries; the house special squid with a dark, spicy sauce; exotic salads; an Indonesian beef curry called *rendang;* and enormous fried "oatmeal" shrimp, all washed down with umbrella drinks. The open kitchen makes things loud but exciting. ⊠ *685–691 Washington St.,* ☎ *617/451–6372. Reservations accepted for six or more only. MC, V.*

Downtown

Boston's downtown scene revs up at lunchtime, but the streets get very quiet after five o'clock, when everyone goes back to the suburbs. The city center is great for after-hours dining, especially around the artist's colony in the former Leather District.

Continental

$$$$ ✕ **Locke-Ober Café.** It used to be that the only times the downstairs Men's Café was open to women were the night of the Harvard-Yale game and New Year's Eve, when the nude painting of "Mademoiselle Yvonne" was draped. That changed in 1972, one of the few alterations since Louis Ober's Restaurant Parisien (founded 1875) was merged with Frank Locke's Wine Rooms in 1894. The ancient kitchen struggles to put out traditional Continental favorites, like a flashy steak tartare, and unique Victoriana like Lobster Savannah (lobster with pimiento, green pepper, mushroom, sherry wine, and Parmesan cheese). If you want to eat here for the experience, stick to simple steaks and seafood. There is valet parking after 6 PM. ⊠ *3 Winter Pl.,* ☎ *617/542–1340. Reservations essential. AE, D, DC, MC, V. No lunch weekends.*

French

$$$$ ✕ **Julien.** Start with the handsomest dining room in the city—a soar-
★   ing space that used to be the boardroom of the Federal Reserve Bank, complete with Renaissance-revival gilded cornices and limestone walls. Then top it all off with some of the best French food in Boston, mas-terminded by French-trained chefs (currently Eric Truglas) advised by a succession of Michelin-starred consulting chefs from France who like to do something nouvelle with the lobsters. Little wonder Julien has become a favorite with French business travelers and Boston Francophiles who enjoy the detail of a great Parisian restaurant in their own home-town. The menu marries modern French cuisine and native New En-gland ingredients. ⊠ *Hotel Meridien, 250 Franklin St.,* ☎ *617/451–1900, ext. 7120. Reservations essential. Jacket and tie. AE, D, DC, MC, V. Closed Sun. No lunch Sat.*

$$$ ✕ **Les Zygomates.** *Zygomates,* in French, are the muscles on the human
★   face that make you smile—and this combination wine bar/bistro will certainly do that. In a world of culinary overstatement, Les Zygomates serves up classic French bistro fare that dares to be simple and simply delicious. The menu is clearly designed to match up beautifully with the ever-changing wine list, with all wines served by the two-ounce taste, six-ounce glass, or bottle. Most bottles are priced at retail or just a bit above. Les Zygomates offers prix-fixe menus at both lunch and din-ner. Pan-seared catfish with house vinaigrette and roasted rabbit leg stuffed with vegetables typify the taste. ⊠ *129 South St.,* ☎ *617/542–5108. Reservations essential. AE, DC, MC, V. No lunch weekends.*

Japanese

$$ ✕ **Tatsukichi-Boston.** Sushi and sashimi are specialties, as are pot-cooked dinners and *kushiagi* (deep-fried kebabs). Meals are served in a modern Japanese setting with Western or tatami room seating. Up-stairs is a popular karaoke lounge. It's a favorite with Japanese busi-ness travelers and tourists. ⊠ *189 State St.,* ☎ *617/720–2468. AE, D, DC, MC, V. No lunch weekends.*

Thai

$$ ✕ **Montien.** A favorite with theatergoers, Montien serves Southeast Asian classics like *pla sarm ros* (spicy whole fish) and *pad thai* (noodles with shrimp, tofu, and peanut sauce) as well as dishes seldom seen on Thai menus: *kat thuong-tong* (chicken tartlets with corn and coriander) and cupid wings (stuffed boneless chicken wings). With its canopied booths, chandeliers, and large silk-flower table arrangements, the dining room has a romantic atmosphere. ⌧ *63 Stuart St.,* ☎ *617/338–5600. AE, D, DC, MC, V. No lunch weekends.*

Faneuil Hall

Perfect for fueling up for the Freedom Trail, this attraction is a tourist magnet and packed with people eating from its fast-food concessions inside. There are a number of more serious alternatives, though, if you're not on a schedule, and if you've seen enough of Faneuil Hall and want a change of scene, you shouldn't rule out a walk under the express-way to the North End (☞ *below*).

American

$$ ✕ **Durgin Park.** Diners here should be hungry enough to cope with enor-mous portions, yet not so hungry they can't tolerate an intolerably long wait. Durgin Park was serving its same hearty New England fare (In-dian pudding, baked beans, corned beef and cabbage, and a prime rib hanging over the edge of the plate) back when Faneuil Hall was a working market instead of a tourist attraction. The service is famously brusque bordering on rude bordering on good-natured. ⌧ *340 Faneuil Hall Mar-ketplace, North Market Bldg.,* ☎ *617/227–2038. AE, D, DC, MC, V.*

$$ ✕ **Union Oyster House.** Established in 1826, the Union Oyster House is Boston's oldest continuing restaurant. My advice is to have what Daniel Webster had—oysters on the half-shell at the ground-floor raw bar, which is the oldest part of the restaurant, and still the best. The rooms at the top of the narrow staircase are dark and have low ceilings—very Ye Olde New England—and plenty of non-restaurant history. Uncom-fortably small tables and chairs tend to undermine the simple, decent, but expensive food. There is valet parking after 6 PM. ⌧ *41 Union St.,* ☎ *617/227–2750. AE, D, DC, MC, V.*

North End

The North End is Boston's oldest immigrant neighborhood. At the end of the 19th century, Paul Revere's house was a crowded tenement, and black-clad Italian grandmothers still push past suburban foodies to get the best of the local groceries. Boston's most authentic Old Country restaurants are here (as you might guess, the smaller the place, the bet-ter the kitchen is), along with charming coffee shops serving up great espresso and cannoli. In recent years, small storefront restaurants have been converting from red-sauce tourist traps to innovative trattoria. In summer, the area hosts a series of patron-saint festivals, which draw the hordes for fun and food.

Italian

$$$ ✕ **Mamma Maria.** What happens when an Italian restaurant has an Irish chef? Chianti mashed potatoes. No joke. Despite the clichéd name, Mamma Maria is one of the most elegant and romantic restau-rants in the North End, from the homemade pasta to the innovative sauces and entrées, to the North End's best desserts; you can't go wrong with the daily tiramisu or specials like chocolate hazelnut cake with a cold champagne sabayon and raspberry compote. ⌧ *3 North Sq.,* ☎ *617/523–0077. AE, DC, MC, V.*

$$$ ✕ **Rabia's Ristorante.** Inside this perfectly good red-sauce spaghetti-and-veal joint is a serious, seasonal seafood restaurant at almost twice the price. Watch the sandwich board outside for specials like softshell crabs, yellowfin tuna steak, or frutti di mare and make your move early. Many North End restaurants are cutting out dessert, but Rabia's has made it a strength. ⌧ *73 Salem St.,* ☎ *617/227-6637. Reservations essential. AE, D, DC, MC, V.*

$$ ✕ **Marcuccio's.** Chef Charles Draghi is a pioneer in the use of transparent, highly flavored broth-sauces, as weirdly effective as transparent beer. His rosewater-tinged desserts, his veal marsala, and the grilled vegetables among his many antipasti also stand out. There is a tasting menu, so you needn't miss anything. The space is post-modern art, in an appetizing way. ⊠ *125 Salem St.,* ☎ *617/723–1807. No credit cards. Sun. brunch but no lunch. Closed Mon. and Tues.*

$$ ✕ **Pomodoro.** Because it's right next door to the Daily Catch (☞
★   *below*), crafty couples can beat the odds against a long wait by splitting up, with one person in line for seafood and the other in line for Pomodoro. This tiny gem of a trattoria is worth the wait, with excellent country Italian favorites such as white beans with various pastas, roasted vegetables, and a fine salad of field greens. The walls are decorated with lacquered cutlery, and the wine list is exceptional. Best choice could well be the clam and tomato stew with herbed flat bread—don't forget to enjoy it with a bottle of Vernaccia. ⊠ *319 Hanover St.,* ☎ *617/367–4348. No credit cards.*

Seafood

$$ ✕ **Daily Catch.** Shoulder-crowding small, this storefront restaurant
★   specializes in calamari dishes, lobster *fra diavolo* (in spicy marinara sauce), and linguine with clam sauce. You've just got to love this place—for the noise, the intimacy, and above all, the food. There's something about a big skillet of linguine and calamari that would seem less perfect if served on fine white china. ⊠ *323 Hanover St.,* ☎ *617/523– 8567. Reservations not accepted. No credit cards.*

South End

Boston's South End is a highly mixed neighborhood, home to a large number of the city's lesbian and gay professionals, and it is continuing to experience an upscaling trend, with more and better restaurants opening all the time. Eventually, Back Bay prices may infiltrate the South End, but until then, enjoy all the great food at something of a discount— even at the Soho-like restaurant row at the bend of Tremont Street.

Contemporary

$$$ ✕ **Hamersley's Bistro.** Gordon Hamersley has earned a national rep-
★   utation, thanks to such signature dishes as grilled mushroom-and-garlic sandwich and cassoulet of duck confit, pork, and garlic sausage. He's one of Boston's great chefs and likes to sport a Red Sox cap instead of a toque. His place has a full bar, a café area with 10 tables for walk-ins, and a larger dining room that's a little more formal and decorative than the bar and café, though nowhere near as stuffy. ⊠ *553 Tremont St.,* ☎ *617/423–2700. D, MC, V.*

$$ ✕ **Franklin Cafe.** Among the dozens of new bistros in Boston, Franklin Cafe has jumped to the head of the class by keeping things simple yet effective. Beans and lentils as a side-dish/sauce for fish is a typical idea of this unpretentious bar, as is anything with its great garlic mashed potatoes. No desserts may be keeping it a little too simple, as the café is in a deserted block, not a desserted block. ⊠ *267 Shawmut Ave.,* ☎ *617/350-0010. No reservations. AE, MC, V.*

$$$ ✕ **Icarus.** Be ready for an exotic menu of real intensity. Inventive touchstones such as grilled shrimp with mango, jalapeño sorbet, and polenta with braised exotic mushrooms form the basis of the seasonally changing menu. The romantic two-tier dining room offers excellent service, and you're within walking distance of the theater district. An extensive wine list complements the fare. A different menu is served at Sunday brunch. Jazz is offered on Friday nights. ⊠ *3 Appleton St.,* ☎ *617/426–1790. Reservations essential. AE, DC, MC, V. No lunch Mon.–Sat.*

Italian

$$ ✕ **Appetito.** Sienese colors and hand-painted murals of people eating and imbibing set off a conditioned reflex for garlic-olive hunger, which this kitchen answers well with grilled seafood, gourmet pizzas, a very good plate of grilled vegetables, and an even better mixed grill of seafood over a terrific seafood risotto. It is much less formal than its neighbor Icarus (☞ *above*), so you can use it simply for a pizza stop, a late dessert, or an inexpensive theater restaurant, as it is just enough out of the theater district to make finding parking easier. Brunch is served on Sunday. ✉ *1 Appleton St.,* ☎ *617/338–6777. Reservations essential. AE, DC, MC, V. No lunch.*

Mediterranean

$$$ ✕ **Claremont Café & Lounge.** In a city full of bistros with limited service and Mediterranean food, this one is outstanding. Every stew and salad is ripe with flavor, and the intensely potent coffee and desserts don't let down that impression. Maybe the potato salads are the crucial clue, as the Peruvian-born owners have started to work a few dishes from that great cuisine into the evening menu, such as *aji de gallina,* a chicken fricaseed in mild chilis and garlic. It opens daily for breakfast at 7:30, and is open for brunch only on Sunday. ✉ *535 Columbus Ave.,* ☎ *617/423–2700. No credit cards.*

Mexican

$$ ✕ **Baja Mexican Cantina.** Anything-but-traditional Mexican food is served in a post-modern Southwest decor. Start with a margarita made from your choice of premium tequilas. All the Cal-Mex food that follows is quite good, with lots of vegetarian options. If you're health-conscious, go for the salads, relatively low-fat burritos, or the lean hamburger served in a tortilla. It's a good bet if you're looking for fresh air and an inexpensive meal near Copley Place, as this is just across the street and down the block. ✉ *111 Dartmouth St.,* ☎ *617/262–7575. AE, D, DC, MC, V.*

Pan-Asian

$$ ✕ **Jae's Café.** Jae's Korean-Californian fusion has a definite way of bringing the taste buds back to life. That's one reason why a young, happening crowd fills the place. They cram the sushi bar, delight in the dishes served in hot-stone pots, and like their rice noodles served with shrimp and dusted with sugar. The main dining room is adorned with a big fish tank, while outside a garden beckons (seating there is forbidden by their license). Upstairs, the joint is jumping with a big take-out and delivery business. In the summer, there's lots of sidewalk seating, the best spots of all. ✉ *520 Columbus Ave.,* ☎ *617/338–8586. AE, DC, MC, V.*

Waterfront

Tourists flock to Faneuil Hall and the Marketplace almost year-round, so tried-and-true cuisine tends to dominate. Some of Boston's most famous seafood restaurants live on the waterfront, naturally, and that's a big draw for the district.

Contemporary

$$$ ✕ **Rowes Wharf Restaurant.** Rowes Wharf itself is stunning, and the ★ restaurant in the Boston Harbor Hotel takes advantage of this, offering perhaps the city's finest waterfront view. The decor is highly traditional with plush upholstered armchairs, exquisite mahogany paneling, and shaded wall sconces. Chef Daniel Bruce creates scintillating modern menus between the field trips on which he takes his staff to hunt wild mushrooms—his personal passion. Sautéed local wild mushrooms over stone-ground polenta is, naturally, his signature composition. The Maine lobster sausage over lemon pasta has intense flavors and unforgettable essences of the sea. The restaurant has Boston's most extensive list of American wines. ⊠ *70 Rowes Wharf,* ☎ *617/439–3995. Reservations essential. Jacket required. AE, D, DC, MC, V.*

Seafood

$$$ ✕ **Anthony's Pier 4.** This massive theme park of a restaurant rolls along, somewhat uncertainly, hosting celebration dinners for Bostonians and visitors alike. The main drawback: the famous long wait for a table, designed—some complain—to sell drinks. Once seated you can dine very well on the top-quality seafood if you remember that simple preparations tend to be the best here. Watch for seasonal specials on swordfish, stone crabs, or soft-shell crabs—Anthony's likes to buy up the best. The wine list is remarkable, and there are scads of older wines at low prices. ⊠ *140 Northern Ave.,* ☎ *617/423–6363. Reservations essential. Jacket required. AE, D, DC, MC, V.*

$$$ ✕ **Jimmy's Harborside.** Rivaling Anthony's for celebrations and power-lunches, this exceedingly popular seafood establishment has aged more gracefully. The fish chowder is as fresh and bright-tasting as ever, and seasonal fish specials simply broiled or fried are excellent. You will fish through a lot of cream sauce to find the traditional finnan haddie, however. The wine list is almost all-American, with oversized bottles a specialty, and wisely divided by match-ups, although we would reverse things and have chardonnay with oysters and Reisling with lobster. ⊠ *242 Northern Ave.,* ☎ *617/423–1000. Reservations essential. AE, DC, MC, V. No lunch Sun.*

$$ ✕ **The Barking Crab Restaurant.** It is, believe it or not, a seaside clam shack plunk in the middle of Boston with a stunning view of the downtown skyscrapers. An outdoor lobster tent in summer, in winter it retreats indoors to a warm-hearted version of a waterfront dive, with chestnuts roasting on a cozy wood stove. In these surroundings, you'll want the classic New England clambake—chowder, lobster, steamed clams, corn on the cob—or the spicier crab boil. The fried food lags. ⊠ *88 Sleeper St. (Northern Ave. Bridge),* ☎ *617/426–2722. AE, DC, MC, V.*

$$ ✕ **No-Name Restaurant.** Famous for not being famous, the No-Name has been serving fresh seafood, simply broiled or fried, since 1917. Being right on the fish pier has its advantages, but the troubled New England fishing fleet provides fewer fish than it once did. Like they say, it is what it is, but it ain't what it used to be. ⊠ *15½ Fish Pier, off Northern Ave.,* ☎ *617/423–2705. No credit cards.*

BROOKLINE

Brookline is a nice way to get out of town without really leaving town. Although it's surrounded by Boston on all sides, this neighborhood has its own suburban flavor, seasoned with a multitude of historic—and expensive—residential houses and garnished with a diverse ethnic population that supports a string of sushi bars and an expanding list of kosher restaurants.

Cambodian/French

$$$ ✕ **Elephant Walk.** The Brookline location of Elephant Walk carries on
★ the tradition of its home base in Somerville (☞ *below*), except it's above ground, much larger, and goes deeper into both modern French platters and what the menu calls "challenging tastes"—such as a dip made from Cambodian shrimp paste. Elephant Walk teases the palate with an exotic assortment of dumpling appetizers, spring rolls that you wrap in fresh lettuce leaves, and outstanding coq au vin. The airy atmo-

sphere evokes a British Colonial hotel; the food reminds you of why Phnom Penh was "the Paris of Asia." ⊠ *900 Beacon St.,* ☎ *617/247–1500. AE, D, DC, MC, V.*

Contemporary

$$$ ✕ **Providence.** Chef Paul O'Connell had to wait out a recession as sous
★ chef for other top restaurants, but now he has established his own reputation with such dishes as smoked veal brisket with potato dumplings and crisp cod cheeks and lobster. The ambience is exotic with columns galore, a midnight-blue ceiling, and wrought-iron details. Brunch is served on Sunday. ⊠ *1223 Beacon St.,* ☎ *617/232–0300. AE, DC, MC, V. Closed Mon. No lunch.*

$$ ✕ **Zaftigs.** Here's something new and different, a contemporary version of a Jewish delicatessen. This food is almost never served without a thick sauce of nostalgia, so it is almost refreshing to have genuinely lean corned beef, a modest slice of cheesecake, low-sugar home-made borscht, and a lovely whitefish salad sandwich. Of course, a day later you're hungry again.⊠ *335 Harvard St.,* ☎ *617/975–0075. AE, D, DC, MC, V.*

Indian

$$ ✕ **Bombay Bistro.** One of Brookline's more pleasing and unusual restaurants, Bombay Bistro offers excellent north Indian cuisine with a couple of hot and spicy south Indian dishes like lamb vindaloo on the menu for good measure. Diners unfamiliar with Indian food should try any of the combination plates, especially the tandoori mix (an assortment of chicken, lamb, and shrimp cooked in a clay oven). The variety of specialty breads is impressive. ⊠ *1353 Beacon St.,* ☎ *617/734–2879. AE, D, DC, MC, V.*

Irish

$$ ✕ **Matt Murphy's Pub.** There are dozens of Irish pubs in Boston, some catering to Irish expatriates, some serving a well-drawn pint of Guinness (itself a gourmet item for aficionados). But none of these dozens of Irish pubs is notable for food, with this one exception. Despite servers with a brogue, Matt Murphy's makes real poetry out of thick slabs of bread and butter, giant soups, fish and chips served in a twist of newspaper, shepherd's pie, and hot rabbit pie—all served in enormous portions. Don't miss the homemade ketchup with your french fries. ⊠ *14 Harvard St., Brookline Village,* ☎ *617/232–0188. No credit cards.*

Japanese

$$$ ✕ **Ginza.** The Chinatown branch (⊠ 14 Hudson St., Boston, ☎ 338–
★ 2261) is thought to have the most advanced sushi in town and serves until 3:30 AM, but the Brookline location is just as good and gains extra points for its selection of 15 brands of hot sake. Avant-sushi these days include hot spices, fried morsels, boozy marinades, and presentations with props like a martini glass. A quick anthology is the "Ginza Surprise," consisting of a daily assortment of chef's eccentricities, such as "caterpiller maki," with avocado scales. There are lots of good appetizers and hot dinners as well, including teriyaki, tempura, and nabemono. ⊠ *1002 Beacon St. ,* ☎ *617/566-9688. AE, DC, MC, V.*

Kosher

$$ ✕ **Rubin's.** The last Jewish delicatessen in Boston serves a hand-cut pastrami sandwich a New Yorker can respect. There are kasha varnishkes (buckwheat with bow-tie noodles), hot brisket, and many other high-cholesterol classics, but, of course, no real cream for your coffee or dairy desserts. ⊠ *500 Harvard St.,* ☎ *617/731–8787. No credit cards. Closed Sat. No dinner Fri.*

$ ✕ **Rami's.** This small room is the best of all the falafel restaurants in Boston; its authentic *Zhoug* (Yemenite-style hot sauce) is green with fresh cilantro. The grilled chicken and the *bourekas* (savory pastries) are also stellar. The service tends to be quick and somewhat hurried, but Rami's is still a bit of a home-away-from-home for Israeli expatriates in the neighborhood. ✉ *324 Harvard St.,* ☎ *617/738–3577. No credit cards. Closed Sat. No dinner Fri.*

Malaysian

$$ ✕ **Pandan Leaf.** This highly popular Malaysian restaurant has good versions of the roti canai, coconut shrimp, and the yummy taro pots Boston knows from Penang, plus new specialties of its own: a mild barbecued stingray, sweet-and-spicy fried Indonesian chicken, and a very complicated and delicious raw fish salad served for two or more. Pleasant service warms noticeably when patrons are enthusiastic about the more exotic dishes. ✉ *250 Harvard St.,* ☎ *617/566-9393. AE, MC, V.*

Pan-Asian

$$$ ✕ **Bok Choy.** Siobhan Carew is the amazing Irishwoman who not only
★   set up an Irish bar with good food (Matt Murphy's) and an Italian success in the North End (Pomodoro), but now aspires to produce the best new Pan-Asian fusion menu in Boston. Bok Choy is dark and calm, less dressy than it would be in the South End, and no brogue shows in the scallion rice cake with spicy long beans, the fire roasted lamb with Malaysian red curry sauce, or the fried banana wontons. Many small plates can make this a less expensive stop for nibblers as well. ✉ *202 Washington St.,* ☎ *617/738–9080. No credit cards.*

Russian

$$ ✕ **Café St. Petersburg.** "Imperial Russian cuisine" is how it's billed, but the sprightly and elegant food is even better than how it sounds. Certainly the betuxed servers (in black tie even during lunch) spare us the Dostoevskian gloom and the Tolstoyan ironies. This tiny café is just a great place to eat, from the opening shot of frozen cranberry vodka and the superb "venigret" salad of beets and potatoes, to clean-tasting borscht, a neat *pozharski* (chicken burger) cutlet, and vegetarian treats like beet pancakes, vegetarian-stuffed cabbage with raisins, and dill-flavored eggplant caviar. Turkish coffee is the best dessert. There is live music many nights, and impressive modern Russian art on the walls. ✉ *236 Washington St., Brookline Village,* ☎ *617/277–7100. D, DC, MC, V.*

Seafood

$$ ✕ **Village Fish.** With one of the few raw bars west of Boston's waterfront, the Village Fish serves nothing but classic seafood, including terrific versions of fried calamari and the best grilled shrimp around. Best seats in the house are either at the bar or at a handful of tables on the bar side. ✉ *22 Harvard St., Brookline Village,* ☎ *617/566–3474. No credit cards.*

Thai

$$ ✕ **Sawasdee.** The dining room is chic but informal, and the food is outstanding and prettily decorated even compared with the other excellent Thai restaurants in the city. Multiple curries are the specialty of the house: red, green, or yellow, they pack an aromatic, spicy punch. Other recommendations include the Golden Bags appetizer (a deep-fried tofu pouch stuffed with seafood and vegetables) and the boneless spareribs, which are extremely spicy. ✉ *320 Washington St., Brookline Village,* ☎ *617/566–0720. AE, D, DC, MC, V.*

CAMBRIDGE/SOMERVILLE

Among other collegiate enthusiasms, Cambridge has a long-standing fascination with ethnic restaurants. A certain kind of great restaurant has also evolved here, mixing world-class cooking with a studied informality. Famous chefs, attired in flannel shirts, are reviving the craft of cooking with wood fires and borrowing flavors from every continent. For posher tastes and the annual celebrations that come with college life (or the end of it), Cambridge also has its share of linen-clothed tables.

Afghan

$$ ✕ **The Helmand.** Boston's first Afghan restaurant is named after a province of Afghanistan south of Kabul. It's run by refugees who came packing an exquisite cuisine, the plans for a lovely room built around a wood hearth, and a vision of service. They also arrived with recipes for three kinds of great rice, some fine sour soups, terrific *aushak* (ravioli stuffed with leeks), the various kebabs you might expect, and an excellent vegetarian menu you might not expect, with a number of choices grilled and stewed in novel ways. ⊠ *143 1st St. ,* ☎ *617/492–4646. AE, MC, V. No lunch.*

American

$ ✕ **Bartley's Burger Cottage.** It may be perfect cuisine for the student metabolism, but watch out for the huge variety of variously garnished thick burgers and the french fries and onion rings. There is a competent veggie burger for aging Harvard dons. The nonalcoholic "raspberry lime rickey," made with fresh limes, raspberry juice, sweetener, and soda water, is the must-try classic drink. Tiny tables in a crowded space make it a convenient place for phi beta eavesdropping. ⊠ *1246 Massachusetts Ave.,* ☎ *617/354–6559. Reservations not accepted. No credit cards. Closed Sun.*

Cambodian/French

$$$ ✕ **Elephant Walk.** The first location of the popular Cambodian-French
★ restaurant (Brookline, *above*), this one is based in multiethnic Union Square, an exciting tangle of restaurants and Italian, Portuguese, and Indian specialty groceries and shops just outside Cambridge. The chef, Langtaine de Monteiro, learned to manage a Cambodian kitchen as the wife of a diplomat, and for a time ran a restaurant in Provence. The common element is garlic, from a French appetizer like *moules* (mussels) swimming in garlic butter, to superb Cambodian spring rolls, delicate salads, and a red curry of surpassing fresh flavor. ⊠ *70 Union Sq., Somerville,* ☎ *617/623–9939. Reservations not accepted.AE, D, DC, MC, V.*

Caribbean

$$ ✕ **Rhythm & Spice.** Enjoy mild-mannered Jamaican-style food and soca music in this pretty restaurant, which has become the gathering spot for Boston's growing coterie of African-American academics and their friends. The best food includes the Gundy appetizer (a spread of chopped herrings and apples), gentle curries, and "festival" cakes made with cornmeal. When the soca DJ comes on later in the evening, the dance floor gets hot, hot, hot. ⊠ *315 Massachusetts Ave.,* ☎ *617/ 497–0977. MC, V. Closed Mon. No lunch.*

Chinese

$ ✕ **Lucky Garden.** A modest holdover from the first, golden period of Szechuan food in Cambridge, Lucky Garden still serves excellent hot-and-sour soup, *yu hsiang* scallops (with garlic, hot pepper, and ginger), chicken and peanuts, and fried dumplings in a pleasant, comfortable

Cambridge Dining

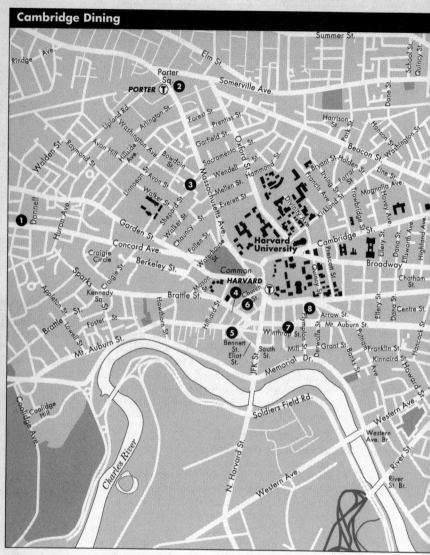

Bartley's Burger Cottage, **8**
Blue Room, **19**
Border Café, **6**
Casa Portugal, **13**
Casablanca, **4**
Chez Henri, **3**
Cottonwood Café, **2**
Daddy-O's Bohemian Café, **14**
East Coast Grill, **11**

Elephant Walk, **10**
Green Street Grill, **15**
The Helmand, **20**
La Groceria, **17**
Legal Sea Foods, **22**
Lucky Garden, **1**
Mary Chung Restaurant, **16**
Rialto, **5**
Rhythm & Spice, **18**
Salamander, **21**

Sandrine's Bistro, **7**
Sunset Café, **12**
Union Square Bistro, **9**

LECHMERE

CENTRAL

KENDALL

Massachusetts
Institute of
Technology

Charles River

Harvard
Bridge

Storrow
Drive

**HYNES CONVENTION CENTER/
ICA (AUDITORIUM)**

550 yards

500 meters

atmosphere. Liquor isn't served. ⊠ *282 Concord Ave.,* ☎ *617/354–9514. AE, D, MC, V.*

$ ✕ **Mary Chung Restaurant.** In the 1970s, Szechuan food was all the rage in Cambridge. Mary Chung's was one of the last high-quality restaurants to open, and became the chosen spot for a generation of MIT students. When Mary closed down, they set up their own Internet news group to reminisce about the Peking ravioli, *dun-dun* noodles (a cold appetizer of noodles in sesame paste), and other spicy delights. Mary finally had to reopen, and the meatiest "ravs" in Boston are back, along with the spicier *suan la chow show* (dumplings in soy soup), and such lesser-known specialties as toothsome chicken velvet (chicken blended with egg whites and stir-fried) and gingery-hot *yu hsiang* broccoli. ⊠ *464 Massachusetts Ave., Central Sq.,* ☎ *617/864–1991. Reservations not accepted. No credit cards.*

Contemporary

$$$$ ✕ **Salamander.** With an airy yet intimate layout of atrium seating, the
★ main dining room is expansive and paneled in dark woods—better yet, it's enticingly filled with aromas of wood and spice from a visible complex of wood-fired grills and ovens. Entrées are generous and appetizers are eccentric and flavorful, often Asian influenced. Favorites are the wood-grilled squid with coconut sauce and the pepper tenderloin over a ragout of wild mushrooms. For dessert, the banana wontons are deliciously indescribable. Best of all, the service is extremely well-paced. Salamander's wines by the glass are perhaps the best in town. ⊠ *1 Atheneum St.,* ☎ *617/225–2121. Reservations essential. AE, D, DC, MC, V. Closed Sun.*

$$$$ ✕ **Union Square Bistro.** A floor above the ethnic markets of Union Square
★ in Somerville is this airy room, true in spirit to the bistro ideal of offering warming foods to small, convivial groups. New chef David Smoke McCluskey's "native nouvelle" cuisine emphasizes American foodstuffs and game, prepared with a nod to his Native American heritage. Recent dishes have included venison with pemmican sauce made of black cherries and venison jerky, roast pumpkin and hazelnut soup, and sweet corn and walnut pudding with an Indian berry cream. Although familial service is an official cliché of the bistro movement, Union Square does it with some heart. Brunch is served on Sunday. ⊠ *16 Bow St., Union Sq., Somerville,* ☎ *617/628–3344. Reservations essential. AE, D, DC, MC, V.*

$$$ ✕ **Blue Room.** Totally hip, funky, and Cambridge, the Blue Room, led by Steve Johnson, the convivial owner-chef, blends a whole world of ethnic cuisines, with a new emphasis on Mediterranean small plates. Brightly colored furnishings, counters where you can meet others while you eat, and a friendly staff add up to a good-time place that's serious about the food it serves. A word of warning: At peak hours it can be a little too loud. An extraordinary brunch with a buffet of grilled meats and vegetables as well as regular breakfast fare plus a gorgeous array of desserts is served on Sunday. ⊠ *1 Kendall Sq.,* ☎ *617/494–9034. AE, D, DC, MC, V. No lunch Mon.–Sat.*

$$$ ✕ **East Coast Grill.** Owner-chef-author Chris Schlesinger built his na-
★ tional reputation on grilling and red-hot condiments. The Jamaican jerk, the North Carolina pulled pork, and the habañero-laced "pasta from Hell" are still here, but this restaurant has made an extraordinary play to establish itself in the front ranks of fish restaurants. Spices and condiments are more restrained, and Schlesinger has compiled a wine list bold and flavorful enough to share a table with the still highly spiced food. The dining space is completely informal. This is surely the best restaurant in America that also has a motorized wiggling fish as a bathroom joke. Brunch is served on Sunday. ⊠ *1271 Cambridge St.,* ☎ *617/491–6568. AE, D, MC, V. No lunch.*

$$$ ✕ **Green Street Grill.** The tables are small, the room is very plain, the
★   service is casual, and the bar next door mixes Bohemians with just-
plain drunks, but Caribbean-born co-owner-chef John Levins is one
of the living masters of mixing hot spices with other distinctive flavors.
A recent example: "Punished conch meat finished in sugar cane, curry,
coconut milk, Meyer's rum, grated cassava & lots of hot chili peppers."
But expect an entirely different—and elaborate—preparation with
Caribbean grouper or Muscovy duck. ✉ *280 Green St.,* ☎ *617/876–
1655. AE, MC, V. No lunch.*

$$ ✕ **Cottonwood Café.** This is Tex-Mex pushed to the next dimension.
★   The atmosphere is Nuevo-Wave-o, with exotic architectural touches
and rustic Southwestern details. Best of all is the Snake Bite appetizer:
deep-fried jalapeños stuffed with shrimp and cheese—impossible to re-
sist yet nearly too spicy-hot to eat. The Cambridge café is close to the
Porter Square stop on the T's Red Line, and another has opened in
Boston's Back Bay. ✉ *1815 Massachusetts Ave.,* ☎ *617/661–7440.*
✉ *Back Bay: 222 Berkeley St.,* ☎ *617/247–2225. Reservations essential.
AE, D, DC, MC, V.*

$$ ✕ **Daddy-O's Bohemian Café.** Decorated with soft-sculpture beatniks
and very popular with other chefs on their nights off, this is a relaxed
place with mildly pretentious home-style food, much of it in the key
of starch. Garlic mashed potatoes, four-cheese macaroni and cheese,
latkes, and bread puddings are justly popular, as are the mussel frit-
ters and the vast homemade pies. Sunday brunch is particularly pop-
ular. ✉ *134 Hampshire St., Inman Sq.,* ☎ *617/354–8371. D, MC, V.
No lunch.*

French

$$$ ✕ **Sandrine's Bistro.** Chef Owner Raymond Ost goes to his Alsatian
★   roots for flavors easy and intense, but this is a bistro only in the way
that little palace at Versailles was a country house. An early hit has
been flammekuche, the Alsatian onion pizza, but much else is haute
cuisine, like the trout Napoleon, or the *turbotin* (chicken turbot, or
small turbot) soufflé, for which you must call in advance. ✉ *8 Holyoke
St.,* ☎ *617/497–5300. AE, DC, MC, V. Closed Sun.*

French/Cuban

$$$ ✕ **Chez Henri.** Weird combination, but it works for this comfortable
room, with a separate bar serving turnovers, fritters, and grilled three-
pork Cuban sandwiches. The dinner menu gets serious with duck
tamale with ancho chili, upscaled paella, and truly French desserts.
Brunch is served on Sunday. ✉ *1 Shepard St.,* ☎ *617/354–8980. AE,
DC, MC, V. No lunch.*

Italian

$$ ✕ **La Groceria.** A trattoria before trattoria was cool, this place draws
loyal lovers of Italian food. Instant favorites are the homemade pasta,
the table of cold antipasti, veal dishes, and homemade cheesecake and
cannoli. ✉ *853 Main St.,* ☎ *617/547–9258 or 617/876–4162. AE,
D, DC, MC, V.*

Mediterranean

$$$$ ✕ **Rialto.** The ultra-posh Charles Hotel dining room continues a pleasant drift from its Mediterrannean beginnings toward more French
techniques and more New England ingredients, such as Maine crab cakes
and macomber turnips. But the savory tarts and the Tuscan-style sir-
loin steak with sliced portabella mushrooms and arugula salad are life-
time commitments. ✉ *Charles Hotel, 1 Bennett St., Harvard Sq.,* ☎
617/661–5050. AE, DC, MC, V. No lunch.

$$$ ✕ **Casablanca.** Long before *The Rocky Horror Picture Show,* Harvard and Radcliffe types would put on trench coats, lip cigarettes, and head to the Brattle Theatre to see *Casablanca,* rising to recite the Bogart and Bergman lines in unison. Then it was on to this restaurant for more of the same fantasy. The theater and restaurant have both been refurbished, and the restaurant, under chef Ana Sortun, has evolved the best and most authentically Mediterranean food of its long run. Typical entrées include cassoulet and grilled skewered lamb. There are perfectly good crab cakes or skillet crisped trout if you happened to see a different movie. The half-dozen desserts—such as homemade cannoli or Syrian spice cake—are substantial. The Casablanca murals by David Omar White are mostly in the lively central bar area. ⊠ *40 Brattle St.,* ☎ *617/876–0999. AE, MC, V.*

Mexican/South American

$$ ✕ **Border Café.** Reasonably priced Sunbelt fare—Tex-Mex with Cajun and Caribbean influences—and a tightly packed, Margaritaville bar scene has the Harvard Square crowd thronging here on weekends. The fried shrimp is a particular favorite, as is the burro (a burrito with enchilada sauce). ⊠ *32 Church St.,* ☎ *617/864–6100. AE, DC, MC, V.*

Spanish/Portuguese

$$ ✕ **Casa Portugal.** The oldest continuing Portuguese restaurant in the Azorean neighborhood east of Inman Square serves specialties like pork with clams and squid stew simmered to tenderness and complexity. You'll find great fried potatoes (brought to your table with every dinner order), and the Portuguese wines are excellent bargains for the price, too. ⊠ *1200 Cambridge St.,* ☎ *617/491–8880. AE, D, MC, V. No lunch.*

$$ ✕ **Sunset Café.** The lively atmosphere here may make you feel as
★ though you're attending a giant Portuguese wedding. Entire families come, and on a Friday or Saturday night (when they have guitarists and singers), it's not unusual to see little girls in frilly dresses and little boys in jackets and ties. Specialties include kale soup thickened with potatoes, *mariscada a chefe* (a great seafood combination in a casserole with fine spices) and shrimp Ana María (pan-fried shrimp in seafood stock). The bargain-priced wines on the list include some of the best Dão reds available anywhere outside Portugal. ⊠ *851 Cambridge St.,* ☎ *617/547–2938. AE, D, DC, MC, V.*

ALLSTON/BRIGHTON

Approximately northwest from downtown, this densely packed little enclave of grunge mixes twentysomething college students with immigrants from four continents. In general, the restaurants are homey and cheap, but the best offer a culinary world tour. A number of places allow low-key BYOB; Blanchard's and Marty's on Harvard Avenue are both great wine stores. If you've sampled Boston's past, this is the place to come to taste its future.

Chinese-Vietnamese

$$ ✕ **Ducky Wok.** Despite the silly name, this is an outstanding restau-
★ rant, the first outside Chinatown to feature live-tank seafood, and one of the few Chinese-Vietnamese restaurants whose menu is equally strong with both cuisines. Don't miss the daily tank seafood special, the stir-fried peapod stems, or the sautéed chicken with lemongrass. ⊠ *122-126 Harvard Avenue, Allston,* ☎ *617/782-8868. AE, DC, MC, V.*

Contemporary

$$ ✕ **North East Brewing Company.** Bright, hoppy ales and a fresh, rich stout complement some very good American bistro cooking. The crab

Allston, Brighton, Brookline, and Jamaica Plain Dining

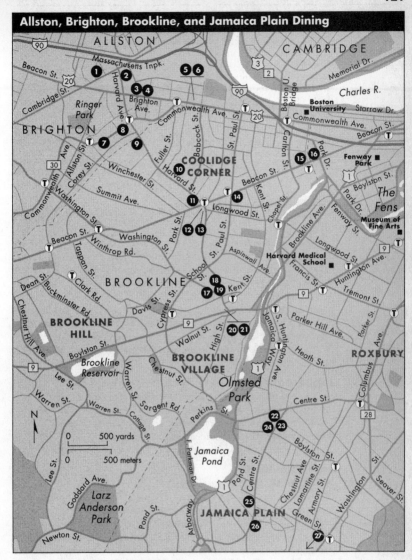

cakes and grilled chicken on polenta are immediate knockouts, and the thin-crust pizza is excellent. ✉ *1314 Commonwealth Ave., Allston,* ☎ *617/566–6699. AE, DC, D, MC, V.*

Indian

$$ ✕ **Rangoli.** Most of what Americans think of as Indian food is decidedly northern Indian, so Rangoli offers a nice alternative journey into the hot and spicy (and relatively vegetarian) world of southern Indian cooking. Specialties include curries wrapped in *dosa* (sourdough pancakes) and *idli sambar* (fiery vegetable soup with soothing dumplings). If you might like something hot and spicy and crunchy and sweet all at the same time, the amazing *bhel* appetizer (a novel curry with bits of fried turnovers worked in) is the dish for you. ✉ *129 Brighton Ave.,* ☎ *617/562–0200. AE, DC, MC, V.*

Italian (Contemporary)

$$$ ✕ **Uva.** A little piece of the South End in Allston, Uva serves up dishes
★ that land somewhere between new American and new Italian; delightfully, the emphasis is always on the new. Try one of Uva's special pasta plates which you construct from dozens of different sauces and garnishes, or delve into such lively entrées as roast leg of lamb over shallot mashed potatoes. This little bistro has embraced a radical wine-pricing scheme: $10 over wholesale, which puts $40 and $50 bottles in the $25 price range (making this a mecca for all wine-lovers). Uva remains a favorite destination for BU and BC parents after dropping off their precious college-bound cargo. ✉ *1418 Commonwealth Ave.,* ☎ *617/566–5670. Reservations essential for 6 or more. AE, D, DC, MC, V. Closed Sun. No lunch.*

Japanese/Korean

$ ✕ **Choe's Café.** Although it's housed in a funny-shaped space, Choe's serves outstanding Korean food and very good sushi. The seafood scallion pancake and hot spicy squid are simply outstanding. The food is kept honest by Korean students who drift up from Boston University. ✉ *957 Commonwealth Ave.,* ☎ *617/783–8702. MC, V. No lunch Sun.*

South American

$$ ✕ **Café Brazil.** This little place has a full slate of terrific meaty entrées from Brazil's ranching province of Minas Gerais, including a fine mixed grill and a couple of fish stews from the neighboring province of Bahia. There is also a great version of the fried yucca appetizer, *mandioca.* The decor is basic travel posters, but the down-home Brazilian cooking is almost as good as a trip to the scenes they depict. ✉ *421 Cambridge St.,* ☎ *617/789–5980. AE, D, DC, MC, V.*

Thai

$$ ✕ **Siam Cuisine.** The names of Thai restaurants are hard to keep straight, but it's not a problem because almost all of them in Allston are very good. Just watch out for those chili-pepper icons next to certain dishes—they mean spicy and they mean business. Siam Cuisine is notable both for the food and for the beautifully decorated dining room full of large Thai art pieces and antiques. Reserve one of the special floor tables for even more atmosphere. ✉ *961 Commonwealth Ave.,* ☎ *617/254–4335. AE, MC, V.*

Vietnamese

$ ✕ **Pho Pasteur.** Outstanding Vietnamese food in a less-crowded space than at their Chinatown location. The specialty, *pho* (beef bouillon), arrives in a huge bowl, delicately spiced and full of noodles and a selection of meat garnishes, with side salads you can toss into the bowl as well. For most diners, pho is a full meal. There are also savory rice plates and fine salads (Vietnamese is the one Asian cuisine that gets into salads). For dessert, try the fruit smoothies described as "milkshakes." ⊠ *137 Brighton Ave., ☎ 617/783–2340. AE, DC, MC, V.*

JAMAICA PLAIN

This neighborhood is a kind of mini-Cambridge, multiethnic and filled with radicals, cutting-edge artists, starving college students, and political idealists. There are no large restaurants, so dining out tends to the unusual and is usually pretty affordable.

American (New)

$$ ✕ **Black Crow Caffé.** It starts the day as a coffee shop, selling pastries, breads, and rolls with the java. Around lunch time, the Black Crow turns into a jumping sandwich spot. By dinner, it takes on a bistro flair, serving hot Caribbean and Mediterranean dishes and innovative salads from its constantly changing menu. Its progressive, multiracial atmosphere is the very soul of Jamaica Plain. ⊠ *2 Perkins St., ☎ 617/ 983–9231. AE, MC, V. Closed Mon.*

$$ ✕ **Five Seasons.** Five Seasons is the last and very best of Boston's macrobiotic restaurants. The cuisine is substantially vegetarian and subtly Japanese-influenced; it offers outstanding fish and chicken dishes, yet no dairy. Everything comes out of the kitchen fresh-tasting and light. The tempura is a highlight. There is always a line out onto the sidewalk at night, but it tends to be very sociable, so you'll feel like a local. ⊠ *669A Centre St., ☎ 617/524–9016. Reservations not accepted. MC, V.*

Caribbean

$$ ✕ **El Oriental de Cuba.** A small haven for a large variety of excellent Cuban food, including a healing chicken soup, a classic Cuban sub, superb rice and beans (opt for the red beans over the black beans), sweet "tropical shakes," and the *tostones* (twice-fried plantains) beloved during the cold New England winter by the many Cuban transplants to Boston. It also makes a good breakfast spot. ⊠ *416 Centre St., ☎ 617/524–6464. No credit cards.*

Italian (Contemporary)

$$ ✕ **Bella Luna.** A great stop in Jamaica Plain, it has eccentric pizzas and calzones. The walls exhibit the works of local artists, while local musicians play live music: Monday it's vocalists in a variety of styles; Tuesday and Wednesday, jazz and world-beat; Sunday there's a jazz brunch; and the last Saturday of the month look for rock. ⊠ *405 Centre St., ☎ 617/524–6060. AE, MC, V.*

Seafood

$$ ✕ **JP Seafood Café.** This neighborhood jewel has one chef for sushi and one for spicier Korean dishes, both of whom draw heavily on the adjoining fish store. You'll find top quality sushi, popular tempura, and a terrific *bi bim bop* (Korean you-mix assorted rice platter) served in a hot stone bowl. The service is informal but friendly. ⊠ *730 Centre St., ☎ 617/983–5177. DC, MC, V.*

Soul Food

$$ ✕ **Jake's Boss BBQ.** Right next to Doyle's, Jamaica Plain's great neigh-
★ borhood bar, Jake's fills the food side of the equation with impressive Texas-style smoked meats and some North Carolina pulled pork that Kenton Jacobs picked up during a stint with the East Coast Grill. The brisket sandwich is perfection of its kind.⊠ *3294 Washington St., ☎ 617/983-3701. No credit cards.*

5 Lodging

For every cramped dorm room in Boston, there's a cozy and cosmopolitan hotel room awaiting. No matter where you hang your hat, the selection of core-city lodging options is choice— grande dames like the Ritz-Carlton, jewel-size B&Bs, and Back Bay buys accommodate every budget. Many of the city's hostelries have welcoming lounges, ideal for enjoying a Paul Revere Alarm over ice and simply taking in the city's understated Yankee gentility.

Updated by
Fawn Fitter

AS THEY GLOWER AT EACH OTHER ACROSS the public garden, two of Boston's best and brightest hotels—the dowager Ritz-Carlton and the upstart Four Seasons—typify the diversity and conflict that dominate all aspects of the city. The Ritz, built in 1927, has been here forever, at least by American standards; the Four Seasons sprang up in 1985, and proceeded to grab a five-star rating, while at about the same time the Ritz inconceivably lost one of its own stars.

The Four Seasons might be said to have it all: huge rooms, a 51-foot-long pool, a Presidential Suite (with accommodation for state dinners), and room service for pets. An average room at the Ritz, by comparison, borders on the small, while the atmosphere verges on the stuffy. And yet here, as in other venues of Boston, reputation often wins out. No number of lavish blandishments can persuade the city's old-line society matrons away from those white-gloved elevator operators, to exchange tea at the Ritz for dinner at the Four Seasons.

If your biggest dilemma is deciding whether to spend $300-plus per night on old-fashioned elegance or extravagant modernity, you've come to the right city. The bulk of Boston's accommodations are not cheap; nevertheless there are abundant less-expensive choices among the smaller, older establishments, modern motels, or—perhaps the best option (if you can take early-morning small talk)—the bed-and-breakfast. Less expensive than most hotels, and more stylish than most HoJos (which kids will prefer), B&Bs are becoming increasingly popular in the Boston area and give visitors the chance to experience Boston's famous neighborhoods, from the increasingly hip South End to the hallowed, gaslit streets of Beacon Hill or ethnic enclaves like Brookline.

One last thought before waving a sad farewell to deluxe anonymity and committing yourself to breakfast chitchat: Check out the promotional packages. Weekend rates at some of the city's best hotels can be far below so-called standard or rack rates and often include free perks like parking, breakfast, or cocktails. If you look hard enough, you can find great deals for family groups, lovers, shoppers, theatergoers, sailors, probably even politicos, in this straitlaced yet liberal, snobby yet accommodating, altogether young-spirited city.

The following prices are regular weekday rates, and the number of rooms available at this rate may be limited.

A few lodging establishments in the guide offer a Modified American Plan (MAP; noted as such in our italicized service information). MAP rates include two meals, generally breakfast and dinner, but be sure to ask for details about the plan when you call to make your reservations.

CATEGORY	COST*
$$$$	over $220
$$$	$160–$220
$$	$110–$160
$	under $110

All prices are for a standard double room, excluding 9.7% tax and service charges.

HOTELS

What with the density of colleges, conventions, and tourist attractions, hotels are generally well booked for the spring, summer, and fall (especially in early October during foliage season). When considering prices, remember that room rates rarely include parking, which can cost more than $20 per night.

Boston

Back Bay

$$$$ 🏨 **The Colonnade.** Not quite Back Bay, not quite the South End, this small, relatively nonhectic modern hotel across from the Hynes Convention Center and next to Copley Place has more personality than some of the larger business-oriented high-rises on the other side of Huntington Avenue. In summer, the rooftop swimming pool is open, with live entertainment in the evenings. Complete executive services include multilingual translation and foreign currency exchange. Children under 12 stay free in their parents' room. ✉ *120 Huntington Ave., 02116,* ☎ *617/ 424–7000 or 800/962–3030,* FAX *617/424–1717. 285 rooms, 10 suites. Restaurant, bar, minibars, pool, barbershop, beauty salon, exercise room, baby-sitting, concierge, business services. AE, D, DC, MC, V.*

$$$$ 🏨 **Fairmont Copley Plaza.** A top-to-bottom renovation completed in
★   early 1998 only burnished the opulence of this stately landmark, built in 1912 and taken over by the Fairmont hotel group in 1996. The public spaces recall an era long gone, with high gilded and painted ceilings, mosaic floors, marble pillars, and crystal chandeliers; the guest rooms have custom furniture from Italy, elegant marble bathrooms, and fax machines in every room. One of the restaurants, now called the Oak Room to match its mahogany-paneled twin in New York's Plaza Hotel, has a new dance floor, a new raw bar, and a new menu; the other, the Copley Room, has also been given a facelift. Despite the imposing Victorian surroundings, the atmosphere is utterly gracious and welcoming, thanks to the multilingual staff. Children under 18 stay free in their parents' room, and pets are welcome. ✉ *138 St. James Ave., 02116,* ☎ *617/267–5300 or 800/527–4727,* FAX *617/247–6681. 379 rooms, 51 suites. 2 restaurants, 2 bars, in-room modem lines, minibars, no-smoking floors, 24-hour room service, barbershop, beauty salon, exercise room, baby-sitting, laundry service and dry cleaning, concierge, business services, parking (fee). AE, D, DC, MC, V.*

$$$$ 🏨 **Four Seasons.** The only hotel in Boston other than the Ritz-Carlton
★   to overlook the Public Garden is also, to the Ritz's chagrin, the only five-star hotel in the city. The Four Seasons is famed for luxurious personal service of the sort demanded by celebrities and heads of state. It boasts huge rooms with king-size beds, HBO, 24-hour concierge and room service, and a fully equipped health club on the eighth floor with whirlpool, sauna, and a heated 51-foot swimming pool with a view of the Public Garden. The antique-filled public spaces are serenely elegant, and Aujourd'hui (☞ Back Bay *in* Chapter 4) is one of Boston's best restaurants. The Bristol Lounge serves high tea daily at 3 PM. Pets are welcome. ✉ *200 Boylston St., 02116,* ☎ *617/338–4400 or 800/ 332–3442,* FAX *617/423–0154. 216 rooms, 72 suites. 2 restaurants, in-room modem lines, in-room safes, minibars, no-smoking floors, 24-hour room service, indoor pool, health club, baby-sitting, laundry service and dry cleaning, concierge, business services, parking (fee). AE, D, DC, MC, V.*

$$$$ 🏨 **Radisson 57 Hotel.** A former Howard Johnson's, now run by the Radisson chain, this hotel is in Park Square on the edge of the theater district, which makes it popular with business travelers. The hotel also houses a small theater that often hosts off-Broadway shows. All rooms have air-conditioning and private balconies. Children under 18 stay free in their parents' room. Pets are permitted. ✉ *200 Stuart St., 02116,* ☎ *617/482–1800 or 800/333–3333,* FAX *617/451–2750. 354 rooms. 2 restaurants, indoor pool, sauna, theater, free parking. AE, D, DC, MC, V.*

$$$$ ✱ 🏨 **Ritz-Carlton.** Despite the attractions of the upstart Four Seasons, many visitors to Boston would never dream of staying anywhere but the Ritz, thanks to its unmatched location, dignified elegance, and fierce devotion to its guests' comfort and privacy. Suites in the older section have parlors with working fireplaces and wonderful views of the Public Garden. The three top floors cost extra but have butler service and a private club with complimentary food and drinks, newspapers, and games. And the child with everything will love the Junior Presidential Suite's scaled-down kids' bedroom with furniture and bath fixtures in proportions to suit the smaller set, all for a most adult-size $600. Public rooms include the elegant café; the sedate bar; and The Lounge. A Chanel boutique opened in 1997 on the ground floor, naturally bearing the address of No. 5 Arlington Street. Small pets are welcome. ✉ *Arlington and Newbury Sts., 02117,* ☎ *617/536–5700 or 800/241–3333,* FAX *617/536–1335. 236 rooms, 42 suites. Restaurant, bar, lobby lounge, in-room safes, no-smoking rooms, refrigerators, room service, beauty salon, exercise room, baby-sitting, laundry service, concierge, parking (fee). AE, D, DC, MC, V.*

$$$$ 🏨 **Sheraton Boston Hotel & Towers.** The twin 29-story towers of New England's largest hotel connect directly to the Hynes Convention Center and the Prudential Center. Rooms are decorated in hushed pastels, with mahogany furniture and wide windows displaying panoramic city views—ask for a room facing the Christian Science Center or the Charles River. The top three floors, known as the Towers, are more luxurious (with butler service and a VIP lounge) and expensive. The hotel also has the city's largest indoor/outdoor swimming pool; it has poolside service. Small pets are allowed. Children under 17 stay free in their parents' room. Parking, with unlimited in and out, is $22 a day. ✉ *Prudential Center, 39 Dalton St., 02199,* ☎ *617/236–2000 or 800/ 325–3535,* FAX *617/236–1702. 1,187 rooms, 158 suites. 2 restaurants, 2 bars, in-room modem lines, no-smoking rooms, room service, indoor-outdoor pool, hot tub, exercise room, laundry service and dry cleaning, concierge, business services, parking (fee). AE, D, DC, MC, V.*

$$$$ 🏨 **Westin Copley Place.** One of the two anchor hotels of Copley Place, with its own skybridge connection to the shopping galleries, the 36-story Westin is one of Boston's tallest hotels. The rooms are large and handsomely furnished in an updated Queen Anne style; those on the Charles River side offer wonderful views. Non-smoking rooms are available, and 40 rooms are specially designed to accommodate people with disabilities. The restaurants include the popular Turner Fisheries Bar and Restaurant (☞ Back Bay/Beacon Hill *in* Chapter 4), which has an oyster bar and live jazz nightly at 8. Small pets are welcome. ✉ *Copley Pl., 02116,* ☎ *617/262–9600 or 800/228–3000,* FAX *617/424–7483. 756 rooms, 48 suites. 3 restaurants, indoor pool, hot tub, sauna, health club, parking (fee). AE, D, DC, MC, V.*

$$$–$$$$ 🏨 **Back Bay Hilton.** The 26-story Hilton occupies a corner pocket between the Prudential Center and the Christian Science Church complex and is close to the Hynes Convention Center. An addition completed in mid-1998 added 44 rooms and a dramatic glassed-in facade to the previously unremarkable building, and most of the older rooms have been renovated. All are soundproof and have panoramic views from bay windows that open; many rooms even have balconies. The hotel has an enclosed year-round swimming pool, a warm-weather outdoor sun deck, and a full-service health club. Ask about discount coupons at the Sony Cheri, a first-run movie theater next door. Children under 18 stay free in their parents' room. Small pets are permitted. ✉ *40 Dalton St., 02115,* ☎ *617/236–1100 or 800/874–0663,* FAX *617/867–6104. 385 rooms, 5 suites. Restaurant, 3 bars, in-room modem lines, room service, no-smoking floors, indoor pool, exercise room, dance club,*

Boston Lodging

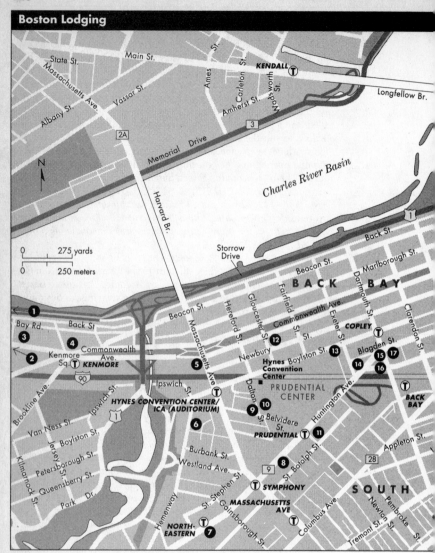

Airport Holiday Inn, **36**

Back Bay Hilton, **9**

Beacon Hill Bed and Breakfast, **19**

Berkeley YWCA, **21**

Best Western Terrace Motor Lodge, **2**

Boston Harbor Hotel at Rowes Wharf, **40**

Boston International Hostel, **6**

Boston Park Plaza Hotel & Towers, **25**

Chandler Inn, **22**

Clarendon Square B&B, **24**

The Colonnade, **11**

Copley Square Hotel, **14**

Doubletree Guest Suites, **1**

82 Chandler Street, **23**

Eliot Hotel, **5**

Fairmont Copley Plaza, **17**

Four Seasons, **26**

Greater Boston YMCA, **7**

Harborside Hyatt Conference Center and Hotel, **38**

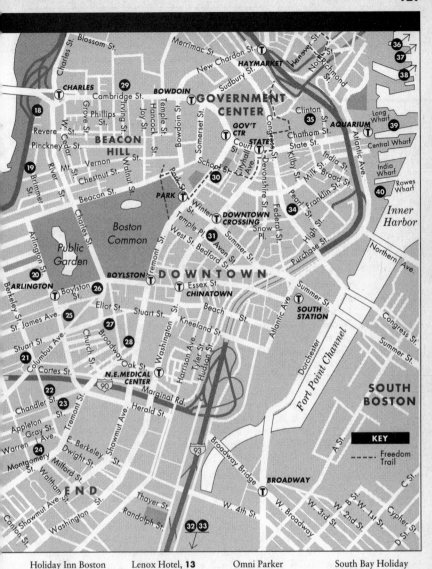

Holiday Inn Boston
Government
Center, **29**

Hotel Buckminster, **4**

Howard Johnson's
Kenmore Square, **3**

John Jeffries
House, **18**

Le Meridien
Hotel, **34**

Lenox Hotel, **13**

Logan Airport
Ramada Inn, **37**

Marriott Hotel at
Copley Place, **16**

Marriott Long
Wharf, **38**

Midtown Hotel, **8**

Newbury Guest
House, **12**

Omni Parker
House, **30**

Radisson 57
Hotel, **27**

The Regal
Bostonian, **35**

Ritz-Carlton, **20**

Sheraton Boston
Hotel & Towers, **10**

South Bay Holiday
Inn, **33**

Susse Chalet Motor
Lodges, **32**

Swissôtel, **31**

Tremont House, **28**

Westin Copley
Place, **15**

laundry service and dry cleaning, concierge, parking (fee). AE, D, DC, MC, V.

$$$–$$$$ 🏨 **Boston Park Plaza Hotel & Towers.** The Park Plaza's original decorative plaster moldings and chandeliered gilt-and-cream lobby with piano bar remain charmingly elegant, but overall, this circa-1297 hotel is a bit more worn around the edges than top-priced accommodations should be. The huge Starwood hotel group took over in 1997, and renovations scheduled to begin in the summer of 1998 include full soundproofing, more contemporary decor in every guest room, and enlargement of some of the rooms, which tend to be on the small side. The location is stellar, one block from the Public Garden and a short walk from Beacon Hill, the theater district, Newbury Street, and public transportation. The branch of Legal Sea Foods (☞ Back Bay/Beacon Hill *in* Chapter 4) on the premises is one of Boston's most popular spots for seafood. If you're traveling with children, ask about the "Cub Club" package including a fully child-proofed room with two bathrooms, discount coupons for local attractions and babysitting, and a daily story hour. ⊠ *64 Arlington St., 02116, ☎ 617/426–2000 or 800/ 225–2008, ℻ 617/426–5545. 960 rooms, 36 suites. 2 restaurants, bar, in-room modem lines, no-smoking floor, no-smoking rooms, room service, beauty salon, exercise room, theater, dry cleaning, laundry service, concierge, business services, meeting rooms, travel services, parking (fee). AE, D, DC, MC, V.*

$$$–$$$$ 🏨 **Copley Square Hotel.** The circa 1891 Copley Square, one of the city's oldest hotels, is busy, comfortable, and extremely popular among those who appreciate its Old World style, quirky turn-of-the-century charm, winding corridors, and convenient location in the center of the Back Bay. Each of the idiosyncratic rooms has an automatic coffee maker (with coffee and filters, of course) in addition to all the ordinary amenities. The quietest rooms are on the top floor overlooking the courtyard. Café Budapest, which serves Hungarian food, is just right for romantic dinners; there's also a coffee shop and a sports bar. Children under 17 stay free in their parents' room. ⊠ *47 Huntington Ave., 02116, ☎ 617/536–9000 or 800/225–7062, ℻ 617/267–3547. 143 rooms, 12 suites. 2 restaurants, 2 bars, coffee shop, in-room modem lines, in-room safes, no-smoking rooms, room service. AE, D, DC, MC, V.*

$$$–$$$$ 🏨 **Eliot Hotel.** The Eliot has gone upscale, emerging from a comprehensive 1995–96 renovation as a luxurious all-suite hotel with Italian marble bathrooms, two cable-equipped televisions in every room, and tasteful pastel-hued decor. The split-level marble lobby, with its vast chandelier, has also been spruced up. The Eliot Lounge, where Marathoners once slaked their thirst, has been replaced by Clio, an airy new restaurant garnering rave reviews for its serene ambience and contemporary French-American cuisine. The Eliot is steps from Newbury Street and a short walk to Kenmore Square. Children under 16 stay free in their parents' room. ⊠ *370 Commonwealth Ave., 02215, ☎ 617/267– 1607 or 800/443–5468, ℻ 617/536–9114. 95 suites. Restaurant, in-room modem lines, minibars, no-smoking rooms, room service, baby-sitting, laundry service and dry cleaning, concierge, valet parking (fee). AE, D, DC, MC, V.*

$$$–$$$$ 🏨 **Lenox Hotel.** A major renovation completed in early 1997 has trans-
★ formed the Lenox into a first-class selection. The updated, soundproof guest rooms have custom-made traditional furnishings, spacious walk-in closets, and marble baths. Structural changes to the 1900 building uncovered a number of handsome archways and elaborate moldings, particularly in the airily spacious corner rooms, a number of which have working fireplaces. The Samuel Adams Brew House, a brewpub, and Anago, a popular bistro transplanted from Cambridge in 1997, add the finishing touches to the metamorphosis. Children under 18 stay

free in their parents' room. ⊠ *710 Boylston St., 02116,* ☎ *617/536–5300 or 800/225–7676,* FAX *617/236–0351. 209 rooms, 3 suites. 2 restaurants, bar, in-room modem lines, no-smoking floor, room service, exercise room, baby-sitting, dry cleaning, concierge, parking (fee). AE, D, DC, MC, V.*

$$$–$$$$ 🏨 **Marriott Hotel at Copley Place.** This "megahotel," the second-largest in the city, has three impressive entrances: through a four-story greenhouse atrium complete with waterfall, via a glass skybridge from the Prudential Center/Hynes Auditorium complex, or directly from the upscale Copley Plaza shopping mall. Guest rooms have Queen Anne-style furnishings, cable TV with free HBO, and views of the Charles. The 28th floor, dubbed the Concierge Level, has special amenities and a private lounge. Four entire floors are set aside for nonsmokers, and 30 rooms are specially designed for people with disabilities. ⊠ *110 Huntington Ave., 02116,* ☎ *617/236–5800 or 800/228–9290,* FAX *617/578-0685. 1,109 rooms, 38 suites. 2 restaurants, bar, sushi bar, coffee shop, in-room modem lines, no-smoking floors, 24-hour room service, indoor pool, health club, video games, laundry service and dry cleaning, concierge, business center, parking (fee). AE, D, DC, MC, V.*

$$–$$$ 🏨 **Midtown Hotel.** This aging motel-style hotel holds its own against its large, expensive neighbors by offering comfortable rooms at reasonable rates in a convenient location near the Prudential Center, Symphony Hall, and the Christian Science Center. Rooms are good-quality, motel-style, with color TV and air-conditioning. Children under 18 stay free in their parents' room. ⊠ *220 Huntington Ave., 02115,* ☎ *617/262–1000 or 800/343–1177,* FAX *617/262–8739. 159 rooms. Restaurant, in-room modem lines, no-smoking rooms, room service, pool, barbershop, beauty salon, baby-sitting, business services, free parking. AE, D, DC, MC, V.*

$–$$ 🏨 **Chandler Inn.** This cozy little hotel with economical rates and a friendly staff is one of the best bargains in the city. Located near an overpass away from the Back Bay, at the end of one of the South End's prettiest streets, it's an easy walk to the T, the Amtrak station, Newbury Street's boutiques, or any of Tremont Street's trendy restaurants. Rooms are small but comfortable. The bar is a popular neighborhood hangout all week; weekends it serves brunch. The Chandler Inn is gay-friendly and often hosts a huge crowd during Gay Pride Week. Small pets are welcome. ⊠ *26 Chandler St., 02115,* ☎ *617/482–3450,* FAX *617/542–3428. 56 rooms. Restaurant (weekends only), bar. AE, D, DC, MC, V.*

Beacon Hill

$–$$ 🏨 **John Jeffries House.** This turn-of-the-century house across from
★ Massachusetts General Hospital has been renovated into an elegant inn with a Federal-style double parlor and guest rooms with French country decor. Triple-glazed windows block virtually all noise from busy Charles Circle. Most rooms have kitchenettes and many have views of the Charles River. At the foot of Beacon Hill, it's an easy walk from public transportation and most of downtown. There's a free Continental breakfast as well as 24-hour coffee service. ⊠ *14 Embankment Rd., 02114,* ☎ *617/367–1866,* FAX *617/742–0313. 23 rooms, 23 suites. No-smoking floors, parking (fee). AE, D, DC, MC, V.*

Downtown

$$$$ 🏨 **Boston Harbor Hotel at Rowes Wharf.** Travelers who arrive from
★ Logan Airport via water shuttle come straight to the door of this deluxe harborside hotel, docking amid a slew of luxury yachts and powerboats. (One of these, the *Odyssey* (☎ 800/946–7245), offers a dinner/dance cruise popular with hotel guests and locals alike.) Everything here is done on a grand scale, starting with the dramatic entrance through an 80-foot archway topped by a rotunda. Guest rooms—decorated

in shades of mauve, green, and cream—have either city or water views, and some have balconies. The Rowes Wharf Restaurant offers a spectacular, if pricey, Sunday brunch as well as seafood and American cuisine. The Boston Harbor Hotel is within walking distance of Faneuil Hall, the North End, the New England Aquarium, and the Financial District. Small pets are welcome. ⊠ *70 Rowes Wharf, 02110,* ☎ *617/439–7000 or 800/752–7077,* ℻ *617/345–6799. 230 rooms, 26 suites. 2 restaurants, bar, outdoor café, no-smoking rooms, room service, indoor lap pool, beauty salons, spa, health club, concierge, business services, valet parking. AE, D, DC, MC, V.*

$$$$ ⊞ **Marriott Long Wharf.** This airy, multitier redbrick hotel juts out into the bay like a big ship (it's meant to look like one) and is convenient to the Aquarium, Quincy Market, and the North End. The hotel abuts Christopher Columbus Park, one of the most romantic places to stroll in the city. Most rooms offer limited views of the harbor; all open onto a five-story-high atrium. A small surcharge will elevate you into concierge class on the top floor, with free Continental breakfast, cocktail hour, a business center, and the best views. Children under 18 stay free in their parents' room, and the hotel offers attractive weekend and vacation packages. ⊠ *296 State St., 02109,* ☎ *617/227–0800 or 800/ 228–9290,* ℻ *617/227–2867. 400 rooms, 2 suites. 2 restaurants, no-smoking rooms, room service, indoor pool, sauna, health club, recreation room, laundry service and dry cleaning, concierge, parking (fee). AE, D, DC, MC, V.*

$$$$ ⊞ **Le Meridien Hotel.** Once the Federal Reserve Building, this 1922 Re-
★   naissance Revival landmark in the center of the Financial District still exudes an almost intimidating aura of money and power—everyone seems to be stiffly suit-clad even on weekends (does anyone *ever* stay here with kids?), and Julien(☞ Downtown *in* Chapter 4), one of the city's best French restaurants, demands jacket and tie. But Le Meridien has a hidden light side: The informal Café Fleuri hosts an all-chocolate buffet each Saturday afternoon, a favorite, even with locals, especially around Valentine's Day. Most rooms, including some cleverly designed bilevel, skylighted suites, have queen-size or king-size beds; all have a small sitting area. Some pets are permitted. ⊠ *250 Franklin St., 02110,* ☎ *617/451–1900 or 800/543–4300,* ℻ *617/423–2844. 326 rooms, 17 suites. 2 restaurants, 2 bars, in-room modem lines, minibars, no-smoking floors, room service, indoor pool, health club, laundry service and dry cleaning, concierge, parking (fee). AE, D, DC, MC, V.*

$$$$ ⊞ **The Regal Bostonian.** The small luxury hotel is an intriguing blend
★   of old and new: The Harkness Wing, built as a warehouse in 1824, has rooms with working fireplaces, exposed beamed ceilings, and brick walls, while the newer wing with its glass-and-steel atrium has sleekly contemporary decor. Every room gets fresh-cut flowers daily. Seasons, the hotel's rooftop restaurant, overlooks Quincy Market. The Bostonian is also adjacent to Government Center and the Financial District, and just an underpass away from the old-world Italian North End. Request a room facing away from the street if you'd rather not awaken with Quincy Market at dawn. Children under 12 stay free in their parents' room. Some pets are allowed. ⊠ *Faneuil Hall Marketplace, 02109,* ☎ *617/523–3600 or 800/222–8888,* ℻ *617/523–2454. 152 rooms, 11 suites. Restaurant, lobby lounge, in-room modem lines, no-smoking rooms, room service, laundry service and dry cleaning, concierge, valet parking. AE, D, DC, MC, V.*

$$$ ⊞ **Swissôtel.** This quietly posh 22-story European hotel a block from Downtown Crossing has a handsome mahogany lobby with Waterford crystal chandeliers—even in the elevators—and one of Boston's most regal ballrooms. It's the sort of place where housekeepers turn down the bedcovers and leave "sweet dreams" chocolates on the pillows.

Rooms are appointed with Chippendale reproductions; some are equipped for people with disabilities. The hotel is on the edge of the former Combat Zone, a neighborhood that can be slightly dicey at night, but the otherwise excellent location is a short stroll from Boston Common, the Financial District, and the restaurants of Chinatown. Pets are welcome. ⊠ *1 Ave. de Lafayette, 02111,* ☎ *617/451–2600 or 800/ 621–9200,* FAX *617/451–0054. 497 rooms, 23 suites. Restaurant, bar, in-room modem lines, no-smoking floor, room service, indoor pool, health club, laundry service and dry cleaning, concierge, business services, meeting rooms, parking (fee). AE, D, DC, MC, V.*

$$–$$$$ 🏨 **Omni Parker House.** The oldest continuously operating hotel in America, having sheltered the likes of Charles Dickens and actress Sarah Bernhardt, the Parker House opened in 1855. This particular building went up in 1927 and has been extensively renovated. The Parker House is known for two things: Parker House rolls and Boston cream pie, both of which were invented here. (The rolls and cream-filled cake are still served in the restaurant, as is a bountiful Sunday brunch.) Eighty percent of the smallish, quaint rooms are non-smoking. They are in need of renovations, which were underway at press time. Appropriately, this historic hotel stands opposite old City Hall, near Government Center, and right on the Freedom Trail. ⊠ *60 School St., 02108,* ☎ *617/227– 8600 or 800/843–6664,* FAX *617/742–5729. 552 rooms, 26 suites. Restaurant, lounge, in-room modem lines, 24-hour room service, exercise room, baby-sitting, concierge, business services, valet parking (fee). AE, D, DC, MC, V.*

Kenmore Square

$$–$$$ 🏨 **Howard Johnson's Kenmore Square.** Boston University's campus, Fenway Park, and the city's vibrant nightlife scene stretched along Lansdowne Street are all nearby. The rooms have modern furnishings, color TV, and air-conditioning. Small pets are allowed. Children under 18 stay free in their parents' room. One note of caution: Because of its proximity to BU, the hotel can fill up with students, especially during breaks, and they may not share your desire for a peaceful night's sleep. ⊠ *575 Commonwealth Ave., 02215,* ☎ *617/267–3100 or 800/654– 2000,* FAX *617/424–1045. 170 rooms. Restaurant, no-smoking rooms, indoor pool, baby-sitting, free parking. AE, D, DC, MC, V.*

$–$$ 🏨 **Hotel Buckminster.** Once a residential hotel, the Buckminster has been transformed into an economical and tastefully decorated European-style inn, with maids but no bellhops. Breakfast is by room service only. Though there's no restaurant in the hotel, the ground floor of the building houses a branch of the Pizzeria Uno chain as well as an excellent sushi restaurant, and Kenmore Square itself offers a wide range of cuisines. The Buckminster is two blocks from the nightlife of Lansdowne Street and the grassy outfield of Fenway Park. Small pets are welcome. ⊠ *645 Beacon St., 02215,* ☎ *617/236–7050 or 800/727–2825,* FAX *617/236–0068. 120 rooms. AE, D, DC, MC, V.*

Old West End

$$–$$$$ 🏨 **Holiday Inn Boston Government Center.** This 14-story hotel is near Massachusetts General Hospital, state and city offices, and Beacon Hill. It's also a brisk walk from Faneuil Hall and the Boston Common. All rooms have air-conditioning and TV. Children under 18 stay free in their parents' room. ⊠ *5 Blossom St., 02114,* ☎ *617/742–7630 or 800/465–4329,* FAX *617/742–4192. 303 rooms, 13 suites. Restaurant, bar, no-smoking floor, room service, pool, exercise room, baby-sitting, coin laundry, dry cleaning, concierge, parking (fee). AE, D, DC, MC, V.*

Theater District

$$$–$$$$ 🏨 **Tremont House.** The 15-story Tremont House, in the center of the Theater District, is a popular home-away-from-home for the casts of

current shows. The lobby here is grand, with a 16-foot-high crystal chandelier (a replica of the original), high ceilings, marble columns and staircase, and liberally applied gold leaf. Built in 1925 as the national headquarters for the Benevolent Protective Order of Elks and transformed into a hotel in the 1950s, the building retains some hints of its past—look for the original Elks Club brass doorknobs in the guest rooms. All rooms have color TV with movie channels and individual climate control. It is also home to Boston's biggest nightclub, the Roxy (☞ Dance Clubs *in* Chapter 6). ⊠ *275 Tremont St., 02116, ☎ 617/426–1400 or 800/331–9998,* ⅢⅩ *617/482–6730. 322 rooms, 25 suites. Restaurant, in-room modem lines, 2 no-smoking floors, room service, exercise room, nightclub, laundry service and dry cleaning, concierge, valet parking (fee). AE, D, DC, MC, V.*

Boston Outskirts

Brighton

$$ 🏨 **Best Western Terrace Motor Lodge.** Incongruously sited in a residential neighborhood between Boston University and Boston College, on the line dividing Boston from Brookline, this motel is inexpensive, clean, and refurbished in 1997. Some rooms have kitchenettes, and there's a supermarket 2 blocks away. The T is less than a block away. (And with its ethnic shops, cafés, many restaurants, and Olmsted and Kennedy sights [☞ The "Streetcar Suburbs" *in* Chapter 2], Brookline itself is worth exploring.) Children under 18 stay free in their parents' room. ⊠ *1650 Commonwealth Ave., 02135, ☎ 617/566–6260 or 800/242–8377,* ⅢⅩ *617/731–3543. 73 rooms. Free parking. AE, D, DC, MC, V.*

Dorchester

$ 🏨 **South Bay Holiday Inn.** Standard-quality motel rooms with air-conditioning are offered in this lodging, just off the Southeast Expressway I–93, 4 mi south of Logan Airport. Children under 18 stay free in their parents' room. The property had just joined the Holiday Inn chain at press time, so call to check prices and amenities, which may have changed. ⊠ *5 Howard Johnson's Plaza, 02125, ☎ 617/288–3030,* ⅢⅩ *617/265–6543. 97 rooms. Restaurant, free parking. AE, D, DC, MC, V.*

$ 🏨 **Susse Chalet Motor Lodges.** Two practically identical motels sit side by side, just off I–93 in Dorchester. They are 5 mi from downtown Boston and 1 mi from the John F. Kennedy Library and Museum. The rooms are clean, serviceable, and dependable; they also have cable TV (with free HBO) and air-conditioning. Children under 18 stay free in their parents' room. ⊠ *800 and 900 Morrissey Blvd., 02122, ☎ 617/287–9100 or 617/287–9200,* ⅢⅩ *617/265–9287 or 617/282–2365. 282 rooms. 2 restaurants, piano bar, pool, coin laundry, free parking. AE, D, DC, MC, V.*

Logan Airport (East Boston)

$$$–$$$$ 🏨 **Harborside Hyatt Conference Center and Hotel.** The city's newest luxury hotel, which resembles a giant glass lighthouse, is perfectly situated at Logan Airport on a point of land separating Boston Harbor from the Atlantic Ocean. The best rooms have either a sweeping view of the Boston skyline or a panoramic sea vista. It's easy to get anywhere from here; the Hyatt operates its own shuttle to all Logan Airport terminals and the Airport T stop, and guests get a discount on the water shuttle that runs between the airport and downtown. All floors but one are nonsmoking, and all rooms are soundproof. The restaurant puts on a chocolate buffet each night starting at 6 PM. ⊠ *101 Harborside Dr., 02128, ☎ 617/568–1234 or 800/233–1234,* ⅢⅩ *617/567–8856. 270 rooms, 11 suites. Restaurant, bar, in-room modem lines, room service, indoor pool, sauna, exercise room, laundry service and dry cleaning, concierge, business services, parking (fee). AE, D, DC, MC, V.*

$$–$$$ ▦ **Airport Holiday Inn.** This Holiday Inn is in East Boston, 1½ mi from the airport and near the Suffolk Downs racetrack. Other than horse racing, the hotel is not local to any attractions, save for a mammoth statue of the Madonna. All rooms have color TV and air-conditioning. The hotel's "Park and Fly" package allows you to leave your car free for up to 10 days, after staying one night at the Inn. Children under 18 stay free in their parents' room. ⊠ *225 McClellan Hwy., East Boston, 02128,* ☎ *617/569–5250 or 800/798–5849,* ☒ *617/569–5159. 351 rooms. Restaurant, bar, no-smoking rooms, room service, pool, exercise room, airport shuttle. AE, D, DC, MC, V.*

$$$ ▦ **Logan Airport Ramada Inn.** It's not within walking distance of any tourist activities, but this hotel is very convenient indeed for early morning departures or late-night arrivals. The only hotel actually on the airport grounds, it operates a free round-the-clock shuttle service to all terminals and the T. The modern, air-conditioned, sound-proof rooms keep out airport noise. Naturally, given the location, the staff is multilingual. Parking is free for the length of your stay. Pets are allowed, and children stay free in their parents' room. ⊠ *75 Service Rd., Logan International Airport, East Boston, 02128,* ☎ *617/569–9300 or 800/272–6232,* ☒ *617/569–3981. 516 rooms, 15 suites. Restaurant, sports bar, no-smoking rooms, room service, pool, exercise room, laundry service, business services, airport shuttle, free parking. AE, D, DC, MC, V.*

Cambridge

$$$$ ▦ **Cambridge Center Marriott Hotel.** This modern 26-story hotel in Kendall Square, Cambridge's high-tech district, is just steps from MIT and the subway, which can whisk you straight to downtown or out to Harvard Square. All rooms have two double beds or a king, plus color TV with free HBO. Two floors are designated concierge level—more services at a higher price. The city's best cineplex, Kendall Square Cinemas (☞ Film *in* Chapter 6), is a short walk away. Children under 18 stay free in their parents' room. ⊠ *2 Cambridge Center, 02142,* ☎ *617/ 494–6600 or 800/228–9290,* ☒ *617/494–0036. 431 rooms, 12 suites. 2 restaurants, lobby lounge, in-room modem lines, no-smoking rooms, room service, indoor pool, sauna, exercise room, dry cleaning, concierge floors, parking (fee). AE, D, DC, MC, V.*

$$$$ ▦ **The Charles Hotel.** You can't stay much closer to the center of Har-
★ vard Square than at this first-class hotel adjacent to the Kennedy School of Government. The interior is contemporary, yet homey, with antiques and work by local artists. Guest rooms, which were all renovated in 1998, are equipped with terry robes, quilted down comforters on every bed, and Bose radios instead of standard-issue alarm clocks; suites have fireplaces. If you haven't read any good books lately, "Room Service Books" provides prompt delivery of phone orders from Harvard Square's many bookstores. Kids can also dial up a recorded bedtime story. Both restaurants (☞ Rialto, *in* Dining, Cambridge/ Somerville, Mediterranean, *above*) are excellent, and the Regattabar (☞ Jazz Clubs *in* Chapter 6) attracts world-class musicians. ⊠ *1 Bennett St., 02138,* ☎ *617/864–1200 or 800/882–1818,* ☒ *617/864– 5715. 296 rooms, 44 suites. 2 restaurants, bar, in-room modem lines, in-room safes, minibars, no-smoking rooms, 24-hour room service, pool, spa, health club, nightclub, baby-sitting, laundry service and dry cleaning, concierge, business services, parking (fee). AE, DC, MC, V.*

$$$$ ▦ **Hyatt Regency.** A glass-walled elevator ascends through the central 14-story atrium of this dramatic ziggurat on the Charles River to a revolving rooftop lounge and Italian restaurant. Some rooms have private balconies, and many have views of Boston across the river. Fif-

Cambridge Lodging

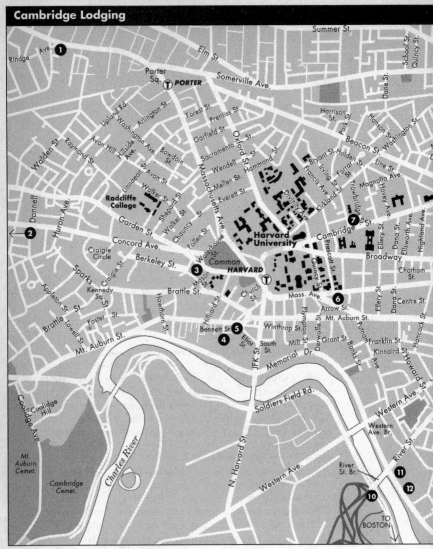

Cambridge Center
Marriott Hotel, **9**

A Cambridge House
Bed and Breakfast, **1**

The Charles Hotel, **4**

Doubletree Guest
Suites, **10**

Harvard Square
Hotel, **5**

Howard Johnson's
Cambridge, **11**

Hyatt Regency, **12**

Inn at Harvard, **6**

Irving House, **7**

Royal Sonesta
Hotel, **8**

Sheraton
Commander, **3**

Susse Chalet Inn, **2**

0   550 yards
0   500 meters

Walnut St.
Bow St.
Sloane Ave.
Somerville Ave.
Washington St.
Medford St.
Mansfield St.
Rossmore St.
Meacham St.
Linden St.
Allen St.
Linwood St.
Poplar St.
Joy St.

Marion St.
Concord Ave.
Newton St.
Oak St.
Tremont St.
South St.
Porter St.
Warren St.
Winter St.
LECHMERE
Gore St.
Cambridge St.
Otis St.
Sciarappa St.
3rd St.

Dimick St.
Dickinson St.
Houghton St.
Webster Ave.
Willow St.
Berkshire St.
Thorndike St.
Spring St.
Hurley St.
7th St.
Fulkerson St.
Charles St.
2nd St.
1st St.
Commercial Ave.
Charlestown Ave.

Cambridge St.
Maple Ave.
Fayette St.
Antrim St.
Amory St.
Prospect St.
Hampshire St.
Lincoln St.
Windsor St.
York St.
Portland St.
Bristol St.
Bent St.
Roger St.
Binney St.
Munroe St.
Athenaeum St.
5th St.
6th St.

Inman St.
Norfolk St.
Elm St.
Market St.
Binney St.
Broadway
Kendall Sq.

West St.
Lee St.
Clifton St.
Bigelow St.
Prospect St.
Essex St.
Pine St.
Harvard St.
9
KENDALL
Howard St.
Carleton St.
Ames St.
Amherst St.

Bishop Richard Allen Dr.
Washington St.
Massachusetts Institute of Technology
Main St.

CENTRAL
Massachusetts Ave.
Green St.
Franklin St.
Western Ave.
Auburn St.
Sidney St.
Landsdowne St.
Cross St.
Memorial Dr.

River St.
Pearson St.
Magazine St.
Pearl St.
Brookline St.
Sidney St.
Purrington St.
Albany St.
Vassor St.
Pacific St.
Harvard Bridge
Storrow Drive

Allston St.
Putnam St.
Waverly St.
Amherst Alley
Beacon St.
BACK BAY

Henry St.
Charles River
Massachusetts Ave.
Boylston St.

N

8

HYNES CONVENTION CENTER/ ICA (AUDITORIUM)

teen rooms on the third floor are designed for people with disabilities; the 10th floor offers special amenities at a premium. There's also a well-equipped outdoor playground. Children under 18 stay free in their parents' room. ⊠ *575 Memorial Dr., 02139,* ☎ *617/492–1234 or 800/ 233–1234,* FAX *617/491–6906. 469 rooms, 10 suites. 2 restaurants, sports bar, in-room modem lines, no-smoking floors, room service, indoor-outdoor pool, health club, bicycles, laundry service and dry cleaning, concierge, business center, parking (fee). AE, D, DC, MC, V.*

$$$$ ★ 🏨 **Inn at Harvard.** This understated four-story property built in the 1990s on the edge of Harvard Yard is operated by Doubletree Hotels for Harvard University. Guest rooms are decorated with original 17th- and 18th-century sketches, on loan from the nearby Fogg Art Museum, as well as with contemporary watercolors. Many rooms have tiny balconies and all possess oversize windows with views of Harvard Square or Harvard Yard. Six of the rooms look out over the Inn's glass-roofed atrium lobby. Guests have access to the Cambridge YMCA a few blocks away in Central Square. ⊠ *1201 Massachusetts Ave., 02138,* ☎ *617/ 491–2222 or 800/458–5886,* FAX *617/491–6520. 109 rooms, 4 suites. Restaurant, in-room modem lines, no-smoking floors, room service, dry cleaning, business services, parking (fee). AE, D, DC, MC, V.*

$$$$ 🏨 **Sheraton Commander.** This sedate brick hotel named for George Washington, built in 1926, overlooks Cambridge Common and is just a block from Harvard Yard and a short stroll from the many unusual shops on Massachusetts Avenue. Rooms are decorated in Colonial style, often with four-poster beds and rocking chairs. Several rooms have been renovated for people with disabilities. Cambridge Common is a venue for wonderful free concerts in the summer; if you aren't a music fan, ask for a room on the other side of the hotel. Children under 17 stay free in their parents' room. ⊠ *16 Garden St., 02238,* ☎ *617/547–4800 or 800/325–3535,* FAX *617/868–8322. 176 rooms, 20 suites. Restaurant, kitchenettes, no-smoking floor, exercise room, concierge, business services, free parking. AE, D, DC, MC, V.*

$$$–$$$$ ★ 🏨 **Doubletree Guest Suites.** Technically, this 15-story hotel, just off Storrow Drive and overlooking the Charles River, is in Boston, but it's actually handier to Cambridge. Every unit is a suite consisting of a living room (with refrigerator and sofa bed), a bedroom with a king-size bed, and a bathroom with a phone. The excellent Sculler's Jazz Club (☞ Jazz *in* Chapter 6) is frequented by visitors and locals alike and is one of the best places in town to catch a national act. Children under 18 stay free in their parents' room. ⊠ *400 Soldiers Field Rd., Boston, 02134,* ☎ *617/783–0090 or 800/222–8733,* FAX *617/783–0897. 305 suites, 5 bilevel penthouses. Restaurant, bar, in-room modem lines, minibars, no-smoking rooms, refrigerators, room service, indoor pool, sauna, exercise room, recreation room, nightclub, laundry service and dry cleaning, concierge, parking (fee). AE, D, DC, MC, V.*

$$$–$$$$ ★ 🏨 **Royal Sonesta Hotel.** There are superb views of Beacon Hill across the Charles River from this 10-floor building, which is near the Museum of Science and adjacent to the CambridgeSide Galleria. An impressive collection of modern art is displayed throughout the hotel. Some suites have kitchenettes. Children under 18 stay free in their parents' room, and the hotel offers superb family excursion packages that include boat rides, ice cream, and bicycles. ⊠ *5 Cambridge Pkwy., 02142,* ☎ *617/491–3600 or 800/766–3782,* FAX *617/661–5956. 400 rooms, 26 suites. 2 restaurants, 2 bars, in-room modem lines, in-room safes, minibars, no-smoking rooms, room service, indoor-outdoor pool, spa, health club, bicycles, laundry service and dry cleaning, business services, parking (fee). AE, DC, MC, V.*

$$–$$$$ 🏨 **Howard Johnson's Cambridge.** This modern 16-story hotel overlooks the Charles River. Some rooms have private balconies; ask for a river view. Children under 18 stay free in their parents' room. Pets are allowed. ✉ *777 Memorial Dr., 02139,* ☎ *617/492–7777 or 800/654–2000,* 𝔽𝔸𝕏 *617/492–6038. 204 rooms. 2 restaurants, 2 bars, no-smoking floors, indoor pool, baby-sitting, laundry service, free parking. AE, D, DC, MC, V.*

$$–$$$ 🏨 **Harvard Square Hotel.** This four-story motel-style hotel in the center of Harvard Square is, like the Inn at Harvard, owned and managed by Doubletree Hotels for Harvard University. Despite a complete refurbishing in 1996, prices here remain lower than at many nearby establishments. All rooms have color TV, air-conditioning, irons, and coffeemakers. Children under 16 stay free in their parents' room. ✉ *110 Mt. Auburn St., 02138,* ☎ *617/864–5200 or 800/458–5886,* 𝔽𝔸𝕏 *617/864–2409. 73 rooms. Café, in-room modem lines, no-smoking rooms, car rental, parking (fee). AE, D, DC, MC, V.*

$ 🏨 **Susse Chalet Inn.** This is a typical Susse Chalet operation: clean, economical, and spare. It is isolated from most shopping and attractions, being a 10-minute drive from Harvard Square, but it is within walking distance of the Red Line terminus, offering T access to Boston and Cambridge sights. All rooms have color TV and air-conditioning. A free Continental breakfast is served in the lobby each morning. ✉ *211 Concord Turnpike, 02140,* ☎ *617/661–7800 or 800/524–2538,* 𝔽𝔸𝕏 *617/868–8153. 78 rooms. In-room modem lines, no-smoking rooms, coin laundry, dry cleaning, free parking. AE, D, DC, MC, V.*

BED-AND-BREAKFASTS

Agencies

Despite their names, many of the following agencies also handle apartment, cottage, and house rentals throughout greater Boston and on the North and South shores.

🏨 **ABC: Accommodations of Boston and Cambridge** (✉ 335 Pearl St., Cambridge, 02139, ☎ 617/491–0274 or 800/253–5542, 𝔽𝔸𝕏 617/547–5478).

🏨 **Bed & Breakfast Agency of Boston** (✉ 47 Commercial Wharf, Boston, 02110, ☎ 617/720–3540 or 800/248–9262, 𝔽𝔸𝕏 617/523–5761) lists 120 homes in the most-visited areas of the city.

🏨 **Bed & Breakfast Associates Bay Colony Ltd.** (✉ Box 57166, Babson Park Branch, Boston, 02157, ☎ 617/449–5302 or 800/347-5088, 𝔽𝔸𝕏 617/449–5958) has more than 150 listings in Boston, Cambridge, the North and South shores, and Cape Cod and the islands.

🏨 **Bed and Breakfast Cambridge and Greater Boston** (✉ Box 1344, Cambridge, 02238, ☎ 617/576–1492 or 800/888–0178, 𝔽𝔸𝕏 617/227–0021) lists rooms in 60 homes in Cambridge, Boston, and the suburbs.

🏨 **Bed and Breakfast Cape Cod** (✉ Box 341, West Hyannisport, 02672, ☎ 508/775–2772 or 800/686–5252, 𝔽𝔸𝕏 508/775–2884) has 100 lodgings on the Cape, Martha's Vineyard, and Nantucket.

🏨 **Bed and Breakfast Marblehead & North Shore, Greater Boston and Cape Cod** (✉ Box 35, Newtonville, 02160, ☎ 617/964–1606 or 800/832–2632 outside MA, 𝔽𝔸𝕏 617/332–8572) handles weekly and monthly rentals as well as overnights.

🏨 **Bettina Network, Inc.** (✉ Box 585, Cambridge 02238, ☎ 617/497–9166 or 800/347–9166), a national organization, offers a personal lodging and events service for a network of private homes and inns.

Cambridge Discovery (☎ 617/497–1630). The kiosk in Harvard Square lists a dozen B&Bs in the Cambridge area.

Citywide Reservations Services (✉ 25 Huntington Ave., Suite 500, Boston, 02116, ☎ 617/267–7424 or 800/468-3593) books rooms at inns, B&Bs, and hotels all over Greater Boston.

Host Homes of Boston (✉ Box 117, Waban Branch, Boston, 02168, ☎ 617/244–1308, ℻ 617/244–5156) has listings for about 40 rooms in Boston, Cambridge, Brookline, Newton, and around Route 128.

New England Bed and Breakfast, Inc. (✉ 1045 Center St., Newton, 02159, ☎ 617/244–2112) lists 20 homes in Boston and Cambridge.

B&Bs

Boston

$$$ **Beacon Hill Bed and Breakfast.** Staying at this six-story Victorian rowhouse on Beacon Hill will give you a tiny taste of the elegant Brahmin lifestyle. In front, it overlooks a narrow cobblestone street with gaslights. From the rear, bay windows look out on the Charles River Esplanade. The three guest rooms are huge, with built-in bookcases, couches, and Victorian antiques. Don't bring a car; there's nowhere to park in this neighborhood, and you can walk everywhere from here anyway. ✉ *27 Brimmer St., Boston, 02108, ☎ 617/523–7376. 3 rooms. Full breakfast included. No pets. No smoking. No credit cards.*

$$ **Clarendon Square B&B.** A gut rehab in 1994 transformed a decrepit 1885 rowhouse into a B&B with light-filled rooms, a sundeck on the roof, and a working fireplace in the living room. The guest rooms have private baths—one with a silver-leaf vaulted ceiling! The best (and most expensive) room is a suite with a kitchen and its own private entrance. The minimum stay is three nights; longer stays are discounted. Children "of well-behaved parents" are welcome. As with most South End establishments, the Clarendon Square is gay-friendly. ✉ *81 Warren Ave., Boston 02115, ☎ 617/536–2229. 3 rooms. Continental breakfast included, air-conditioning. No pets. No smoking. AE, D, DC, MC, V.*

$$ **82 Chandler St.** The 1863 redbrick row house in Boston's South End
★   is just a five-minute walk from Copley Square and Amtrak's Back Bay station. Rooms color-coordinated in green, red, blue, or yellow open off the main staircase; all are spacious and sunny and have pedestal sinks, Oriental rugs, and a discreetly placed kitchen area with fridge and microwave oven. The best room—whose wide bay windows overlook downtown—is on the top floor and has a working fireplace and a skylight in the bathroom. Like this alternative, yuppie, racially mixed neighborhood, 82 Chandler is gay-friendly. ✉ *82 Chandler St., Boston, 02115, ☎ 617/482–0408. 5 rooms. Full breakfast included, air-conditioning. No pets. No smoking. No credit cards.*

$–$$ **Newbury Guest House.** This elegant redbrick and brownstone row
★   house was built in 1882, opened as a B&B in 1991, and expanded in 1994 when the father and son owner-manager team bought the house next door. It's wildly successful and always full, because it's smartly managed, well furnished, and ideally located on Boston's most fashionable shopping street. Rooms with elegant reproduction Victorian furnishings open off a carved oak staircase, and prints from the Museum of Fine Arts enliven the walls. Limited parking is available at $10 for 24 hours, a good deal for a Boston hotel, especially on Newbury Street. ✉ *261 Newbury St., Boston, 02116, ☎ 617/437–7666, ℻ 617/ 262–4243. 32 rooms. Continental breakfast included, parking (fee). No pets. AE, D, DC, MC, V.*

Boston Outskirts

$ ⊞ **Beacon Inns.** A B&B budget option, these two guest houses in the streetcar suburb of Brookline, owned by the same family, are convenient to several local colleges and to the T, which stops just outside and will get you downtown in 15 minutes. 1087 Beacon Street is a Victorian brick townhouse with period detailing and large rooms; 1750 Beacon Street is a bit shabby but still clean and spacious. Parking is available and inexpensive.⊠ *1087 and 1750 Beacon St., Brookline, 02146,* ☎ *617/566–0088 or 800/726–0088,* ᴵᴬˣ *617/397–9267. 1087: 11 rooms (3 share baths); 1750: 13 rooms (7 share baths). Continental breakfast included, parking (fee). AE, MC, V.*

Cambridge

$$–$$$$ ⊞ **A Cambridge House Bed and Breakfast.** A gracious 1892 Greek Revival home listed on the National Register of Historic Places, A Cambridge House is on busy Massachusetts Avenue but set well back from the road. Inside, it's a haven of peace and otherworldliness, with richly carved cherry paneling, a grand mahogany fireplace, elegant Victorian antiques, and polished wood floors overlaid with Oriental rugs. The best of the 16 antiques-filled guest rooms is referred to as "the suite" (actually one room), with fabric-covered walls, a working fireplace, and a four-poster canopy bed. Rooms in the adjacent carriage house, however, are small. There's a reservations center here for other host homes in the area. Harvard Square is a distant walk, but public transportation is nearby. ⊠ *2218 Massachusetts Ave., Cambridge, 02140,* ☎ *617/491–6300 or 800/232–9989,* ᴵᴬˣ *617/868–2848. 16 rooms (4 share baths). Full breakfast included, parking (free). No pets. No smoking. MC, V.*

$–$$ ⊞ **Irving House.** This friendly, affordable B&B is a bit larger than a house, a bit smaller than a hotel. It's on a quiet residential street just three blocks from Harvard Square. The cozy lobby is furnished with antiques and reproductions. Some guest rooms have kitchenettes; most have private baths. Children 6 and under stay free, and those aged 7–15 stay at a discount. There's even limited free off-street parking, a real coup in car-clotted Cambridge. ⊠ *24 Irving St., Cambridge 02138,* ☎ *617/547–4600,* ᴵᴬˣ *617/576–2814. 40 rooms. Continental breakfast included, air-conditioning, kitchenettes. No pets. No smoking. AE, D, DC, MC, V.*

HOSTELS

Boston

$ ⊞ **Boston International Hostel.** Run by American Youth Hostels, this very low-cost option near the Museum of Fine Arts is ideal if you're on a budget and don't mind sharing space with strangers. Guests sleep three to five people to a dormitory with shared bath and must provide their own sheets or sleep sack (no sleeping bags allowed). The maximum stay is three nights in summer and two weeks the rest of the year. During peak season, AYH membership is required; you can apply on the spot. Member or not, it's best to make reservations. Doors are locked at midnight (2 AM on weekends), so arrive before then. ⊠ *12 Hemenway St., 02115,* ☎ *617/536–9455,* ᴵᴬˣ *617/424–6558. Capacity 205. Lounge, kitchenette. No pets. MC, V.*

⊞ **Greater Boston Council of American Youth Hostels** (⊠ 1020B Commonwealth Ave., Boston, 02215, ☎ 617/731–5430) provides information on membership and on hostels in the Boston area.

YMCAS AND YWCAS

Boston

$ 🏨 **Berkeley YWCA** Located just where the Back Bay meets the South End, this facility has single rooms ($42), doubles ($64), and triples ($75) for adult women only; non-members pay a $2 surcharge. The desk is staffed around the clock for guests' safety. A dining room serves inexpensive meals. Guests have access to an indoor pool and a fully equipped nearby health club. The Copley Square T station is just a block away. For stays of more than a few nights, you must apply at least three weeks in advance. Pets are not allowed. ✉ *40 Berkeley St., 02116,* ☎ *617/482–8850,* 🖷 *617/482–9692. 200 rooms with shared baths. Lounge, laundry. MC, V.*

$ 🏨 **Greater Boston YMCA,** near the Museum of Fine Arts and Symphony Hall, is a coed facility with single ($38), double ($56), and triple ($76) rooms. A major refurbishment program finished in 1996 upgraded the rooms, and guests benefit from a free breakfast, in-room TV, and excellent fitness facilities. The Y is open to guests only between June and September; for the rest of the year, its rooms have been given over to students. You must write in advance to reserve a room, especially if you plan to bring children. ✉ *316Huntington Ave., 02115,* ☎ *617/ 536–7800. 180 rooms, most with shared baths. Cafeteria, indoor pool, sauna, health club, indoor track, coin laundry. No pets. MC, V.*

6 Nightlife and the Arts

Including Cafés and Coffeehouses

From cafés to concert halls, churches to comedy clubs, Boston offers as wide a variety of entertainment as you'll find in any American metropolis. For devotees of high art, a night out can mean Bach cantatas performed by an early music group at a small church, Beethoven at the BSO, Balanchine at the ballet, or a film classic at a Cambridge repertory house. Night crawlers can start the evening at a neighborhood café or bar and move on to one of the city's many comedy, jazz, rock or dance clubs. Whether it's high culture or low life you're after, New England's liveliest cultural calendar offers something to please everyone.

By Jeanne
Cooper

Updated by
Fawn Fitter

BOSTON HAS ALWAYS HAD AN ACTIVE—and traditional—performing arts circuit, but in recent years
it has been rewired to reflect the adventurous in-
fluence of college students, ethnic immigrants, city newcomers, and the
increasingly visible gay community. Good sources of information are
the *Boston Globe* Calendar section and the weekly listings of the
Boston Phoenix (both published on Thursday). The Friday Music and
Sunday Arts sections in the *Boston Globe* also contain recommendations for the week's top events. *Boston* magazine's "On the Town" feature gives a somewhat less detailed but useful monthly overview.

Boston's supporters of the arts are an avid group, and tickets often sell
out well in advance of an event. If you want to attend a specific performance, it is wise to buy tickets when you make your hotel reservations. Most theaters and music presenters will take telephone orders
and charge them to a major credit card, generally with a service fee of
several dollars per ticket. If you order far enough in advance, your tickets will be mailed to you; otherwise they will be held at the box office.

Bostix is Boston's official entertainment information center and the city's
largest ticket agency. It is a full-price TicketMaster outlet, and, beginning at 11 AM, it sells half-price tickets for same-day performances; the
"menu board" in front of the booth announces the available events.
Only cash and traveler's checks are accepted. People often begin queu-
ing up well before the agency opens. ⊠ *Faneuil Hall Marketplace,* ☎
617/723–5181 recorded message. ⊙ *Tues.–Sat. 10–6, Sun. 11–4.* ⊠
Copley Sq., near corner of Boylston and Dartmouth Sts. ⊙ *Mon.–Sat.
10–6, Sun. 11–4.*

Out of Town Tickets and Sports Charge (☎ 617/497–1118), in the Harvard Square T station, is open weekdays 9–6 and Saturday 9–1 and
takes major credit cards.

Ticketmaster (☎ 617/931–2000 or 617/931–2787) allows phone
charges to major credit cards, weekdays 9 AM–10 PM, weekends 9–8.
No refunds or exchanges. It also has outlets in local stores; call for nearest address.

NIGHTLIFE

Boston is a city segregated into neighborhoods, and its nightclubs are
divided into crowds. Armani'd international students head out late, after
taking over one of the chichi restaurants along Newbury Street for pre-
clubbing martinis. After dinner, they climb into luxury cars, press
fifties into the palms of doormen to get in ahead of the queue, and spend
1 AM to 2 AM swilling champagne and grinding to imported techno jams
at a downtown club. Baseball cap–sporting students fill up clubs and
pubs along Lansdowne Street, and hipsters bar-hop from Cambridge
clubs to Kenmore Square to catch live bands. Some clubs do double
duty, scheduling live music early, then packing in a late-night dance
crowd. "Theme" nights change frequently, as do clientele, so call first
or check Thursday's *Boston Globe* Calendar or the *Boston Phoenix*.
Most bars open daily for lunch around 11:30 and stay open until 1 or
2 AM, but may close earlier if business is slow (usually because of bad
weather). Almost all accept major credit cards; cash-only places are
noted. Note that while Boston's past has been prim and proper, its present
and future can be as raucous as any other happening city: The music
can be louder in nightclubs where people expect to converse than it is
at rock concerts, where they don't.

Bars

Boston

Alley Cat Lounge (✉ 1 Boylston Pl., ☎ 617/351–2510) is part of an alley of nightclubs in the Theater District. Most of the music is contemporary rock, and in the early evening, pub grub here is decent.

Atrium Lounge (✉ Bostonian Hotel, North and Blackstone Sts., ☎ 617/523–3600) is an elegant room overlooking Faneuil Hall Marketplace. A pianist plays nightly 6:30 to 10:30, joined by a cabaret artist Saturday night at 9.

Bay Tower Room (✉ 60 State St., ☎ 617/723–1666). By day, it's a private corporate dining room atop a landmark skyscraper in the Financial District. By night, you can sip a cocktail and watch the sun set through windows two stories high, or dance on Fridays and Saturdays to a live swing quartet. Closed Sunday; dress to enchant.

Black Rose (✉ 160 State St., Faneuil Hall, ☎ 617/742–2286). Walking into this Irish pub decorated with family crests, pictures of Ireland, and portraits of the likes of Samuel Beckett, Lady Gregory, and James Joyce, is like walking into a pub in Dublin. Its location draws as many tourists as locals, but it has one of the liveliest scenes in the city. On Sunday nights, a Celtic fiddler encourages patrons to dance on the tabletops.

Boston Beer Works (✉ 61 Brookline Ave., Kenmore Sq., ☎ 617/536–2337) is a "naked brewery," with all the works exposed—the tanks, pipes, and gleaming stainless steel and copper kettles used in producing beer. Seasonal brews, in addition to a regular selection, are the draw here for students, young adults, and fans from nearby Fenway Park. The menu has pastas and pub fare.

Bull & Finch Pub (✉ 84 Beacon St., at Hampshire House, ☎ 617/227–9605) was dismantled in England, shipped to Boston, and reassembled here, an obvious success. This place was the inspiration for the TV series *Cheers*. An international crowd of tourists and students often lines up out the door. Karaoke and live bands add to the hubbub Thursday–Saturday.

Clerys (✉ Dartmouth St. and Columbus Ave., Back Bay/South End, ☎ 617/262–9874) is one of Boston's many Irish pubs. Clerys has an informal atmosphere, Irish coats of arms hanging by the bar, and moderately priced American cuisine served in two rooms.

Club Café (✉ 209 Columbus Ave., Back Bay/South End, ☎ 617/536–0966) is one of the smartest spots in town for gay men and lesbians. The front end of the bar area, popular with suits after work, is the most mixed gay/lesbian. In the back is a video bar open only Thursdays–Sundays. An upscale new-American restaurant is part of the package.

Delux Café (✉ 100 Chandler St., South End, ☎ 617/524–4494) is a perfect spot to mix with the locals or to grab a chicken sandwich with homemade chutney. It's decorated with old record album covers and Christmas lights and populated by hipsters in their twenties and thirties.

Library Grill at the Hampshire House (✉ 84 Beacon St., ☎ 617/227–9600), above the Bull & Finch Pub, has, like the rest of the Hampshire House, the atmosphere of an old Back Bay drawing room, with paneled walls, moose heads, and paintings. There's nightly piano music, a dance combo on Friday and Saturday evenings, and a Sunday jazz brunch. Open till 10:30 nightly.

Mercury Bar (✉ 116 Boylston St., Downtown/Back Bay, ☎ 617/482–7799), popular among well-heeled young professionals and theatergoers, has a sleek 100-ft bar facing a row of raised, semicircular booths and a more private dining room off to the side. Bar patrons may order from the extensive tapas menu: anything from mixed olives to grilled Portuguese sardines—food salty enough to encourage imbibing.

Napoleon Club (⌗ 52 Piedmont St., Back Bay/Downtown, ☎ 617/338–7547), the city's oldest gay bar, is a former speakeasy with three separate, quietly elegant sections, each with its own piano. The crowd tends to be well-dressed, over 30, and uninhibited about crooning both show tunes and ballads. The top floor is Josephine's, a tiny dance floor open only on weekends.

Punch Bar (⌗ Sheraton Hotel & Towers, 39 Dalton Street,☎ 617/236–2000) is considered one of the country's best cigar bars, with private humidors for regular patrons' personal smokes as well as a selection of cigars for visitors. It also boasts Scotch (of course) and imported beers, a circular bar, overstuffed chairs and couches, and an air of retro ever-so-British manliness.

The Spot (⌗ 1270 Boylston St., Back Bay, ☎ 617/424–7747) is that new hybrid in the bar world: It's both a straight *and* a gay bar. Monday the crowd is gay male, Friday attracts both gay men and lesbians; Thursday, Saturday, and Sunday the bar attracts a lively straight crowd. During good weather, everyone comes to enjoy the un-Bostonian roof deck.

Tim's Tavern (⌗ 329 Columbus Ave., Back Bay/South End, ☎ 617/247–7894) is a working-class pub that pours its liquor from gallon jugs and offers arguably the best burgers in town—both at very low prices (no credit cards). Other fare, chicken and fish, is similarly reliable and simply served.

Top of the Hub (⌗ Prudential Center, ☎ 617/536–1775) has a wonderful view over the entire city; that and the sounds of hip jazz make the pricey drinks worth it. The 52nd-floor lounge is open weeknights till 12:45 and weekends till 1:30 AM.

Cambridge

Cambridge Brewing Company (⌗ 1 Kendall Sq., Bldg. 100, where Hampshire meets Broadway, ☎ 617/494–1994) is a microbrewery where beer lovers can order a hamburger and wash it down with a beer sampler, a pint of Cambridge Amber, or one of the other standards. The dark Charles River porter is one of which the owners are especially proud. Next to the popular Blue Room restaurant, near the new Kendall Square Cinema, it's a favorite among the twentysomething crowd. Open Sunday through Tuesday till 11:30; Wednesday through Saturday till 1.

Cantab Lounge (⌗ 738 Massachusetts Ave., near Central Sq., ☎ 617/354–2685) has a local band playing nightly from 9:30 until closing, with a cover charge. Upstairs, Monday and Tuesday are folk and blues nights, while other nights the mix includes rock and jazz. The downstairs bar often hosts poetry slams and low-budget cabaret. It's friendly and informal; no credit cards.

John Harvard's Brew House (⌗ 33 Dunster St., Harvard Sq., ☎ 617/868–3585) dispenses from behind its long, dark bar a range of ales, lagers, pilsners, and stouts brewed on the premises. The Brew House, frequented by a crowd in its twenties, smells like a real English pub; the food is so-so but plentiful. Stained-glass windows of modern figures add to the mock-antique air.

Plough & Stars (⌗ 912 Massachusetts Ave., just outside Central Sq., ☎ 617/492–9653) is a traditional Irish bar with Guinness and Bass on tap and Irish, country, and bluegrass music daily from 9 PM to 1 AM. It's a comfortable, friendly, noisy place popular with students. Sometimes there's a cover charge; no credit cards.

Sazarac Grove(⌗ One Kendall Sq., ☎ 617/577–7850) is a former warehouse transformed into a hip yet low-key modern bar. It's full of sharp angles and a youngish crowd that wanders over before or after art flicks at the Kendall Square Cinema.

Blues/R&B Clubs

House of Blues (⊠ 96 Winthrop St., Harvard Sq., Cambridge, ☎ 617/491–2583) is co-owned by Dan Aykroyd and the late John Belushi's wife, Judy, plus other celebrity investors. They opened this venue in 1992, considering it a headquarters for blues lovers, with a museum, store, restaurant, and recording facility in the compact space. Live music begins at 10 PM; Sunday offers a gospel brunch. The cover charge varies.

Johnny D's (⊠ 17 Holland St., Davis Sq., Somerville, ☎ 617/776–9667) brings an eclectic blend of performers from around the world to play in this restaurant-cum-music hall with a small stage but not a bad seat in the room. Sunday afternoon is a blues jam; Monday night is swing dancing (with lessons before the show); Tuesday is acoustic music night. Come early for dinner and stay for the performance. It's close to the Davis Square T stop. Cover varies.

Marketplace Café (⊠ 300 Faneuil Hall, ☎ 617/227–9660) is a "no cover" treasure in the North Market building amid the bustle of Faneuil Hall. It offers a blues/jazz format, with music every night from 9, and nouvelle American cuisine.

Cafés and Coffeehouses

If you just want a cup of coffee, you'll find plenty of Starbucks cafés and Au Bon Pains. However, the atmosphere at most of those establishments won't encourage you to linger; you may not even be able to find a seat. But there is a more welcoming group of cafés and coffeehouses in the city, listed here. Only Club Passim feels like a true old-fashioned coffeehouse, complete with live folk music. At the rest, you can relax in between or after sightseeing, enjoying your thoughts (or pretending to enjoy those of your date). To eavesdrop on the liveliest conversations—some in Italian—head to the many espresso bars on Hanover Street in the North End.

Boston

Caffé Vittoria (⊠ 296 Hanover St., ☎ 617/227–7606) is the biggest and the best of the North End cafés, with gleaming espresso machines going nonstop. Many Italian-restaurant patrons head here for dessert and coffee after dining elsewhere.

Daily Grind (⊠ 168 Cambridge St., ☎ 617/367–3233) is a welcome bit of funkiness on the edge of Beacon Hill. Suffolk University students, State House types, and hospital workers enjoy the well-prepared coffee drinks, the fresh pastries, and the small but intriguing selection of sandwiches and other lunch fare, all at low prices. It's open weeknights till 8 (6 in winter) and weekends till 4 PM. No credit cards.

Other Side Cosmic Café (⊠ 407 Newbury St., ☎ 617/536–9477) offers college-dorm ambience, a good cup of java, a fruit and vegetable juice bar, and no-frills soup and sandwiches. The first floor feels like a warehouse; the second floor has low ceilings, red velvet curtains, and mismatched furniture. Open daily till midnight; no credit cards.

Roasters (⊠ 85 Newbury St., ☎ 617/867–9967) has outdoor seating for sunny days. Inside is 1930s-sleek, with an art deco-style mural and a huge bay window from which to people-watch while nibbling pastry and sipping coffee roasted on the premises. Open till 10PM on weeknights, 11PM on Fridays and Saturdays.

Trident Booksellers Café (⊠ 338 Newbury St., ☎ 617/267–8688) is bohemian-cool with a New Age sensibility. You'll find esoteric books, a great selection of magazines, and a lot of journal-writing. It's open daily till midnight.

Cambridge

Café Algiers (⊠ 40 Brattle St., ☎ 617/492–1557) is a genuine Middle Eastern café with a choice of strong coffees and tea and pita-bread lunches. The decor is plain and the service is rather relaxed; go for conversation. It's open daily till midnight; no credit cards.

Club Passim (⊠ 47 Palmer St., ☎ 617/492–7679), formerly Passim's, is one of the country's first and most famous venues for live folk music. The spare, light basement room has tables close together, with wait service, and a separate coffee bar/restaurant counter.

Someday Café (⊠ 51 Davis Sq., Somerville, ☎ 617/623–3323) is a funky Seattle-style coffeehouse next to the Somerville Theater right off the Davis Square station on the T's Red Line. The drinks menu is extensive, with Italian sodas and a dozen types of tea alongside the requisite coffees, but the munchies are limited and usually sell out early. It's open daily 7 AM till 11 PM, except Friday, when it closes at midnight; no credit cards.

1369 Coffee House (⊠ 757 Massachusetts Ave., Central Square, ☎ 617/576–4600) is popular with Cambridge eccentrics and college professors. There are plenty of plugs for laptop work, and the coffee is fresh-brewed in individual pots.

Comedy Clubs

Comedy Connection (⊠ Faneuil Hall Marketplace, ☎ 617/248–9700) offers a mix of local and nationally known acts, seven nights a week (two shows Friday and Saturday), with a cover charge.

Nick's Comedy Stop (⊠ 100 Warrenton St., ☎ 617/482–0930) presents local comics every night except Monday, and occasionally a well-known comedian pops in. Reservations advised on weekends, as it's in the heart of the theater and bar district; cover charge varies.

Dance Clubs

Axis (⊠ 13 Lansdowne St., ☎ 617/262–2424) is one of Boston's largest clubs. Near Kenmore Square, it has high-energy disco and a giant dance floor that can accommodate more than 1,000 people. Friday is "X Night," starring DJs from alternative radio station WFNX. At Sunday's "Gay Night," Axis and neighboring megaclub Avalon combine and let dancers circulate between the two for one cover charge. Some nights are 18+; others are over-21 only. Cover charge varies.

International (⊠ 184 High St., ☎ 617/542–4747) is a strikingly elegant, multifaceted club in the ordinarily staid Financial District. Wednesdays are jazz nights, Thursdays are "Soul International," with soul, acid jazz, and house music. Fridays feature dance hits of the '70s, and Saturdays are "Tribe," with two DJs improvising with two percussionists. Cover charge.

Joy (⊠ 533 Washington St., ☎ 617/424–7747) draws a fashionable crowd: Two levels of wealthy international students and their well-dressed companions move to a techno or acid jazz beat—once they make it out of the line to get in. Cover charge.

Karma Club (⊠ 11 Lansdowne St., Kenmore Sq., ☎ 617/421–9678) is an exotic fantasyland with incense, carved temple doors from East Asia, and an immense stone Buddha who watches the proceedings with a beatific smile from Thursday until Sunday night.

Man-Ray (⊠ 21 Brookline St., Inman Sq., Cambridge, ☎ 617/864–0400) is the home of Boston's underground scene, where the Gothic, glam, and alternatively lifestyled go for long nights of industrial, house, techno, disco, and trance music. Friday night is "Fetish Night." You needn't participate in the staged spankings—just don't stare. Wear black. Closed Monday and Tuesday.

Roxy (✉ 279 Tremont St., Theater District, ☎ 617/338-7699) is the biggest nightclub in Boston. On Thursday nights, the club caters to an upscale African-American crowd, and on Fridays, the international students take it over. Saturday nights are popular with sports stars and celebrities, who congregate in the club's VIP room.

Jazz Clubs

Clubs often alternate jazz with other kinds of music; always call ahead for program information and times.

Regattabar (✉ Charles Hotel, Bennett and Eliot Sts., Cambridge, ☎ 617/864-1200; 617/876-7777 for tickets) headlines some of the top names in jazz. Even when there's no entertainment, the spacious, low-ceilinged club is a pleasant (if expensive) place for a drink. It's closed Sunday and Monday.

Ryles (✉ 212 Hampshire St., Inman Sq., Cambridge, ☎ 617/876-9330) has soft lights, mirrors, and greenery to set the mood for first-rate jazz by local and national groups. This is one of the best places for new music and musicians, with a different group playing on each floor. Open nightly at 7, with a cover charge (no reservations).

Scullers Jazz Club (✉ DoubleTree Suites Hotel, 400 Soldiers Field Rd., ☎ 617/783-0811) has made a very strong name for itself by hosting such well-knowns as Herb Pomeroy and the Victor Mendoza Quintet. Shows are Tuesday through Thursday at 8 and 10 PM and Friday and Saturday at 8:30 and 10:30; reservations advised (cover charge varies).

Turner Fisheries Bar (✉ Westin Hotel, 10 Huntington Ave., ☎ 617/262-9600, ext. 7425) has live jazz nightly from 8 till midnight. A pianist plays Sunday through Wednesday; Thursday through Saturday the Debra Mann Trio backs varying soloists, and plays till 1 AM. The sleek but comfortable room is hung with modern art and adjacent to a handsome oyster bar. No cover charge.

Wally's (✉ 427 Massachusetts Ave., ☎ 617/424-1408) is a Boston rarity—a racially well-integrated bar in the South End—with a loyal clientele hooked on jazz and blues. Performers are mostly local musicians. No cover charge.

Other Attractions

Jillian's (✉ 145 Ipswich St., ☎ 617/262-0300), a 70,000-sq-ft entertainment complex on the corner of club-hopping Lansdowne Street, has a third-floor pool hall with 52 tables and a second-floor virtual-reality game arcade, each with a bar. The Atlas Bar & Grill is on the first floor. Everything's open until 2 AM. The pool hall opens at 11 AM Monday through Saturday and noon Sunday; the games open at 5 PM weekdays, 11 AM Saturday, and noon Sunday.

Joey & Maria's Italian Comedy Wedding (✉ New Tremont Playhouse, Tremont House Hotel, 275 Tremont St., ☎ 800/733-5639) is dinner cabaret at its participatory best. You're a wedding guest—dancing the tarantella, eating the buffet dinner (provided by a well-known North End restaurant), and getting drawn into the action—as Joey, Maria, and their respective off-the-wall families are overwhelmed by the emotion of this special day.

Rock Clubs

Avalon (✉ 15 Lansdowne St., ☎ 617/262-2424) is one of two clubs in this building outside Kenmore Square. Avalon hosts concerts by alternative, rock, and dance acts, then turns into a dance club. Sunday is gay night when next-door Axis and Avalon combine forces and permit dancers to circulate between the two clubs. Concert show times vary; Ticketmaster (☎ 617/931–2000) sells advance tickets. Closing at 2 AM each night, the dance club opens at 10:30 PM Thursday, 9:30 PM Friday and Saturday, and 9 PM Sunday, with cover charge.

Bill's Bar (✉ 5 Lansdowne St., ☎ 617/421–9678), near Kenmore Square, has live rock seven nights a week (reggae on Sunday) as well as dancing, listening, and DJ formats. Cover charges vary. Bill's is open from 8 PM till 2 AM; the live rock is usually over by midnight.

Causeway (✉ 65 Causeway St., North Station, ☎ 617/367–4958) is one of the most authentic rock bars in town, housed in a tiny room barely identifiable from the street. One of the pierced doormen will be your guide upstairs—all you have to do is ask. This is often a great place to celebrity-spot after a rock show at the FleetCenter.

Mama Kin (✉ 36 Lansdowne St., ☎ 617/536–210) is jointly owned by members of the Boston-based rock group Aerosmith and a local impresario. It puts on local bands and artists from other genres. The long, narrow club room, in gothic black and red, has a stage at one end, a CD jukebox, and a custom-built bar with the names of Aerosmith's hit songs inscribed in gold.

The Middle East (✉ 472 Massachusetts Ave., Central Sq., ☎ 617/497–0576) manages to be both a Middle Eastern restaurant and an eclectic rock club, with three rooms showcasing live local and national acts. There's also belly dancing, folk, jazz, and even the occasional country-tinged rock band. With the demise of Kenmore Square's venerable Rathskeller (The Rat), the Middle East is hands-down the heart of the local rock scene. There's usually a different cover charge for each stage.

The Paradise (✉ 967 Commonwealth Ave., ☎ 617/254–3939) is a small club known for having hosted such big-name talent as Matthew Sweet, Soul Coughing, and the Finn Brothers. National and local rock, jazz, folk, blues, alternative, and country acts all take their turn here. Inside, two tiers of booths overlook the dance floor, and four bars quench the crowd's thirst. Tickets may be purchased in advance at Ticketmaster (☎ 617/931–2000) or at the box office.

Singles

Avenue C (✉ 5 Boylston Place, Back Bay, ☎ 617/423-3832) caters to the older members of Generation X with a music mix heavy on hits from the '80s. This is a great place to meet like-minded potential significant others while mashing up against them on the overcrowded dance floor or waiting for a pool table in the side room.

Buzz (✉ 67 Stuart St., ☎ 617/267–8969), one of the city's trendiest gay clubs, stands just where the South End gives way to the Theater District. Bump and grind with the wall-to-wall hardbodies on the dance floor, or simply savor the sights from the bar. Saturday nights are the week's peak.

Frogg Lane Bar and Grille (✉ Faneuil Hall Marketplace, ☎ 617/720–0610) is a popular spot with tourists and singles in the heart of Quincy Market. The jukebox is very loud. It's open Sunday through Thursday until 11, Friday and Saturday until 12:30.

Il Panino (✉ 295 Franklin St., Post Office Sq., Financial District, ☎ 617/338–1000) attracts a nonstudent, more mature and upscale crowd. The first two floors in this five-floor complex offer informal and formal dining, the third has a jazz bar, and the top two are dance floors. No cover charge.

Sonsie (✉ 327 Newbury St., ☎ 617/351–2500) has no music except a stereo system that diners at the hip restaurant often drown out. The bar crowd, which spills into the sidewalk café, is full of trendy, cosmopolitan types and professionals.

THE ARTS

Dance

Ballet

Boston Ballet (✉ 19 Clarendon St., ☎ 617/695–6950). The city's premier dance company performs at the Wang Center for the Performing Arts and the Shubert Theater (☞ *below*). In addition to a fine repertory of classical and high-spirited modern works, it presents an elaborate *Nutcracker* every Christmas.

Ballet Theatre of Boston (✉ 186 Massachusetts Ave., ☎ 617/262–0961). The company's Cuban-born resident artistic director and choreographer, José Mateo, presides over a young troupe that is building an exciting, contemporary repertory—including an original *Nutcracker*. Performances take place at the Emerson Majestic Theatre (☞ *below*).

Contemporary

Beth Soll and Company (☎ 617/547–8771). The choreographer, who teaches at MIT, draws on everyday life for dance themes; her style has been linked to European expressionism. The company performs at theaters all over Boston.

Dance Collective (✉ 33 Richdale Ave., Cambridge, ☎ 617/576–2737) comprises three local choreographers who since 1974 have explored themes from contemporary life in collaborative works.

Dance Umbrella (✉ 380 Green St., Cambridge, ☎ 617/492–7578), one of New England's largest presenters of contemporary dance performances, provides services and advocacy for the area's dance companies and puts together national and international touring companies.

Folk

Folk Arts Center of New England (✉ 1950 Massachusetts Ave., Cambridge, ☎ 617/491–6083) sponsors participatory international folk dancing at locations throughout the city.

Mandala (☎ 617/868–3641), a popular group of dancers and musicians, performs lively international folk dances in full costume at different venues.

Multicultural

Art of Black Dance and Music (☎ 617/666–1859) performs the music and dance of Africa, Latin America, and the Caribbean at venues across the area.

Cambridge Multicultural Arts Center (✉ 41 2nd St., Cambridge, ☎ 617/577–1400) hosts local performers in ethnic music and dance; two galleries showcase the visual arts.

Film

With its large population of academics and intellectuals, Boston has its share of discerning moviegoers. Several first-run and art-house theaters have closed in recent years, however, and many of the remaining theaters are small or poorly divided into multiplexes. Theaters at suburban malls offer better screens, if less adventurous fare. The *Boston Globe* has daily listings in the Living/Arts section.

Brattle Theater (✉ 40 Brattle St., Cambridge, ☎ 617/876–6837) is a small downstairs cinema catering to classic-movie buffs and fans of new foreign and independent films.

Ciné Club at the French Library (✉ 53 Marlborough St., ☎ 617/266–4351) shows a different French film (usually subtitled) every week, with screenings Thursday at 8 and Friday at 6 and 8:30.

Coolidge Corner Theater (✉ 290 Harvard St., Brookline, ☎ 617/734–2500) offers an eclectic and frequently updated bill of art films, foreign films, cult flicks, and classics. In 1997, the non-profit group that runs the Coolidge hired the owners of the Brattle Theater (*above*) to do promotions and programming. With its shabby velvet seats and striking vintage murals, it's one of the few grand movie houses left in the area.

Goldwyn/Landmark Kendall Square Cinema (✉ 1 Kendall Sq., Cambridge, ☎ 617/494–9800) opened its well-designed nine-screen theater, devoted to independent and foreign films, to ecstatic reviews in 1995. There's free validated parking; 1 Kendall Square is actually at Hampshire and Broadway, not near the Kendall Square T.

Harvard Film Archive (✉ Carpenter Center for the Visual Arts, 24 Quincy St., Cambridge, ☎ 617/495–4700) screens the works of directors not usually shown at commercial cinemas; there are two or more programs daily in the comfortable downstairs theater.

Museum of Fine Arts (✉ 465 Huntington Ave., ☎ 617/369–3306, ext. 3) screens international and avant-garde films, early cinema, and the work of local filmmakers in Remis Auditorium.

Sony Nickelodeon Cinema (✉ 606 Commonwealth Ave., ☎ 617/424–1500) is one of the few theaters in the city that shows first-run independent and foreign films as well as revivals.

Wang Center for the Performing Arts (✉ 270 Tremont St., ☎ 617/482–9393) annually revisits its movie-palace days with a classic movie series, usually suitable for families.

Music

For its size, Boston is the most musical city in America. Only New York has more events, perhaps twice as many, but it has 10 times the population. Most of the year the music calendar is crammed with both classical and pop events. Jazz, blues, folk, and world music fans have plenty to keep them busy as well. Supplementing appearances by nationally known artists are performers from the area's many colleges and conservatories, which also provide music series, performing spaces, and audiences.

The jewel in Boston's musical crown is the multifaceted Boston Symphony Orchestra, which presents more than 250 concerts annually, led by its music director, Seiji Ozawa, and other distinguished guest conductors. The season at Symphony Hall runs from late September to late April. In July and August, the activity shifts to the orchestra's beautiful summer home at the Tanglewood Music Center in Lenox, Massachusetts. A favorite of television audiences, the Boston Pops presents concerts of "lighter music" from May 8 through June 30, followed by outdoor concerts at the Hatch Memorial Shell. These outdoor concerts are free of charge and among greater Boston's most popular summertime activities.

But pop orchestral arrangements and the warhorses of the 19th-century symphonic repertoire aren't Boston's only classical musical offerings today. The city has emerged as the nation's capital of early music performance. Dozens of small groups, often made up of performers who have one foot in the university and another on the concert stage, are rediscovering pre-18th- and 19th-century composers, whose works they play on period instruments, often in small churches where the acoustics resemble the venues in which some of this music was first performed. If you're a die-hard early-music devotee, plan to visit Boston in odd-numbered years, when the biannual Early Music Festival takes over the city for two weeks in June.

Concert Halls

Berklee Performance Center (✉ 136 Massachusetts Ave., ☎ 617/266–1400 or 617/266–7455 for recorded information), associated with Berklee College of Music, is best known for its jazz programs.

Boston Conservatory of Music (✉ 31 Hemenway St., ☎ 617/536–6340) presents many free musical events. Tickets are also available at the box office around the corner at 8 The Fenway (☎ 617/536–3063, ext. 42).

Boston University Concert Hall (✉ Tsai Performance Center, School for the Arts Bldg., 685 Commonwealth Ave., ☎ 617/353–8724), associated with Boston University, presents many free concerts.

Harborlights (✉ Fan Pier off Northern Ave., ☎ 617/737–6100 or 443–0161) presents top pop, R&B, and country artists in a picturesque white tent on the waterfront.

Hatch Memorial Shell (✉ Off Storrow Dr. at Embankment, ☎ 617/727–9548) is a jewel of an acoustic shell where the Boston Pops perform their famous free summer concerts. Local radio stations also put on music festivals here many weekend evenings, April through October.

Isabella Stewart Gardner Museum (✉ 280 The Fenway, ☎ 617/734–1359 for schedule information) holds classical concerts by up-and-coming artists in its beautiful Tapestry Room weekends at 1:30 PM, for an additional charge to the museum admission.

Jordan Hall at the New England Conservatory (✉ 30 Gainsborough St., ☎ 617/536–2412) is one of the world's acoustic treasures, ideal for chamber music yet large enough to accommodate a full orchestra. Restored in 1995, the hall is home to the **Boston Philharmonic** (☎ 617/868–6696).

Kresge Auditorium (✉ 77 Massachusetts Ave., Cambridge, ☎ 617/253–2826 or 617/253–4003) is MIT's hall for pop and classical concerts.

Museum of Fine Arts (✉ 465 Huntington Ave., ☎ 617/369–3306, ext. 2) puts on jazz and folk concerts in its outdoor courtyard every Wednesday evening at 7:30 from late June through mid-August (bring a blanket and a picnic). The Boston Museum Trio and numerous guest artists appear on Sunday afternoons in **Remis Auditorium** from late September to mid-May.

Orpheum Theatre (✉ 1 Hamilton Pl., off Tremont St., ☎ 617/482–0650), a once-ornate theater, is cramped, shabby, and occasionally overheated, but nonetheless a popular forum for national and local rock acts avoiding the stadium scene.

Pickman Recital Hall (✉ 27 Garden St., Cambridge, ☎ 617/876–0956, ext. 991) is Longy School of Music's excellent acoustical setting for smaller ensembles and recitals.

Sanders Theater (✉ Cambridge and Quincy Sts., Cambridge, ☎ 617/496–2222) at Harvard provides a fine stage for local and visiting classical and folk performers.

Somerville Theater (✉ 55 Davis Sq., Somerville, ☎ 617/625–5700) occasionally interrupts its second-run movie schedule to present blues, folk, and world music. It's two stops from Harvard Square on the Red Line.

Symphony Hall (✉ 301 Massachusetts Ave., ☎ 617/266–1492 or 800/274–8499), one of the world's most perfect acoustical settings, is home to conductor Seiji Ozawa, the **Boston Symphony Orchestra**, and the **Boston Pops** (conducted by Keith Lockhart). It is also used by visiting orchestras, chamber groups, and soloists, and for presentations by many Boston performing groups. The Pops concerts take place in May and June.

Chamber Music

Boston is blessed with an impressive array of talented chamber groups, some of them the product of successful undergraduate alliances. Many colleges have their own resident string quartets and other chamber ensembles, and concerts, often free to the public, are given almost every night of the week.

Alea III (⌗ 685 Commonwealth Ave., ☎ 617/353–3340), associated with Boston University, presents a season of chamber music performances here.

Boston Chamber Music Society (⌗ 286 Congress St., ☎ 617/422–0086), under the artistic direction of Ronald Thomas, gives a 12-concert series each year at Sanders Theater and Jordan Hall.

Boston Museum Trio (⌗ 465 Huntington Ave., ☎ 617/369–3306, ext. 2), in residence at the Museum of Fine Arts, garners high praise for skilled performances of baroque chamber music.

Boston Musica Viva (⌗ 25 Huntington Ave., ☎ 617/353–0556) performs contemporary masterpieces and newly commissioned works at Tsai Performance Center.

Boston Symphony Chamber Players (⌗ 301 Massachusetts Ave., ☎ 617/266–1492), an outstanding ensemble, comprises members of the Boston Symphony Orchestra.

Longy School of Music (⌗ 27 Garden St., Cambridge, ☎ 617/876–0956, ext. 991) gives a continuing series of free chamber music performances almost every week.

Choral Groups

It's hard to imagine another city's having more active choral groups. Many outstanding choruses are associated with Boston schools and churches. *See* also Church Concerts, *below,* and Early Music Groups, *below* for additional venues and vocal groups.

Boston Cecilia (⌗ 1773 Beacon St., Brookline, ☎ 617/232–4540), dating back to 1875, this group holds regular concerts at Jordan Hall and is especially noted for its period instrument performances of Handel.

Cantata Singers (⌗ Box 375, Cambridge, 02238, ☎ 617/267–6502) perform music dating from the Renaissance to the present.

Chorus Pro Musica (⌗ 645 Boylston St., ☎ 617/267–7442), a large chorus with more than 100 singers, appears with various symphony orchestras.

Church Concerts

Boston's churches offer outstanding music programs. The Saturday *Boston Globe* provides a current listing.

Emmanuel Church (⌗ 15 Newbury St., ☎ 617/536–3355) is known as "the Bach church" for its Holy Eucharist services on Sundays at 10AM. A professional chamber orchestra and chorus performs a Bach cantata each week from mid-September to mid-May.

King's Chapel (⌗ 58 Tremont St., ☎ 617/227–2155) has acoustics so excellent that when local classical performers put on half-hour concerts each Tuesday at 12:15PM, they need no microphone.

Trinity Church (⌗ Copley Sq., ☎ 617/536–0944) presents a free half-hour organ recital each Friday at 12:15PM.

Concert Series

BankBoston Celebrity Series (⌗ Statler Bldg., Suite 832, 20 Park Plaza, ☎ 617/482–2595 or 617/482–6661) presents 50 events annually— renowned orchestras, chamber groups, recitalists, vocalists, and dance companies.

***Boston Globe* Jazz Festival** (☎ 617/523–4047), an annual event sponsored by the city's leading newspaper, brings in prominent jazz musicians and attracts thousands of fans from across the country. Performances take place over a week in mid-June, at venues throughout the city.

Charles River Concerts (⌂ 729 Boylston St., ☎ 617/262–0650) presents young and lesser-known classical musicians whose careers merit greater exposure; concerts are given at Jordan Hall and elsewhere.

Midday Performances (⌂ Federal Reserve Bank of Boston, 600 Atlantic Ave., ☎ 617/973–3453) are 40-minute lunchtime programs of music, dance, opera, and such, in the ground-floor auditorium at 12:30 on Thursdays.

Early Music Groups

Boston Camerata (⌂ 140 Clarendon St., ☎ 617/262–2092) has become a worldwide favorite thanks to its popular recordings. Founded in 1954, it offers a series of medieval, Renaissance, baroque, and early American vocal and instrumental concerts at various venues.

Boston Early Music Festival (⌂ Box 2632, Cambridge, 02238, ☎ 617/661–1812) focuses on medieval, Renaissance, and baroque music, with eight events throughout the year at concert halls and churches. The festival also hosts the city's biannual weeklong early music festival in early June in odd-numbered years. Dozens of concerts, master classes, and lectures culminate in a rarely performed, fully staged Baroque opera. (Past productions have included Monteverdi's *Orfeo* and Purcell's *King Arthur.*)

Cambridge Society for Early Music (⌂ Box 336, Cambridge, 02238, ☎ 617/423–2808) has promoted the performance and appreciation of early music since 1951 and deserves much of the credit for early music's preeminence in Boston's musical scene. The society administers the annual Erwin Bodky competition.

Handel & Haydn Society (⌂ 300 Massachusetts Ave., ☎ 617/266–3605), America's oldest musical organization, has a history of performances dating from 1815. It presents instrumental and choral performances at Symphony Hall.

Opera

Boston Lyric Opera Company (⌂ 114 State St., ☎ 617/542–6772), is a professional company staging three full productions each season, usually including one 20th-century work. In recent years, it's performed classics by Mozart and Strauss as well as lesser-knowns. For opera-lovers, the Lyric is the only professional show in town; the bankrupt Opera Company of Boston has temporarily shut down until it finds funding and a new home.

Theater

Boston once played the role of tryout town, a place where producers shaped their productions before taking them on to Broadway. Although fewer shows come to Boston's theater district in this way today, local troupes are growing in sophistication and number. The rehabilitation of the Boston Center for the Arts has created a range of performance spaces for fledgling troupes, while established companies such as American Repertory Theatre and the Huntington Theatre Company now include pre-Broadway premieres of works by leading playwrights such as David Mamet, August Wilson, and Horton Foote.

Commercial Theaters

Charles Playhouse (⌂ 74 Warrenton St., ☎ 617/426–6912) is home to two of Boston's most popular long-running shows. *The Blue Man Group,* a loud, messy, exhilarating trio of playful performance artists painted vivid cobalt, has been appearing on Stage I since 1995. *Shear Madness* (☎ 617/426–5225) an audience-participation whodunit set in a hair salon, is an 18-year-old institution on Stage II.

Colonial Theatre (✉ 106 Boylston St., ☎ 617/426–9366) is one of Boston's most lavish proscenium theaters even though it is situated within an office building. Designed by Charlence H. Blackhall and opened in 1900, the Colonial remains the home of major productions, often on the way to or from Broadway. The period decor has been richly restored and preserved, but the balconies are cramped.

Emerson Majestic Theatre (✉ 219 Tremont St., ☎ 617/578–8727), a 1903 beaux arts building, has undergone a multimillion-dollar restoration, thanks to Emerson College (which is devoted exclusively to communications and performing arts). The Majestic hosts professional and student productions from dance to drama and opera.

Huntington Theatre Company (✉ 264 Huntington Ave., ☎ 617/266–0800), occupying a theater opened in 1925 by Henry Jewett's repertory group, is Boston's largest professional resident theater company. Under the auspices of Boston University, with Peter Altman as producing director, the company performs five plays annually, a mix of established 20th-century plays, new works, and classics.

Loeb Drama Center (✉ 64 Brattle St., Cambridge, ☎ 617/495–2668) has two theaters, the smaller one an experimental stage. This is the home of American Repertory Theatre, the long-established resident professional repertory company founded by Robert Brustein, one of the artistic directors and a playwright. The highly respected ART stages both classic and experimental plays at the Loeb, plus puts new works and visiting artists on stage at other venues in Boston and Cambridge.

Shubert Theatre (✉ 265 Tremont St., ☎ 617/426–4520), a quietly elegant circa-1910 theater with just 1,700 seats, spent much of the last decade dark and empty, but theatergoers lined up for its reopening in early 1997 when it hosted the touring company of the Broadway blockbuster *Rent*. The Boston Ballet now holds its repertory performances here—a move that promises to keep the Shubert lit for some time to come.

Wang Center for the Performing Arts (✉ 270 Tremont St., ☎ 617/482–9393), a huge theater designed by Blackhall, first opened in 1925 as a movie palace. Restructured today for opera, dance, and drama, it stages large-scale productions—notably the Boston Ballet season and Andrew Lloyd Webber extravaganzas—and conducts guided tours of its splendid building.

Wilbur Theatre (✉ 246 Tremont St., ☎ 618/423–7440), the smallest of the traditional theater houses in the Theater District, has been in and out of foreclosure in recent years, but now seems to be making a comeback with off-Broadway hits like *Stomp* and *Defending the Caveman*.

Small Theaters and Companies

Boston Center for the Arts (✉ 539 Tremont St., ☎ 617/426–7700) houses more than a dozen quirky low-budget troupes in four performance areas: a basic 40-seat theater, a 90-seat "black box," a fully equipped 140-seat stage, and the massive Cyclorama, built to hold a 360-degree mural of the Battle of Gettysburg (the painting is now at the battlefield). Performances, which go on year-round, range from Coyote Theater, the in-house Equity troupe, to the contemporary SpeakEasy Stage Company, to innovative, explicit one-person shows.

Harvard's Hasty Pudding Theatricals/Cambridge Theatre Company (✉ 12 Holyoke St., Cambridge, ☎ 617/496–8400 or 617/576–7638). The first troupe, the "oldest theatrical organization in the United States," produces one show annually; it usually runs from late February to the end of March, then goes on tour. The latter is a professional company that often uses the Hasty Pudding Theater to present solo artists like Spalding Gray and Mort Sahl and to mount its own productions.

Le Grand David and His Own Spectacular Magic Company (Cabot Street Cinema Theater) (⊠ 286 Cabot St., Beverly, ☎ 508/927–3677) stages an eye-opening performance that mixes magic, music, and comedy in the lavish style of the turn of the century. On Sunday the company performs on Cabot Street; on selected Saturdays and holidays, at the restored Larcom Theater (⊠ 13 Wallis St., Beverly). Both theaters are a 35-minute drive from downtown Boston.

Lyric Stage (⊠ 140 Clarendon St., ☎ 617/437–7172), on the second floor of the YWCA building, presents New England and American premieres as well as the classics. The annual production of *A Child's Christmas in Wales* is a holiday favorite.

New Repertory Theatre (⊠ 54 Lincoln St., Newton Highlands, ☎ 617/332–1646), convenient to the Green Line's D trolley, is often the first repertory company in the area to present popular off-Broadway comedies and dramas, and it's also one of the best.

Nora Theatre Company (⊠ Harvard Union, Harvard and Quincy Sts., Cambridge, ☎ 617/491–2026) has won local acting and directing awards for its thoughtful stagings of modern drama from Arthur Miller to Terrence McNally.

Puppet Showplace Theatre (⊠ 32 Station St., Brookline, ☎ 617/731–6400) since 1974 has drawn on puppeteers from far and near. Performances in the 120-seat theater are given every weekend and holiday weekdays; ticket prices are under $10.

Triangle Theater Company (⊠ 58 Berkeley St., ☎ 617/426–3550) presents well-designed plays and musicals with gay and lesbian themes in a small South End theater.

7 Outdoor Activities and Sports

Boston is the city where Larry Bird once showed mere mortals the art of basketball, where Babe Ruth was traded as a rookie to the Yankees, where Ivy Leaguers still let off steam at Harvard–Yale games. The Bruins rule the ice and as for the Celtics—well, they ran out of room in the rafters of the old Garden for their championship flags. The Red Sox? Natives have their fingers crossed. If the pro games are sold out, there are always the college games. When you're ready to trade a bleacher seat for a bit of sporting yourself, choose from a variety of outdoor delights, from biking to tennis, in-line skating to rowing.

SPECTATOR SPORTS

SPORTS ARE AS MUCH A PART of Boston as codfish and Irish Democrats. Everything you have heard about the zeal of Boston fans is true; if you're an out-of-towner and want to avoid controversy, you'd best not flaunt your partiality to the team back home. College teams are followed with enthusiasm, especially Boston College and Harvard football. College hockey fans look forward to the Beanpot Tournament in February.

By Michele
McPhee

Updated by
Carolyn Heller

Baseball

Boston Red Sox, American League (⊠ Fenway Park, ☎ 617/267–1700 for tickets). Baseball season begins early in April and finishes in late September or early October. The Sox won the American League pennant in 1967, 1975, and 1986, though they haven't won a World Series since 1918. (See Dan Shaugnessy's excellent book, *The Curse of the Bambino,* published by Penguin, 1991, for a full explanation of the fix Boston baseball fans are in.) The small ballpark is the country's oldest (Fenway Park and Detroit's Tiger Stadium opened the same day in 1912) and is most infamous for the 37-ft-high left-field wall affectionately known as the "Green Monster," as well as for the fans who occupy the seats nearby, who have been dubbed "Bleacher Creatures." In July 1999, Fenway Park hosts the annual Major League All-Star Game.

Basketball

Boston Celtics, NBA (⊠ FleetCenter, ☎ 617/624–1000; 617/931–2000 Ticketmaster for tickets). Basketball season runs from October to May, though it used to run longer during the Celtics' heyday, and fans firmly believe they'll soon get a taste of post-season play. The Celts have won the NBA championship 16 times since 1957, the last time in 1986.

New England Blizzard, American Basketball League (⊠ Springfield Civic Center, 1277 Main St., Springfield, 01103, ☎ 860/522–4667). New England's professional women's team plays occasional exhibition games in Boston, although its home arenas are in Springfield (90 miles west of Boston) and Hartford. Regular season runs from October through February.

Football

New England Patriots, NFL (⊠ Foxboro Stadium, Foxboro, ☎ 800/543–1776). Having solved their coaching problem in 1993 and their ownership problem early in 1994, in 1997 the Patriots went all the way to Super Bowl XXXI, where they were, alas, defeated by the Green Bay Packers.

Boston College Eagles (⊠ Alumni Stadium, Chestnut Hill, ☎ 617/552–3000).

Harvard University Crimson (⊠ Harvard Stadium, North Harvard St. and Soldiers Field Rd., Allston, ☎ 617/495–2211).

Hockey

Boston Bruins, NHL (⊠ FleetCenter, ☎ 617/624–1000; 617/931–2000 Ticketmaster for tickets). The Bruins are on the ice from October until

April, frequently on Thursday and Sunday evenings. The Bruins have won the Stanley Cup five times, the last one in 1972.

In February, Boston area college hockey teams (Boston College, Boston University, Harvard, and Northeastern) face off in the annual **Beanpot Hockey Tournament.** Call the FleetCenter for information (☎ 617/ 624–1000).

Rowing

Rowing is big in Boston; its popularity spawned the country's first rowing club, the Union Boat Club (☎ 617/742–1520), which is one of several organizations that enters rowers in the world's biggest rowing event, started in 1965, the annual **Head of the Charles Regatta** (☎ 617/864–8415 for information). In mid-October more than 5,000 male and female collegiate rowers from all over the world compete, while thousands of spectators line the shores of the Charles River and use the race as a reason to lounge on blankets and drink beer. (Imbibe with caution; the police have been known to disapprove.) The Regatta was canceled for the first time in the history of the event in 1996 due to inclement weather.

Running

Every Patriot's Day (the Monday closest to April 19), fans gather along the Hopkinton-to-Boston route of the **Boston Marathon** to cheer the more than 12,000 runners from all over the world. The race ends near Copley Square in the Back Bay. For information, call the Boston Athletic Association (☎ 617/236–1652).

In October, women runners take the spotlight on Columbus Day for the **Tufts 10K for Women** (☎ 617/439–7700). Starting and ending near the Boston Common, this race typically attracts more than 5,000 entrants and 20,000 spectators.

Soccer

New England Revolution, Major League Soccer (✉ Foxboro Stadium, Foxboro, ☎ 508/384–9164, 800/946–7287; 617/931–2000 Ticketmaster for tickets). New England's professional soccer team, established in 1996, plays from March to September.

In 1999, Foxboro Stadium hosts several world championship women's soccer games, when the **1999 Women's World Cup** (☎ 888/499–2463) comes to town. Games are scheduled on June 20, June 27, and July 4, 1999.

Tennis

The **Longwood Cricket Club** (✉ 564 Hammond St., Chestnut Hill, ☎ 617/731–2900) hosts the weeklong U.S. Pro Tennis Championships in mid-summer.

PARTICIPANT SPORTS AND FITNESS

The mania for physical fitness is big in Boston. Lots of people play racquet sports on their lunch hours, and runners and rollerbladers whiz by constantly on the **Storrow Embankment** or in the **Arnold Arboretum** in Jamaica Plain. Most public recreational facilities, including skating rinks and tennis courts, are operated by the **Metropolitan District Commission** (✕✉ MDC, 20 Somerset St., ☎ 617/727–5114, ext. 555).

Bicycling

The **Dr. Paul Dudley White Bikeway,** approximately 18 mi long, runs along both sides of the Charles River from Watertown Square to the Museum of Science. For other path locations, call the MDC (☞ *above*).

Minuteman Bicycle Trail. The 11-mi trail runs from the Alewife Red Line station in Cambridge through Arlington, Lexington, and Bedford along the bed of an old railroad track.

The **Bicycle Coalition of Massachusetts** (⊠ 214A Broadway, Cambridge 02139, ☎ 617/491–7433), an advocacy group that works to improve conditions for area cyclists, has information on organized rides and sells bike maps of Boston and the state. Thanks in part to their efforts, for $5 you can buy a permit to take your bike on subway and commuter rail trains, subject to certain time restrictions. Call the Bicycle Coalition for details.

In Boston's South End, **Community Bicycle Supply** (⊠ 496 Tremont St. at E. Berkeley St., ☎ 617/542–8623) rents cycles during the spring and summer.

The **Bicycle Workshop** (⊠ 259 Massachusetts Ave., Cambridge, ☎ 617/876–6555) rents city bicycles and fixes flat tires while you wait.

Billiards

Flat Top Johnny's (⊠ 1 Kendall Square, Cambridge, ☎ 617/494–9565) is the hippest billiards hall around. Alternative rock, chosen by the tattooed and pierced staff, blares from behind the bar, which has one of the best selections of draft beers in the city. The exposed brick walls show off the art of local painters, and the red felt-topped tables are an attraction if you're tired of headache green. Members of Boston's better local bands often hang out here on their nights off.

Jillian's Billiard Club (⊠ 145 Ipswich St., ☎ 617/437–0300) is a semi-posh joint with the atmosphere of an English gentleman's library. Professional lessons are available, and the 56-table pool hall also has three bars, a café, darts, shuffleboard, table tennis, a motion simulator, and more than 200 high-tech games.

Boating

On the Charles River and Inner Harbor to North Washington Street, all types of pleasure boats (except inflatables) are allowed on the waters of Boston Harbor, Dorchester inner and outer bays, and the Neponset River from the Granite Avenue Bridge to Dorchester Bay.

Public landings and floats are located at **North End Waterfront Park** (⊠ Commercial St., Boston Harbor), **Kelly's Landing** (⊠ Day Blvd., South Boston), and at these locations along the Charles River: **Clarendon Street,** Back Bay; **Hatch Shell,** Embankment Road, Back Bay; **Pinckney Street Landing,** Back Bay; **Brooks Street,** Nonantum Road, Brighton; **Richard T. Artesani Playground,** off Soldiers Field Road, Brighton.

There is another launching area at the **Monsignor William J. Daly Recreation Center** (⊠ Nonantum Road, Brighton, ☎ 617/727–4708) on the Charles River.

Community Boating (⊠ 21 Embankment Rd., ☎ 617/523–1038), near the Charles Street footbridge that crosses Storrow Drive, has America's oldest public sailing program. From April through October you can have a two-day membership with unlimited boat use for $50 if you are qualified to sail solo. Monthlong memberships, during which you may learn to sail solo, are available for $65; 75 days costs $130.

From April through October, rent your own canoe, kayak, or shell from **Charles River Canoe and Kayak Center** (⊠ 2401 Commonwealth Ave., Newton, ☎ 617/965–5110). A second location (⊠ Soldiers' Field Rd., Allston), closer to the city, is open weekends.

Camping

Of Boston's **Harbor Islands,** Lovells, Peddocks, Grape, and Bumpkin allow camping with a permit. Camping season runs from July through Labor Day. Swimming is available at Lovells, Grape, and Gallups islands, but lifeguards are on duty only at Lovells. Pets and alcohol are not allowed on the Harbor Islands. **Boston Harbor Cruises** (⊠ 1 Long Wharf, ☎ 617/227–4321) provides boat service to the Harbor Islands. For camping reservations, general Harbor Islands information, and specific questions about islands, contact the **Boston Harbor Islands State Park** (☎ 617/727–7676; ☞ Downtown Boston *in* Chapter 2).

Fishing

You can try freshwater fishing along the shores of the Charles River at **Turtle Pond** (⊠ Stony Brook Reservation, Turtle Pond Pkwy., Hyde Park) or at **Jamaica Pond** (⊠ Rte. 1, Jamaica Plain), which is stocked with trout and runs an annual one-day fishing contest. For fishing from shore, try the **John J. McCorkle Fishing Pier** (⊠ Castle Island) and the pier at **City Point,** both located off Day Boulevard in South Boston. The Boston Harbor Islands (☞ Downtown Boston *in* Chapter 2) also permit fishing.

Boston Park Rangers (⊠ Boston Parks and Recreation Dept., ☎ 617/635–7383) offer fishing lessons for youth groups at Jamaica Pond. Call for program information and reservations.

Golfing

Franklin Park William Devine Golf Course (⊠ Franklin Park, Dorchester, ☎ 617/265–4084), a 6,100-yard, par-70 course was created in the early 1900s by Donald Ross. It is open year-round, weather permitting. Greens fees are $11 for 9 holes and $19 for 18 holes on weekdays, and $12 and $22 respectively on weekends (9 holes only after 3 on weekends). Fees are $2 to $3 higher for nonresidents of Boston. The golf course also functions as a family picnic ground and jogging spot for locals.

The **Massachusetts Golf Association** (⊠ 175 Highland Ave., Needham, ☎ 781/449–3000) represents more than 270 clubs in the state and will provide information on courses that are open to the public as well as on equipment rentals. The office is open weekdays 9–4:30.

Hiking

There are excellent footpaths for hikers in the 450-acre **Stony Brook Reservation** (☎ 617/698–1802) in Boston's Hyde Park and West Roxbury sections. A 20-minute drive south of Boston, the **Blue Hills Reservation** (⊠ Exit 3, Houghton's Pond, off Rte. 128, Milton, ☎ 617/698–1802) offers 7,000 acres of woodland and about 150 mi of trails, some ideal for cross-country skiing, some designated for mountain biking. Maps ($1) are always available on the headquarters' front porch.

The **Blue Hills Trailside Museum,** operated by the Massachusetts Audubon Society, presents discussions on natural history, live animals, and such special events as organized hikes and walks. ⊠ *Exit 2B off Rte. 128 to Rte. 138, Milton,* ☎ *617/333–0690.* ⛱ *$3.* ⏱ *Tue.–Sun. 10–5.*

The **Boston Harbor Islands** (☞ Downtown Boston *in* Chapter 2) also provide a convenient and off-the-beaten-path venue for beach walks.

Jogging

Both sides of the **Charles River** are popular with joggers (☞ Bicycling, *above*). For the location of other paths in greater Boston, ask your hotel's concierge for a jogging map. Another great source of information is the **Bill Rodgers Running Center** (⊠ Faneuil Hall Marketplace, ☎ 617/ 723–5612), which also sells running equipment (Bill Rodgers is a four-time marathon winner). At **Castle Island** in South Boston (☞ South Boston *in* Chapter 2), rollerbladers and joggers exercise alongside strolling lovers and mothers pushing baby carriages.

Physical Fitness

Numerous **hotels** offer health club facilities or exercise rooms for guests (☞ Chapter 5): Back Bay Hilton, Boston Harbor Hotel at Rowes Wharf, Boston Park Plaza Hotel & Towers, Cambridge Center Marriott, The Charles, The Colonnade Copley Square Hotel (free use of the Westin's club), Doubletree Guest Suites, Four Seasons, Harborside Hyatt Conference Center and Hotel, Holiday Inn Logan Airport, Holiday Inn Select Government Center, Hyatt Regency Cambridge, Marriott Copley Place, Marriott Long Wharf, Le Meridien, Midtown, Omni Parker House (use of nearby Fitcorp Health and Fitness Center at a discounted rate), Radisson Hotel Boston, Ramada Inn Logan Airport, Ritz-Carlton, Royal Sonesta, Sheraton Boston Hotel & Towers, Sheraton Commander, Swissôtel, The Westin.

Several of these hotels also allow nonguests to use their health club facilities for $10 per day, including the Marriott Copley Place, the Sheraton Boston Hotel & Towers, and the Westin (all in the Back Bay), the Meridien downtown, and the Cambridge Center Marriott in Kendall Square.

The extensive facilities of the **Greater Boston YMCA** (⊠ 316 Huntington Ave., ☎ 617/536–7800) are open for $5 per day (for up to two weeks) to members of other YMCAs in the Boston area; if you have out-of-state YMCA membership, you can use the Boston Y free for up to a week. Nonmembers pay $10 per day or $65 for one month. The site has pools, squash, racquetball courts, cardiovascular equipment, free weights, aerobics, track, and sauna.

The **Boston Athletic Club** (⊠ 653 Summer St., ☎ 617/269–4300) offers use of its facilities, including a pool, to guests of downtown hotels for $20 per day (simply present your hotel key). **Fitcorp** (⊠ 1 Beacon St., ☎ 617/248–9797; ⊠ Prudential Center, ☎ 617/262–2050; ⊠ 350 Longwood Ave., ☎ 617/732–7111; ⊠ 133 Federal St., ☎ 617/542–1010) offers a similar arrangement but does not have a pool; the cost is $12 per day, or $100 for 10 visits.

The daily guest fee is $12 at **Boston Fitness for Women** (⊠ 27 School St., between Tremont and Washington streets downtown, ☎ 617/523–3098).

Rollerblading

From May through October, **Memorial Drive** on the Cambridge side of the Charles River is closed to auto traffic on Sunday from 11 AM to

7 PM, when the area between the Western Avenue Bridge and Eliot Bridge is transformed into **Riverbend Park.** On the Boston side of the river, the **Esplanade** area offers some excellent skating opportunities. **Beacon Hill Skate Shop** (⊠ 135 Charles St. South, off Tremont St. near the Wang Center for the Performing Arts, ☎ 617/482–7400) rents blades for $5 per hour or $15 per day (you need a credit card for deposit) year-round. Safety equipment is included. **Eric Flaim In-Motion Sports** (⊠ 349 Newbury St., ☎ 617/247–3284) also rents in-line skates for $15 per day.

Skating

From late November to early April (weather permitting), skaters can glide across the **Frog Pond** (☎ 617/635–2197) in Boston Common. A warming hut, a concession stand, skate rentals ($5 for adults), lockers ($1), skate sharpening ($6), and lessons are available. Admission is $3 for adults; kids under 14 skate free (kids' rentals are free, too). Frog Pond hours are Mondays 10–5, Tuesdays through Thursdays 10–9, Fridays and Saturdays 10–10, and Sundays 10–9. If the kids get tired of skating, there's a playground adjacent.

In winter, skaters also flock to the frozen waters of the **Boston Public Garden's lagoon.** Ice on one side of the bridge is for figure skating, while the other side is for faster-paced ice hockey. **Beacon Hill Skate Shop** (☞ Rollerblading, *above*) rents skates for use in the Public Garden for $5 per hour or $10 per day.

Listed here are a few of the 19 public ice-skating rinks operated by the MDC. For a complete list of rinks and schedules of hours of operation, contact the Department of Parks and Recreation (☎ 617/727–9547).

Charlestown Rink, Rutherford Avenue near Prison Point Bridge; **Cleveland Circle Rink,** Cleveland Circle, Brighton; **North End Rink,** Commercial St.; **South Boston Rink,** Day Blvd.

Skiing

Blue Hills Ski Area (⊠ Blue Hills Reservation, Washington St., Canton, exit 2B from Rte. 128, just south of Boston city limit, ☎ 781/828–5090 for ticket and ski school information; 781/828–5070 for recorded report on snow conditions) is an MDC-managed downhill facility with a 1,200-ft double chairlift, a j-bar, and two rope tows. Its facilities include seven slopes, snowmaking, a ski school, equipment rentals, and a restaurant.

For serious skiing, **Loon Mountain** (☎ 603/745–8111 or 800/229–5666) and **Waterville Valley** (☎ 603/236–8311 or 800/468–2553) are both about 2½ hours north of Boston in New Hampshire. The Waterville Valley Chamber of Commerce (☎ 603/726–3804) is also a good source for ski information.

Swimming

A number of **hotels** offer swimming pools for guests, but not all are indoors (☞ Chapter 5): Back Bay Hilton, Boston Harbor Hotel at Rowes Wharf, Cambridge Center Marriott Hotel, The Charles, The Colonnade, Doubletree Guest Suites, Four Seasons, Harborside Hyatt Conference Center and Hotel, Holiday Inn Logan Airport, Holiday Inn Select Government Center, Howard Johnson's Cambridge, Howard Johnson's Kenmore Square, Hyatt Regency Cambridge, Le Meridien, Marriott Copley Place, Marriott Long Wharf, Midtown, Radisson Hotel Boston,

Ramada Inn Logan Airport, Royal Sonesta, Sheraton Boston Hotel & Towers, Susse Chalet Motor Lodges, Swissôtel, and The Westin.

The Boston Athletic Club (☞ Physical Fitness, *above*) has an eight-lane, 18.3-m (20-yd) heated pool.

The Central Branch of the **Greater Boston YMCA** (☞ Physical Fitness, *above*) on Huntington Avenue has a 22.9-m (25-yd) heated pool with three wide lap lanes. For outdoor swimming options, *see also* Beaches, *below.*

Tennis

The MDC maintains tennis courts throughout Boston. No permit is required to use these courts, which operate on a first-come, first-served basis. Call ☎ 617/727–9547 for more information on the following and other public courts: **Charlesbank Park** (lighted), along Storrow Drive opposite Charles Street; **North End Park**, Commercial Street; and **Marine Park** (lighted), South Boston.

BEACHES

Yes, Boston is on the ocean, and no, it is not renowned for its beaches. The harbor is a working harbor, with several million people living nearby, and the water is hardly Bahamas-pure. However, beginning in 1988 the city embarked on a massive cleanup of the harbor waters and opened a brand-new sewage works in 1995. Consequently, public beaches have been spruced up, new facilities added, and the former governor has taken a few well-publicized dips in the once-murky waters. Most beaches are in relatively family-oriented sections of town and remain largely neighborhood affairs.

The main beaches are **Malibu Beach, Savin Hill Beach,** and **Tenean Beach,** off Morrissey Boulevard, in Dorchester, near the John F. Kennedy Library; and **Carson Beach, Castle Island Beach, City Point Beach, M Street Beach,** and **Pleasure Bay,** off Day Boulevard, in South Boston. The only swimming off the Harbor Islands is at **Lovells Island, Grape Island,** and **Gallups Island** (lifeguards are on duty only at Lovells).

These beaches are open from the end of June to the beginning of September, when lifeguards are on duty daily from 10 to 6. High temperatures and high tide may cause schedule changes. For further information, call the MDC (Recreation Division: ☎ 617/727–9547, ext. 450).

Several excellent beaches a short distance from the city make lovely day trips. Among the nicest are **Nantasket Beach** in Hull, **Crane's Beach** in Ipswich, **Plum Island** (☞ Chapter 9) in Newburyport, and **Wingaersheek Beach** in Gloucester.

8 Shopping

Boston, Edith Wharton once said,
thought she was too fashionable to be
serious, whereas New York found her
too serious to be fashionable. Today
Boston and Cambridge's tens of
thousands of students set the dress
code—from scrubbed and preppy to the
thrift-store slacker look, accessorized
with tattoos, piercings, and dyed hair—
and there's a store to please them all.
Natives and transplants alike wear
their pride wherever they go: don't
even try to count the T-shirts and
sweatshirts you see emblazoned with
BOSTON or the name of a college or
hometown team. Once you're outfitted
like a native, browse the dozens of
bookstores.

BLAME IT, PERHAPS, ON THE STILL BOOMING business in *Cheers* merchandise. But the last three years
have seen the Boston shopping scene explode—
with both visitor and local business. Now that Boston is a world-class
city, the prevailing attitude is that if the world wants to visit, the world
wants to shop. Purists may bemoan the proliferation of chain stores;
determined shoppers, however, can still find unusual, one-of-a-kind items
in idiosyncratic boutiques and bookstores. The well-heeled may wish
to peruse the top-class designers on Newbury Street, while the more
down-to-earth can head for Downtown Crossing, where department
store giants Macy's and Filene's preside. Upscale mall shoppers can cruise
Copley Place and the Prudential Center, connected by walkways high
above the street. Bargains abound in the used-book and music stores,
thrift shops, and clothing discounters. Closer to the waterfront, the huge
Quincy Market development is a perpetual Christmas morning, with
dozens of trendy little shops waiting to be unwrapped.

Boston's shops and stores are generally open Monday through Saturday from 9 or 10 until 6 or 7; many stay open until 8 one night late
in the week, usually Thursday, and open Sunday at 10 or noon and
close at 5 or 6. Many mall stores are open until 9 PM weekdays. Most
stores accept major credit cards. Traveler's checks are welcome throughout the city (though it may be difficult for a small store to cash a check
of large denomination). The state sales tax of 5% does not apply to
food, except in restaurants, or clothing, except for purchases of more
than $300. Boston's two daily newspapers, the *Globe* and the *Herald,*
are the best places to learn about sales.

Updated by
Stephanie
Schorow

Major Shopping Districts

Boston's shops and department stores are concentrated in the area
bounded by Quincy Market, the Back Bay, and downtown. There are
few outlet stores in center city, but plenty of bargains nevertheless, particularly in the world-famous Filene's Basement and Chinatown's fab-
ric district. In Cambridge, you'll find most of the shopping around
Harvard and Central squares, and along Massachusetts Avenue between
Porter and Harvard squares.

Boston

Boylston Street, in the heart of the Back Bay and parallel to Newbury
Street, is home to more than 100 stores, including Talbot's, Eddie
Bauer, City Sports, and F. A. O. Schwarz. At the east end of Boylston
Street at Arlington Street is a very elegant complex, **Heritage on the
Garden** (⊠ 300 Boylston St., ☎ 617/426–9500), that contains Her-
mès, Saint John's Knits, Sonia Rykiel, and Escada. At the west end of
Boylston Street is the updated and upscale **Prudential Center** complex,
where specialty shops and department stores, among them Saks Fifth
Avenue, cluster under an airy atrium.

Charles Street, in Beacon Hill, draws antiques and boutique lovers. Some
of the city's prettiest shops are here. **River Street,** parallel to Charles
and near the intersection with Chestnut, is also an excellent source for
antiques.

Copley Place (⊠ 100 Huntington Ave., ☎ 617/375–4400), an indoor
shopping mall that connects the Westin and Marriott hotels in Back
Bay, is a blend of the elegant, the glitzy, and the often overpriced. The
Neiman Marcus department store anchors more than 80 stores, restaurants, and cinemas. Prices in the shops on the second level tend to be
a bit lower.

Downtown Crossing, Boston's downtown shopping area, has a festival feeling year-round in its usually crowded pedestrian mall, with outdoor merchandise kiosks, street performers, and benches for people-watchers. The city's two largest department stores, Macy's and Filene's (with the famous Filene's Basement beneath it), are here. Nearby are Loehmann's and Marshall's, discount clothing stores that aim to give Filene's Basement a run for its money.

Faneuil Hall Marketplace (☎ 617/338–2323) has dozens of specialty shops, pushcarts with a variety of wares, street performers, and one of the area's great food experiences, Quincy Market. The intrepid shopper must cope with crowds of people, particularly on weekends. Friday and Saturday are the days to walk through **Haymarket,** a jumble of outdoor fruit and vegetable vendors, meat markets, and fishmongers. **Marketplace Center,** adjacent to Faneuil Hall Marketplace, has more shops and chain stores.

Newbury Street is Boston's eight-block-long version of New York's Fifth Avenue. Near the Public Garden, Newbury Street is quite upscale, with the most stylish clothing boutiques, the most up-to-date art galleries, the most sparkling jewelry, and formal afternoon tea in the Ritz-Carlton Hotel. Toward Massachusetts Avenue, Newbury Street gets funkier with hip clothing stores, ice-cream shops, music stores, bookstores, and Tower Music and Video.

Cambridge

CambridgeSide Galleria (⊠ 100 CambridgeSide Pl., ☎ 617/621–8666) is a three-story mall in East Cambridge, accessible from the Green Line Lechmere T stop and a shuttle from the Kendall T stop. It encompasses about 100 shops, including the anchor stores of Filene's and Sears. Parking costs $1 for the first hour, then $1 per 30 minutes. Weeknights, weekends, and holidays it's a flat $3.

Harvard Square comprises just a few blocks but holds more than 150 stores selling clothes, books and records, furnishings, and a surprising range of specialty items. Three small weatherproof shopping complexes are just off the square: the **Garage** (⊠ 38 John F. Kennedy St.), the **Galeria** (⊠ 57 John F. Kennedy St.), and **The Holyoke Center** (⊠ 1352 Massachusetts Ave). The Holyoke Center now also has an outlet for BosTix, where half price arts and entertainment tickets for Cambridge and Boston venues may be purchased. An eye-catching building has been constructed over the old bus terminal at 1 Brattle Square, housing HMV and the Limited. And, for better or worse, you can find a branch of just about any popular chain within a few blocks, including Urban Outfitters, the Body Shop, and Crate and Barrel. For book lovers, the Cambridge Visitor Information Booth (⊠ Zero Harvard Sq., ☎ 617/497–1630) supplies a wonderful map of bookstores in the area.

Porter Square, west on Massachusetts Avenue from Harvard Square, is home to distinctive clothing stores such as **Susanna** (⊠ 1776 Massachusetts Ave., ☎ 617/492–0334) and **Looks** (⊠ 1607 Massachusetts Ave., ☎ 617/491–4251), plus crafts shops, coffee shops, natural food stores, and restaurants. The other direction on Massachusetts Avenue from Harvard Square leads to the less upscale, funky environs of **Central Square.**

Department Stores

Filene's (⊠ 426 Washington St., ☎ 617/357–2100; ⊠ CambridgeSide Galleria, Cambridge, ☎ 617/621–3800) is a full-service department store that carries a complete line of name-brand and designer-label men's and women's formal, casual, and career clothing. Furs, jewelry, shoes, and cosmetics are found at the Downtown Crossing store, where escalators connect to the famous Filene's Basement, now a separate business entity.

Filene's Basement (⊠ 426 Washington St., ☎ 617/542–2011) has spawned suburban outlets, but this is the only branch where items are automatically reduced in price according to the number of days they've been on the rack. The competition can be stiff for the great values on discontinued, overstocked, or slightly irregular items, especially those from stores such as Neiman Marcus and Henri Bendel. You can enter directly from the Downtown Crossing T station (Red and Orange Lines).

Loehmann's (⊠ 385 Washington St., ☎ 617/338–7177) opened its fourth Massachusetts store just yards from Filene's Basement. The off-price clothing store, long a legend among bargain hunters, has won a few converts here.

Lord & Taylor (⊠ 760 Boylston St., ☎ 617/262–6000) has classic clothing, from casual to elegant, by such designers as Anne Klein and Ralph Lauren, along with accessories, cosmetics, jewelry, and children's clothing.

Macy's (⊠ 450 Washington St., ☎ 617/357–3000) first bought and then renamed Jordan Marsh, New England's largest department store since the mid-19th century. It carries men's and women's clothing, including top designers, as well as housewares, furniture, and cosmetics. Like Filene's, it has direct access to the Downtown Crossing T station.

Neiman Marcus (⊠ 5 Copley Pl., ☎ 617/536–3660), the flashy Texas retailer, has three levels of high fashion, Steuben glass, and gadgetry.

Saks Fifth Avenue (⊠ 1 Ring Rd., Prudential Center, ☎ 617/262–8500) offers top-of-the-line clothing, from more traditional styles to avant-garde apparel, plus accessories and cosmetics.

Food Stores

Baked Goods

Bagel outlets now seem to be as ubiquitous in Boston as Starbucks in Seattle, but many here still opt for old-fashioned sweets and treats at neighborhood institutions.

Finagle a Bagel (⊠ 535 Boylston St., ☎ 617/266–2500; ⊠ Marketplace Center, ☎ 617/367–9720; ⊠ 1 Center Plaza, Government Center, ☎ 617/523–6500) has some of the best bagels in the area, both classic varieties and new flavors such as Super Cinnamon Raisin.

Modern Pastry Shop (⊠ 257 Hanover St., North End, ☎ 617/523–3783) is open till about 9 every night, with a tempting array of authentic Italian desserts such as its unrivaled *torrone* (nougat), tiramisu, and cannoli.

Rosie's Bakery (⊠ 2 South Station, ☎ 617/439-4684; ⊠ 243 Hampshire St., Cambridge, ☎ 617/491–9488) is everyone's sweetheart. Rosie's has tempting cookies, pastries, and cakes, but it's their chocolate chip cookies that have put the shop into *Boston Magazine*'s Best of Boston Hall of Fame. Go for the Chocolate Orgasm brownie, the ultimate experience for the chocoholic.

Candy

Dairy Fresh Candies (⊠ 57 Salem St., ☎ 617/742–2639), a long-standing family-owned business in a tiny store, sells European packaged assortments, truffles, hard candy, dried fruits, nuts, and all kinds of chocolates.

Ice Cream

Herrell's (⊠ 15 Dunster St., Cambridge, ☎ 617/497–2179; ⊠ 155 Brighton Ave., Allston, ☎ 617/782–9599; ⊠ 350 Longwood Ave.,

Boston Shopping

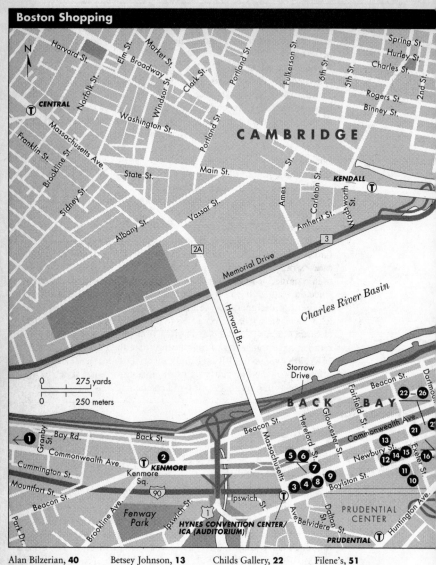

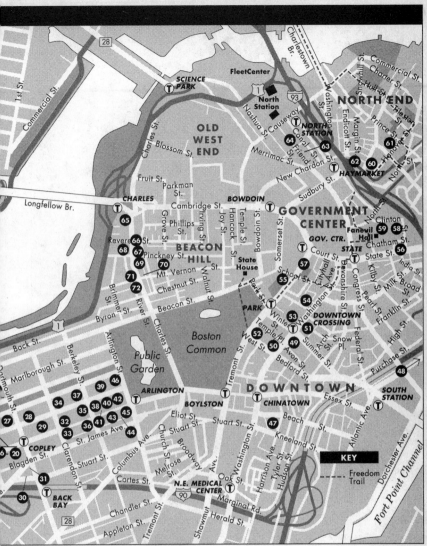

J. P. Licks
Homemade
Ice Cream, **4**
Jos. A. Bank
Clothiers, **41**
Judi Rotenberg
Gallery, **29**
Kenneth Cole, **29**
Kitchen Arts, **26**
Koo de Kir, **72**
Lauriat's, **30**
Loehmann's, **53**
Lord & Taylor, **11**
Louis, Boston, **35**
Macy's, **49**
Modern Pastry
Shop, **61**

Mystery Train, **9**
Neiman Marcus, **31**
Newbury Comics, **4**
Nielsen Gallery, **23**
Niketown, **15**
North End
Fabrics, **47**
Pucker Gallery, **24**
Robert Klein
Gallery, **38**
Rolly-Michaux, **27**
Saks Fifth Avenue, **10**
Savenor's, **65**
Shreve, Crump &
Low, **45**

Society of Arts
and Crafts, **25**
Sweet Peas Home, **32**
Tiffany & Co., **30**
Tower Records
Video Books, **3**
Trident Bookseller
and Café, **8**
Twentieth Century
Limited, **70**
Upstairs
Downstairs, **69**
Vose Galleries, **12**
Waterstone's
Booksellers, **21, 59**
We Think the World
of You, **73**

Women's
Educational and
Industrial
Union, **43**

172

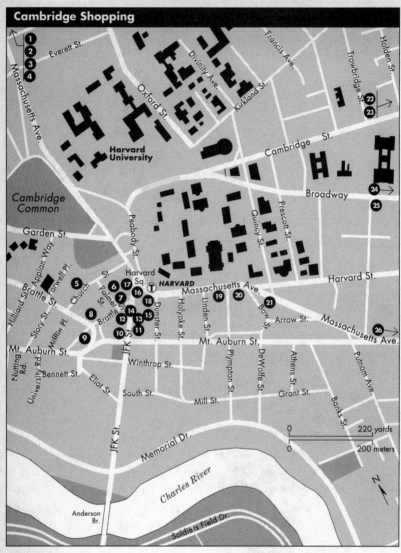

Cambridge Shopping

Bread & Circus, **3**

Buck a Book, **13**

Cambridge Antique
Market, **22**

Cambridge Artists'
Cooperative, **5**

Cardullo's, **7**

The Garment
District, **24**

Globe Corner
Bookstore, **6**

Grolier Poetry
Bookshop, **20**

Harvard
Bookstore, **19**

Harvard Coop
Society, **17**

Herrell's, **15**

HMV, **9**

Jasmine, **8**

Kate's Mystery
Books, **1**

Loulou's Tealuxe, **14**

Marathon Sports, **4**

Mystery Train, **21**

New Words, **25**

Newbury Comics, **11**

Out-of-Town
News, **16**

Rosie's Bakery, **23**

Stereo Jack's, **2**

Toscanni
Ice Cream, **18, 26**

Tower Records
Video Books, **10**

WordsWorth, **12**

Boston, ☎ 617/731–9599) was founded by Steve Herrell, the original creator of Steve's Ice Cream, who, after selling his name, decided to get back in the ice-cream business. Nondairy ice cream and frozen yogurt augment the extensive variety of regular flavors.

J. P. Licks Homemade Ice Cream (✉ 352 Newbury St., ☎ 617/236–1666; ✉ 674 Centre St., Jamaica Plain, ☎ 617/524–6740) has sorbet if you're seeking a light touch, as well as rich desserts.

Toscanni Ice Cream (✉ 899 Main St., Cambridge, ☎ 617/491-5877; ✉ 1320 Massachusetts Ave., Cambridge,☎ 617/354–9350 has long been a popular hangout near MIT and has recently expanded its creamy double dips and creative flavors and sauces to a Harvard Square site.

Specialty Grocers

Cardullo's (✉ 6 Brattle St., Cambridge, ☎ 617/491–8888) purveys exotic imports, sandwiches to go, cheeses, wines, and more than 270 varieties of beer amid impressive clutter.

Bread & Circus (✉ 186 Alewife Brook Pkwy., Cambridge, ☎ 617/491–0040; ✉ 115 Prospect St., Cambridge, ☎ 617/492–0070), one of the original health food/gourmet grocery stores, has organic fruit, fresh herbs and other New Age staples, although prices are steep.

J. Pace & Son (✉ 42 Cross St., ☎ 617/227–9673) is a friendly neighborhood Italian grocer that carries a variety of olive oils, pastas, and cheeses; if you don't feel like making your own lunch, stop at the store's café.

Savenor's (✉ 160 Charles St., ☎ 617/723–6328) carries outstanding cheeses, breads, prime cuts of meat, exotic game, and fine produce in a small but well-organized space.

Specialty Stores

Antiques

There are some excellent antiques stores on Newbury Street and in the South End, but Charles Street—coincidentally, one of the city's oldest streets—is the place to go for a concentrated perusal of antiquities.

Antiques (✉ 125 Newbury St., ☎ 617/424-8823) has a selection of country French and some Italian 18th- and 19th-century antiques and furniture; Chinese lamps and vases; ivory; and silver.

Boston Antique Co-op (✉ 119 Charles St., ☎ 617/227–9810 or 227–9811) is a collection of dealers that occupies two floors, carrying everything from vintage photos and paintings to porcelain, silver, bronzes, and furniture.

Cambridge Antique Market (✉ 201 Msgr. O'Brien Hwy., Cambridge, ☎ 617/868–9655), off the beaten track, has four floors of dealers and pieces ranging from 19th-century furniture to vintage clothing, as well as plenty of reasonably priced items.

Churchill Galleries (✉ 103 Charles St., ☎ 617/722–9490) has fine period furniture, paintings, and decorative objects in a elegant setting.

Eugene Galleries (✉ 76 Charles St., ☎ 617/227–3062) is chockablock with prints, etchings, old maps, city views, and books; it's a place for lovers of both antiques and art.

Shreve, Crump & Low (✉ 330 Boylston St., ☎ 617/267–9100), the jewelry store, also has 18th- and 19th-century English and American furniture, silver, Chinese export porcelain, and decorative lamps.

Upstairs Downstairs (✉ 93 Charles St., ☎ 617/367–1950) has the atmosphere of an upscale country store, with a Portuguese duck pitcher next to a hand-painted Mexican chair, plus cabinets, chests, and other furniture.

Art Galleries

Alpha Gallery (⌧ 14 Newbury St., ☎ 617/536–4465) sells 19th- and 20th-century American and European painting, sculpture, and master prints.

Barbara Krakow Gallery (⌧ 10 Newbury St., 5th floor, ☎ 617/262–4490) deals in contemporary, generally minimalist or conceptual, American and European paintings, photographs, drawings, and prints.

Childs Gallery (⌧ 169 Newbury St., ☎ 617/266–1108) carries paintings, prints, drawings, watercolors, and sculpture from the 16th to the 20th centuries.

Copley Society of Boston (⌧ 158 Newbury St., ☎ 617/536–5049) presents the works of well-known and aspiring New England artists. The nonprofit membership organization was founded in 1879.

Gallery NAGA (⌧ 67 Newbury St., ☎ 617/267–9060) offers contemporary paintings, sculpture, and furniture.

Guild of Boston Artists (⌧ 162 Newbury St., ☎ 617/536–7660), a nonprofit gallery, sells representational watercolors, oils, graphics, and sculpture by guild members.

Haley and Steele (⌧ 91 Newbury St., ☎ 617/536–6339) specializes in 19th-century British sporting, historical New England, and marine prints.

Judi Rotenberg Gallery (⌧ 130 Newbury St., ☎ 617/437–1518) represents painters Zygmund Jankowski, Oliver Balf, Roz Farbush, Charles Movalli, Jason Berger, and Harold and Judi Rotenberg, and sculptor Marianna Pineda.

Nielsen Gallery (⌧ 179 Newbury St., ☎ 617/266–4835) showcases established and aspiring artists, as well as representative and abstract paintings and prints.

Pucker Gallery (⌧ 171 Newbury St., ☎ 617/267–9473) sells contemporary paintings, sculpture, ceramics, and prints, plus Inuit and African works.

Robert Klein Gallery (⌧ 38 Newbury St., ☎ 617/267–7997) stocks contemporary and vintage photographs by international and national photographers, including Ansel Adams, Diane Arbus, and Edward Weston.

Rolly-Michaux (⌧ 290 Dartmouth St., ☎ 617/536–9898) has 20th-century paintings, graphics, silk screens, and sculpture including works by Moore, Calder, Picasso, Chagall, Miró, and Matisse. It also sells 18th-century French antiques.

Vose Galleries (⌧ 238 Newbury St., ☎ 617/536–6176), established in 1841, specializes in 19th- and 20th-century American art, including the Hudson River School, Boston School, and American Impressionists.

Books

If Boston and Cambridge have bragging rights to anything, it would be to their bookstores, many of which stay open late into the evening. Many stores sponsor author readings and literary programs.

Avenue Victor Hugo (⌧ 339 Newbury St., ☎ 617/266–7746) has two crowded floors of quality used books and a great selection of old magazines.

Barnes & Noble at BU (⌧ 660 Beacon St., Kenmore Sq., ☎ 617/267–8484), among New England's largest bookstores, has three floors of best-sellers, out-of-print collections, magazines, maps, and a café catering to Boston University students.

Borders Books and Music (⌧ Corner of Washington and School Sts., ☎ 617/557–7188), in a former bank, is a combination bookstore, music store, and café, Borders has a large selection of art and travel books.

Brattle Bookstore (⌧ 9 West St., ☎ 617/542–0210 or 800/447-9595) was built by the late George Gloss into Boston's best used and rare book shop. Today, his son, Kenneth, fields the queries from passionate book lovers. If the book they want is out of print, Brattle has it or can probably find it.

Buck a Book (⊠ 125 Tremont St., ☎ 617/357–1919; ⊠ 38 Court St., ☎ 617/367–9419; ⊠ 30 JFK St., Cambridge, ☎ 617/492–5500) is the ultimate discount bookstore, with overstocked fiction, nonfiction, and children's books, plus stationery and gift wrap. "Better" books run $3 and up, but there is always a find for a buck.

Globe Corner Bookstore branches (⊠ 500 Boylston St., ☎ 617/859–8008; ⊠ 28 Church St., Cambridge, ☎ 617/497–6277) are the best sources by far for domestic and international travel books and maps; they also carry very good selections of books about New England and by New England authors.

Grolier Poetry Bookshop (⊠ 6 Plympton St., Cambridge, ☎ 617/547–4648), founded in 1927, specializes in the writings of those whose vice is verse.

Harvard Bookstore (⊠ 1256 Massachusetts Ave., Cambridge, ☎ 617/661–1515) serves the intellectual and academic community with new titles upstairs and used and remaindered books downstairs.

Harvard Coop Society (⊠ 1400 Massachusetts Ave., Cambridge, ☎ 617/499–2000; ⊠ MIT, 3 Cambridge Center, ☎ 617/499–3200), begun in 1882 as a nonprofit service for students and faculty, is now managed by Barnes & Noble. They offer a large selection of books (most at discounts), textbooks, stationery, and music.

Kate's Mystery Books (⊠ 2211 Massachusetts Ave., Cambridge, ☎ 617/491–2660), a favorite Cambridge haunt, is a good place to find mysteries by local writers; look for the authors in person at one of the shop's frequent readings and events.

Lauriat's (⊠ Copley Pl. at 100 Huntingon Ave., ☎ 617/262–8858) is a popular spot for book browsers, conveniently located in the Copley Square complex.

New Words (⊠ 186 Hampshire St., Cambridge, ☎ 617/876–5310) is New England's largest and oldest women's bookstore; it also sells gifts, stationery, and children's books.

Trident Bookseller and Café (⊠ 338 Newbury St., ☎ 617/267–8688) offers browsers an eclectic collection of books, tapes, and magazines, as well as a limited but tasty selection of homemade items on the café menu.

Waterstone's Booksellers (⊠ 26 Exeter St., ☎ 617/859–7300; ⊠ Quincy Market, Faneuil Hall Marketplace, ☎ 617/589–0930) has its flagship outlet in a former spiritualist temple and movie theater (☞ Exeter Theater *in* the Back Bay *in* Chapter 2) on the corner of busy Newbury Street. It has three floors offering an excellent selection of literature, health books, children's books, and journals, and hosts an extensive reading series.

We Think the World of You (⊠ 540 Tremont St., ☎ 617/423–1965), in the heart of the South End's gay neighborhood, specializes in travel literature and books with gay and lesbian themes and is a source of community news and tickets to gay and lesbian events.

WordsWorth (⊠ 30 Brattle St., Cambridge, ☎ 617/354–5201) is the biggest bookstore in Harvard Square, with 100,000 titles, most of them discounted. It's easy to get lost among the narrow stacks. Just down the block is **Curious George Goes to WordsWorth** (⊠ 1 John F. Kennedy St., ☎ 617/498–0062), an annex devoted entirely to children's books and an eclectic selection of book-related toys and activity sets.

Clothing

The terminally chic shop on Newbury Street, the hip hang in Harvard Square, and everyone goes Downtown for the real bargains.

Alan Bilzerian (⊠ 34 Newbury St., ☎ 617/536–1001) is the place to go for the most avant-garde and au courant men's and women's clothing in Boston.

Back Bay Harley-Davidson (⊠ 160 Newbury St., ☎ 617/236–0840) features hats, jackets, and other apparel with the distinctive Harley-Davidson logo.

Betsey Johnson (⊠ 201 Newbury St., ☎ 617/236–7072) is the place to take your teen-age daughter—if you dare—to finger leopard print tops and short, flirty dresses, and to remember your youth—or recapture it!

Chanel (⊠ 5 Newbury St., ☎ 617/859-0055), which opened at No. 5 in honor of its famous perfume, carries Chanel dresses, separates, bags, and shoes.

Brooks Brothers (⊠ 46 Newbury St., ☎ 617/267–2600; ⊠ 75 State St., ☎ 617/261–9990) offers traditional formal and casual clothing for men and women.

Emporio Armani (⊠ 210 Newbury St., ☎ 617/262–7300) sells sportier versions of the Italian designer's clothing, in addition to jeans, children's apparel, and home furnishings. The café next door, which spills out onto the sidewalk in warm weather, is popular with the store's international clientele.

Giorgio Armani (⊠ 22 Newbury St., ☎ 617/267–3200) is a top-of-the-line couture boutique of the Italian designer.

Jasmine (⊠ 329 Newbury St., ☎ 617/437–8466; ⊠ 37A Brattle St., Cambridge, ☎ 617/354–6043) has the work of current designers from New York and Los Angeles. The Cambridge store includes the Sola and Sola Men shoe boutiques; it wins raves for having the best shop windows in the Square.

Jos. A. Bank Clothiers (⊠ 399 Boylston St., ☎ 617/536–5050) is the store where Bostonians head for reasonably priced classic men's and women's apparel.

Louis, Boston (⊠ 234 Berkeley St., ☎ 617/262–6100) is the city's ultrapricey clothing store for men and women. You'll find elegantly tailored designs and a wide selection of imported clothing and accessories, including the latest Italian styles and subtly updated classics in everything from linen to tweeds. In the rear of the handsome brownstone building, the pricey **Café Louis** (☎ 617/266–4680) serves lunch and dinner.

Crafts

Alianza (⊠ 154 Newbury St., ☎ 627/262–2385) displays contemporary crafts including glowing glasswork, ceramics, and whimsical clocks.

Artful Hand (⊠ 36 Copley Pl. at 100 Huntington Ave., ☎ 617/262–9601) displays and sells jewelry, glass, glass sculpture, wood, pottery, lamps, and furniture by American artisans. There's also a wedding registry.

Artsmart (⊠ 272 Congress St., ☎ 617/695–0151) deals in high-quality art, including furniture, sculpture, jewelry, and designer home accessories. The emphasis here is on affordable, accessible art.

Cambridge Artists' Cooperative (⊠ 59A Church St., Cambridge, ☎ 617/868–4434) has innovative jewelry, ceramics, glass, weavings, quilts, leather, and woodwork. It tends to be expensive, but most of the items are truly one of a kind.

Society of Arts and Crafts (⊠ 175 Newbury St., ☎ 617/266–1810; ⊠ 101 Arch St., ☎ 617/345–0033) has an excellent assortment of high-quality ceramics, jewelry, leather, batik, weaving, and furniture by some of the country's finest craftspeople.

Fabrics

North End Fabrics (⊠ 31 Harrison Ave., ☎ 617/542–2763) has almost everything in fabrics, including bridal materials, imported laces, designer fabrics, fun furs, theatricals, and woolens.

Gifts

Bellezza Home and Garden (⊠ 129 Newbury St., ☎ 617/266-1183) sells exquisitely painted Italian bowls, plates, vases, planters, and tiles for inside and outside the home.

Black Ink (⊠ 101 Charles St., ☎ 617/723–3883) has reasonably priced rubber stamps, distinctive stationery, and funky gifts made from unusual materials.

Loulou's Lost & Found (⊠ 121 Newbury St., ☎ 617/859–8593) and **Loulou's Tealuxe** (⊠ Zero Brattle St., Cambridge, ☎ 617/441-0077) are the places to pick up Jazz-era tableware, salt and pepper shakers, and other items scavenged from old ships and hotels. The Tealuxe outlet sells 140 premium teas and tea accessories; you can also stop here for a cup of tea.

Women's Educational and Industrial Union (⊠ 356 Boylston St., ☎ 617/536–5651) sells cards, gifts, decorative items, children's clothing, and accessories on behalf of the social and educational organization founded in 1877. There is an excellent needlework department and a second-floor antiques shop. Look for the large gold swan above the door.

Home Furnishings

Kitchen Arts (⊠ 161 Newbury St., ☎ 617/266–8701) Here's where to find all sorts of gadgets, gizmos, and do-dads for culinary success and style.

Koo de Kir (⊠ 34 Charles St., ☎ 617/723–8111) has offbeat and modernistic furniture, lamps, chairs, candles, wineracks and other urban necessities.

Sweet Peas Home (⊠ 216 Clarendon St., ☎ 617/247–2828) offers colorful and whimsical handpainted furniture, plus vases, mirrors, and other accessories.

Jewelry

Dorfman Jewels (⊠ 24 Newbury St., ☎ 617/536–2022) is an elegant shop with first-class watches, pearls, and precious stones.

Shreve, Crump & Low (⊠ 330 Boylston St., ☎ 617/267–9100) sells the finest jewelry, stationery, china, crystal, and silver and an extensive collection of clocks and watches.

Tiffany & Co. (⊠ Copley Pl. at 100 Huntington Ave., ☎ 617/353–0222) is Fifth Avenue come to Boston, with the finest in gems and precious metal jewelry as well as flatware, crystal, china, stationery, and fragrances.

Twentieth Century Limited (⊠ 73 Charles St., ☎ 617/742–1031) has every kind of rhinestone concoction imaginable—perfect for the funky chic bauble babe in your life.

Newspapers and Periodicals

Out-of-Town News (⊠ Zero Harvard Sq., Cambridge, ☎ 617/354-7777) has a staggering cross section of the world's newspapers and magazines on sale here daily 6 AM–11:30 PM, and until midnight on Friday and Saturday.

Records, Tapes, and Compact Discs

As befitting a town with more than 20 colleges, music of all kinds is never far away, including a hot market in used vinyl.

HMV (⊠ 24 Winter St., ☎ 617/357–8444; ⊠ 1 Brattle Sq., Cambridge, ☎ 617/868–9696) is the British rival to Tower Records: a large selection of CDs and tapes of every sort, with listening stations to sample the wares.

Mystery Train (⊠ 306 Newbury St., ☎ 617/536–0216; ⊠ 1208 Massachusetts Ave., ☎ 617/536–0216) sells used and collectible CDs, tapes, and vinyl in some very hip settings.

Newbury Comics (⊠ 332 Newbury St., ☎ 617/236–4930; ⊠ 36 John F. Kennedy St., Cambridge, ☎ 617/491–0337) has a very friendly, very cool staff that sells the best selection of new rock and roll, especially independent pressings. Frequent sales keep prices down.

Stereo Jack's (⊠ 1686 Massachusetts Ave., Cambridge, ☎ 617/497–9447) has used and new vinyl records and CDs, particularly jazz, blues, and classical.

Tower Records Video Books (⊠ 360 Newbury St., ☎ 617/247–5900; ⊠ 95 Mt. Auburn St., Cambridge, ☎ 617/876–3377) has its second-largest store in the nation (after New York's Lincoln Center branch) in the Back Bay. Three enormous floors stock every kind of music imaginable, plus books, magazines, and videos.

Shoes

El Paso (⊠ 154 Newbury St., ☎ 617/536–2120) has cowboy boots wild—look for the green and white or the orange and white—and sober, plus belts and cowboy shirts.

Helen's Leather Shop (⊠ 110 Charles St., ☎ 617/742–2077) is one of New England's biggest Western boot dealers for men and women, with a variety of exotic animal-skin boots. There are leather jackets, belts, luggage and accessories, briefcases, sandals, and leather backpacks. Boots are from Lucchese, Larry Mahan, Dan Post, Tony Lama, Justin, and Frye.

Kenneth Cole (⊠ 128 Newbury St., ☎ 617/867–0836; ⊠ Copley Pl. at 100 Huntington Ave., ☎ 617/867–9580) sells comfortable classic and hip footwear.

Souvenirs

Boston City Store (⊠ Faneuil Hall basement, ☎ 617/635–2911) has a delightfully offbeat assortment of Boston souvenirs and memorabilia. It sells surplus municipal items such as vintage street signs, school supplies, and furniture, promotional posters, buttons, and pens. Profits from the store support neighborhood youth programs; it is closed Sundays. Enter on the north side of the hall.

Sporting Goods

Bill Rodgers Running Center (⊠ North Market, Faneuil Hall Marketplace, ☎ 617/723–5612) is a destination for Boston Marathon runners and wanna-bes. While you may not see champion Rodgers, the attentive staff will help you pick the best shoes or training regimens.

Eastern Mountain Sports (⊠ 1041 Commonwealth Ave., Brighton, ☎ 617/254–4250) offers tons of gear for the backpacker, camper, climber, or skier. The stock includes everything from tents and sleeping bags to technical mountaineering equipment—and a wide selection of casual clothing. The store is also a good source for books and maps for planning trips into the New England backcountry.

Eric Flaim In-Motion Sports (⊠ 349 Newbury St., ☎ 617/247–3284) is where to buy or rent Rollerblades and other in-line skates, young Boston's preferred mode of transportation and recreation.

Hilton's Tent City (⊠ 272 Friend St., Downtown, ☎ 617/227–9242), an out-of-the-way store in an old building, is stuffed to the gills with an excellent selection of hiking, backpacking, and camping equipment, boots and clothing, and hard-to-find items.

Marathon Sports (⊠ 1654 Massachusetts Ave., ☎ 617/354–4161) is the place to go for personalized services in choosing the perfect running shoe, as well as other sports gear.

Niketown (⊠ 200 Newbury St., ☎ 617/267–3400), a kind of temple to marketing hype, has sports apparel, gear, and shoes in a huge, flashy store.

Thrift Shops

Boomerangs (⊠ 60 Canal St., ☎ 617/723–2666) sells clothing as well as home furnishings and collectibles at bargain rates. All proceeds go to the AIDS Action Committee.

Chic Repeats (⊠ 117 Newbury St., ☎ 617/536–8580), run by the Junior League of Boston, sells donated or consigned clothing of high quality, often with designer labels.

The Garment District (⊠ 200 Broadway, Cambridge, ☎ 617/876–9795) has vintage, used, and new clothing and accessories for that post-grunge industrial student look.

Toys

Eric Fuchs (⊠ 28 Tremont St., ☎ 617/227–7935) specializes in model trains, planes, and automobiles, with some dollhouse miniatures, Dungeons and Dragons paraphernalia, and hobby materials.

F. A. O. Schwarz (⊠ 440 Boylston St., ☎ 617/266–5101), a branch of the famed New York toy emporium, sells all kinds of toys—trains, dolls, stuffed animals, games, and other intriguing playthings—of the highest quality, at the highest prices. The giant teddy bear sculpture outside is a popular photo spot.

Henry Bear's Park (⊠ 361 Huron St., Cambridge, ☎ 617/547–8424; ⊠ 81 Union St., Newton Centre, ☎ 617/969–8616) is a charming neighborhood children's store that carries books, toys, dinosaurs, party favors, games, such specialty items as Carolle dolls and the Muffy Vander Bear Collection—but nothing that hints of violence.

9 Side Trips

West of Boston, the North Shore, South of Boston

If your vision of an ideal New England includes pre-Revolutionary inns, seriously scenic surroundings, and towns right out of a Currier & Ives print, then head west for the historic towns of Lexington and Concord and nearby Walden Pond. Heading north leads you to the ocean, and cozy inns, seafood stands, crafts shops, art galleries, and coastal walks that offer a relaxing contrast to Boston's urbanity. In Salem, revisit the sites important to the witch trials. South of Boston, travel back in time at Plimoth Plantation, an unerring re-creation of New England's first settlement in 1627, seven years after the Mayflower landed.

Updated by
Anne Stuart

SOME OF THE MOST IMPORTANT SITES in early American history are within shouting distance of Boston. Whether you spend a day or a long weekend visiting these places, you will come away with an enriched sense of history—a deeper view made possible after walking across a dewy battlefield, ducking through the abbreviated door frame of a 300-year-old house, strolling through the woods or along the seashore, or envisioning inhabitants of bygone eras that, truth be told, are much closer to our own than we typically imagine.

You might begin at the beginning, 40 mi south in Plymouth, where a living history center known as Plimoth Plantation re-creates the 17th-century everyday life of the Pilgrims. The quintessential New England towns of Lexington and Concord offer a glimpse of the American Revolution as well as homes of and small museums devoted to some of the country's first literary luminaries—Ralph Waldo Emerson, Nathaniel Hawthorne, Louisa May Alcott, and Henry David Thoreau. Walden Pond, which occasioned the eponymous book, is now a state park. A national historic park in the town of Lowell commemorates the Industrial Revolution. About 35 mi north of Boston, you'll find "the other Cape"—Cape Ann, home to Gloucester, the oldest seaport in the United States, and charming Rockport, crammed with crafts shops and art galleries. Elsewhere on the North Shore, there's Salem, overcome by witchcraft hysteria in the 17th century. And don't miss Newburyport, with its redbrick town center and rows of clapboard Federal mansions.

Pleasures and Pastimes

By the Sea

Bostonians usually visit the North Shore for its beaches, especially those around Gloucester and Rockport. Others enjoy discovering the pretty New England coastal towns with colorful clapboard cottages, narrow streets, and antiques stores; these are found in greatest concentration inland around Essex—but there are plenty sprinkled elsewhere on Cape Ann as well.

Many of the area's attractions—swimming, boating, and fishing—focus on the water: deep-sea fishing trips are plentiful and surf casting is popular, as is freshwater fishing in the Parker and Ipswich rivers. If you prefer to observe sea life rather than fish for it, take a whale-watching trip. Several breeds of whale feed locally between May and October, so you're practically guaranteed to see a few—and on a good day you may see upwards of 40. Organized boat trips leave from many of the coastal towns; they usually last three to four hours, including travel time to and from the whales' feeding grounds.

Dining

The North Shore offers these destinations' most distinctive dining. In addition to the plethora of seafood restaurants big and small, look for traditional "seafood in the rough" eating places. These establishments serve generous, inexpensive seafood on paper plates, often at wooden picnic tables and frequently outdoors. Menus favor plenty of fried fish dishes and usually fried clams, "invented" in Essex at the turn of the century. The following price chart is applicable for all regions covered in this chapter.

CATEGORY	COST*
$$$$	over $40
$$$	$25–$40
$$	$15–$25
$	under $15

*per person for a three-course meal, excluding drinks, service, and 5% sales tax

Literary Haunts

The 1994 movie version of Louisa May Alcott's *Little Women* sent the number of visitors to Orchard House in Concord skyrocketing. Not only did Alcott use the house as the setting for her beloved book, she wrote it on a semicircular shelf-desk set between two second-floor windows that is still there. This entire region is dotted with literary landmarks. In Concord alone, you may visit in one afternoon Alcott's Orchard House, Nathaniel Hawthorne's Wayside, the Ralph Waldo Emerson House, and Henry David Thoreau's Walden Pond.

Lodging

In the areas around Concord and Lexington, you'll find country inns and bed-and-breakfasts—many with a delightful personal touch. The North Shore, meanwhile, is home to distinctive seaside inns. Some are converted sea captains' mansions, others were once grand summer homes, a few were built as hotels. The best successfully combine country and oceanside ambience. Cedar shingles, ships' lanterns, and pineapple motifs (a pineapple on the doorstep showed that seafarers were safely returned from exotic lands) combine with patchwork quilts, shining hardwood floors, and open fireplaces to offer some outstanding accommodations. Less expensive options—waterfront motels and bed-and-breakfast homes—are also widely available in summer. But be sure to make reservations early. The North Shore tourist season ends earlier than those in other areas, with many places closing down from late October until April or May. The following price chart is applicable for all regions covered in this chapter.

CATEGORY	COST*
$$$$	over $100
$$$	$70–$100
$$	$40–$70
$	under $40

*All prices are for a standard double room, excluding 9.7% tax.

The Spirit of 1775

To better understand the Boston Tea Party, the Battle of Bunker Hill, and the "Massacre," visit Lexington and Concord, the towns where Boston's, and the country's, freedom trail truly began in 1775. These communities quietly embody the region's character traits: charm, reserve, fierce independence, and, above all, deep pride in their history. (But be warned: Even in traditional New England, quaintness does beget some development.) Here history is a multifaceted experience; you can explore Revolutionary battlegrounds, taverns, and houses as well as several excellent museums that emphasize both content and context.

WEST OF BOSTON

West of Boston lie a group of historic sites known by every American schoolchild as the birthplace of the American Revolution. Synonymous with patriotism, daring deeds, and heroic horsemanship, the quintessential New England towns of **Lexington** and **Concord** are where the Revolution's first military encounters took place.

If your interests lean more toward literature and philosophy, you'll find abundant evidence here of an intellectual revolution as well. Lofty

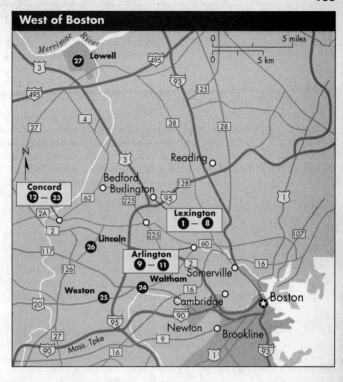

West of Boston

thinkers like Thoreau and Emerson, and writers like Nathaniel Hawthorne and Louisa May Alcott, turned Concord into a think—and literary—tank. These famed figures of American culture were nurtured in these unassuming small towns, now comfortable green commuter suburbs.

Waltham, Weston, and **Lincoln**—also west of Boston—offer a number of other attractions, although they lack the historical and literary significance of either Lexington or Concord.

Farther west and north, **Lowell** underwent still another revolution—theIndustrial Revolution—and its legacy is considerably less picturesque. But despite its derelict mills and canals, and its high quotient of crime and poverty, Lowell offers an imaginatively restored downtown area, including a large, compelling urban national park.

Lexington

Numbers in the margin correspond to points of interest on the Lexington and Arlington map.

1 *16 mi northwest of Boston.*

The events of the American Revolution are very much a part of present-day Lexington. The town comes alive each Patriot's Day (the Monday nearest April 19) when groups of costume-clad "Minutemen" participate in re-created battle maneuvers, "Paul Revere" reenacts his midnight ride, and the town turns out for a parade, pancake breakfasts, and other celebrations.

The real Paul Revere roused patriots John Hancock and Sam Adams—who were in Concord to attend the Provincial Congress then in session—from their sleep at the eight-room **Hancock-Clarke House,** a parsonage built in 1698. Revere rode out from Boston to "spread the alarm" that the British were approaching "through every Middlesex village and farm." Both Hancock and Adams fled to avoid capture. The house, a 10-minute walk from Lexington Common, displays the pistols of the British major John Pitcairn as well as period furnishings and portraits. A 20-minute tour is offered. ⊠ *36 Hancock St.,* ☎ *781/ 861–0928.* ⊑ *$3.*☉ *Mid Apr.-Oct., Mon.-Sat. 10–5, Sun. 1–5; Nov.– mid-April, by appointment.*

Downtown Lexington bustles with ice cream and coffee shops, clothes stores, bookstores, restaurants, and a great little movie theater. During warm weather, the town fills with bicyclists—taking a break for an ice-cream fix—from the nearby **Minuteman Trail,** an 11-mi biking, in-line skating, and jogging path that follows an abandoned railroad route running from Somerville through Cambridge, Arlington, and Lexington to Bedford. A trail map is available at the **Lexington Visitors Center** (☞ *below*).

❸ On the east side of the Green is the **Buckman Tavern,** built in 1690, where the Minutemen gathered on the morning of April 19, 1775. A 40-minute tour takes in the tavern's seven rooms. Display items include an old front door with a hole made by a British musket ball. ⊠ *1 Bedford St.,* ☎ *781/862–5598.* ⊑ *$3.*☉ *Mid-Apr.–Oct., Mon.–Sat. 10–5, Sun. 1–5. Special hours and tours during winter holidays.*

❹ Minuteman captain John Parker assembled his men out on **Battle Green,** a 2-acre, triangular piece of land, to await the arrival of the British, who were marching from Boston toward Concord to "teach rebels a lesson." Parker's role is commemorated in Henry Hudson Kit-
❺ son's renowned sculpture, the **Minuteman Statue,** standing at the tip of the Green, facing downtown Lexington. Because it's in a traffic island, it doesn't present a natural photo op. The **Revolutionary Monument,** near the Minuteman Statue, marks the burial site of Minutemen killed that day. Captain Parker's command that morning to his 77 men, who formed two uneven lines of defense, is emblazoned on the **Line of Battle boulder,** to the right of the Minuteman Statue: "Stand your ground, don't fire unless fired upon; but if they mean to have war, let it begin here." The British major John Pitcairn ordered his troops to surround the Minutemen and disarm them, but not to fire. A shot did ring out, and the rest is history. Two questions remain unanswered: Who fired that first shot? And why did Parker, a seasoned veteran of the French and Indian Wars, position his men behind the two-story, barnlike meetinghouse that stood on the spot where the Minuteman Statue stands today? (A memorial behind the statue marks the site.) From there, the Minutemen weren't able to see the British advancing, much less make a show of resistance. Indeed, why didn't Captain Parker tell his men to take to the hills overlooking the British route? It was an absurd situation: 77 men against 700, turning it into one of history's most notorious mishaps. Even in modern times, the green has been the site of patriotic public gatherings: In 1942, residents gathered to pledge support for the Allies, and during the 1960s, it saw demonstrations on civil rights and the Vietnam War. The pleasant **Visitor Center** nearby has a diorama of the 1775 clash on the green, plus a gift shop. *Visitor Center (Lexington Chamber of Commerce):* ⊠ *1875 Massachusetts Ave.,* ☎ *781/862-1450.* ☉ *Mid-Apr.–Oct., daily 9–5; Nov.–mid-Apr., generally weekdays 10–3, weekends 10–4.*

As April 19 dragged on, British forces met far fiercer resistance in Concord. Dazed and demoralized after the battle at Old North Bridge (☞
❻ Concord, *below*), the British backtracked and regrouped at the **Munroe Tavern** (built in 1695) while the Munroe family hid in nearby woods;

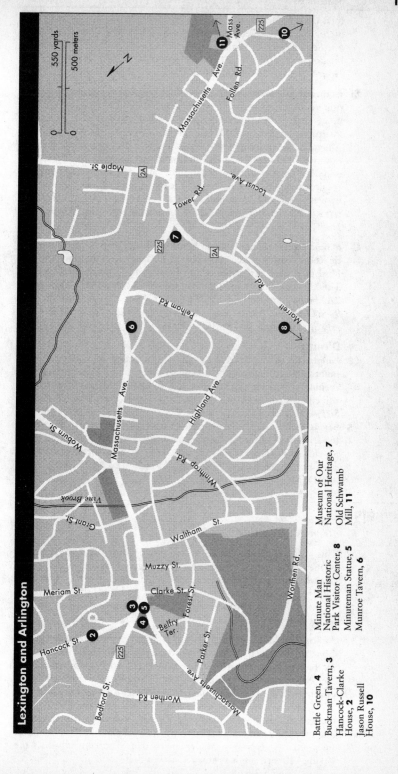

550 yards

500 meters

Battle Green, **4**
Buckman Tavern, **3**
Hancock-Clarke
House, **2**
Jason Russell
House, **10**

Minute Man
National Historic
Park Visitor Center, **8**
Minuteman Statue, **5**
Munroe Tavern, **6**

Museum of Our
National Heritage, **7**
Old Schwamb
Mill, **11**

then the troops retreated to Boston. The tavern is 1 mi east of Lexington Common. ⊠ *1332 Massachusetts Ave.,* ☎ *781/674–9238.* ⌦ *$3; Lexington Historical Society offers a combination ticket for admission to Munroe Tavern, Buckman Tavern, and Hancock-Clarke House.* ⊙ *Mid-Apr.–Oct., Mon.–Sat. 10–5, Sun. 1–5.*

★ ❼ Ironically, the **Museum of Our National Heritage,** devoted to the nation's cultural heritage and located in one of its oldest towns, is housed in a contemporary brick-and-glass building. This small but dynamic institution superbly displays items and artifacts from all facets of American life, putting them in social and political context. An ongoing exhibit, "Lexington Alarm'd," illustrates Revolutionary-era life through everyday household objects. Another ongoing exhibit highlights the country's fraternal organizations. The museum also hosts lectures, family programs, and films; there's a well-stocked gift shop. ⊠ *33 Marrett Rd.,* ☎ *781/861–6559.* ⌦ *Free; donation suggested.* ⊙ *Mon.–Sat. 10–5, Sun. noon–5.*

❽ **Minute Man National Historical Park Visitor Center,** formerly the Battle Road Visitor Center, is part of the 800-acre Minute Man National Historical Park that extends into Lexington, Concord, and Lincoln. The center's exhibits and film focus on the Revolutionary War. ⊠ *Rte. 2A, ½ mi west of Rte. 128,* ☎ *781/862–7753.* ⊙ *Mid-April–Oct., daily 9–5; Oct.–mid-April, contact North Bridge Visitor Center,* ⊠ *174 Liberty St., Concord,* ☎ *781/369–6993..*

Dining

$$ **Yangtze River.** The Yangtze is a big, contemporary-style Chinese restaurant that serves a good luncheon on weekdays and a dinner buffet every evening. If you don't like fried foods, skip the buffet and try a steamed fish entry instead. ⊠ *25 Depot Sq. (off Massachusetts Ave.),* ☎ *781/ 861–6030. AE, D, MC, V.*

$ **Bertucci's.** Part of a popular chain, this Italian restaurant offers good food, reasonable prices, a large menu, and a family-friendly atmosphere. Specialties include ravioli, calzones, and a wide assortment of brick-oven baked pizzas. ⊠ *1777 Massachusetts Ave.,* ☎ *781/860–9000. AE, D, MC, V.*

Arlington

❾ *10 min. northwest of Boston.*

This bustling suburb, between Cambridge on the east and Lexington on the west, contains a favorite haunt among moviegoers, the discounted **Capitol Theatre.** Like Lexington, the small but packed town center hosts a burgeoning number of coffee, ice cream, and bagel shops, as well as access to the 11-mi **Minuteman Trail** (☞ Lexington, *above*), a pleasant and scenic path for walking, biking, skating, and jogging.

Although seldom mentioned in the same breath as Lexington and Concord, the town played an important role in Revolutionary history. As the Redcoats retreated during that fateful April 1775 battle, Minutemen peppered them with musket fire from behind stone walls and

❿ pine trees. The bulletridden **Jason Russell House** marks the spot where 10 Minutemen and more than 20 British soliders were killed during the Battle of the Foot of the Rocks. Today, the interior displays period kitchenware, spinning wheels, even a stray cannonball. Adjoining the Jason Russell House, a modern barn-shaped structure houses the **George Abbott Smith History Museum,** with changing exhibits examining both contemporary and historic American cultural phenomena. ⊠ *7 Jason St., near the corner of Massachusetts Ave.,* ☎ *781/*

648–4300. ✆ *$2.* ☉ *Tues.–Fri. 1–5 and by appointment. Jason Russell House closed Nov.–mid-Apr. Tours available.*

⑪ In Arlington Heights, explore the utterly fascinating **Old Schwamb Mill** gristmill, which exhibits a trove of Industrial Revolution-ear machinery. The mill has been featured on television's *New Yankee Workshop* and *This Old House.* ✉ *7 Mill La. (take Massachusetts Ave. to Lowell St. to Mill La.),* ✆ *781/643–0554.* ✆ *Free.* ☉ *Weekdays 10–2; some weekends by appointment.*

Concord

Numbers in the margin correspond to points of interest on the Concord map.

⑫ *About 10 mi west of Lexington, 21 mi northwest of Boston.*

To reach Concord from Lexington, take Routes 4/225 through Bedford and Route 62 west to Concord; or take Massachusetts Avenue to Route 2A west at the Museum of Our National Heritage. The latter route is a longer but charming drive that takes you through parts of The **Minute Man National Historical Park,** a two-parcel park with more than 800 acres straddling Lexington, Concord, and Lincoln. Stop off at the point where Revere's midnight ride ended with his capture by the British; it's marked with a boulder and plaque. The park contains many of the sites important to Concord's role in the story of the Revolution, such as the Old North Bridge, Fiske Hill, and Hartwell Tavern, plus two visitor centers. It is laced with hiking trails and crossed by Battle Road, which roughly follows the path the British took to and from Boston during the battle of Lexington and Concord. (You can attempt to drive it; watch for the distinctive signs.) The National Park Service has also recently built a 5-mi asphalt trail for bikes and foot: the **Battle Road Trail,** which lets the more intrepid see the park sans auto. *North Bridge Visitor Center,* ✉ *174 Liberty St.,* ✆ *978/369–6993.* ✆ *Free.* ☉ *Mid-Jun.–Nov. 9–5, Nov.–mid-Jun. 9–4. Audiovisual programs; printed material; lectures in summer.*

You can reach the park by water if you rent a canoe at **the South Bridge Boat House** and paddle along the Sudbury and Concord Rivers to a park entrance near the Old North Bridge. ✉ *496 Main St.,* ✆ *978/369-9438.*

Concord may also be reached from Cambridge and Boston via Route 2 west. Autumn lovers, take note: Concord is a great place to start a fall foliage tour. Head west to find harvest stands along Route 2 and do-it-yourself apple-picking around Harvard and Stow.

While the initial Revolutionary War sorties were in Lexington, word of the American losses spread rapidly to surrounding towns: When the British marched into Concord, more than 400 Minutemen were waiting. A marker set in the stone wall along Liberty Street, behind the Old North Bridge Visitors Center, announces: "On this field the Minutemen and militia formed before marching down to the fight at the bridge."

⑬ At the **Old North Bridge,** ½ mi from Concord center, the Concord Minutemen turned the tables on the British in the morning hours of April 19, 1775. The Americans did not fire first, but when two of their own fell dead from a Redcoat volley, Major John Buttrick of Concord roared, "Fire, fellow soldiers, for God's sake, fire." The Minutemen released volley after volley, and the Redcoats fled. Daniel Chester French's famous statue of *The Minuteman* (1875) honors the country's first freedom fighters. The creek underneath the bridge and the

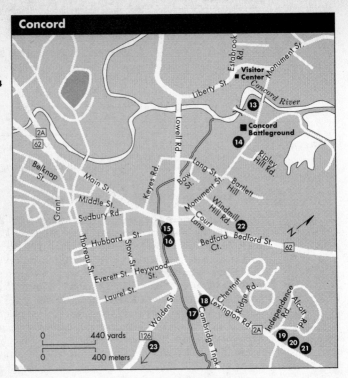

lovely wooded surroundings give a sense of what the landscape was like in more rural times.

Of the confrontation, Ralph Waldo Emerson wrote in 1837: "By the rude bridge that arched the flood/Their flag to April's breeze unfurled/Here once the embattled farmers stood/And fired the shot heard round the world." (The lines are inscribed at the foot of *The Minuteman*) statue. Hence, Concord claims the right to the "shot," believing that native son Emerson was, of course, referring to the North Bridge standoff. Park Service officials skirt the issue, saying the shot could refer to the battle on Lexington Green, when the very first shot rang out from an unknown source, or to Concord when Minutemen held back the Redcoats in the Revolution's first major battle, or even to the Boston Massacre. What's important is Emerson's vision that here began the modern world's first experiment in democracy.

The Reverend William Emerson, ancestor of Ralph Waldo Emerson, watched rebels and Redcoats battle from behind his home, the **Old Manse,** on Monument Street, within sight of the Old North Bridge. The house, built in 1770, was occupied by the family except for a period of 3½ years, when renter Nathaniel Hawthorne lived and wrote short stories here. Furnishings date from the late 18th century. ⊠ *Monument St.,*☎ *978/369–3909.* 🎫 *$5.* 🕐 *Mid-Apr.–end Oct., Mon.–Sat. 10–5, Sun. and holidays, noon–5. 30-min. tours.*

The **Wright Tavern** (⊠ 2 Lexington Rd.), built in 1747, served as headquarters first for the Minutemen, then the British, both on April 19. It is closed to the public.

Now displaying a series of rotating art exhibits, the **Jonathan Ball House,** built in 1753, was a station on the underground railroad for runaway slaves during the Civil War. Ask to see the secret room. The garden and waterfall are refreshing sights. ⊠ *Art Association, 37 Lexington Rd.,* ☎ *978/369–2578.* ▨ *Free.* ⊘ *Tues.–Sat. 10–4:30, Sun. 2–4:30.*

The 19th-century essayist and poet Ralph Waldo Emerson, grandson of William Emerson, lived briefly in the Old Manse in 1834–1835, then moved to what is known as the **Ralph Waldo Emerson House,** where he lived until his death in 1882. Here he wrote the *Essays* ("To be great is to be misunderstood"; "A foolish consistency is the hobgoblin of little minds"). Except for Emerson's study, now at the nearby Concord Museum, *below,* the Emerson House furnishings have been preserved as the writer left them, down to his hat resting on the newel post. ⊠ *28 Cambridge Tpke., on Rte. 2A,* ☎ *978/369–2236.* ▨ *$4.50.* ⊘ *Mid-Apr.–late Oct., Thurs.–Sat. 10–4:30, Sun. 2–4:30. 30-min. tours.*

The original contents of Emerson's private study are in the **Concord Museum,** just east of the town center. In a 1930 Colonial Revival structure, the museum houses 15 period rooms, ranging in decor from Colonial to Empire. It has the world's largest collection of Thoreau artifacts, including furnishings from the Walden Pond cabin, as well as a diorama of the Old North Bridge battle, Native American artifacts, and one of two lanterns hung at Boston's Old North Church on the night of April 18, 1775. ⊠ *200 Lexington Rd.,* ☎ *978/369-9763.* ▨ *$6.* ⊘ *Apr.–Dec., Mon.–Sat. 9–5, Sun. noon–5.; Jan.–Mar., generally Mon.–Sat. 10–4, Sun. noon–4.*

The dark rusty-brown exterior of Louisa May Alcott's family home, **Orchard House,** poses a sharp contrast to the light, wit, and energy so much in evidence inside. Named for the apple orchard that once surrounded it, Orchard House was home for the Alcott family from 1857 to 1877. Here Louisa wrote *Little Women,* based on her life with her three sisters, and her father, Bronson, founded his school of philosophy; the building remains behind the house. (Earlier, Bronson, along with Emerson, Thoreau, and English reformer Charles Lane, had established a Utopian community at Fruitlands, a farm farther west in rural Harvard; it is now a museum.) Because Orchard House had just one owner after the Alcotts left and because it became a museum in 1911, many of the original furnishings remain. Portraits and watercolors by May Alcott (the model for Amy) abound; in her room you can see where she sketched figures on the walls—the Alcotts encouraged such creativity. The gift shop has a generous selection of Alcott books, as well as videos of the 1994 movie of *Little Women,* which contributed to the revival of interest in the Alcotts. ⊠ *399 Lexington Rd.,* ☎ *978/369–4118.* ▨ *$5.50.* ⊘ *Apr.–Oct., Mon.–Sat. 10–4:30, Sun. 1–4:30; Nov.–Mar., weekdays 11–3, Sat. 10–4:30, Sun. 1–4:30. Closed Jan. 1–15.*

Nathaniel Hawthorne lived at the Old Manse in 1842–1845, working on stories and sketches; he then moved to Salem (where he wrote *The Scarlet Letter*) and later to Lenox (*The House of the Seven Gables*). In 1852 he returned to Concord, bought a rambling structure called **The Wayside,** and lived here until his death in 1864. The subsequent owner, Margaret Sidney (author of *Five Little Peppers and How They Grew*), kept Hawthorne's tower-study intact—to the fascination of visitors today. Prior to Hawthorne's ownership, the Alcotts lived here, from 1845 to 1848. ⊠ *455 Lexington Rd.,* ☎ *978/369–6975.* ▨ *$4.* ⊘ *Mid-Apr.–Oct., daily except Wed., 10–5. Guided tours until 4:30.*

A Concord curiosity, the yard of the privately owned **Grapevine Cottage** has the original Concord grapevine, the grape that the Welch's jams and jellies company made famous. In 1983, Welch's moved its corporate headquarters from New York to Concord to bring the com-

pany "back to its roots." A plaque on the fence tells how Ephraim Wales
Bull began cultivating the Concord grape. ⊠ *491 Lexington Rd.* ☉
Not open to the public.

㉒ Each Memorial Day, Louisa May Alcott's grave in the nearby **Sleepy
Hollow Cemetery** (⊠ Entrance on Rte. 62 W) is decorated in commemoration of her death. Like Emerson, Thoreau, and Nathaniel
Hawthorne, Alcott is buried in a section of the cemetery known as **Author's Ridge.**⊠ *Bedford St.,* ☎ *978/371–6299.* ☉ *Generally, weekdays 7–dusk.*

㉓ A trip to Concord can also include a pilgrimage to **Walden Pond,**
Henry David Thoreau's most famous residence. Here, in 1845, at age
28, Thoreau moved into a one-room cabin—built for $28.12½—on the
shore of this 100-ft-deep kettle hole, formed 12,000 years ago by the
retreat of the New England glacier. Living alone over the next two years,
Thoreau discovered the benefits of solitude and the beauties of nature.
"Thank God they can't cut down the clouds," he once remarked; such
sentiments—so effectively seeded at Walden—made him into the philo-
sophical godfather of the 20th-century ecological movement. Thoreau
later published *Walden* (1854), a collection of essays on observations
he made while living here. The site of that first cabin—only discovered a few decades ago—is staked out in stone. A full-size, authenti-
cally furnished replica of the cabin stands about ½ mile from the
original site, near the Walden Pond State Reservation parking lot.
Even when it's closed, you can peek through its windows. Its sparse-
ness is stirring, even if—truth be told—Thoreau was not actually that
far from civilization: The railroad ran nearby and he could walk into
town. Nevertheless, standing at the pond, particularly in cold weather
when the tourist throngs are gone, you may be moved to "simplify,
simplify" your life.

Modern conservationists have fought long and hard, as did Thoreau,
to keep commercial development at bay. One only has to notice the
huge sanitary landfill just ¼ mi from the park's entrance to realize that
Thoreau's legacy meant little when a fast buck was to be made. Now,
however, through the Walden Woods Project spearheaded by singer Don
Henley, about 90 acres of the area surrounding the 333-acre Walden
Pond Reservation have been set aside in perpetuity. (Henley's forces
battled those of a developer who sought to open an office park across
Route 2 from the pond.)

Now, as in Thoreau's time, the pond is a delightful summertime spot
for swimming, fishing, and rowing, and there's hiking in the nearby
woods. To get to Walden Pond State Reservation from the center of
Concord—a trip of only 1½ mi—take Concord's Main Street a block
west from Monument Square, turn left onto Walden Street and head
for the intersection of Routes 2 and 126. Cross over Route 2 onto Route
126, heading south for ½ mi. The entrance to the state reservation is
on the left. Parking is extremely tight in summer; it's a good idea to
call ahead to find out the next hour at which the lot will open again
(only a certain number of visitors are allowed in at a time). ⊠ *Rte. 126,*
☎ *978/369–3254.* ▨ *Free; parking across road from pond, $2 per
vehicle.*☉ *Daily until approximately ½ hr after sunset. Replica of
Thoreau's cabin: End May–mid-Oct., daily 1–3; closed mid-Oct.–end
May.*

Dining and Lodging

$–$$ ✕ **Walden Grille.** In an old brick firehouse, Walden Grille prepares
contemporary dishes including fresh seafood. ⊠ *24 Walden St.* ☎ *978/
371–2233. AE, D, DC, MC, V.*

$$$ ✕⌂ **Colonial Inn.** Traditional fare—from prime ribs to scallops—is served in the gracious dining room of this 1716 inn (reservations are essential). Lighter meals are offered in the lounge. Rooms in the main inn have Colonial elegance, with exposed beams and antique furniture. The 1960s Prescott Wing has a cozier, more modern country-inn-floral feel. ✉ *48 Monument Sq.,* ☎ *978/369–9200 or 800/370–9200,* ⨳ *978/369–2170. 49 rooms. 2 restaurants, bar, laundry service. AE, D, DC, MC, V.*

Waltham

⑳ *12 mi west of Boston on Route 20 near the Charles River.*

Waltham's role today is primarily as a commuter suburb of Boston on the Charles River, but back in 1813, the local Boston Manufacturing Company experimented with an "industrial revolution" of its own: producing a product—machine-made cloth—from start to finish under one roof. When it became obvious that the waters of the Charles were inadequate to supply enough energy to produce cloth on the scale intended, however, Boston Manufacturing moved its operations north to Lowell, on the Merrimack River. The **Charles River Museum of Industry** houses a history of American industry, from 1800 to the present, with an emphasis on steam-powered machinery. Exhibits include automobile manufacturing, watchmaking, and power looms. ✉ *154 Moody St.,* ☎ *781/893–5410.* ⌸ *$4.* ⊙ *Mon.–Sat, 10–5.*

Besides its landmarks of the industrial revolution, Waltham's past has another side, captured in two well-preserved pieces of architecture. One, the **Lyman Estate,** or The Vale, was built in 1793 by Theodore Lyman, a wealthy Boston merchant and entrepreneur. The Salem architect Samuel McIntire designed the elegant country house and the surrounding grounds in accordance with English design principles. An enthusiastic horticulturist and gentleman-farmer, Lyman erected **greenhouses** for the cultivation of exotic fruits and flowers. Many of the camellias and grapevines growing here today are more than 100 years old. The property is run under the supervision of the Society for the Preservation of New England Antiquities (SPNEA), which has a **Conservation Center** here. The house, substantially enlarged in 1882, is rented out for special events from May through November. ✉ *185 Lyman St.,* ☎ *781/891–7095 greenhouses; 781/893–7232 house.* ⌸ *Greenhouses: $2 donation.* ⊙ *Greenhouses, Mon.–Sat. 9:30–3:30; house, by appointment for groups of 10 or more.*

Waltham's other distinctive building is **Gore Place,** a 22-room Federal-period mansion built in 1805, accented by a "flying staircase" that spirals three full flights upward. Built originally as the country house of Governor Christopher Gore, it now houses a museum devoted to early American and European antiques. The 40 acres of grounds comprise cultivated fields, gardens, and woodlands. ✉ *52 Gore St.,* ☎ *781/894–2798.* ⌸ *$4, includes guided tour; grounds free.* ⊙ *Mid-Apr.–mid-Nov., Tues.–Sat. 11–5, Sun. 1–5 (last tour leaves at 4); mid-Nov.–mid-Apr., tours by appointment. Grounds and gift shop open daily.*

Weston

㉕ *5 mi from Waltham, 16 mi west of Boston on Route 20.*

A rich, rambling country suburb characterized by gracious homes on large rural lots, Weston is the site of **Case Estates** (✉ 135 Wellesley St.), a smaller version of Jamaica Plain's 265-acre Arnold Arboretum

(☞ The "Streetcar Suburbs" *in* Chapter 2). Unusual perennials are for sale here Maythrough October.

The **Cardinal Spellman Philatelic Museum,** on the campus of **Regis College,** displays more than 3.5 million stamps. Director Joseph Muller's enthusiasm for the permanent collection and the special exhibits—everything from Walt Disney–theme stamps to flower stamps—is contagious. ⊠ *235 Wellesley St.,* ☎ *781/894–6735.* 🎫 *Free.* ⊙ *Wed. 9–4, Sat. 10–4, Sun. 1–4; gallery and shop have additional hours..*

Beyond Weston on Route 20 in Sudbury is **Longfellow's Wayside Inn,** which was restored, beginning in 1923, by auto titan Henry Ford. Known originally, in 1661, as John How's Black Horse Tavern, the tavern became forever linked with the name of the poet Henry Wadsworth Longfellow, when his *Tales of a Wayside Inn* was published in 1863. ⊠ *Boston Post Rd. (off Rte. 20), Sudbury,* ☎ *978/443–8846.*

Within walking distance are a working reproduction of an 18th-century **gristmill;** the **schoolhouse** that "Mary" and her "little lamb" reportedly attended (moved here from Sterling by Henry Ford in 1926); and the **Mary Martha Chapel.**

Lincoln

㉖ *15 mi from Boston, west of I–95 and mostly south of Route 2.*

Lincoln is an elegant suburban hamlet that preserves more than 7,000 acres of land in conservation areas and is home to several interesting sites.

The Massachusetts Audubon Society's **Drumlin Farm** is a 180-acre working New England farm with domestic and wild animal exhibits, nature trails, hayrides, and a gift shop. ⊠ *South Great Rd., Rte. 117,* ☎ *781/259–9807.* 🎫 *$6.* ⊙ *Mar.–Oct., Mon. holidays and Tues.– Sun. 9–5; Oct.–Mar., Mon. holidays and Tues.–Sun. 9–4.*

The **DeCordova Museum and Sculpture Park** is worth a morning or afternoon, especially on a sunny day when you can walk around the modern sculptures set on 30 acres of parkland overlooking Sandy Pond. Indoors, the museum offers rotating contemporary art exhibitions. Outdoor concerts take place on weekends in warm weather. ⊠ *Sandy Pond Rd.,* ☎ *781/259–8355.* 🎫 *Museum $4, grounds free.* ⊙ *Museum Tues.– Sun., noon–5, selected Mon. holidays; grounds open daily.*

The **Codman House,** originally a two-story, L-shaped Georgian structure set amid agricultural fields, was more than doubled in size in 1797– 1798 by John Codman. (The design for the expansion is attributed to Charles Bulfinch.) The house is preserved with evidence of every period, from the original Georgian paneled rooms to a Victorian dining room, and it is run under the supervision of SPNEA. Codman also landscaped the grounds to resemble those of an English country estate. ⊠ *Codman Rd.,* ☎ *781/259–8843.* 🎫 *$4.* ⊙ *June–mid-Oct., Wed.–Sun. 11–5; last tour departs at 4 PM.*

The **Gropius House** was the family home of the architect Walter Gropius (1883–1969), director of the Bauhaus, the celebrated modernist school of design in Germany, from 1919 to 1928. This was the first building he designed on his arrival in the United States in 1937; he used components available from catalogs and building-supply stores in a revolutionary manner; the results were faithful to the Bauhaus principles of functionality and simplicity. The house is under the supervision of SPNEA. ⊠ *68 Baker Bridge Rd.,* ☎ *781/259–8843 or 781/227–3956.* 🎫 *$5.* ⊙ *June–mid-Oct., Fri.–Sun. noon–5; mid-Oct.–May, weekends 11–4. Tours available.*

Lowell

 30 mi northwest of Boston.

Everyone knows that the American Revolution began in Massachusetts. But the Commonwealth, and in particular the Merrimack Valley, also nurtured the Industrial Revolution. Lowell's first mill opened in 1823; by the 1850s, 40 factories employed thousands of workers and produced 2 million yards of cloth every week. By the mid-20th century, much of the textile industry had moved South, but the remnants of redbrick factories and murky canals remain as testaments to Lowell's role in American industrial history. The **Lowell National Historical Park** tracks the history of a gritty era when the power loom was the symbol of economic power and progress.

Part of Lowell's fascinating character stems from its broad ethnic diversity, a legacy of the days when immigrants from all over North America and Europe came to work in the textile mills. (The current influx is from Cambodia, but it was a Chinese immigrant, Dr. An Wang, who established a computer company here.) Lowell now holds a city celebration for the Cambodian New Year every April. One major ethnic group to migrate to Lowell in its mill days was the French Canadians; a noted son of French-Canadian Lowell was the late Beat poet and novelist Jack Kerouac, born here in 1922. Kerouac's memory is honored in the Eastern Canal Park on Bridge Street, where plaques bear quotes from his Lowell novels and from *On the Road*. Every October "Lowell Celebrates Kerouac" offers academic symposia, music, and coffeehouse poetry. Why October? "I was going home in October. Everyone goes home in October," he wrote in *On the Road*. His grave is in **Edson Cemetery,** 2 mi south of the Lowell Connector, the highway linking Lowell with I–495.

The National Park Visitor Center in the Market Mills Complex offers a thorough orientation to the city. The building was the headquarters of the Lowell Manufacturing Company at the height of Lowell's mill days. Pick up a self-guiding brochure at the Visitor Center for a walking tour that highlights aspects of local history, from the ubiquitous "mill girls" (young women who toiled up to 13 hours a day in factories) to the city's 5½ mi of canals. Park rangers offer guided tours on foot year-round and on turn-of-the-century trolleys and canal barges in summer and fall. ✉ *246 Market St.,* ☎ *978/970–5000.* 💲 *Free, except for trolley and barge tours.* ☉ *Daily 9–5.*

The **American Textile History Museum,** near the **Boott Cotton Mills Museum** (☞ *below*), enhances the city's position as a major interpreter of the industrial revolution and gives new meaning to the phrase "hands-on exhibits." Housed in a former Civil War-era mill, the museum's collection of working machines ranges from an 18th-century water wheel to an 1860s power loom to a 1950s "weave room" where fabrics are still made. Designs are drawn from the museum's extensive collection of period textiles, and some museum-produced products, such as blankets and tablecloths, are for sale onsite. ✉ *491 Dutton,* ☎ *978/441–0400.* 💲 *$5.* ☉ *Mon. holidays, Tues.–Fri. 9–4, weekends 10–4.*

The **Boott Cotton Mills Museum** is the first major National Park Service museum devoted to the history of industrialization. You know you're in for an unusual museum experience when you're handed ear plugs with your admission ticket. (The plugs are needed for walking through an authentic re-creation of a 1920s weave room, complete with the deafening roar of 88 working power looms. Today's visitors are luckier than the workers who were never issued protective ear gear.) Other exhibits at the Boott Mills complex, which dates from the mid-19th century, include weaving artifacts, cloth samples, video interviews with workers, and a large, meticulous scale model of 19th-century production. Images have not been prettified; the textile worker's grueling life is shown with all its grit, noise, and dust. The complex housing the museum also holds the **Tsongas Industrial History Center,** an educational center named for the late former U.S. Sen. Paul Tsongas, a Lowell legend, and the **New England Folklife Center.** ⊠ *400 block of John St.,* ☎ *978/970–5000.* 🎫 *$4.* ☉ *Daily 9:30–5.*

Just outside the Boott Cotton Mills Museum is **Boarding House Park,** an open space bordered by the former boarding houses where many millworkers lived and dotted with contemporary sculptures and structures that pay homage to working men and women.

The **Brush Art Gallery,** in **Market Mills,** offers visitors a chance to see and buy local artists' work. The gallery has changing exhibitions and demonstrations of weaving, papermaking, painting, sculpture, and other arts. ⊠ *256 Market St.,* ☎ *978/459–7819.* ☉ *Tues.–Sat 11–5, Sun. 12–4, and by appointment.*

The **New England Quilt Museum** is a small but charming museum that displays historical and contemporary examples of the art of quilting, banishing forever doubts about whether quilting is an art form. ⊠ *18 Shattuck St.,* ☎ *978/452–4207.* 🎫 *$4.* ☉ *Tues.–Sat. 10–4. Call for Sun. hrs.*

The Sports Museum of New England moved to Lowell in 1997 and provides an option for partners of quilt enthusiasts (☞ New England Quilt Museum, *above*) who'd rather view basketballs than blankets. ⊠ *25 Shattuck St.,* ☎ *978/452–6775.* 🎫 *$3.* ☉ *Tues.–Sat 10–5; Sun. noon–5.*

The **Working People Exhibit,** in a restored Boott Mills boardinghouse, records the triumphs, sorrows, and daily experiences of both women mill workers and immigrants. Upstairs, there's a poignant display of letters and books belonging to several mill girls; downstairs, a kitchen and parlor show how they lived; there's even a display on the food they gulped down during 30-minute breaks in their grueling work days. Immigrants, from the Irish to Cambodians, are celebrated with photos, video, and historical artifacts. ⊠ *40 French St.,* ☎ *978/970–5000.* 🎫 *Free.* ☉ *June–Oct., daily 9–5; Nov.–May, daily 1–5.*

NEED A BREAK?   For coffee, quiche, and muffins baked on the premises, stop at **The Coffee Mill** (⊠ 23 Palmer St., ☎ 978/458-8852), a storefront café and sandwich shop.

Two blocks from the Market Mills entrance to the Lowell National Historical Park is the birthplace and museum of American artist James McNeill Whistler. Despite Whistler's claim that he was a Baltimore native, the Lowell Art Association purchased the gray clapboard Whistler house (built in 1823) to preserve the painter's roots in his real hometown. Inside, the **Whistler House Museum of Art** displays the museum's permanent collections; the **Parker Gallery** in an adjacent building has temporary exhibits of contemporary and historic arts. ⊠ *243 Worthen St.,* ☎ *978/452–7641.* 🎫 *$3.* C *Wed.–Sat. 11–4, Sun. 1–4. ; Generally closed Jan. and Feb. 1-hr. tours available.*

Dining

$$ ✕ **The Olympia.** Lowell's diverse population includes a large Greek-American community. Specialties at this friendly, family-run Greek restaurant—a favorite of employees at the nearby museums—include lamb, moussaka, and fish dishes. ⊠ *453 Market St.,* ☎ *978/452–8092. MC, V.*

West of Boston A to Z

Arriving and Departing

The **MBTA** (☎ 617/722–3200) operates buses to Arlington, Lexington, and Boston's western suburbs from Alewife and Harvard Square stations in Cambridge. Travel time is about one hour. You can also catch buses along Massachusetts Avenue (Route 2A).

To get to Lexington by car from Boston, cross the Charles River at the Massachusetts Avenue Bridge and proceed on Massachusetts Avenue through Cambridge, passing Harvard Square and then Porter Square. Cross the Fresh Pond Parkway into Arlington and continue through Arlington Center on Mass. Ave. Alternatively, take Route 2 as far as I–95, then head north on I–95 until you see the Lexington exit. Once in Lexington, follow Mass. Ave. as it bears to the right leading through Lexington Center. Just beyond is Battle Green. To reach Concord or Lincoln by car, take Route 2 out of Boston. Or take I–90 (the Massachusetts Turnpike) to I–95 north, then exit at Route 2, heading west.

The fastest way to reach Weston or Waltham is the Massachusetts Turnpike westbound, then I–95 north to Route 20 (head west for Weston and east for most Waltham addresses).

Lowell lies at the intersection of I–495 and Rte. 3. From Boston, take the Mystic Bridge to I–93 and stay on I–93 to the junction of I–495. Go south on I–495 to the exit for Rte. 3–Lowell. Travel time is one hr.

The **"purple line,"** the T's commuter rail, runs from North Station(⊠ 150 Causeway St., ☎ 617/722–3200) to Concord in about 37 minutes and to Lowell in about 45 minutes. Also from North Station, the commuter rail to Fitchburg runs through Waltham and on to Weston. Travel time to Weston is 30 minutes.

Getting Around

Lexington and Arlington are each easily accessible by the MBTA and bus service and are both compact enough to be explored on foot. The sights in Concord, however, are more spread out, so either plan to visit by car or wear substantial walking shoes. The historic sections of Lowell are all easily reached on foot from the National Park Visitor Center. Waltham, Weston, and Lincoln are not considered walking towns; you should plan to visit by car.

Guided Tours

Brush Hill Tours and Bean-Town Trolley Tours (⊠ 435 High St., Randolph 02368, ☎ 781/986–6100) offers several daily motorcoach tours from the Transportation Building in downtown Boston to Lexington's Battle Green and Concord's Old North Bridge area in spring, summer and fall.

Visitor Information

Concord Chamber of Commerce ⊠ 2 Lexington Rd., Concord, ☎ 978/369–3120. ⊗ Daily 9:30–4:30). **Lexington Chamber of Commerce and Visitor Center** (⊠ 1875 Massachusetts Ave., Lexington, ☎ 781/862–1450; ⊗ Visitor Center, mid-Apr.–Oct., daily 9–5; Nov.–mid-Apr., generally weekdays 10–3; weekends 10–4). **National Park Visitors Center** (⊠ 246 Market St., Lowell, ☎ 978/970–5000; ⊗ daily 9–5).

THE NORTH SHORE

The slice of Massachusetts's Atlantic Coast known as the North Shore extends from Boston's well-to-do northern suburbs past grimy docklands to the picturesque **Cape Ann** region, and beyond the Cape to Newburyport, just south of the New Hampshire border. It takes in the historic town of **Salem,** which thrives on a history of witches, millionaires, and the maritime trades; **Gloucester,** the oldest seaport in America; quaint, colorful **Rockport,** crammed with lobster pots, crafts shops, and artists' studios; and **Newburyport,** with its redbrick center and rows of clapboard Federal mansions. Bright and bustling during the short summer season, the North Shore is tranquil between November and June, with many restaurants, inns, and attractions operating during reduced hours or closing down entirely. It's worth calling ahead off-season.

Marblehead

Numbers in the margin correspond to points of interest on the North Shore map.

28 *17 mi north of Boston.*

Marblehead, with its old clapboard houses and narrow, winding streets, retains much of the character of the village as settled in 1629 by fishermen from the Cornwall coast and the Channel Islands. It's a sign of the times that today's fishing fleet is small compared to the armada of pleasure craft anchored in the harbor. This is one of New England's premiere sailing capitals, and Race Week (usually the last week of July) attracts boats from all along the Eastern seaboard. The proud spirit of the hardworking, ambitious merchant sailors who made Marblehead prosper in the 18th century can still be felt in many of the impressive Georgian mansions that line the downtown streets.

You should really walk through Marblehead's streets to appreciate their charm. Park wherever you can, perhaps in the public lot at the end of Front Street; if you park on the street, watch the time to avoid being ticketed. The Chamber of Commerce (☞ North Shore A to Z, *below*) has a complete visitor guide with a suggested walking tour of the city.

NEED A
BREAK?
To experience the fisherman's Marblehead, visit the **Driftwood**(⊠ 63 Front St., ☎ 781/631–1145), a simple, red-clapboard restaurant by the harbor, whose ceiling is draped with fishnet, where you can get excellent, inexpensive homestyle breakfasts and lunches.

The town's Victorian-era municipal building, **Abbott Hall,** built in 1876, houses Archibald Willard's painting *The Spirit of '76,* one of the country's most beloved icons of patriotism. Many visitors, familiar since childhood with this image of the three Revolutionary veterans with fife, drum, and flag, are surprised to find the original in an otherwise unassuming town hall. Other artifacts on display include the original deed to Marblehead from the Nanapashemet Indians. There's also a gift shop. ⊠ *Washington St.,* ☎ *781/631–0528.* ☺ *Generally, Mon., Tues., Thurs. 8–5, Wed. 7:30–7, Fri. 8–1; check for summer weekend hours.*

Dining and Lodging

$$$–$$$$ 🏨 **Harbor Light Inn.** This is one of the best places to stay on the North
   ★   Shore. Some rooms have Jacuzzis, and there are skylights, working fireplaces, rooftop decks, and spacious, modern bathrooms in addition to antique mahogany furnishings, four-poster beds, and other traditional touches. A family suite is available. Continental breakfast is included. ⊠ *58 Washington St., 01945,* ☎ *781/631–2186,* ⨳ *781/631–2216.21 rooms. Pool, meeting rooms. AE, MC, V.*

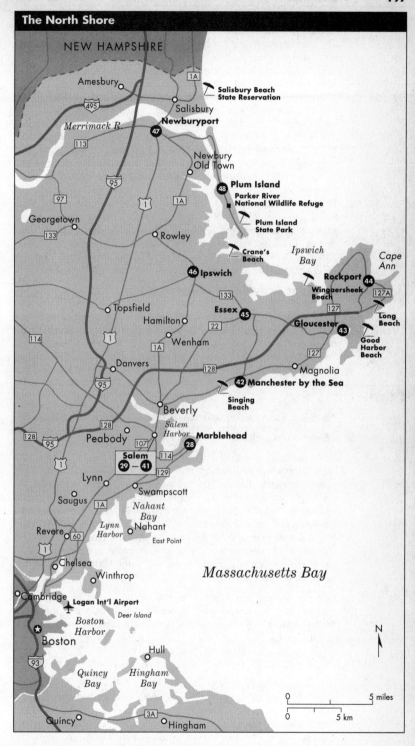

The North Shore

NEW HAMPSHIRE

Amesbury

495

Merrimack R.

113

Salisbury
Salisbury Beach
State Reservation

1A

Newburyport

47

Newbury
Old Town

1A

95

48 **Plum Island**
Parker River
National Wildlife Refuge

Plum Island
State Park

97

Georgetown

1

133

Rowley

Crane's
Beach

*Ipswich
Bay*

*Cape
Ann*

Topsfield

46 **Ipswich**

Rockport **44**

Wingaersheek
Beach

127A

133

Hamilton

Essex **45**

127

Long
Beach

1

Wenham

22

Gloucester **43**

Good
Harbor
Beach

114

1A

127

Danvers

128

Magnolia

95

42 **Manchester by the Sea**

Beverly

Singing
Beach

128

*Salem
Harbor*

Peabody

107

Marblehead

128

95

Salem
29 — **41**

114

28

1

129

Lynn

Swampscott

Saugus

1A

*Nahant
Bay*

Revere

60

*Lynn
Harbor*

Nahant

East Point

Chelsea

Winthrop

Massachusetts Bay

Cambridge

✈ **Logan Int'l Airport**

Deer Island

★

*Boston
Harbor*

93

Boston

Hull

N

*Quincy
Bay*

*Hingham
Bay*

0   5 miles

0   5 km

Quincy

3A

Hingham

$$$ ✕ **The Landing.** Right on Marblehead harbor and still in the historic district, this pleasant, small restaurant has indoor and outdoor dining. The chef prepares clam chowder, local scrod, filet mignon, seafood casseroles, and lobster. The entertainment is live Friday and Saturday. There's also a British-style pub and Sunday brunch. ⌧ *81 Front St.,* ☎ *781/631–6268. AE, DC, MC, V.*

$$–$$$ ▣ **Harborside House.** In Marblehead's historic district, Harborside House was built in 1850 by a ship's carpenter. The downstairs living room has a working brick fireplace; there's also a deck, a porch, a garden patio, and a sitting room with TV. Bedrooms have polished wideboard floors and overlook Marblehead harbor and its hundreds of sailboats. Continental breakfast is included. ⌧ *23 Gregory St., 01945,* ☎ *781/631–1032. 2 rooms. Breakfast room, parking. No credit cards. No smoking.*

$$–$$$ ▣ **Pleasant Manor Inn.** Off the main road between Salem and Marblehead, this rambling Victorian mansion has large guest rooms (some with pineapple four-poster beds) and a carved mahogany staircase. Continental breakfast is included. ⌧ *Rte. 114, 264 Pleasant St., 01945,* ☎ *781/631–5843 or 800/399–5843. 12 rooms. Breakfast room, tennis court, parking, outside tables. No credit cards. No smoking.*

Outdoor Activities and Sports
BOATING

Marblehead is one of the North Shore's pleasure-sailing capitals, but don't count on finding mooring space here. Like many nearby communities, the town has long waiting lists. The town harbormaster (☎ 781/631–2386) can inform you of nightly fees at public docks when space is available.

Salem

Numbers in margin correspond to points of interest on the Salem map.

㉙   *16 mi northeast of Boston, 4 mi west of Marblehead.*

Underneath its tarnished, slightly industrial exterior, Salem is a gem: full of compelling museums; trendy waterfront stores and restaurants; a shopping area closed to traffic; and a wide, open common with a children's playground and a jogging path. Settled in 1626, the town became infamous for the witchcraft hysteria of 1692, its rich maritime tradition, and the architectural splendor of its Federal houses. Frigates out of Salem opened the Far East trade routes and generated the wealth that created America's first crop of millionaires. Among its native sons were writer Nathaniel Hawthorne, navigator Nathaniel Bowditch, and architect Samuel McIntire.

One way to explore Salem is to follow the 1.7-mi Heritage Trail (painted in red on the sidewalk) around town. If you prefer, the **Salem Trolley**) leaves every hour for a guided tour from near the National Park Service Visitor Center at Essex Street Mall. You may get off and back on the trolley at any point with your original ticket. ☎ *978/744–5469.*☉ *Apr.–Oct., daily 10–4; Nov., Mar., weekends 10–4.*

Salem unabashedly calls itself "Witch City." Logos bearing witches astride broomsticks identify the police cars; witchcraft shops and local practitioners recall the city's infamous connection with the trials of 1692 that resulted in the hanging of 19 innocent people. The commercialization—some would say trivialization—of the victims led in part to the dedication of a somber, reflective monument—The Salem Witch Trials Memorial (☞ *below*)—in 1992.

㉚   A good place to start your tour is at the large **National Park Visitor Center,** which has a wide variety of booklets and pamphlets, includ-

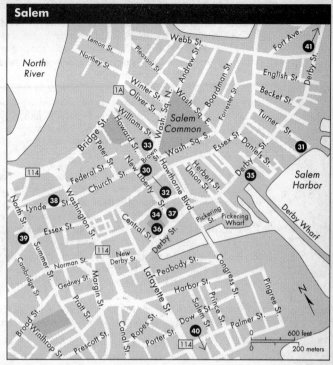

Salem

ing a "Maritime Trail" and "Early Settlement Trail" for Essex County, as well as a free 27-minute film. ⊠ *2 New Liberty St.,* ☎ *978/740-1650.* ☾ *Daily 9–5.*

❸① The **House of the Seven Gables,** immortalized in the classic by Nathaniel Hawthorne, should not be missed. Interesting sights on the tour are the period furnishings, a secret staircase, and the garret, containing an antique scale model of the house. The complex of 17th-century buildings includes the small house where Hawthorne was born in 1804; it was moved to the site from its original location elsewhere in Salem. ⊠ *54 Turner St.,* ☎ *978/744–0991.* ☜ *$7.* ☾ *July–Oct., daily 9–6; Nov.–June, daily 10–4:30; Sun. 12–4:30; closed first 2 wks in Jan.*

❸② Salem's vast, dazzling maritime riches are the focal point of the **Peabody Essex Museum,** celebrating its 200th anniversary in 1999. The **East India Hall Galleries** on Liberty Street are filled with maritime art and history and spoils of the Asian export trade—ranging from 16th-century Chinese blue porcelain to an entire Japanese carrying litter to Indian colonial silver. **Plummer Hall** on Essex Street contains New England portraits and Revere silver. Scrimshaw, a whale's jaw, and boat models illustrate Salem's seafaring past. The museum created a major new exhibition space for Native American art in 1998. There are gift shops and a café. ⊠ *East India Sq.,* ☎ *978/745-9500 or 800/745–4054.* ☜ *$7.50.* ☾ *Memorial Day–Oct., Mon.–Sat. 10–5, Fri. until 8, Sun. noon–5; Nov.–Memorial Day, Tues.–Sat. 10–5, Sun. noon–5.; closed Thanksgiving, Dec. 25, and Jan. 1.*

❸③ The **Salem Witch Museum,** offers a multisensory re-creation of the 1692 witchcraft hysteria with 13 stage sets and life-size models. ⊠ *Washington Sq. N.,* ☎ *978/744–1692.* ☜ *$4.50.* ☾ *Aug.–June, daily 10–5; July–Aug., daily 10–7.Presentations in French, German, Japanese, Spanish, and Italian.*

❸❹ The Salem Witch Trials Memorial. Dedicated in 1992, on the 300th anniversary of the witchcraft trials, the memorial honors those who died not because they were witches, but because they refused to confess. Next to the central burial ground, this melancholy space provides an antidote to the relentless marketing of the merry witches motif. An ancient-looking stone wall is studded with 20 stone benches, each inscribed with a victim's name. Flagstones at one end of the plot are engraved with protestations of innocence, sometimes cut off in mid-sentence. Black locust trees, reputedly the kind used for the hangings, are planted here. The monument was dedicated by Holocaust survivor Elie Wiesel, who drew parallels at the ceremony to other historical atrocities. ⊠ *Off Liberty St., near corner of Charter St.,* ⊙ *Daily.*

Putting its macabre past behind it, Salem went on to become a major seaport, with a thriving overseas trade. That heritage is the focus of ❸❺ the **Salem Maritime National Historic Site,** a 9.2-acre historic site along Derby Wharf, run by the National Park Service. The site includes the 1762 home of Elias Derby, America's first millionaire; the 1819 Customs House, made famous in Nathaniel Hawthorne's *The Scarlet Letter*; the 1671 Narbonne-Hale House, three sites relating to sea trade: the 1819 Public Stores, the 1826 Scale House, and the West India Goods Store. You can stroll for almost ½ mi along Derby Wharf, where a replica of *The Friendship*, a 171-ft, three-masted 1797 trader merchant vessel, was scheduled to open for tours in 1998. ⊠ *175 Derby St.* ☎ *978/740–1660.* 🎟 *$3.* ⊙ *Daily 9–5. Tours of historic site and ship available.*

❸❻ The **Salem Wax Museum of Witches and Seafarers** offers a multimedia presentation of sights and sounds culled from a century of Salem's tragedies and triumphs. A hands-on activity area will entertain the youngsters. ⊠ *288 Derby St.,* ☎ *978/740–2929.* 🎟 *$4.50, or with combination pass to Salem Witch Village.* ⊙ *Nov.–June, daily 10–4:30; July–Oct., daily 10–6.*

❸❼ Next to the wax museum, at the recently created **Salem Witch Village,** visitors may learn about historic and modern witchcraft's spiritual and religious practices. ⊠ *282-288 Derby St.,* ☎ *978/740–9229.* 🎟 *"Hysteria Pass" ($6.95) gives access to both village and wax museum.* ⊙ *Daily 10–5.*

❸❽ The **Witch Dungeon Museum** features a guided tour of dungeons where accused witches were kept and a live reanctment of one trial, as adapted from 1692 transcripts. ⊠ *16 Lynde St.,* ☎ *978/741–3570.* 🎟 *$4.50.* ⊙ *Apr. 1–Nov. 1, daily 10–5; evening hours around Halloween. Continuous performances.*

❸❾ No witch ever lived at **The Witch House,** the former home of witch trial magistrate Jonathan Corwin, but more than 200 accused witches were questioned on the premises. It's the only remaining structure with direct ties to the 1692 trials; decor remains authentic to the period. Tours offered. ⊠ *310½ Essex St.,* ☎ *978/744–0180.* 🎟 *$5.* ⊙ *Mar.–June and Labor Day–Dec. 1, daily 10–4:30; July–Aug., daily 10–6.*

Ⓒ ❹❶ Children will enjoy the **Salem 1630 Pioneer Village and Forest River Park** which, with costumed "interpreters," re-creates the Salem of the early 17th century, when it was a fishing village and the Commonwealth's first capital. Replicas of thatched-roof cottages, period gardens, and wigwams have been constructed at the site. ⊠ *Jct. Rtes. 1A and 129,* ☎ *978/745–0525 or 978/744-0991.* 🎟 *$5.* ⊙ *May–Oct., Mon.–Sat. 10–5, Sun. noon–5.*

🎈 ㊵ **Salem Willows Park** (⊠ at the eastern end of Derby St.) has picnic grounds, beaches, food stands, amusements, games, boat rentals, and fishing bait. It is some distance from the historical sites.

OFF THE
BEATEN PATH

DANVERS– Although Salem became famous as the witch-trials city, it is Danvers (Old Salem) that has the real relics of the witchcraft episode. The house where the black slave, Tituba, told her tales to two impressionable girls—beginning the whole sorry business—has long been demolished, but its foundations were excavated in 1970; they can be viewed behind 67 Center Street. A monument to the victims was dedicated in 1992 near 178 Hobart Street.

Also in Danvers, the **Rebecca Nurse Homestead** was the home of aged, pious Rebecca, a devout churchgoer whose accusation of being a witch caused shock waves in the community. Her trial was a mockery (she was first pronounced innocent, but the jury was urged to change its verdict), and she was hanged in 1692. Her family secretly buried her body somewhere on the grounds of this house, which has period furnishings and 17th-century vegetable and herb gardens. ⊠ 149 Pine St., ☎ 978/774-8799. 🎫 $3.50. ⊘ May–Labor Day, Tues.–Sun. 1–4:30; Labor Day–Oct., weekends 1–4:30 or by appointment; May–mid-June, by appointment; closed Nov.–Apr.

Dining and Lodging

$$$ ✕ **Nathaniel's.** Chandelier-bedecked and formal, this restaurant has an ambitious menu, including lobster, swordfish in mustard cream, prime rib, and poached sole on spinach with a champagne cream sauce. Also at Nathaniel's are a cozy tavern and Sunday brunch. It's part of the Hawthorne Hotel on Salem Common. ⊠ 18 Washington Sq. W, ☎ 978/744–4080. AE, D, DC, MC, V.

$$ ✕ **Chase House.** On Pickering Wharf overlooking the harbor, this restaurant is extremely busy in summer. The menu emphasizes steaks, seafood, and pasta. A house specialty is the baked lobster stuffed with still more lobster and, for the abstemious, the "heart-healthy" scrod. ⊠ Pickering Wharf, ☎ 978/744–0000. AE, D, DC, MC, V.

$$ ✕ **Lyceum Bar & Grill.** The Lyceum's claim to fame is that Alexander Graham Bell made his first public phone call from the building, in 1877. The decor is warm and inviting, with a pressed-tin ceiling, a dark wood bar, and a fireplace. Favorites include baked scrod, fish chowder, grilled pork tenderloin, and garlic mashed potatoes. ⊠ 43 Church St., ☎ 978/745–7665. Reservations essential. AE, D, MC, V.

$$$$ ✕🏨 **Hawthorne Hotel.** This imposing redbrick structure stands on the green, just a short walk from the commercial center, the waterfront, and other attractions. Guest rooms are appointed with reproduction 18th-century antiques, armchairs, and desks. The hotel restaurant, Nathaniel's, is one of the more elegant eateries in Salem. There's live entertainment on weekends in the bar. ⊠ 18 Washington Sq. W, 01970, ☎ 978/744–4080 or 800/729–7829., ℻ 978/745–9842. 83 rooms, 6 suites. Restaurant, bar, lounge, exercise room, meeting rooms. AE, D, DC, MC, V.

$$$ 🏨 **Inn at Seven Winter St.** Built in 1870, this inn has been authentically restored to re-create the Victorian era. Rooms are spacious and well furnished, with heavy mahogany and walnut antiques. Some open to a deck, some have Jacuzzis, some have fireplaces. Rates include a Continental breakfast buffet. In the middle of town, it's better for couples than for families. ⊠ 7 Winter St., 01970, ☎ 978/745–9520, ℻ 978/745–5052. 8 rooms, 2 suites. Breakfast room, parlor, parking. MC, V. No smoking or pets permitted.

$$–$$$ 🏠 **Amelia Payson Guest House.** This elegantly restored 1845 Greek
Revival house has been converted into a bright, airy bed-and-breakfast;
it is near all historic attractions. The pretty rooms are decorated with
floral-print wallpaper, brass and canopy beds, nonworking marble
fireplaces, and white wicker furnishings. The downstairs parlor has a
grand piano. Rates include Continental breakfast. ⊠ *16 Winter St.,
01970,* ☎ *978/744–8304. 3 rooms, 1 studio. Breakfast room, parking. AE, MC, V . No smoking.*

Nightlife and the Arts

The **North Shore Music Theatre** (⊠ 62 Dunham Rd., Beverly, ☎ 978/
922–8500) puts on celebrity concerts, musicals, and children's theater
from May through December.

The **Salem Beer Works** (⊠ 278 Derby St., ☎ 781/745-2337), a microbrewery restaurant, offers eclectic Americancuisine and fresh-
brewed beers in a historic merchants' warehouse with high
ceilings,exposed brick walls and ductwork, mahogany paneling, and
live music weekends.

Shopping

Salem is the center for a number of offbeat shops whose goods have a
distinct relationship to the city's witchcraft history. The best known su-
pernatural store is **Crow Haven Corner** (⊠ 125 Essex St., ☎ 978/745–
8763), the former haunt of Laurie Cabot, once dubbed Salem's "official"
witch. Her daughter, Jody, now presides over a wide selection of crystal balls, herbs, tarot decks, healing stones, and books about witchcraft.
The **Broom Closet** (⊠ 3 and 5 Central St., ☎ 978/741–3669) stocks
250 varieties of dried herbs, aromatic oils, candles, tarot cards, New
Age music, and witchcraft supplies. The friendly, knowledgeable staff
is happy to educate shoppers about their wares. **Pyramid Books** (⊠
214 Derby St., ☎ 978/745–7171) stocks publications on New Age and
metaphysical topics.

Somewhat more conventional than Salem's witchcraft stores are the
waterside gift and antiques shops on sparkling, restored **Pickering
Wharf,** which also has moorings for private boats and a slew of bars
and restaurants. The **Pickering Wharf Antique Gallery** (☎ 978/741–
3113), a 4,000-sq-ft former theater-in-the-round, now houses about
50 dealers.

Manchester by the Sea

*Numbers in the margin correspond to points of interest on the North
Shore map.*

42 *29 mi from Boston, 13 mi northeast of Salem, via Beverly on Route
127.*

Bostonians visit the small seaside town of Manchester by the Sea for
its lovely, long, wooded Singing Beach, so-called because of the sound
the wind makes against the white sand. The beach has lifeguards, food
stands, and rest rooms, but no parking; there is a private pay ($15 per
day) lot for nonresidents by the town railroad station—a ½-mi hike.

Lodging

$–$$ 🏠 **Old Corner Inn.** Built in 1865 and once used as the Danish Embassy,
the Old Corner Inn has bedrooms with bird's-eye maple floors, four-
poster beds, brass gaslight-era fixtures, featherbeds, and claw-foot
tubs. Some rooms have working fireplaces. The low rates reflect the
fact that, although the country location is attractive, it's a mile walk
from the village center and a mile from the nearest beach. An apartment with bedroom, sitting room, private bath, and kitchenette is

available. Continental breakfast is included in the rate. ⊠ *2 Harbor St., 01944,* ☎ *978/526–4996. 6 rooms with bath, 3 rooms share 2 baths. AE, MC, V.*

Gloucester

❹③ *37 mi from Boston, 8 mi from Manchester.*

The first sight you'll see as you enter Gloucester along a fine seaside promenade is the statue of a man steering a ship's wheel, his eyes searching the horizon. The statue, which honors those "who go down to the sea in ships," was commissioned by the town citizens in 1923 in celebration of Gloucester's 300th anniversary. The oldest seaport in the nation, this is a workaday town and still a major fishing port. The creative side of its personality is illuminated by **Rocky Neck,** the first-settled artists' colony in the United States. Its alumni include Winslow Homer, Maurice Prendergast, Jane Peter, and Cecilia Beaux. Today Rocky Neck remains home to many artists; its galleries are usually open daily 10 AM to 10 PM during the busy summer months.

Hammond Castle Museum, a stone "medieval" castle built in 1926 by the inventor John Hays Hammond, Jr., contains medieval-style furnishings and paintings. The Great Hall houses an organ impressive for its 8,200 pipes. From the castle you can also see "Norman's Woe Rock," made famous by Longfellow in his poem *The Wreck of the Hesperus.* ⊠ *80 Hesperus Ave., Gloucester,* ☎ *978/283–2080.* ⌸ *$6.* ☺ *June 1–Labor Day, daily 9–6; Labor Day–mid-Oct, Wed.–Sun. 10–4; Nov. 1–June 1, weekends 10–5; closed mid-Oct.–Nov. 1.*

The **Cape Ann Historical Museum** has a large collection of paintings by the19th-century master Fitz Hugh Lane and other artists associated with Cape Ann, including Winslow Homer and Maurice Prendergast, in a furnished Federal period house. ⊠ *27 Pleasant St.,* ☎ *978/283–0455.* ⌸ *$3.50.* ☺ *Tues.–Sat. 10–5; closed Feb.*

The **Sargent House Museum** was home to sea merchants and high-minded community leaders. The Georgian house, built in 1782 for writer and activist Judith Sargent Murray and her husband John Murray, founder of Universalism in America, is furnished with 1790s textiles, personal items, and china and includes works by Judith's great-great nephew, John Singer Sargent. ⊠ *49 Middle St.,* ☎ *978/281–2432.* ⌸ *$3.* ☺ *June 1–Columbus Day, Fri.–Mon. noon–4.*

Dining and Lodging

$$$ ✕ **White Rainbow.** The dining room in this excellent restaurant is in
★   the basement of a downtown store, and candlelight provides a romantic atmosphere. Specialties include Maui onion soup, grilled beef with a zinfandel-based wine sauce, lobster, and fresh fresh fish of the day. ⊠ *65 Main St.,* ☎ *978/281–0017. AE, D, DC, MC, V.*

$$–$$$ ✕ **Thyme's on the Square.** A cozy, bistro-style restaurant, with high ceilings, large windows, and walls covered with paintings, it offers creative American cuisine. Menu choices include crawfish corncake with celeriac slaw appetizer; wood-grilled black Angus top sirloin with olive risotto, arugula, and truffle oil; and, for vegetarians, grilled vegetable gratin with wild mushroom etouffée. On the dessert menu are bread pudding, chocolate soufflé, and upside-down apple pie. ⊠ *197 E Main St.,* ☎ *978/282–4426. AE, D, M, V.*

$$ ✕ **Evie's Rudder.** Quaint and quirky, this family-owned restaurant has been dishing up good food and entertainment in a century-old former fish-packing plant for 40 years. You can sit on a wharf-side deck to feast on seafood, chicken, steak, and New England clam chowder. The final touch: free, offbeat entertainment, such as a flaming baton-

twirling act by the owner's daughter. ⊠ *Rocky Neck,* ☎ *978/283–7967. D, MC, V. Closed Nov.–Mar.; Apr. and Oct., reduced hours.*

$$$ 🏨 **Cape Ann Motor Inn.** On the sands of Long Beach, the Cape Ann operates year-round and offers guest rooms with balconies and ocean views. Some rooms have kitchenettes equipped with appliances and cooking paraphernalia. The Honeymoon Suite has a full kitchen, a fireplace, a whirlpool bath, a king-size bed, and a private balcony. Rates include free Continental breakfast. Pets are welcome. ⊠ *33 Rockport Rd., 01930,* ☎ *978/281–2900 or 800/464–8439. 29 rooms. AE, D, MC, V.*

$$$ 🏨 **Vista Motel.** The name is apt, because every room in this motel perched atop a small, steep hill overlooks the sea and Good Harbor Beach, just a few minutes' walk away. Some rooms have decks and all have refrigerators. ⊠ *22 Thatcher Rd., 01930 ,* ☎ *978/281–3410. 40 rooms (30 in winter). Pool. AE, MC, V.*

$$ 🏨 **Cape Ann's Marina Resort.** This year-round hostelry less than a mile from Gloucester really comes alive in summer, when a full-service restaurant, a whale-watch boat, and deep-sea fishing excursions operate on and from the premises. The rooms, with views of the water, have color TVs, balconies, and air-conditioning, should the Atlantic breezes be insufficient. ⊠ *75 Essex Ave., 01930,*☎ *978/283–2116,* ⨳ *978/281–4905. 52 rooms. Restaurant (mid-Apr.–mid-Nov.), indoor pool. AE, D, MC, V.*

$$ 🏨 **Captain's Lodge.** This pleasant, modern motel has rooms with cathedral ceilings, air-conditioning, and cable-equipped color TVs. On Route 127, between Gloucester and Rockport, it's just a mile from Good Harbor Beach. ⊠ *237 Eastern Ave., 01930,* ☎ *978/281–2420. 47 rooms (7 with kitchenettes). Coffee shop, pool, tennis court. AE, MC, V.*

Nightlife and the Arts

The **Hammond Castle Museum** (⊠ 80 Hesperus Ave., Gloucester, ☎ 978/283–2080) has a summer chamber-music concert series. The **Gloucester Stage Company** (⊠ 267 E. Main St., Gloucester, ☎ 978/281–4099) is a nonprofit professional group that stages new plays and revivals May–September. The **Rhumb Line** (⊠ 40 Railroad Ave., ☎ 978/283–9732) offers good food and live rock music several nights a week.

Outdoor Activities and Sports

BEACHES

Gloucester has some of the best beaches on the North Shore. **Wingaersheek Beach** (⊠ Exit 13 off Rte. 128) is a picture-perfect, well-protected cove of white sand and dunes, with the white Annisquam lighthouse in the bay. **Good Harbor Beach** (⊠ Signposted from Rte. 127A), is a huge, sandy, dune-backed beach with a rocky islet just offshore. Parking for Gloucester beaches costs about $10 on weekdays and about $15 on weekends, when the lots often fill by 10 AM. **Long Beach** (⊠ Off Rte. 127A on Gloucester/Rockport town line) is another excellent place for sunbathing; expect to pay less for parking here.

BOATING

If you prefer sailing, consider a two-hour sail along the harbor and coast aboard the schooner **Thomas E. Landon.** ⊠ *37 Rogers St., Seven Seas Wharf,* ☎ *978/281–6634. Reservations usually required.*

FISHING

Gloucester has a great fishing tradition, and many fishermen in the town's busy working harbor offer fishing trips. Try **Captain Bill's Whale Watch** (⊠ 33 Harbor Loop, ☎ 978/283–6995) for full-and half-day excursions.

Rockport

44 *41 mi northeast of Boston, 4 mi northeast of Gloucester on Route 127.*

Rockport, at the very tip of Cape Ann, derives its name from the local granite formations, and many Boston-area structures are made of stone cut from its long-gone quarries. Today, the town is a tourist center, with hilly rows of colorful clapboard houses, historic inns, artists' studios, and bathing beaches. The town has wisely refrained from going overboard with T-shirt emporia and other typical tourist-trap landmarks. Shops sell good crafts, clothing, and cameras, but not trashy souvenirs, and the restaurants serve quiche, seafood, or home-baked cookies rather than fast food. The best time to visit Rockport is during the uncrowded off-season, when many of the shops remain open. Walk out to the end of Bearskin Neck for an impressive view of the open Atlantic and the old, weatherbeaten lobster shack known as "Motif No. 1" because of its popularity as a subject for amateur painters. Other sights include the **Rockport Art Association Gallery** (⊠ 12 Main St., ☎ 978/546–6604), open all year, which displays the best work of local artists.

Dining and Lodging

$$ ✕ **Brackett's Oceanview Restaurant.** A big bay window in this quiet, homey restaurant allows an excellent view across Sandy Bay. The menu includes scallop casserole, fish cakes, and other seafood dishes. ⊠ *29 Main St.,* ☎ *978/546–2797. DC, MC, V. Closed Mon. and Nov.–Mar.*

$$ ✕ **My Place by the Sea.** This restaurant is perched right at the tip of Bearskin Neck, with a lower deck on rocks over the ocean. The menu offers New England seafood specialties such as lobster, plus steaks, pasta, salads, and sandwiches. ⊠ *Bearskin Neck,* ☎ *978/546–9667. Closed Tues. and Nov.–Apr.; no dinner weekdays Apr.–June. AE, D, DC, MC, V.*

$ ✕ **Portside Chowder House.** This great little hole-in-the-wall is one of the few restaurants in Rockport that remains open year-round. The tiny dining room with wood beams and low ceilings has partial sea views. Chowder is the house specialty; also offered are lobster and crab plates, salads, burgers, and sandwiches. The seafood is caught and served fresh daily. ⊠ *Bearskin Neck,* ☎ *978/546–7045. No credit cards. Reduced hours during winter.*

$$$$ ⊞ **Yankee Clipper Inn.** The imposing Georgian mansion, built as a private home, that forms the main part of this perfectly located inn sits
★ surrounded by gardens on a rocky point jutting into the sea. Guest rooms vary somewhat in size, but most are spacious. Furnished with antiques, they contain four-poster or canopy beds, and all but one have an ocean view. In the Quarterdeck, a newer building across the lawn, all rooms have fabulous sea views; the decor here is more modern, and rooms are spacious with large picture windows. The Bullfinch House across the street is an 1840 Greek Revival house, tastefully appointed with antique furnishings but with less-grand views. Rates include full breakfast in season. ⊠ *96 Granite St., 01966,* ☎ *978/546–3407,* fax *978/546–9730. 27 rooms, 6 suites. Restaurant, pool. AE, D, MC, V. Closed mid-Dec.–Mar. 1.*

$$$–$$$$ ⊞ **Seacrest Manor.** The distinctive inn, surrounded by large gardens, sits atop a hill overlooking the sea. Two elegant sitting rooms are furnished with antiques and leather chairs; one has a huge looking glass salvaged from the old Philadelphia Opera House. The hall and staircase are hung with paintings—some depicting the inn—done by local artists. Guest rooms vary in size and character and combine traditional and antique furnishings; upstairs, two have large, private decks with sea views. Rates include full breakfast and afternoon tea. ⊠ *131*

Marmion Way, 01966, ☎ 978/546–2211. 8 rooms, 2 with shared bath. Dining room, 2 lounges. No credit cards. Closed Dec.–Apr. 1. Ask about minimum-night stays.

$$$ 🛏 **Addison Choate Inn.** This historic inn sits inconspicuously among
★   private homes, just a minute's walk from the center of Rockport. The spacious rooms, with large tile bathrooms, are beautifully decorated; the navy-and-white captain's room contains a canopy bed, handmade quilts, and rag rugs. Other rooms—all with polished pine floors—have their share of wicker, antique furniture, and local seascape paintings. The two luxuriously appointed duplex stable-house apartments have skylights, cathedral ceilings, and exposed wood beams. Rates include breakfast. ⊠ *49 Broadway, 01966, ☎ 978/546–7543 or 800/245–7543, FAX 978/546–7638. 7 rooms, 2 apartments. Dining room, pool. D, MC, V. No smoking.*

$$–$$$ 🛏 **Bearskin Neck Motor Lodge.** Set almost at the end of Bearskin Neck, this small gray-shingled motel is within a short hike of many gift and craft shops and eateries. Rooms are comfortably but simply appointed with plain wood furnishings; their real attraction is the view: All face the water. From the windows and private balconies all you see is sea, and at night you can hear it rolling in—or thundering—against the rocks below. You can sun or read on the motel's large deck. ⊠ *74 South Rd., 01966, ☎ 978/546–6677. 8 rooms. No credit cards. Closed mid-Dec.–Mar. 30.*

$$ 🛏 **Inn on Cove Hill.** This Federal building set on a picturesque hillside
★   dates from 1792. Its construction was reportedly paid for with gold from a pirate's booty. Some of the guest rooms are small, but all are cheerful and pretty, have wood floors, and are appointed with bright, floral-print paper, Oriental rugs, patchwork quilts, and old-fashioned beds—some brass, others canopy four-posters. Rates include Continental breakfast; smoking is not permitted. ⊠ *37 Mt. Pleasant St., 01966, ☎ 978/546–2701. 11 rooms, 9 with bath. MC, V. Closed late-Oct.–Mar.*

$$ 🛏 **Sally Webster Inn.** Sally Webster was a member of Hannah Jumper's
★   so-called hatchet gang, which smashed up the town's liquor stores in 1856 and turned Rockport into the dry town it remains today. Sally lived in this house for much of her life, and the guest rooms are named for members of her family. They contain rocking chairs; nonworking brick fireplaces; pineapple four-poster, brass, canopy, or spool beds; and pine wide-board floors covered with Oriental rugs. Rates include breakfast. ⊠ *34 Mt. Pleasant St., 01966, ☎ 978/546–9251. 6 rooms. Dining room, lounge. D, MC, V. Closed Dec. 20–Feb. 1.*

Shopping

An artist's colony, Rockport has a tremendous concentration of **studios** and **galleries** selling the work of local artists. Most of these are on Main Street near the harbor and on Bearskin Neck. The *Rockport Fine Arts Gallery Guide,* available from the Rockport Chamber of Commerce (☞ Visitor Information, *below*), lists some 30 reputable galleries in town.

Essex

45 *30 mi northeast of Boston, 12 mi west of Rockport. Head west out of Cape Ann on Route 128, turning north on Route 133.*

The small town of Essex, once an important shipbuilding center, is surrounded by salt marshes and is filled with antiques stores and seafood restaurants. The **Essex Shipbuilding Museum** has exhibits on 19th-century shipbuilding, including displays of period tools and ship models. In 1998, staffers were building a replica of a 19th-century fishing vessel, to be docked outside the museum and sailed in maritime events. ⊠ *Rte. 133, Essex, ☎ 978/768–7541. 🎫 $2. ◷ Daily 1–5.*

Dining

$$ ✕ **Jerry Pelonzi's Hearthside.** This 250-year-old converted farmhouse is the epitome of coziness with its small dining rooms that have exposed beams and open fireplaces. Entrées include baked stuffed haddock, seafood casserole, sirloin steak, lobster, and chicken. ✉ *Rte. 133,* ☎ *978/768–6002. AE, MC, V.*

$$ ✕ **Tom Shea's.** Picture windows in this expanded two-story, cedar-shingle restaurant overlook the salt marsh. Seafood is the main fare, including shrimp in coconut-beer batter, scallop-stuffed sole, Boston scrod, lobster, and, of course, the fried clams for which Essex is famous. ✉ *122 Main St., Rte. 133,* ☎ *978/768–6931. AE, D, MC, V.*

$ ✕ **Woodman's of Essex.** Back in 1916, Lawrence "Chubby" Wood-
★   man dipped a shucked clam in batter and threw it into the french fryer as a kind of joke, apparently creating the first fried clam in town. Today, this large wooden shack with unpretentious booths is *the* place for seafood in the rough. The menu includes lobster, a raw bar, clam chowder, and, of course, fried clams. ✉ *Rte. 133,* ☎ *978/768–6451 or 800/649–1773. No credit cards.*

Outdoor Activities and Sports

CANOEING

Canoeing is available on the Ipswich and Parker rivers; for saltwater canoeing and kayaking, the waters of the Essex River Estuary are generally calm and protected. The **Harold Parker State Forest** (✉ Middleton Rd., ☎ 978–686–3391) in North Andover also permits canoeing.

POLO

The one spectator sport of note on the North Shore is polo. The very grand **Myopia Hunt Club** (☎ 978/468–4433)—one of the most exclusive clubs in America—stages polo matches on weekends in warm weather at its grounds along Route 1A in Hamilton.

Ipswich

46   *36 mi north of Boston, 6 mi northwest of Essex.*

Quiet little Ipswich, settled in 1633 and famous for its clams, is said to have more 17th-century houses standing and occupied than any other place in America; more than 40 were built before 1725. Information and walking maps are available at the Visitor Information Center (☞ Visitor Information, *below*). Nearby Crane's Beach is long and sandy, backed by dunes and a nature trail.

New England Alive is a petting farm and nature study center with New England wild animals as well as farm animals and some reptiles. ✉ *189 High St. (Rtes. 1A and 133),* ☎ *978/356–7013.* ✏ *$5.* ☉ *Apr.– Nov., weekdays 10–5, weekends 9:30–6.*

Wolf Hollow, in Ipswich, has an unusual exhibit depicting the North American gray wolf in its natural habitat and describing its role in our environment. ✉ *114 Essex Rd. (Rte. 133),* ☎ *978/356–0216.* ✏ *$4.* ☉ *Weekends 1–5.*

Nightlife and the Arts

Castle Hill (✉ Argilla Rd., ☎ 978/356–7774) holds an annual summer festival of pop, folk, and classical music, plus a jazz ball and winter-holiday concert.

Outdoor Activities and Sports

HIKING

Ipswich, with its miles of unique salt marshes, is one of the best places to hike on the North Shore. The Massachusetts Audubon's **Ipswich River Wildlife Sanctuary** has a variety of trails through marshland hills, where there are remains of early Colonial settlements as well as abundant wildlife. Get a self-guiding trail map from the office. The Rockery Trail takes walkers to the perennial rock garden and the Japanese garden; the map details a further 10 mi of walking trails. You can also fish in the Parker and Ipswich rivers, both of which are stocked with trout each spring. ⊠ *87 Perkins Row, Topsfield (1 mi off state Rte 97),* ☎ *978/887–9264. Office and trails closed Mondays.*

Newburyport

47 *38 mi north of Boston, 12 mi north of Ipswich on Route 1–A.*

Newburyport's High Street is lined with some of the finest examples of Federal-period (roughly, 1790–1810) mansions in New England. The city was once a leading port and shipbuilding center; the houses were built for prosperous sea captains. You'll notice widow's walks perched atop many of the houses, providing views of the port and the sea beyond.

Although Newburyport's maritime significance came to a close with the decline of the clipper ships, an energetic downtown renewal program has brought new life to the town's brick-front center. Renovated buildings now house an assortment of restaurants, taverns, and shops that sell everything from nautical brasses to antique Oriental rugs. The civic improvements have been matched by private restorations of the town's housing stock, much of which dates from the 18th century, with a scattering of 17th-century homes in some neighborhoods.

Tiny Newburyport is a good walking city, and there is all-day free parking down by the water. A stroll through the **Waterfront Park and Promenade** gives a super view of the harbor and the fishing and pleasure boats that moor here. Walking to the left as you leave the parking lot will take you to the **Custom House Maritime Museum.** Built in 1835 in Classic Revival style, it contains exhibits on maritime history, ship models, tools, and paintings. ⊠ *25 Water St.,* ☎ *978/462–8681.* ☒ *$3.* ☉ *Apr.–Dec., Mon.–Sat. 10–4, Sun. 1–4.*

48 A causeway leads from Newburyport to a narrow spit of land known as **Plum Island,** which harbors a summer colony (rapidly becoming year-round) at one end. The **Parker River National Wildlife Refuge** is at the other end of Plum Island. The refuge has 4,662 acres of salt marsh, freshwater marsh, beaches, and dunes; it is one of the few natural barrier beach–dune–salt marsh complexes left on the Northeast coast. The choice of bird-watching, surf fishing, plum and cranberry picking, and swimming is exhilarating. The refuge is such a popular place in summer, especially on weekends, that cars begin to line up at the gate before 7 AM. Only a limited number of cars are let in, although there's no restriction on the number of people using the beach. ☎ *978/465–5753.* ☒ *$5 per car; $2 for bicycles and walk-ins; annual passes available.* ☉ *Dawn to dusk. Beach sometimes closed during endangered species nesting season in spring and early summer. No pets.*

Dining and Lodging

$$$ ✕ **Scandia.** This restaurant is well known locally for its fine cuisine;
★   house specialties include rack of lamb and lobster ravioli. The dining room is small, narrow, and dimly lit with candles on the tables and chandeliers with candle bulbs. The Sunday brunch has hot entrées, cold salads, crêpes, waffles, and omelets. ⊠ *25 State St.,* ☎ *978/462–6271. Reservations essential. AE, D, DC, MC, V.*

$$–$$$ ✕ **David's and Downstairs at David's.** These two restaurants at the Garrison Inn (☞ *below*) are top-of-the-line for both food and service. If you dine upstairs in the formal room—furnished with chandeliers and white linen, damask-covered chairs and draperies—you will have a difficult time choosing among entrées such as sautéed lobster, scallop and shrimp with roasted vegetables, crisp ravioli in rich lobster cream sauce with sherry and fine herbs, and sautéed breast of duck. Downstairs at David's is less formal, with a tavern offering some of the same dishes served upstairs, as well as full- or half-portions of Maine seafood. Both supply supervised child care for $5 per youngster, allowing kids to play and eat while parents enjoy their meals in peace. ⊠ *11 Brown Sq.,* ☎ *978/462–8077. Reservations essential. AE, MC, V.*

$ ✕ **East End Seafood Restaurant.** For a true dining "in the rough" experience, visit this restaurant just south of Newburyport in the village of Rowley. Dining is on wooden picnic tables, and the fare is deep-fried seafood. It closes at 7:30 PM. ⊠ *Corner Rte. 1A and Railroad Ave., Rowley,* ☎ *978/948–7227. Reservations not accepted. No credit cards.*

$$$ 🏠 **Garrison Inn.** This four-story Georgian redbrick building is set back from the main road on a small square. Inside, an elegant lounge and formal dining room (☞ David's, *above*) are smartly furnished with reproductions; the basement tavern (☞ Downstairs at David's, *above*) is more casual. Guest rooms vary in size; all have handsome antique replicas, and some have working fireplaces. The best rooms are the top-floor suites, set on two levels. ⊠ *11 Brown Sq., 01950,* ☎ *978/465–0910,* 𝖥𝖠𝖷 *978/465–4017. 18 rooms, 6 suites. Bar, room service. No pets. AE, DC, MC, V.*

$$–$$$ 🏠 **Clark Currier Inn.** This 1803 Federal mansion has been restored with
★   care, taste, and imagination, making it one of the best inns on the North Shore. Guest rooms are spacious and partly furnished with antiques, including one with a glorious sleigh bed dating from the late 19th century. Rates include Continental breakfast and afternoon tea. ⊠ *45 Green St., 01950,* ☎ *978/465–8363. 8 rooms. AE, D, MC, V.*

Nightlife

The Grog Shop (⊠ 13 Middle St., Newburyport, ☎ 978/465–8008) hosts a variety of blues and rock bands several nights weekly.

Outdoor Activities and Sports

FISHING

Surf casting is popular—bluefish, pollack, and striped bass can be taken from the ocean shores of Plum Island; if you enter the refuge with fishing equipment in the daylight you can obtain a free permit to remain on the beach after dark. You don't need a permit to fish from the public beach at Plum Island; the best spot is around the mouth of the Merrimack River.

HIKING

At the **Parker River National Wildlife Refuge** (⊠ Plum Island, ☎ 978/465–5753), deer and rabbits share space with thousands of ducks and geese, many of them migrating. The 2-mi Hellcat Swamp Trail cuts through the marshes and sand dunes, taking in the best of the sanctuary. Trail maps are available at the office.

WHALE-WATCHING

Between May and October **Newburyport Whale Watch** (⊠ 54 Merrimac St., ☎ 978/465–9885 or 800/848–1111) conducts daily whale-watching trips. Reservations are required.

North Shore A to Z

Arriving and Departing

BY BOAT

A boat leaves Boston daily for Gloucester during July and August (also, weekends during June). The round-trip lasts approximately 7½ hours, including a 2½ hour stopover in Gloucester. For information, call **A. C. Cruise Lines** (⊠ 28 Northern Ave., Pier 1, Boston, ☎ 617/261–6633 or 800/422–8419).

BY BUS

The **Coach Company** bus line (☎ 800/874–3377) runs an express commuter bus between Boston and Newburyport twice each weekday.

The **Cape Ann Transportation Authority** (CATA, ☎ 978/283–7916) covers the Gloucester/Rockport region with buses and water shuttles.

BY CAR

The primary link between Boston and the North Shore is Route 128, which, just inland, follows the line of the coast as far north as Gloucester. To reach Newburyport directly from Boston, take I–95. The more scenic coastal road (it doesn't become scenic until you're north of Lynn) is Route 1A, which leaves Boston via the Callahan Tunnel. Beyond Beverly, Route 1A goes inland, and the coastal route connecting Beverly, Gloucester, and Rockport is Route 127.

To reach Salem, follow Route 114 out of Marblehead and turn right on Route 1A. From the west take Route 114 from Route 128 into Salem. A word of caution: This route is confusing and poorly marked, particularly on the return to Route 128.

BY TRAIN

Massachusetts Bay Transportation Authority (MBTA) trains leave North Station, Boston, for Salem, Beverly, Gloucester, Rockport, and Ipswich. Call ☎ 617/722–3200 for schedules.

Guided Tours

The **Brush Hill/Gray Line Tour Company** (⊠ 439 High St., Randolph, 02368, ☎ 781/986–6100) runs a daily North Shore tour, including Salem and Marblehead, in warm weather.

WHALE-WATCHING

The most popular special-interest tours on the North Shore are whale-sighting excursions. Some of the more reputable whale-watch operations include **Cape Ann Whale Watch** (⊠ Rose's Wharf, Box 345, Gloucester, 01930, ☎ 978/283–5110 or 800/877-5110), **Captain Bill's Whale Watch** (⊠ 33 Harbor Loop; mailing address: 9 Travers St., Gloucester, 01930, ☎ 978/283–6995), **Newburyport Whale Watch** (⊠ 54 Merrimac St., Newburyport, 01950, ☎ 978/465–9885 or 800/848–1111), and **Yankee Whale Watch** (⊠ 75 Essex Ave., Gloucester, 01930, ☎ 978/283–0313 or 800/942-5464).

Out of Boston, **A. C. Cruise Lines** (☞ Arriving and Departing, *above*) also offers whale-watching excursions weekends April–June and September–October, daily during July and August.

Contacts and Resources

EMERGENCIES

Police (☎ 911). **Beverly Hospital** (⊠ Herrick St., Beverly, ☎ 978/922–3000). **CVS Pharmacy** (⊠ Dodge St., Beverly,☎ 978/927-3291) is open 24 hours a day. **Walgreen's** (⊠ 201 Main St., Gloucester, ☎ 978/283–7361) is open until 9 weeknights, 6 on weekends.

STATE PARKS

Of the numerous parks in the area, the following have particularly varied facilities: **Halibut Point State Park** (⊠ Rte. 127 to Gott Ave., Rockport, ☎ 978/546–2997). **Harold Parker State Forest** (⊠ Rte. 114, North Andover, ☎ 978/686–3391). **Maudslay State Park** (⊠ Curzon Mill Rd. Newburyport, ☎ 978/465–7223). **Parker River National Wildlife Refuge** (⊠ Plum Island, off Rte. 1A, Newburyport, ☎ 978/465–

5753). **Plum Island State Reservation** (⊠ Off Rte 1A, Newburyport, ☎ 978/462–4481). **Salisbury Beach State Reservation** (⊠ Rte. 1A, Salisbury, ☎ 978/462–4481). **Willowdale State Forest** (⊠ Linebrook Rd., Ipswich, ☎ 978/887–5931).

Visitor Information

The umbrella organization for the whole region is the **North of Boston Visitors and Convention Bureau** (⊠ Box 642, 248 Cabot St., Beverly, 01915, ☎ 978/921–4990 or 800/742–5306, FAX 978/921–4956). The following cover more specific areas:

Cape Ann Chamber of Commerce (⊠ 33 Commercial St., Gloucester, 01930, ☎ 978/283–1601). **Greater Newburyport Chamber of Commerce and Industry** (⊠ 29 State St., Newburyport, 01950, ☎ 978/462–6680). **Ipswich Visitor Information** (⊠ S. Main St., ☎ 978/356–8540). **Marblehead Chamber of Commerce** (⊠ 62 Pleasant St., Box 76, Marblehead, 01945, ☎ 781/631–2868). **National Park Service Visitor Information** (⊠ 2 New Liberty St., Salem, 01970, ☎ 978/740–1650). **Rockport Chamber of Commerce Visitor's Booth** (⊠ Box 67, 3 Main St., Rockport, 01966, ☎ 978/546–6575). **Salem Chamber of Commerce and Visitor Information** (⊠ 32 Derby Sq., Salem, 01970, ☎ 978/744–0004 or 800/777–6848). **Salem Maritime National Historic Site** (⊠ 174 Derby St., Salem, 01970, ☎ 978/740–1660). **Salisbury by the Sea Chamber of Commerce** (⊠ Town Hall, Beach Rd., Salisbury, 01952, ☎ 978/465–3581 or 800/779–1771).

SOUTH OF BOSTON

The towns south of Boston make an enjoyable day trip or a convenient stop on your way down to the Cape or Martha's Vineyard. If you're a history buff or are seeking to give children an educational experience they won't soon forget, take the 40-mi trip south to **Plymouth**, the community natives proudly call "America's Home Town." Here you can see the monument you've heard about since childhood—Plymouth Rock. A couple of miles down the road at Plimoth Plantation you can stroll through a re-creation of a 17th-century Puritan village that puts new meaning into the word *authentic,* or walk the decks of the *Mayflower II.* Most important, with its historical accuracy, Plymouth dispels many myths about the first English settlers. The truth, you're likely to find, is far more fascinating.

If you're more ambitious, take a drive into the seafaring towns of **New Bedford** and **Fall River.** In Fall River, history has taken a macabre turn with the ever-burgeoning interest in the Trial of the Century—the 19th century, that is. Fall River is the home town of Lizzie Borden—she who was accused, and acquitted, of dispatching her parents with "40 whacks"—and Borden history has become a cottage industry here. New Bedford is a center of seafaring history.

Plymouth

Numbers in the margin correspond to points of interest on the South of Boston map.

49 *40 mi south of Boston.*

On December 21, 1620, 102 weary men, women, and children disembarked from the *Mayflower* to found the first permanent European settlement north of Virginia. Today, Plymouth is characterized by narrow streets, clapboard mansions, quaint shops, and antiques stores. Some commecial names would make the Pilgrims shudder: The John Alden Gift Shop, Mayflower Seafoods, and, incongruously, Pocahontas Gifts, Sportswear and Sundries. (She was from Virginia.) But it's easy to overlook these and admire the picturesque waterfront—on a fine fall day, the view from the harbor is spectacular. The town, which bustles with tourists all summer, also offers a parade, historic-house tours, and other activities to mark Thanksgiving.

A variety of **historic statues** dot the town, including ones of William Bradford on Water Street, a Pilgrim Maiden in Brewster Gardens, Massasoit on Carver Street, and the largest freestanding granite statue in the country, the National Monument to the Forefathers, on Allerton Street. A variety of historical houses are also open for visits, including the 1640 **Sparrow House,** Plymouth's oldest structure. ⊠ 42 Summer St., ☎ 508/747–1240. ⌷ $1.50. ⊘ Thurs.–Tues. 10–5.

The 1749 **Spooner House,** home to the same family for 200 years, has guided tours, historic recipes, and a garden. ⊠ 27 North St., ☎ 508/ 746-0012. ⌷ Donation. ⊘ June–mid–Aug., Thurs.–Sat 10–3:30 or 4.

★ ☾ Over the entrance of the **Plimoth Plantation** is the caution: "You are now entering 1627." Believe it. Against the backdrop of the Atlantic Ocean, a Pilgrim village has been painstakingly re-created, from the thatched roofs, cramped quarters, and open fireplaces to the long-horned livestock. Throw away your preconception of white collars and funny hats; through ongoing research, the Plimouth staff has developed a portrait of the Pilgrims richer and more complex than the dour folk in elementary school textbooks. Listen to the quaint accents and mannerism of the "residents," who never break out of character. You might see them plucking ducks, cooking rabbit stew, or tending garden. Feel free to engage them in conversation about their life, but expect only curious looks if you ask about anything that happened later than 1627.

Elsewhere on the plantation is **Hobbamock's Homestead,** where descendants of the Wampanoag Indians re-create the life of a Native American who chose to live near the newcomers. In the **Carriage House Craft Center** visitors may see such items created using the techniques of 17th-century English craftsmanship—that is, what the Pilgrims might have imported. (You can also buy samples.) At the **Nye Barn,** you can see goats, cows, pigs, and chickens bred from 17th-century gene pools or bred to represent animals raised in the original plantation. The visitor center has gift shops, a cafeteria, and multimedia presentations.⊠ Warren Ave. (Rte. 3A),☎ 508/746–1622. ⌷ $18.50 (includes entry to Mayflower II); Plantation only: $15. ⊘ Apr.–Nov., daily 9–5.

One of the country's oldest public museums, the **Pilgrim Hall Museum,** established in 1824, transports visitors back to the time before the Pilgrims' landing, with items carried by those weary travelers to the New World. Included are a carved chest, a remarkably well-preserved wicker cradle, Myles Standish's sword, John Alden's Bible, Native American artifacts, and the remains of the Sparrow Hawk, a sailing ship that was wrecked in 1626. There are also changing exhibits.⊠ 75 Court St. (Rte. 3A), ☎ 508/746–1620. ⌷ $5. ⊘ Daily 9:30–4:30; closed Jan.

From the Pilgrim Hall Museum, it's a short walk to the harbor and the **Mayflower II,** an exact replica of the 1620 Mayflower. Like Plimoth Plantation 2 miles down the road, the ship is staffed by Pilgrims and hearty mates in period dress. The ship was built in England through research and a bit of guesswork, then sailed across the Atlantic in 1957. ⊠ State Pier, ☎ 508/746–1622. ⌷ $5.75 or as part of Plimoth Plantation fee. ⊘ Apr.–Nov., daily 9–5 (until 7 in July and Aug.).

A few dozens yards from the Mayflower II is **Plymouth Rock,** popularly believed to have been the Pilgrims' stepping stone when they left the ship. Given the stone's unimpressive appearance—many visitors are dismayed that it's little more than a boulder—and dubious authenticity

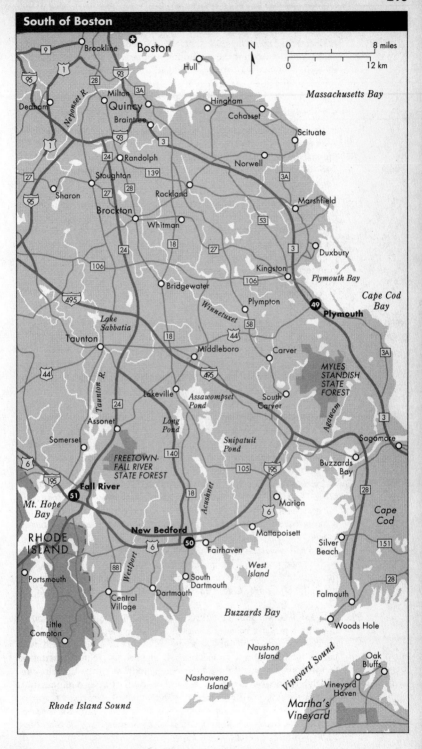

(as explained on a nearby plaque), the grand canopy overhead seems a trifle ostentatious. Across the street from Plymouth Rock is **Cole's Hill,** where the company buried their dead—at night, so the Native Americans could not count the dwindling numbers of survivors. Just past the hill, on what was once called locally "First Street," is the site of the original settlement; in 1834, the street was named Leyden Street in honor of the Dutch city that sheltered the Pilgrims. Look for plaques designating the locations of the original lots and their owners.

For a more traditional view of the Pilgrims, visit the **Plymouth National Wax Museum,** on the top of Cole's Hill. It contains 26 scenes with 180 life-size models that tell the Pilgrims' story. ⊠ *16 Carver St.,* ☎ *508/746–6468.* ⌸ *$5.* ⊙ *Mar.–May and Nov., daily 9–5; June, Sept.–Oct., daily 9–7; July–Aug, daily 9–9.*

Imagine an entire museum devoted to a Thanksgiving side dish. But the Ocean-Spray–operated **Cranberry World** is amazingly popular. For one thing, it's free. After viewing details of how the state's local crop is grown, harvested, and processed, you can sip juices and sample products made from *Vaccinium macrocarpon* (the Latin name for cranberries). In October, you can see harvesting techniques and attend local cranberry festivals. ⊠ *225 Water St.,* ☎ *508/747–2350.* ⌸ *Free.* ⊙ *May–Nov., daily 9:30–5.*

<table>
<tr><td>NEED A
BREAK?</td><td>Sample some cranberry wine—it's oddly refreshing, and free—at the Plymouth Bay Winery (⊠ Village Landing Marketplace,170 Water St., ☎ 508/746-2100). For more substantive fare, the Lobster Hut (☎ 508/746-2270), open year-round on Town Wharf at the waterfront, offers seafood in classic breaded and fried style, plus sandwiches and luncheon specials.</td></tr>
</table>

Dining and Lodging

$$–$$$ **Bert's Cove.** This local landmark, just off the entrance to Plymouth Beach, has great ocean views along with a menu listing choices from veal medallions, sirloin steak, and risotto to fresh seafood. ⊠ *Warren Ave., Route 3A.* ☎ *508/746–3330. AE, D, MC, V.*

$$ ✕ **Iguana's.** A good spot for both lunch and late-night dining, Iguana's serves fajitas, burritos, and other Mexican-Southwestern fare, plus burgers, sandwiches, and chicken, steak, and rib dishes. There's a bar, a patio, ocean views—and a live iguana. ⊠ *Village Landing Marketplace, 170 Water St.,* ☎ *508/747–4000. AE, DC, MC, V.*

$–$$ ✕ **The All-American Diner.** The look is nostalgia—red, white, and blue with movie posters. The specialty here is beloved American foods— omelets and pancakes for breakfast; burgers, salads and soups for lunch. ⊠ *60 Court St.,* ☎ *508/747–4763. Closed dinner. DC, MC, V.*

$$$ ✕🖫 **John Carver Inn.** This three-story Colonial-style redbrick building with a massive pillared facade is just a few steps from Plymouth's main attractions. The public rooms and dining rooms are lavish, with period furnishings and stylish drapes. The rooms are more matter-of-fact, but ask for one of the six environmentally sensitive alpine rooms, which have filtered air and water and in-room exercise equipment. At its Hearth 'n Kettle Restaurant, a huge menu of American favorites, including hearty sandwiches and a broad range of seafoods, is served by a staff dressed in colonial attire. ⊠ *25 Summer St.,* ☎ *508/746–7100 or 800/274–1620,* FAX *508/746–8299. 79 rooms. Restaurant, bar, pool, meeting rooms. AE, D, DC, MC, V.*

$$$ 🖫 **Governor Bradford Motor Inn.** On the waterfront directly across from the *Mayflower II,* this two-story inn has 94 rooms (some non-smoking are available), each with two double beds, a small refrigerator, instant coffee service, and free HBO. ⊠ *98 Water St.,* ☎ *508/746–6200 or 800/332–1620,* ℻ *508/747–3032. 94 rooms. Pool. AE, D, MC, V.*

New Bedford

⑤⓪ *45 mi southwest of Plymouth, 50 mi south of Boston.*

New Bedford is home to the largest fishing fleet on the East Coast. Although much of the town is industrial, the restored historic district near the water is a delight. It was here that Herman Melville set his masterpiece, *Moby Dick,* a novel ostensibly about whaling. The **New Bedford Whaling Museum,** established in 1902, is the largest American museum devoted to the 200-year history of whaling. Exhibits include ship models, whaling gear, scrimshaw, paintings, and photographs. A 22-minute film depicting an actual whaling chase is shown in July and August at 10:30 and 2, on weekends at 2 in other months. **Seaman's Bethel,** the small chapel described in *Moby Dick,* is across the street from the whaling museum. ⊠ *18 Johnny Cake Hill,* ☎ *508/997–0046.* ⊡ *$4.50.* ☉ *Memorial Day–Labor Day, Fri.–Wed. 10–5, Thurs. 10–8; Labor Day–Memorial Day, daily 10–5.*

Dining

$$$ ✕ **Davy's Locker.** A huge seafood menu is the main draw at this spot overlooking Buzzards Bay. Choose from more than a dozen shrimp preparations or a healthy choice entrée—dishes prepared with olive oil, vegetables, garlic, and herbs. For landlubbers, chicken, steak, ribs, and the like are also served. You can park or dock your boat at the restaurant's private pier. ⊠ *1480 E. Rodney French Blvd.,* ☎ *508/992–7359. AE, D, MC, V.*

$$$ ✕ **Rosie's Restaurant.** Some New Orleans–style seafood dishes—blackened catfish and gumbo soup—enliven the Cajun-focused menu, which also includes lots of pastas and sandwiches. Live jazz and piano music on weekends and some weeknights make this a cut above the competition. ⊠ *380 Hathaway Rd.,* ☎ *508/990–3700. D, MC, V.*

Fall River

⑤① *54 mi south of Boston, 15 mi northwest of New Bedford.*

Every schoolchild can recite this rhyme of woe: "Lizzie Borden took an axe / And gave her mother 40 whacks. / When she saw what she had done, / She gave her father 41." And yet Lizzie, the maiden daughter of the town's prominent banker, was found innocent of the 1892 bludgeoning deaths of her father and stepmother in the most sensational trial of its time. She went on to spend the rest of her life quietly in **Fall River,** today a fading port and factory town. But the Borden tragedy continues to draw the curious, while the city's burgeoning factory-outlet centers continue to draw bargain-hunters.

The best place to learn about the Borden case is the **Fall River Historical Society,** which has the world's largest collection of Borden artifacts, including courtroom evidence, photographs, and the handleless hatchet suspected to be the murder weapon. The Greek Revival–style mansion, built in 1843, also displays artifacts related to Fall River's days as home of the world's largest cotton cloth manufacturer. Tours are available. ⊠ *451 Rock St.,* ☎ *508/679–1071.* ⊡ *$3.50.* ☉ *Apr.–May and Oct.–Dec., Tues.–Fri. 9–4:30; June–Sept. Tues.–Fri. 9–4:30, weekends 1–5.*

If you're strong of heart and stomach, you may also want to take in the **Lizzie Borden Bed & Breakfast Museum** (☞ Dining and Lodging, *below*). In 1996, the Borden home, the site of the murders, was transformed into a New England B&B . Even if you don't spend the night here, you can still drop by to see the display of Lizzie-related items. ✉ *92 Second St.,* ☎ *508/675–7333.* 🎫 *$7.50.* ⊙ *11–3; tours on the ½ hr.*

Another Lizzie highlight is the **Borden burial plot** in the Oak Grove Cemetery on Prospect Street. Lizzie's home after her acquittal was at **306 French Street** (a private residence), where she lived until her death in 1927.

A visit to Fall River can skirt Lizzie Borden's sad saga entirely. The town's industrial docks and enormous factories recall the city's past as a major textile center in the 19th and early decades of the 20th century. It also served as a port; today the most interesting site is **Battleship Cove,** a "floating" museum complex docked on the Taunton River. In addition to several museums, the cove is home to the 35,000-ton battleship USS *Massachusetts;* the destroyer USS *Joseph P. Kennedy, Jr.;* a World War II attack sub, the USS *Lionfish;* two PT boats from World War II; and a Cold War–era, Russian-built warship. ✉ *Davol St., just off state Rte 79,* ☎ *508/678–1100 or 800/533–3194.* 🎫 *$9.* ⊙ *Daily 9–4:30.*

From May through October, the **HMS Bounty** of *Mutiny on the Bounty* fame, is docked adjacent to Battleship Cove. Visitors can participate in sails organized by the Tall Ship Bounty Foundation; call for details. ☎ *508/673–3886.* 🎫 *$4.* ⊙ *Daily 10–6; call ahead, as ship is often on sail.*

The **Fall River Carousel,** built in the 1920s, was rescued from the defunct Lincoln Amusement Park in 1992 and moved to Battleship Cove. The glorious restoration is now housed dockside. ✉ *Battleship Cove,* ☎ *508/324–4300.* 🎫 *Rides: 75¢.* ⊙ *Mid-Apr.–May and Labor Day–end Oct., weekends noon–4; June, daily noon–6; July–Labor Day, daily noon–8.*

The **Marine Museum at Fall River.** This museum celebrates the age of sail and steamship travel, especially the lavishly fitted ships of the Old Fall River Line, which operated until 1937 between New England and New York City. The museum also contains the 28-ft-long, 1-ton model of the *Titanic* used in the 1952 movie. ✉ *70 Water St.,* ☎ *508/674–3533.* 🎫 *$4.* ⊙ *Mon.–Fri. 9–5; Sat. 12–5; Sun. 12–4.*

Also at riverside, the **Fall River Heritage State Park** tells the story of Fall River's industrial past, focusing on the city's textile mills and their workers. The park has a visitors center, sailboat rentals, a concert series, and exhibits. ✉ *200 Davol St. W,* ☎ *508/675–5759.* 🎫 *Free.* ⊙ *Daily 10–4.*

Dining and Lodging

$$$–$$$$ ✕🏨 **Lizzie Borden Bed & Breakfast Museum.** Could you stand to sleep in the same house where Lizzie Borden's father and stepmother met a bloody end? Choose from one of the four original bedrooms, two of which are suites, or two rooms converted from attic space. Non-guests may tour the place between 11 and 3. Neither pets nor smoking are permitted. ✉ *92 Second St.,* ☎ *508/675–7333. AE, D, MC, V. Overnight guests must be 12 and over.*

Shopping

Fall River is home to the **Quality Factory Outlets** (✉ 638 Quequechan, ☎ 508/677–4949), a group of more than 70 brand–name factory outlet stores housed in original granite mills that once turned out cotton.

South of Boston A to Z

Arriving and Departing

BY BUS

American Eagle Motorcoach Inc. (☎ 800/453–5040)offers service from Boston. **Bonanza Busline** (☎ 800/556–3815) offers service from New York and Providence. **Plymouth & Brockton Street Railway** (☎ 508/746–0378) links Plymouth and the South Shore to Boston with frequent service.

BY CAR

To get to **Plymouth,** take the Southeast Expressway I–93 south to Route 3(toward Cape Cod); exits 6 and 4 lead to downtown Plymouth and Plimoth Plantation, respectively. To get to **Fall River** and **New Bedford** take I–93 to Route 24 South to I–195.

BY TRAIN

MBTA (☎ 617/722–3200 or 800/392–6100) commuter rail service is available to Attleboro and Plymouth. Plans are underway to increase commuter rail service to Taunton, Fall River, and New Bedford.

Guided Tours

Colonial Lantern Tours (⊠ 98 Water St., Plymouth, ☎ 508/747–4161) offers guided evening tours of the original Plymouth plantation site and historic district.

WHALE-WATCHING

Capt. John Boats (☎ 508/746–2643) offers several daily whale-watch cruises from April to November. **Andy Lynn Boats** (☎ 508/540–3474 or 508/746–7776), at Plymouth Town Wharf, offers daily trips.

Contacts and Resources

EMERGENCIES

Police (☎ 911 or dial township station).

CVS Pharmacy (⊠ 2100 Acushnet Ave., New Bedford,☎ 508/995–2653) is open until 10 daily. **CVS Pharmacy,** ⊠ State Road, Manomet (Plymouth), ☎ 508/224–3312.

St. Luke's Hospital (⊠ 101 Page St., New Bedford,☎ 508/997–1515). **Jordan Hospital,**⊠ 275 Sandwich St., Plymouth, ☎ 508/746–2000.

STATE PARKS

Fort Phoenix State Beach Reservation (⊠ Green St., Fairhaven, ☎ 508/992–4524); **Freetown State Forest** (⊠ Slab Bridge Rd, Assonet, ☎ 508/644–5522); **Horseneck Beach State Reservation** (⊠ Rt. 88, Westport, ☎ 508/636–8816). **Myles Standish State Forest** (⊠ Cranberry Rd., South Carver—exit 5 off Rte. 3), ☎ 508/866–2526) has more than 16,000 acres for hiking, biking, swimming, picnicking, and canoeing. Several ponds are stocked with bass, perch, and pickerel.

Visitor Information

Bristol County Convention and Visitors Center (⊠ 70 N. Second St., Box 976, New Bedford, 02741 ☎ 508/997–1250).
Destination Plymouth (⊠ 225 Water St., Suite 202, Plymouth, 02360, ☎ 800/872–1620).
Fall River Chamber of Commerce (⊠ 200 Pocasset St., Fall River, 02720, ☎ 508/676–8226).
New Bedford Chamber of Commerce (⊠ 794 Purchase St., New Bedford, 02742, ☎ 508/999–5231).

INDEX

NOTES

Looking for a different kind of vacation?

Fodor's makes it easy with a full line of guidebooks to suit a variety of interests—from sports and adventure to romance to family fun.

At bookstores everywhere.
www.fodors.com

WHEREVER YOU TRAVEL, HELP IS NEVER FAR AWAY.

From planning your trip to providing travel assistance along the way, American Express® Travel Service Offices are always there to help.

Boston

American Express Travel Service
One Court Street
617/723-8400

American Express Travel Service
222 Berkeley Street
617/236-1331

American Express Travel Service
170 Federal Street
617/439-4400

Travel